Calvin on the Ropes

A verse by verse exposition of Romans that puts Calvin on the ropes

Volume I
Romans 1:16 - 4:5

Douglas R. Shearer

Dedicated to my wife Sita - without whose help and encouragement I couldn't possibly have completed this book.

Gratefully acknowleging the contribution of Dr. Arnold Fructhenbaum whose scholarship has been a real inspiration to me and who spent many long hours reading through the manuscript; Pastor Ray Stedman who many years ago up on the Rogue River encouraged me to "write theology;" Dr. Earl Radmacher who has been a friend and mentor; Pastor Richard Paradise who has walked alongside me in a friendship most persons hope for, but find ever so elusive; my brother Steve Shearer who first introduced me to Jesus Christ; and, finally, Don Morsey who navigated me through my early years with the Lord.

Front Cover:

The Dempsey-Firpo fight at the Polo Grounds, September 14, 1923
Artist: George Wesley Bellows

Calvin on the Ropes
by Douglas R. Shearer

Printed in the United States of America

ISBN 978-1-60647-979-7

Unless otherwise indicated, Bible quotations are taken from Authorized King James Version.

www.xulonpress.com

Forward by Dr. Arnold Fruchtenbaum

Having read Pastor Shearer's work (Volume I) it is obvious that Pastor Shearer is neither a Calvinist nor an Arminian in the traditional sense of the terms. The focus of this work is evaluating Calvinism and its treatment of Scripture and how it relates to the person's view of Israel and Israelology. The tendency in Covenantal Calvinism has been to impose certain theological presuppositions on the text and interpret the text based upon a preconceived theology rather than letting the text speak for itself in context and application of normal rules of interpreting literature. Such imposition in turn has led to a presuppositional Replacement Theology which in turn rules out any future for ethnic Israel. Furthermore, it has left Israel with the curses and transferred the blessings promised to Israel to the Church. None of this, as Pastor Shearer shows, sits well with what Paul teaches in Romans 9-11. While such an evaluation may not be valid with Dispensational Calvinists, it has certainly been true with the vast majority of Calvinists that follow a Covenant Theology and hence a Covenantal Calvinism.

In his treatment of Romans, Pastor Shearer clearly shows how a number of concepts and statements Paul makes in chapters 1-8 are preliminary to what he will elaborate in Romans 9-11. While I have not yet seen his treatment of Romans 9-11, what Pastor Shearer has written on the preliminary segments of his treatment makes me look forward to see how he will tie everything together in treating those passages.

This book is highly recommended to both Dispensational Calvinists and Covenantal Calvinists as well as to Arminians, and also to all of those who do not see themselves in any of these categories for an honest evaluation of what the Book of Romans really says about God's program for salvation and God's program for Israel.

Arnold Fruchtenbaum
Ariel Ministries

To the Reader

Ordinarily, I'd want to wait on getting this first volume out until completion of the others - carrying us through to the end of Romans; however, in this case I don't believe it's necessary – largely because an exegesis of the first three chapters of Romans invalidates so many of the proof-texts used by Calvinists in Romans 9-11, and conclusively proves that those three chapters are not about God's sovereignty, but the unfettered nature of God's mercy.

But even more importantly, I'm convinced that there's an urgent need to get what I've completed into circulation – and that there's a ready audience for it across a wide spectrum of evangelical Christianity – from Baptists to Pentecostals.

At the moment, there are two powerful trends developing within evangelicalism – and here I'm speaking as a pastor – both of which surfaced initially at the academic level, but today are spilling out into churches and generating a powerful impact there:

- a pernicious postmodernism that demeans moral and intellectual certainty and presses for accommodation among competing "truths" – a postmodernism that's now "institutionalizing" itself in the so-called "emerging churches" – some more so than others; and
- a resurgent five point Calvinism – which, though wrong, nevertheless casts itself in opposition to postmodernism and, therefore, appeals to college Christians who are desperately looking for a spiritual and intellectual mooring - a mooring that will safeguard their beliefs from being swept into the sea of relativism that's engulfing so much of contemporary academic culture.

In short, the one, postmodernism and the relativism it's producing among American intellectuals, has led to the other, a resurgence of five point Calvinism with all its rigor and internal consistency - along, of course, with its moral certainty.

In the past, five point Calvinists, though always scornful of Arminianists, were willing to negotiate a modus vivendi with so-called four point Calvinists who, by and large, shied away from the harsher conclusions that flow so inexorably from "tulip." Now, however, they're far less inclined to do so; they've been buoyed by a confidence they haven't enjoyed for almost a hundred years and see little or no need any longer to rein in their disdain of four point Calvinists.

The resurgence of Five Point Calvinism has aroused my concern along several lines of thought - each of which is related to the other:

- First, is the horrifying portrait it sketches of God - a deity who, as James Montgomery Boice reluctantly acknowledges, assigns human destinies with an apparent indifference that calls into question his compassion and love. It's a portrait that Calvinists, try as they may, can't soften - not at least on an intellectual level. And, indeed, if that were the portrait an accurate exegesis of the New Testament sketched, then that's the portrait we'd be stuck with - regardless of how repulsive it might seem. Simply put, however, it's not an accurate exegesis.
- Second, Five Point Calvinism inevitably denigrates the Cross. For Calvinists, it's election and reprobation that most vividly display God's mercy and his wrath, meaning his hatred of sin. But that runs completely contrary to the whole corpus of the New Testament - which, in no uncertain terms, teaches that it's the Cross, a single event occurring at a single point in time, that most vividly reveals God's mercy and his wrath:
    - his mercy poured out on mankind, and
    - his wrath poured out on Christ.
- Third, Five Point Calvinism, as we shall see, assigns both mercy and faith only bit roles in the drama of salvation. The featured role is reserved exclusively for God's sovereignty; mercy and faith are little more than corollaries of God's sovereignty and can boast no independent reality of their own. In light of the importance Paul gives both mercy and faith in the book of Romans, that's an awfully hard pill to swallow.
- Fourth, Five Point Calvinism makes evangelism superfluous - at least from an intellectual standpoint if not from an ethical one. For Calvinists, the drama of personal salvation is a fiction - because the outcome has already been determined. Yes, many Five Point Calvinists make a real effort to underscore the need for evangelism, but not because it will make any

genuine difference in the lives of those they're evangelizing, but only because it's an all too obvious imperative woven into the fabric of the New Testament. That, however, begs the question, "Why would God send the church off on a wild-goose chase to evangelize the already chosen and the irrevocably damned?" It certainly seems a bit odd - to say the least; and strongly suggests, on the very face of it, that Calvinists have "got it wrong."

- Finally, Five Point Calvinists, with a few exceptions, have never been on "friendly" terms with premillennialism. They have historically aligned themselves with postmillennialism – an eschatology that lends little if any legitimacy to the resurrected state of Israel and the continuing significance of the Jews as "the people of God."

It's with all this in mind that I'm anxious to get this first volume into the hands of American evangelicals without waiting on completion of the remaining volumes - and at every possible level: congregants, pastors and academicians - but especially college students, the pool from which most of our future leaders will be drawn and also the segment of American evangelicals likely to be most influenced by postmodernism and Five Point Calvinism.

May God bless you as you read this study; and may he reveal his staggering mercy to you - and so claim you for the cause of Christ.

Douglas R. Shearer

Table of Contents

Preface

About ten year ago, I was up in Portland, Oregon, at Western Seminary visiting two friends of mine, Dr. Earl Radmacher and Dr. Gerry Breshears. While at Western, I visited the campus bookstore and began browsing through a few of the texts used in the classes taught there. Eventually, I meandered over to a section in the back of the store where the commentaries were shelved. I picked up a couple of commentaries on the Book of Romans - curious to see how the authors handled chapters nine through eleven. In every case, the result was the same - a Calvinist interpretation that stressed the sovereignty of God and little else - certainly not God's faithfulness and only a perfunctory treatment of Israel, though for Paul that's obviously the "raison d'etre" of chapters nine through eleven.

I was shocked. Western is a seminary that by and large eschews hard line Calvinism; but the only commentaries on the Book of Romans there on the shelves and recommended for student use reflected a decidedly Calvinist bent. The Commentary by James Montgomery Boice was a good example. Boice is an unabashed "five point Calvinist" who, driven by his intellectual honesty, doesn't back away from the obvious ramifications that flow inexorably from "double predestination" - most especially the horrifying portrait it sketches of God - as Boice himself reluctantly admits: *"an indifferent deity who sits in heaven arbitrarily assigning human destinies, saying, as it were, 'This one to heaven and I don't care; and this one to hell and I don't care.'"*

I was told later by a few of the professors on campus that the only good commentaries on the Book of Romans are, in point of fact, authored by Calvinists; that, think what you will of a Calvinist frame of reference, they are, by and large, darn good scholars. And, not only that, what other option is there? Arminianism? That, claimed the professors, is hardly a viable alternative for a serious student of scripture. Too many inconsistencies - and not permeated with the intellectual thoroughness so characteristic of Calvinism.

Calvinism is closely argued, tightly bound, and scrupulously logical. That's because it begins with a series of "biblical axioms" summarized in the acronym "tulip"...

- total depravity
- unconditional election
- limited atonement
- irresistible grace
- perseverance of the saints

...and then rigorously spins out carefully reasoned corollaries from them. It's a logician's delight - and because of that it's apt to appeal to anyone whose mind runs in that direction. But its logic is its undoing - because, ultimately, it argues Calvinist conclusions from Calvinist premises that don't always line up with the Biblical text. Therefore, while it boasts an internal consistency that's all but impossible to challenge, it is easily "deconstructed;" in short, the whole edifice rests on a flawed foundation which a verse by verse exegesis of Romans reveals to anyone with enough patience to undertake and actually complete - and who is equipped with a little background in pre-modern thought.

I was hoping to avoid writing this book: a front-line pastor finds himself with little time for that kind of effort. But the more I searched for an already published book reflecting some of my concerns, the more convinced I became that there was no avoiding it. Most of what I found pitted against Calvinism has been authored by Arminian scholars - who buy into conclusions I don't find altogether credible. A few scholars have attempted to construct "theologies" - what they call "Four Point Calvinist theologies" - based around Calvinist doctrines, but avoiding the harsher conclusions that emerge from "tulip." However, that's a mistake - because, as Five Point Calvinists rightly argue, a Four Point Calvinist is like a "half pregnant woman."

I've been locked into this effort for at least the last six years - and am only a third done. This book only gets us through the first part of Chapter Four. That's the bad news. The good news, however, is that only this far into Romans and it's already apparent how easily Calvinism can be discredited and, as that occurs, how many of the difficulties plaguing the interpretation of

Chapters Nine through Eleven are resolved.

Ultimately, however, this book is more than a polemic against Five Point Calvinism. It's...

- First and foremost, a verse by verse exegesis.
- Especially geared to Gen Xers, Gen Yers, and Millennials.
- With diagrams and charts.
- Highlights Paul's train of thought as he moves from topic to topic.
- Highlights the underlying premises that guide and govern that train of thought.
- Highlights Paul's teleological mode of thinking - so contrary to our contemporary western mode of thinking.
- Shows how a teleological mind-set redefines certain concepts that have traditionally caused confusion among Christians - including the concepts of "freedom," "predestination," and the relationship between the individual and the community to which he belongs.
- Allows the text itself to speak against Five Point Calvinism and the interpretive biases that arise from it.
- Highlights lead-ins to Romans 9-11 - how they cue the interpretation of those three chapters.
- Underscores the over arching themes of Romans - especially the theme of God's mercy.
- Highlights Paul's description of the human psyche´.
- Special emphasis on cultural relevance.
- Includes an excursus on faith designed to highlight the important distinction between the ground of our faith and the ground of our hope - and to point out the fallacy of making salvation turn upon belief in the doctrine of eternal security - without at the same time denying the validity of the doctrine itself.

A STUDY OF ROMANS

Chapter One
Including Basic Insights Fundamental to Understanding the Book of Romans

Why?

Why another expository study of the Book of Romans? That's a fair question – and it deserves an honest, straightforward answer. And, really, it's quite simple: I don't know of another book of the Bible that so clearly spells out the central doctrines of the Christian Faith. The Book of Romans is a veritable repository of Christian truth – a repository that, in my opinion, is unmatched by any other book of the Bible.

But there are already many outstanding studies of Romans – by men far better trained than I and far better connected to other men who can provide useful critiques and the kind of balanced perspective so necessary in expositing scripture. Why should I want to add my study to the many already circulating? Simply put, it's because I don't know of another verse by verse exposition of Romans that effectively cuts Calvinism down to size - that dismantles its intimidating edifice and exposes its inconsistencies.

There have been myriads of topical attacks launched against Calvinism; but a topical attack is, by its very nature, piecemeal, and, moreover, plays to the strength of Calvinism - its internal consistency and the rigorous logic used to build it. Calvinism can't be attacked from within; it must be "deconstructed" from without - meaning its basic premises must be invalidated - and not by marshalling an array of "proof texts," but by a careful exegesis of New Testament scripture - in this case, the Book of Romans because it's such a rich mine of New Testament truth.

There is, however, a second reason I've decided to add my study to the many already circulating; and it has to do with the kind of believer now crowding into the church. Let me explain.

I've been teaching Bible studies for about forty years now – both from the pulpit and in small groups; and over the course of those many years, especially the last twenty years, I've noticed a precipitous decline in expository teaching – accompanied, tragically, by a corresponding decline in the knowledge of fundamental Christian doctrine. There's a whole welter of reasons underlying that decline – and I don't want to get bogged down in delineating them all; I only want to mention the three I've found to be the most disturbing – the three that have prompted to me to change the way I exposit[1] scripture.

1. It seems to me that "gen-Xers," persons born between 1961 and 1981, the sons and daughters of the "boomers," don't "connect the dots" as easily as their parents and grandparents did – meaning they find it very difficult to draw logical inferences from general truths. And it's a problem that seems to be getting worse with each passing year.

   I'm not at all suggesting that they can't think inferentially; it's just that they don't. Nor am I suggesting that "gen-Xers" – or the generational cohort following, the "gen-Yers"[2] – can't think conceptually. They certainly can. They're downright good at it. What I am saying, however, is that they seem to have a hard time...
   - reading a passage of scripture and drawing out the general principles imbedded there,
   - spotting those very principles at work within their own cultural milieu, and
   - then applying those principles to their own personal lives.

   And that's precisely what an expository study, to be useful, requires of its readers and listeners – at least in the format that's currently the common coin. If each step[3] isn't carefully walked out, expository studies lose their value[4] and seem almost pointless.

   No doubt much of the problem is rooted in the ever increasing fragmentation that's taking hold in American culture. Gen-Xers[5] are in some respects the living embodiment of that fragmentation. Many of them – indeed almost 50% of them – have grown up in ruptured homes – "latch-key kids" left to fend for themselves long before they were either emotionally or intellectually ready to do so. Consequently, many of them neither live holistically nor think holistically – meaning they grab at bits and pieces of life – bits and pieces of information – without trying to integrate them. Each bit of life – each bit of information – stands pretty much on its own – part of a "stream of consciousness" the meaning of which they seldom if ever pursue. Moreover, the pace of life nipping at their heels is just too frantic to permit quiet reflection – which, of course, only exacerbates their tendency to let all the "loose ends" lie where their busy, topsy-turvy lives cast them.

I certainly don't think the solution is to rail against either them or the powerful cultural forces which have conspired to destroy quiet reflection and holistic thinking. That's too much like trying to sweep back the incoming tide with nothing more than a kitchen broom. The solution, I believe, is to develop a format for expository teaching that takes into account the "gen-X mind-set." In short, the format – however it's put together – must do for them what they're not in the habit of doing for themselves: (1) connect the dots, (2) spot overarching themes, and (3) highlight both personal and cultural relevance.[6]

The alternative is to abandon expository studies altogether and switch over instead to topical studies – which, of course, is already well underway. What we've been getting for the last twenty years or so are bookshelves laden with topical studies – studies, for example, on faith, on marriage and divorce, on stewardship, on parenting, on spiritual gifts, on worship, on God's love, on leadership, on prayer, on the End Times, and so on and so forth.

And I'm not at all suggesting that topical studies aren't worthwhile; they most certainly are. Many of them have proven to be invaluable. But I think that the topical study of scripture, if relied upon too much, lends itself easily to a loss of balance and perspective; moreover, it exacerbates the very fragmentation that's already plaguing gen-Xers and gen-Yers.

The Book of Romans illustrates perfectly what inevitably occurs when expository studies are abandoned. Think about it. The topics found in Romans are myriad – including justification, human psychology, the nature of sin, the dynamics of God's jurisprudence, sanctification, the relationship between the Old and the New Testaments, the two natures and one person of Christ, the Trinity, the dynamics of faith, the continuing significance of Israel, the nature of the church, Christian ethics, stewardship, the nature and relevance of the Law, the meaning of mercy – and so much more. But what's especially fascinating is how, in the mind of Paul, each of those topics leads to or is developed out of the others – how, in short, they're all connected. A simple topical study...

- would never reveal those connections,
- or the overarching themes informing those connections,
- or the priorities they suggest.

Why? Because a topical study doesn't permit us to follow *Paul's train of thought;* only an expository study does that. That's the loss we suffer when expository teaching is abandoned; but I'm afraid only a changed format can save expository teaching for the gen-Xers – at least that's my opinion.

2. The second reason underlying the decline in expository teaching is even more disconcerting – and is, I'm convinced, far more deeply entrenched and deleterious. It's rooted in the postmodern mind-set that has become so chic among American and European intellectuals. Fifty years ago it was *"de rigueur"* for a "Western Lit" college professor to ask his students some such question: "What's Shakespeare's meaning in Act V, scene 3 of King Lear, when the king suddenly appears on stage with the lifeless body of Cordelia in his arms? What terrible truth is Shakespeare telling us?" Today, however, he no longer asks his students that question. Instead, he asks them, "What does Act V, scene 3, mean *to you?"* In short, it's no longer the author's meaning that's pivotal; it's the meaning – whatever it might be – that his readers give to it. And, quite frequently, there's more to it than even that: it's not just that Shakespeare's meaning isn't considered pivotal, it's no longer even probed – often with a caveat from the professor that doing so will prove not just pointless, but detrimental. Why? Because probing the author's intentions will undermine the reader's quest for personal identity and "self-authentication." Think about it! If during the Renaissance, *"man became the measure of all things,"* today *"the individual has become the measure of all things"* – with one person's opinion, however ill informed and poorly grounded it might be, no more valid than anyone else's.

And that same mind-set is, I'm afraid, becoming

all too prevalent within the Evangelical community – especially among the so-called "emerging churches." At least that's what I've observed. All too often, for example, it's not...

- "What does Paul mean in Romans 2:2-16?",
- it's "What does Romans 2:2-16 mean *to you?*"[7]

And since the overriding purpose of expository teaching is to ferret out *the author's* meaning and lay it bare, is it any wonder that it has fallen on hard times? It doesn't cater to the "self-authenticating" impulse now at work in American culture. In short, expository teaching is at odds with the values gen-Xers and gen-Yers have imbibed and have by now thoroughly assimilated.

3. But there's also a third reason[8] underlying the decline in expository teaching: *the inability of gen-Xers to correlate ambiance with the specific underlying values that produce that ambiance.*

Not far from Sacramento – which is where I live and where I've pastored for most of my career – seventy five miles or so to the north-east, is a small town nestled in the gently rolling hills of California's Gold Country. Its name is Nevada City.

It's a Norman Rockwell painting come to life: drug stores with soda fountains and magazine racks; restaurants with fine wines and mouth-watering, though rustic, cuisine; pot belly stoves radiating a warmth that coats and mollifies frayed nerves; book stores where patrons are encouraged to relax in large, overstuffed chairs; clapboard churches with steep roofs and stained glass windows; a WPA-era, art deco grammar school and town hall; painstakingly restored Victorian homes with manicured green lawns. Everywhere, there's a sense of rootedness and belonging.

The ambiance is breathtaking; but it's entirely contrived – and a prolonged stay in Nevada City invariably "pops its bubble." Nevada City is nothing more than a commercial venture designed to produce a *feeling* of community among the alienated denizens of Sacramento and the San Francisco Bay Area. It's a week-end escape put together by slick entrepreneurs who themselves suffer from that very same alienation – that same gnawing sense of loss that dogs their patrons. It's not real – because the values that produce authentic community are so glaringly absent...

- a willingness to both acknowledge and revere authority,
- a willingness to embrace dependency, and
- a willingness to honor constraints that limit personal freedom.

Personal freedom and independence are precisely what no one is willing to surrender – whether it's the entrepreneurs and merchants responsible for producing the ambiance or the patrons who enjoy it. And that makes authentic community impossible. But it doesn't make the *ambiance* of community impossible – at least not in the short run. That's still possible. And there are whole industries geared toward producing that ambiance – along with the advertising and promotional gimmicks that push it. If genuine community is no longer possible, at least its ambiance is within reach – or so we've been led to believe. It's the *feeling* they're after – the *mood*. That and nothing more.

And what's true of that correlation is true also for a whole array of other "correlations" as well...

- the ambiance of success without the hard work to undergird it;
- the ambiance of education and scholarship without the training to undergird it;
- the ambiance of athletic prowess without the fitness to undergird it;
- and so on and so forth.

Ambiance has become a way of life for gen-Xers. They're addicted to it. Many of them aren't even aware of the disjunction they've bought into. Ambiance is all they see – nothing more.[9]

And that same disjunction is at work within the church...

- the ambiance of worship – without the way of life that undergirds it;
- the ambiance of prayer – without the convictions that undergird it;
- the ambiance of leadership and authority – without the character that undergirds it;
- love of Israel – without the underlying theology that informs it.
- and so on and so forth.

Is it any wonder, then, that expository teaching

doesn't generate much resonance in the minds and hearts of gen-Xers? One of the overriding purposes of expository teaching is to reveal general convictions and underlying principles – exactly what gen-Xers care very little about. I don't think it's possible to recover the relevance of expository teaching for them unless we develop a format that hammers away at the vital correlation between the ambiance they're so desperately searching for and the underlying convictions and ethics that produce that ambiance and make it authentic.

The kind of format I'm proposing can assume many different forms. There's no one form that's right. All that matters is that it takes into account the "gen-X mind-set" – their bias against inferential thinking. In short, the format – however it's put together – must do for them what they're not in the habit of doing for themselves: (1) connect the dots, (2) spot overarching themes, and (3) highlight both personal and cultural relevance. There are several techniques I've developed which, I hope, facilitate that. I'm sure, however, there are additional techniques that can be added to the repertoire I've put together – some, no doubt, far more effective than the ones I've formulated.

Connecting the dots:
Connecting the dots assumes that we're able to follow the flow of Paul's thought – and that's not always an easy task. Paul's sentences are often complex – sometimes downright labyrinthine – a maze of subjects, predicates, and modifiers that can bewilder and confuse even the best of scholars. Sorting through them is a very daunting task. I've employed two techniques that I believe will make that task a bit easier.

- Sentence diagramming:
  A complex sentence can be likened to an intricate maze of railroad tracks consisting of a primary trunk-line and a whole array of secondary spurs. Sentence diagramming enables us to distinguish between the trunk-line and the spurs.[10] It's a time honored technique that, regrettably, has fallen into disuse.

  A good example of the use to which I've put sentence diagramming is my analysis of Romans 1:18 found on page 82. An even more effective use of it is found in my analysis of the grammatical structure of verses 18b – 24 found on page 84.

- Graphs:
  Sentence diagramming is best suited for only a few verses. It's far too cumbersome for whole passages of scripture - sometimes extending for several chapters. For that, I've employed graphs - accompanied by legends that explain each step outlined on the graph. A good example of the use to which I've put graphs is found on page 109 - and, again, on pages 162 and 163.

Identifying Underlying Presuppositions

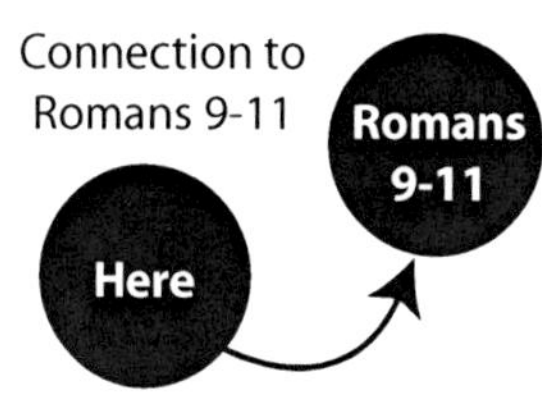

There's a fundamental presupposition that Paul spells out at the very beginning of his teaching - a presupposition that (1) informs almost every topic he raises and (2) comprises the backdrop against which it's meant to be understood. Anyone who loses sight of it is likely to stumble into error[11] – especially along one all-important axis of thought: *Paul's theology of grace – or, perhaps more accurately, Paul's theology of mercy.*

For Paul, mankind's condemnation is a given. It's axiomatic. Put a little differently, man is *not* awaiting trial. He's *not* awaiting an assessment of his standing before God – whether he's innocent or guilty – deserving of life or death. No,
- the trial has *already* occurred;
- a verdict has *already* been rendered – *guilty;* and
- a sentence has *already* been determined – *death.*

The world, then, is precisely what Franz Kafka[12] suggests it is: a holding cell where man awaits execution of the sentence pronounced against him. *That's the fundamental human condition!* And Paul brooks no compromise. It's in this sense that man is what Paul in Romans 9:22 calls *"a vessel of wrath."*

Romans 9:22	What if God, wanting to show His wrath and to make His power known, endured with much longsuffering the *vessels of wrath* fitted for destruction...

It's essentially the same term he uses in Ephesians 2:3, *"children of wrath"* –

Ephesians 2:3	...among whom also *we all* once conducted ourselves in the lusts of

> our flesh, fulfilling the desires of the flesh and of the mind, and *were by nature children of wrath, just as the others.*

...except that in Ephesians 2:3 Paul makes explicit what he leaves implicit in Romans 9:22 – that *all* men, not just *some* men, are, from their very conception,[13] vessels of wrath...

- Isaac no less than Ishmael;
- Jacob no less than Esau;
- Moses no less than Pharaoh.

We all begin the same: ***vessels of wrath.*** There's nothing novel about Paul's presupposition. It's the very same truth Jesus himself affirms in John 3:17-18.

John 3:17	For God did not send His Son into the world to condemn the world, but that the world through Him might be saved.
John 3:18	He who believes in Him is not condemned; but he who does not believe is ***condemned already***, because he has not believed in the name of the only begotten Son of God.

John the Baptist declares the same truth in John 3:36.

John 3:36	He who believes in the Son has everlasting life; and he who does not believe the Son shall not see life, ***but the wrath of God abides on him***."

The meaning here is not that disbelief occasions the wrath of God, but, rather, *belief in Jesus absolves its otherwise intrinsic presence*. The sense of the verse is perhaps better conveyed by a slight change in the wording...

John 3:36	He who believes in the Son has everlasting life; and he who does not believe the Son shall not see life, *but the wrath of God* ***remains*** *upon him.*"

Mankind stands condemned – *that's the starting point of Paul's theology*. It's the very backdrop against which the sum and substance of the messianic mission is cast. And because there's no doubt whatsoever that the trial leading to man's condemnation was altogether fair, God will always dismiss out of hand any appeal grounded in justice. That means man's only hope is God's mercy.

But can an appeal grounded in God's mercy provide any real basis for genuine hope?[14] That question, like a thread, is woven into every chapter of Romans – its entire warp and weft. The answer Paul gives reveals the fundamental nature of God. And, ironically, it's summed up most completely and most definitively in the three chapters many scholars consider parenthetical, Romans 9-11. It's the same answer the Prophet Micah gives...

Micah 7:18	Who is a God like unto you, who pardons iniquity, and passes by the transgression of the remnant of his heritage? He retains not his anger for ever, *because he delights in mercy.*

Chapters Nine through Eleven are not about God's

Already Condemned - A Truth Too Often Overlooked

How often has the straightforward truth of man's intrinsic *condemnation* been overlooked? Not his intrinsic *sinfulness*, but his intrinsic *condemnation*? More frequently than might be imagined - and by theologians who should certainly have known better. It's an oversight that for centuries has bled into the whole fetid controversy that swirls about God's justice and man's moral accountability. *How can God condemn men and women for sins their human frailty makes inevitable? And if God does so, aren't we then led to conclude that God himself is unjust?*

It's the question itself that's off base, not just the answers given to it. It's not that men and women are condemned for sins they can't keep themselves from committing,

- it's that even before committing those sins, they stood helplessly condemned before God;
- it's that condemnation, no less than sinfulness, is woven into the fabric of their human existence;
- it's that they were conceived not just in sin, but in condemnation as well.

How can God condemn men and women for sins their human frailty makes inevitable? It's a question that arises from a misunderstanding of the human condition.

sovereignty, as James Boice and John Piper - along with their fellow Calvinists - would have us believe. They're about God's mercy. And the passages Boice and Piper use to buttress their interpretation are, ironically, the very ones that prove they're wrong.

Identifying Underlying Presuppositions

- ***Teleological Thought***

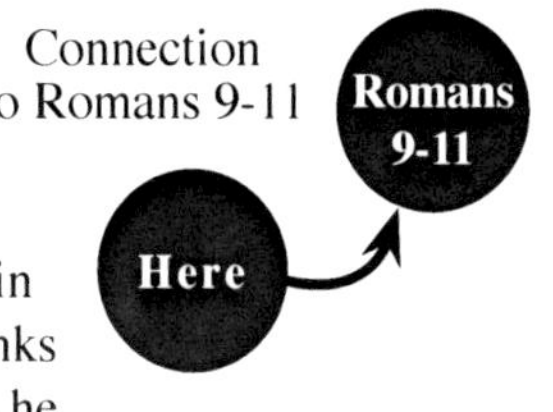

Paul, in common with almost everyone steeped in a pre-modern culture, thinks teleologically – meaning, he assumes that any given phenomenon – whatever it might be – is governed by a *fixed destiny;* and it's *that* destiny – what Aristotle called "telos"[15] – which defines its *real* nature, its consummation, its perfection – or, to use Aristotle's terminology, its *"entelecheia."* Thus, a premodern teacher, like Paul, can hold in his hand an *acorn* and call it an *oak tree* - because its "telos" – meaning its ultimate destiny – is the *form* of an oak tree, not the *form* of an acorn.

That's precisely what Paul does for example in Romans 8:9 – where he categorically asserts that believers *"... are not in the flesh, but in the Spirit."* He's holding, so to speak, *justified* believers in his hands and insisting that they're all fully *sanctified.* Why? Because that's their destiny - that's the "telos" God has imparted to them - that lays claim to, governs, and directs their lives. Believers are – to use another Biblical word laden with teleological meaning – *sealed,* meaning their destiny is fixed.

Likewise, in Romans 6:18 Paul is speaking teleologically.

Rom. 6:18 ...and having been freed from sin,

Did Paul Make Use of Greek Philosophical Categories?

It was my privilege as a young man to have studied Plato and Aristotle under Dr. Marvin Zetterbaum and to have worked as his research assistant for a time. Dr. Zetterbaum himself studied under and was personally mentored by none other than Dr. Leo Strauss of the University of Chicago - who, in Germany, had worked along side Ernst Cassirer and Martin Heidegger. It was also my privilege to have been enrolled in a seminar taught by Leo Strauss for a small number of honors graduate students.

What's particularly fascinating about Strauss is his insistence that neither Plato nor Aristotle was a novel thinker; that the philosophical categories they developed arose from a primordial intuition rooted in premodern culture. That intuition, Strauss contended, is no longer accessible to modern thinkers – because the culture that informs and governs their thoughts is so far removed from antiquity. It's buried under the sophistries that emerged during the Renaissance and Enlightenment - a conviction shared by Ludwig Wittgenstein. What we're left with, Strauss suggested, is a wholly artificial culture stripped of the underpinnings needed to make it truly authentic. The premoderns, both Zetterbaum and Strauss claimed, were far closer to the truth; indeed, their culture was impregnated with it – though even then it was under attack and beginning to dissipate - which is exactly the point Plato was trying to make in so many of the dialogues he attributes to Socrates - especially his dialogue with Thrasymachos recorded in *The Republic*. If Strauss and Zetterbaum are right, there's no need to insist that Paul was either a Platonist or an Aristotelian. The same fundamental presuppositions that guided Greek culture also guided Hebrew culture.

Strauss, of course, didn't play down the difference between, as he and Heidegger put it, "Athens and Jerusalem." Indeed, he was quick to acknowledge that one was a culture of "Reason" and the other a culture of "Faith." Nevertheless, the two cultures were not as radically dissimilar as William Barrett made them out to be in his epic study *Irrational Man, a Study in Existential Philosophy*. That's because both cultures wholly embraced a teleological mind-set - a fact that Barrett mystifyingly overlooked.

you became slaves of righteousness.

The sense here is that believers can't help but be righteous – which is true, but only teleologically. In short, believers are ultimately cast in the form of perfect righteousness. And though their lives may not at present reflect that righteousness, its attainment is a certainty.

A simple "dictionary" definition of "telos" is usually inadequate. Why? Because the lexicologists compiling the dictionary seldom take the time to mention its *dynamic* nature; moreover, many seminary graduates haven't been trained in classical Greek philosophy and are, therefore, unaware of that omission and the inadequate definition they're left to work with. It's certainly true that for Plato telos was, by and large, a static concept[16]; but for Aristotle, whose concept of telos is far closer to the original, more culturally rooted definition, telos is not inert; it's dynamic – an overriding impulse that draws to itself the phenomena possessed of it. Telos, properly defined, then, is not just a fixed destiny, *it's a self-propelling, self-actuating fixed destiny.*

The Doctrine of Immanent Impulse

Ernest Barker, who for years lectured at Wadham College, Cambridge University, and the University of Cologne and who completed one of the finest English translations of Aristotle's *The Politics,* coined a term for the dynamic nature of telos: he called it Aristotle's doctrine of "immanent impulse." Actually, however, it was not at all unique to Aristotle. It was common coin within Attic Greece – most especially Ionia.

The nature of telos is underscored again and again in scripture, but nowhere more emphatically than Romans 5:12 – 5:21 where Paul contrasts Adam's humanity – basically, Adam's telos – to Christ's humanity – basically, Christ's telos; and, then, highlights the irresistible dynamic propelling both. In short, anyone possessed of Adam's telos is destined to sin and death; whereas anyone possessed of Christ's telos is destined to righteousness and life.

It's not just Paul's epistles that reflect a teleological bent, Peter's epistles do so as well - especially 1 Peter 1:23...

1 Pet. 1:23 Being born again, not of corruptible seed, but of incorruptible, by the word of God, which lives and abides for ever.

The "corruptible seed" corresponds, of course, to Adam's telos; whereas the "incorruptible seed" corresponds to Christ's telos - which guarantees a believer's eventual transformation into the image of Christ. Many more examples could be marshalled, but these suffice.

For anyone familiar with Greek philosophy, Aristotle's "telos" is nothing more than Plato's "archetype" rescued from pure transcendence and inserted into existential phenomena. Thus, in some sense, *both* Plato and Aristotle are wholly teleological in their thinking. And it was Platonic and Aristotelian philosophical categories that dominated Hellenic thought and, hence, the entire Roman Empire, including Palestine, at the time of Paul in the First Century. The concept itself, however, was an integral part of both a Greek's and a Jew's cultural baggage long before either Plato or Aristotle got hold of it.[16]

The bottom line is simple: telos was not merely "one of many" concepts swirling about in the minds of premodern scholars and academicians - whether semitic or non-semitic; it was the very framework within which they formulated and developed their concepts; it was the paradigm that governed their intellectual discourse.

Freedom

Connection to Romans 9-11

Romans 9-11

Here

Freedom, for example, is a concept Paul grounds in telos – and not only Paul, but virtually every other premodern thinker as well. For Paul, freedom is not cast in a negative light, *"freedom from,"* but in a wholly positive light, *"freedom for."* I'm truly free only when I've bound myself to the telos God has assigned me. Romans 6:18 is, once again, a case in point.

Rom. 6:18 ...and having been freed from sin,

you became slaves of righteousness.

It's not when I've been liberated from the chains of sin that I'm truly free; it's when I've been enslaved to the righteousness of Christ, the telos that governs and guides redeemed humanity, that I'm truly free. Plato's *Republic* is no different. A citizen is only truly free when he's "enslaved" to whatever political, social, and economic status or role best serves the well being of the "polis."

Modern thinkers – thinkers nourished in the tradition of the Renaissance and the Enlightenment – have severed completely the link that once bound freedom to telos. For us, freedom is not "freedom for;" it's only "freedom from;" it's the freedom of the void.

The distinction Sartre draws between "en soi," "being in itself," and "pour soi," "being for itself," sheds a telling light on just how far contemporary intellectuals have embraced "freedom of the void" and, correspondingly, have distanced themselves from teleological presuppositions – and how terribly difficult it is for us, living in the 21st Century, to accommodate ourselves to a teleological mind-set. "Being in itself" corresponds to Plato's archetype and Aristotle's telos – a fixed destiny; "being for itself" is the very opposite: it's an on-going, never ending "project" with no fixed destiny. Sartre makes "being in itself" the refuge of cowards – anyone who refuses to assume the terrifying burden of continually redefining himself – and that, of course, includes the vast majority of men and women. It's a point he makes the centerpiece of his best known novel, *Les Jeux Sont Fait*. "Being for itself," on the other hand, is embraced only by the courageous few – those willing to shoulder that burden. In short, contemporary intellectuals – from Nietzsche to Sartre and culminating with the postmodernists – have heaped scorn on teleological presuppositions and anyone who embraces them – including, of course, Christians.

That freedom could possibly consist of being bound – of being restricted – that's a wholly alien notion for most of us! That freedom could possibly consist of being "enslaved" – that's hard for us to wrap our minds around! But unless we do, Paul's epistles will always remain a bit enigmatic.

Predestination

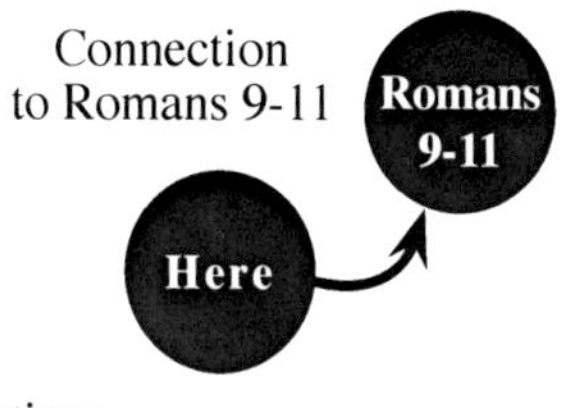

Predestination is still another of Paul's concepts that can only be grasped against the backdrop of telos – its meaning and the implications that follow in its wake. There's no doubt whatsoever that the Bible teaches predestination; but it's not what's usually taught from the pulpit or, for that matter, from the lecterns of many of our best Bible schools and seminaries. Boice and his fellow Calvinist John Piper are two cases in point: for them, specific individuals are the focal point of predestination – the hub around which its meaning revolves; but that's *not* the meaning Paul gives to predestination. Ephesians 1:11 illustrates well the meaning Paul gives to predestination – and it's a meaning grounded in telos...

Eph. 1:11 In Him also we have obtained an inheritance, being predestined according to the purpose of Him who works all things according to the counsel of His will...

The word "purpose" translates the Greek word "προθεσιν" – which can also be translated "plan." The two words are virtually interchangeable. What Paul is saying here is simple and straightforward: it's not the fate of specific individuals that predestination turns upon; it's God's eternal plan – and the purpose that plan reflects. In short, predestination is conceptually grounded in God's plan, not in the fate he supposedly assigns specific individuals. Put slightly differently:

- *God's plan is God's choice* – that's where his sovereignty is anchored – that's its real situs – that's where it's found.
- The fate of specific individuals is left to those individuals – whether or not they choose to conform their lives to that plan. *That's their choice, not God's.*

Calvinists, of course, deny that man is any longer capable of "choosing God" - of seizing the pardon God has graciously tendered him. They insist he's too depraved to make that choice. But Romans One and Two make it abundantly clear that man is not totally depraved; that, even in his fallen state, he's neither devoid of a moral sensitivity or a God consciousness - a point I'll expand upon shortly.

Ephesians 1:4 illustrates just how profoundly a teleological perspective alters the usual interpretation of certain key passages.

> Eph.1:4 ...just as He chose us in Him before the foundation of the world, that we should be holy and without blame before Him in love...

If Ephesians 1:4 is read without imbedding it in a teleological framework, personal choice appears to have been written out of salvation. However, when we set it within a teleological framework, what we have is quite different:

- it's *not* that God has predestined *specific individuals* to be holy and blameless before him in love;
- it's that *God's plan* for man is that he be holy and blameless before him in love – that's the *telos* he has predestined for him – the purpose to which man must conform his life if he's to be truly human.

In the first instance, the focus is on *specific individuals*; however, in the second instance, the focus is on *God's purpose – God's plan.*

In short, Ephesians 1:4 tells us nothing about the personal fate of each individual man or woman. Within a teleological framework, that choice is left to them – whether or not to conform their lives to that telos – and, in so doing, become fully free – meaning fully human. And that's no different from what we find...

- in any of Plato's writings, from *The Apologia* to *The Republic*[17]
- or in any of Aristotle's writings, from *The Politics* to *The Nicomachean Ethics*.[18]

The Individual and Community

Connection to Romans 9-11

Here → Romans 9-11

Individualism, a mind-set virtually unknown to the authors of scripture, is so deeply entrenched in the Western psyche´ that it's seldom called into question; and the few who do challenge it run the risk of being consigned to the margins of intellectual and moral respectability. It has been the organizing principle of Western Culture[19] for at least three hundred and fifty years.[20] Indeed, it's enshrined in the second paragraph of our own country's founding document, *The Declaration of Independence...*

> We hold these truths to be self-evident, that all men are created equal, *that they are endowed by their Creator with certain inalienable rights, ... that to secure these rights, governments are instituted among men.*

There it is: *rights and privileges inhere in individuals; they're not derived from the collective. Moreover, the sole purpose of the collective is to secure those rights.* That's the fundamental precept lying at the heart of individualism. Put a little differently, a social collective – whatever it might be – is subordinate to the individuals who comprise it. It has no life of its own. It's wholly contrived, an artificial construct fabricated by the persons who make it up. It amounts to little more than the sum of its parts. Its key features are so obvious, the very warp and weft of our lives, that we're apt to overlook them...

- Identity is rooted in the parts, not in the whole.
- Individuals don't "belong" to social collectives – not in the sense that they become organically united to them and so lose their autonomy.
- They join them, but aren't "merged" with them, meaning they don't acquire a *corporate* identity that supplants their *personal* identity.
- Finally, social collectives – whether the state, a church, a labor union, whatever – exist for the individual's benefit, not the other way around.

Which is primary? Is it the whole or the parts? Americans and Europeans are apt to reply with knee-jerk alacrity: "***The parts!***"

But that's wholly at odds with Paul's mind-set. For Paul – and virtually every other premodern thinker as well – whatever rights and privileges individuals enjoy are derived from the social collectives to which they belong; it's their class – meaning the social standing to which they're born and the institutions arising from it – that determines their rights and privileges. In short, for Paul, it's not the individual who's imbued with meaning and

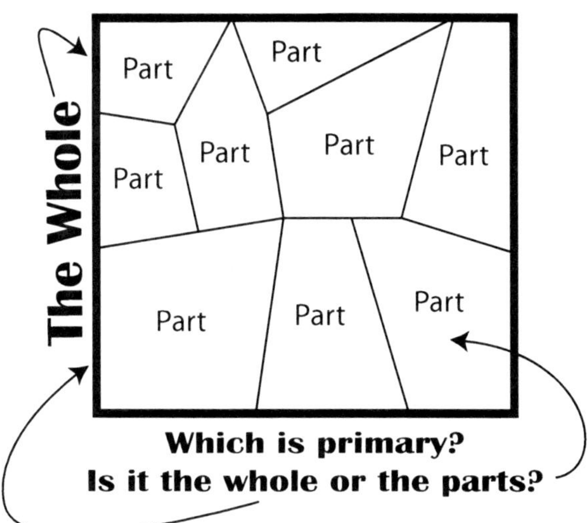

purpose; it's the collective. That's the rationale underlying the importance Paul ascribes to both Israel and the Church.

Israel is much more than merely the sum of her parts. In a very real sense, Israel's existence *lies beyond* the individuals who comprise her. That's why Paul can so confidently assure us in Romans 9:6 that Israel's standing before God has not been jeopardized by the inexcusable failure of so many Jews – indeed the overwhelming majority of them.

> Rom. 9:6 But it is not that the word of God has taken no effect. For they are not all Israel who are of Israel.

The phrase "*... they are not all Israel who are of Israel*" poses no real difficulty for a premodern thinker; that's because, once again, the collective *stands apart from and is prior to* the individuals who make it up.

- Only within Israel can individual Jews live out the telos God has ordained for them.
- Only to the extent that they are *organically* incorporated into her can their lives acquire meaning and purpose.
- Indeed, outside Israel their lives are bereft of any real significance.

The Church is no different. She too, like Israel, exists prior to and apart from the individuals who comprise her. And it's only to the extent that individual Christians are *organically* incorporated into her...

- that their lives acquire significance;
- that they're enabled to live out the telos regeneration has imparted to them.
- Simply put, an individual Christian cannot live out his faith without being built into the church – without committing himself wholly to the church and becoming one with her.

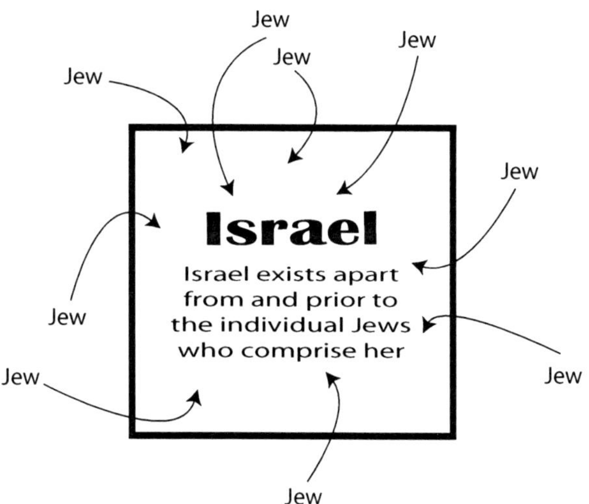

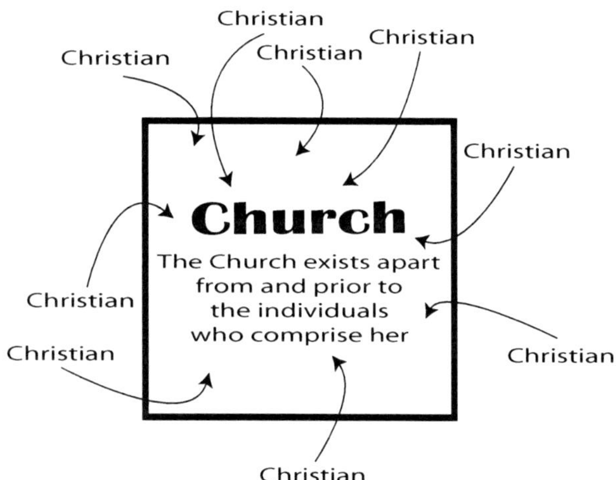

In short, for Paul sanctification is not a solitary quest for personal holiness. It can only be undertaken within the Church – a truth too many pastors fail to teach their congregations. Once again what we have here is a cultural mind-set, a way of thinking common to the entire premodern world, not just the premodern Semitic world. Plato and Aristotle, for example, share the Torah's outlook: individuals alone are unable to lend meaning to their lives. It's the "polis"[21] that supplies their lives with purpose – that imparts to them the full measure of their humanity.

It's hard for 21st Century Americans to grasp the horror the Torah ascribes to being "cut off." For us, it's merely a matter of being unwelcome – no doubt embarrassing, certainly inconvenient, but seldom lethal. It's not the "end of the world" for us. We simply move on to new friendships and new collectives. If the "Lions Club" revokes my membership, I join the "Moose Club" and get on with my life. But for a 1st Century Jew, whose personal identity was derived almost wholly from his corporate identity, being "cut-off" was tantamount to a death sentence. It's not just that his physical well-being was jeopardized – though, no doubt, that was true. The wound he suffered was far deeper and more profound than that: he was alienated from all his emotional and intellectual moorings, and was cast into a terrifying isolation that quite literally *eviscerated his psyche´*. How different for 21st Century Evangelicals! Once again, for us, "excommunication" is more of a "bother" than the terrifying sanction the New Testament meant it to be.

In short, individualism has stripped Christians of the mind-set that at one time enabled them to both grasp the meaning Paul gave to the Church and to live out that meaning in authentic community.

Community - the Depository of Telos

The relationship between discrete individuals, the telos that directs and governs their lives, and the community to which they're linked - *that relationship* is finely balanced and charged with subtle nuances. No one metaphor conveys the full range of meanings that characterizes it. One that comes close, however, is the metaphor of a depository. Though telos is personally possessed by each individual, it can only be "drawn" upon within community. In a sense, therefore, community is where telos is deposited. It can't be actualized apart from community; it can't be made concrete and tangible.

The Communal Nature of Personal Ethics

The train of Paul's thought extending from Romans 5:1 all the way to Romans 15:13 reflects a teleological bent that's very seldom picked up on - though it's so obvious that when pointed out we're left wondering how it's possible to overlook it.

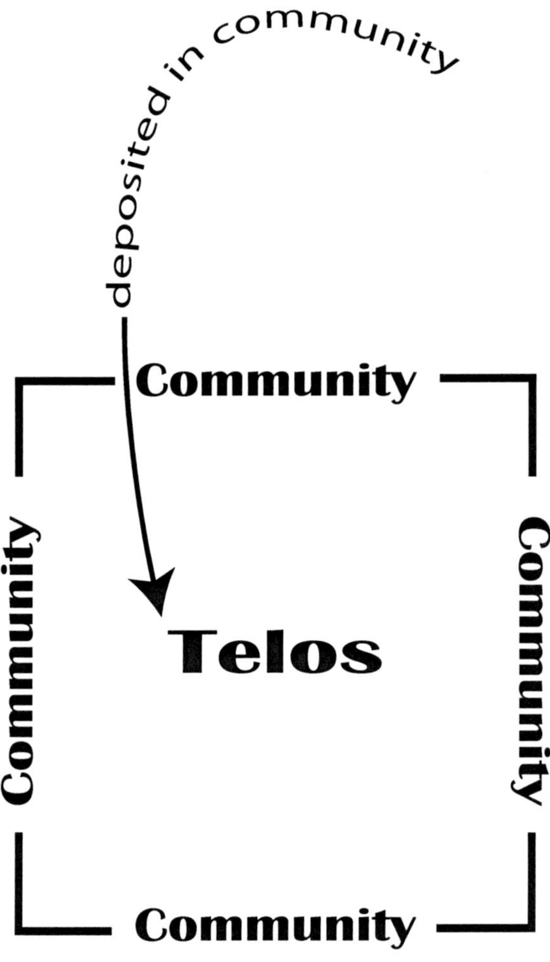

Community is where telos is "deposited" and where men and women can "actualize" it. In short, individual men and women must make themselves a part of community to become truly authentic. It's in this sense that the community is prior to and apart from the individuals who comprise it.

Romans 5 through 8 sums up Paul's teaching on *personal* sanctification - the dynamics underlying the ethical changes justification leads to - what it means to be conformed to the image of Christ and how it occurs. That's all patently clear. But what does *personal sanctification lead to?* That's not as clear - not because Paul doesn't highlight it, but because our non-teleological thought patterns by and large blind us to it. *What it leads to is community!*

In short *personal* sanctification, contrary to what's so commonly taught in Evangelical Bible studies and from Evangelical pulpits, is not meant to produce merely sanctified individuals; it's meant to produce the church - individuals built up with one another - integrated into a whole that's far more than merely the sum of its parts. Romans 5 - 8 leads to Romans 12:1 - 15:13.

And isn't that exactly the truth Jesus himself is pointing to in Matthew 22:37-40?

> Matt. 22:37 Jesus said unto him, You shall love the Lord thy God with all your heart, and with all thy soul, and with all thy mind.
> Matt. 22:38 This is the first and great commandment.
> Matt. 22:39 And the second is like unto it, Thou shalt love thy neighbour as thyself.
> Matt. 22:40 On these two commandments hang all the law and the prophets.

Jesus begins in verses 37-40 with "the personal," each individual's relationship with God, and ends with "the communal," love of neighbor. And he insists that what we have here is the very consummation of the law and the prophets. The personal and the communal can't be divorced from one another. In a very real sense, they're the opposite sides of the same coin.

Not a Matter of Personification

We're often tempted to think that Plato is merely personifying the polis in *The Republic* and that Isaiah is doing the same with Israel in Chapters 40-66. But that misses the point altogether and reflects the linear thought patterns that have developed here in the West since the Enlightenment. Personification implies that the collective is not real; that it's a fiction used to describe a mass of individuals engaged in a joint effort; for example, "*America waged war against Japan from 1941 through 1945.*" It's not that anyone here in the West truly believes there was an actual "America" that fought an actual "Japan" during the four years from late 1941 to 1945. The term "America" is meant only to refer to individual Americans acting in concert with one another, just as the term "Japan" is meant only to refer to individual Japanese acting in concert with one another. That's the way we think in the West That's the way our minds work.

But that's not the way Plato thinks; nor is it the way Isaiah thinks: Plato isn't merely personifying the polis in *The Republic* nor is Isaiah merely personifying Israel in Chapters 40-66.

For Plato, Athens is real corporately; likewise, for Isaiah, Israel is real corporately.

And it's the other way around as well: for Plato a particular individual can embody within himself Athens – not just the meaning of Athens, but Athens herself and all the individuals who comprise her. For example, it's clear from Plato's *Apologia* that Socrates embodies Athens[22] just as Athens embodies Socrates.[23]

And the same holds true for Isaiah. That's why it's so difficult to tell if "The Servant of the Lord" described in Chapters 40-66 is the nation of Israel or an individual Jew. The debate has been endless; but it's largely beside the point; and that's because a premodern thinker has little trouble "shuttling back and forth" between the two. The one entails the other.

And that's characteristic of *all* premodern thinking – not just Isaiah, or Plato, or Aristotle.

Christ is the Church
Paul reflects the very same mind-set. Christ, a single individual, gathers into himself, meaning he embodies within himself, all the discrete individuals who comprise the Church. Indeed, he is the Church – just as in Isaiah 40-66 the "The Servant of the Lord" is Israel. *Thus, Christ's history becomes our history.*

- It's in this sense that we died with Christ on the Cross (Rom. 6:8).
- It's in this sense that we were raised with Christ in the Resurrection (Col. 3:1).
- It's in this sense that we are even now seated with Christ in the heavenlies (Eph. 1:3).

And it's the other way around as well:
- It's in this sense that *we* complete Christ's suffering (Col. 1:24).
- It's in this sense that *we* complete Christ's mission (2 Cor. 5:18-19).

It's the same rationale underlying Paul's claim that Christ is in us and we are in Christ.

Col. 1:27 To them God willed to make known what are the riches of the glory of this mystery among the Gentiles: which is ***Christ in you***, the hope of glory.

Rom. 8:1 There is therefore now no condemnation to ***those who are in Christ Jesus***, who do not walk according to the flesh, but according to the Spirit.

But that's not the end of it. Christ's identification with the church is carried even further: for Paul, the church is not merely a community; it's more than that: it's an extension of Christ himself; it's his body; it's his eyes, his ears, his hands, his arms, etc. Furthermore, it's not just his body figuratively, but actually. For example, when Paul tells us in 1 Corinthians 12:27 that we are the Body of Christ...

1 Cor. 12:27 Now you (plural) are the body of Christ, and members individually.

...he means that quite literally: we ***are*** Christ's hands and feet – ministering reconciliation to a lost and dying world.

Christ is Israel
Not only do the scriptures clearly tell us that Christ embodies the Church, they also tell us – just as clearly – that Christ embodies Israel. Matthew 2:15 is decisive – though its implications are seldom spun out...

> ...and (Jesus) was there (in Egypt) until the death of Herod, that it might be fulfilled which was spoken by the Lord through the prophet, saying, *"Out of Egypt have I called My Son."*
>
> Matthew 2:15

...a quote taken from Hosea 11:1 and there clearly pointing to Israel's exodus from Egypt under Moses, but applied to Christ here in Matthew. In short, *Christ is Israel's telos* – meaning Israel finds her consummation in Christ just as surely as the Church finds her consummation in Christ. Clearly, then, the *Servant of the Lord* Isaiah describes in Chapters 40-66 is none other than Christ himself. And that sheds a new light on Romans 11:16-26 – the implications of which we'll be taking up in our exegesis of Romans 9-11.

Extended through Time - Past • Present • Future
The corporate nature of both Israel and the Church

Israel Finds Her Consummation in Christ

That there is a distinction between the Church and Israel is a truth underscored in the most unmistakable of terms throughout Romans 9 - 11. However, that distinction can be pressed too far. Ultimately, Israel no less than the Church, finds both her identity and her consummation in Christ – meaning Israel will stand incomplete and deficient until she at last acknowledges that Christ is her Messiah.

It's not just a matter of salvation – that salvation is wrought no differently for the Jews than for the gentiles – that the Jews are not provided a means of salvation that circumvents "Christ on the Cross" and their need to embrace that truth openly and plainly. It's that, of course; but it's much more: Christ is Israel's calling – her destiny – the ground of her existence. Christ is what Israel is all about. Without Christ, Israel is broken. It's that simple.

The failure on the part of some Christians – ostensibly, friends of Israel – to proclaim this truth is a sad and tragic fact. Some ignore it all together; others, lacking the courage of their convictions and unwilling to offend Jewish sensitivities and undermine the status they have gained within the Jewish community and among Jewish leaders, play down this truth. Unwittingly, they have become enemies of the Cross.

is not limited to the here and now, but extends through time as well - meaning it embodies not just believers living at the present, but believers who have lived in the past and believers yet unborn. And the metaphors used in Scripture have been carefully crafted to reflect this important truth; for example, the metaphor of "the root and branches" used in Romans Eleven - where the root symbolizes Abraham, the father of faith. (See pages 183-184.)

The Mystery of Israel's Rejection

Connection to Romans 9-11

Here → Romans 9-11

Salvation can't occur apart from a redeeming community – whether Israel or the Church. Given Paul's teleological mind-set, that's unthinkable. It wouldn't even occur to him. And if Israel, for the moment, has repudiated Christ, who is as much her telos as he is the Church's, then the Church, as a redeeming community, becomes the sole repository of that telos – the collective framework within which redemption is both preached and lived out. *And it's precisely here that the meaning of Israel's rejection is found: God, while preserving her, no longer saves individual Jews into her. They're saved into the church. Israel has lost that privileged status - and won't regain it until she at last acknowledges Christ as her Messiah at the end of the Tribulation.*

The Necessity of a Redeeming Community - Eschatological Implications of That Truth

The eschatological implications here are both profound and somewhat disconcerting. Why? Because so many of us were raised to believe in a pre-tribulational rapture; but the necessary correlation between salvation and a redeeming community seems to call that into question. All premillennialists acknowledge that conversions occur during the Tribulation – on a scale that's without precedent – both for Jews and for Gentiles. But if Israel does not turn her heart back to God and embrace Christ until the very end of the Tribulation – a fact that's incontrovertible – then those salvations must surely occur within and through the Church - entailing her presence during almost that entire time-frame. Hundreds of millions of souls redeemed in the absence of either the Church or a redeemed Israel – which is what a pretribulational rapture requires? The very idea is incomprehensible to a premodern, wholly teleological intellect – so much so that Paul wouldn't even bother to stress it – nor would any other author of the New Testament Canon. It would simply be taken for granted.

Telos and the Meaning of Holiness

The Pentateuch, especially Genesis and Leviticus, defines holiness quite differently from what we've grown accustomed to expect. We tend to define holiness along two lines of thought...

1. It's an attribute – an attribute we acquire when we're regenerated – an attribute that makes possible fellowship with God. Ordinarily, we're at a loss to take it any further – meaning we can't quite define what it *specifically* consists of – except to blurt out the word "godliness" – without

defining what *that* means. Rarely, a well trained and perspicacious student of theology will point to Galatians 5:22-23...

> But the fruit of the Spirit is love, joy, peace, longsuffering, gentleness, goodness, faith, Meekness, temperance: *against such there is no law.*
>
> Galatians 5:22-23

...explaining that holiness consists of the "fruit of the Spirit." Why? Because the phrase *"against such there is no law"* is meant to indicate that the Law, which reflects God's holiness, can find no basis for condemning a man whose life displays the fruit of the Spirit.

2. Occasionally, holiness is defined less as a concrete attribute and more as an *absence* – specifically, an absence of sin – without bothering to define exactly what constitutes sin.

And, certainly, there's a modicum of truth in both definitions. But the Pentateuch defines holiness along a different line of thought - in a way that catches contemporary Christians off guard – that seems a bit strange and unsettling. That's because the Pentateuch defines holiness *teleologically*. For Moses, the author of the Pentateuch, holiness consists of living out the *telos* God has sovereignly ordained for every phenomenon that comprises existence; and, correspondingly, sin consists of violating that telos – of overstepping the bounds it defines. Leviticus 19:19 is a good example...

> Lev. 19:19 You shall keep my statutes. You shall not let your cattle gender with a diverse kind: you shall not sow your field with ***mingled*** seed: neither shall a garment ***mingled*** of linen and wool come upon you.

God's statutes are ultimately meant to safeguard the design he has ordained for all creation – which means keeping separate and distinct the various "teloi" that comprise existence. *That's holiness.* Sin, on the other hand and at bottom, consists of a disregard for that design – a disregard that assumes the form of *"mingling"* – in this case...

- *mingling* different species of animals,
- *mingling* different kinds of seed,
- *mingling* different kinds of cloth.

Mingling leads to confusion – and confusion is contrary to holiness. Leviticus 18:23 and Leviticus 20:12 are both good examples...

> Lev. 18:23 Neither shall you lie with any beast to defile yourself therewith: neither shall any woman stand before a beast to lie down thereto: ***it is confusion.***

> Lev. 20:12 And if a man lie with his daughter in law, both of them shall surely be put to death: ***they have wrought confusion***...

- Mankind should never "cross-breed" with another kind of animal. That's sinful. It mingles two distinct "teloi," and, therefore, causes confusion – which is the antithesis of holiness.
- Moreover, the boundaries that comprise a specific telos often include exacting behavioral patterns that must likewise be respected; for example, a father-in-law cannot "marry" his daughter-in-law. That kind of behavior breeds confusion and chaos within the family unit – which, once again, is the antithesis of holiness.

It's this very rationale that underlies the prohibition against cross-dressing...

> Deut. 22:5 A woman shall not wear what pertains to a man, neither shall a man put on a woman's garment; for whosoever does these things is an abomination unto Jehovah your God.

Mingling and confusion – a refusal to honor the unique differences God has assigned men in contrast to women and women in contrast to men – differences grounded in the separate and distinct teloi God has ordained for each.

The prohibition against homosexuality is grounded here as well. A man's physical sexuality finds its consummation in a woman, not another man. That specific expectation is integrated into the telos God has assigned him. Likewise, a woman's physical sexuality finds its consummation in a man, not another woman. Put a little differently: men are *designed* sexually for women and, likewise, women are *designed* sexually for men.

Calvin on the Ropes

Homosexuality is, therefore, contrary to God's design – and reflects a high-handed disregard of God's sovereignty. It leads to confusion and, hence, is contrary to holiness.

Sin, then, finds its roots in *confusion* – which occurs whenever the distinction that contrasts one telos from another is either overlooked or intentionally breached.

- Separation and distinction lie at the heart of holiness;
- mingling and confusion lie at the heart of sin.

Jude 6 is another example of a sin clearly grounded in a high-handed disregard of telos.

Jude 6	And the angels ***which kept not their first estate, but left their own habitation,*** he has reserved in everlasting chains under darkness unto the judgment of the great day.

Here we have angels who overstepped the bounds God had set for them – who contemptuously violated the telos – the "estate," the "habitation" – he had assigned them. It's quite likely that these are the very angels Moses had in mind when he penned Genesis 6...

Gen. 6:1	And it came to pass, when men began to multiply on the face of the ground, and daughters were born unto them,
Gen. 6:2	that the sons of God (angels) saw the daughters of men that they were fair; and they took them wives of all that they chose.

Angels transgressing the teleological distinction between themselves and mankind – "leaving their first estate" – and procreating with the "daughters of men" – a sin so abominable in the eyes of God that it led to the Flood! *Mingling* and *confusion* on a grand scale! A blatant, rebellious disregard for the separate telos he had assigned angels in contrast to mankind – a failure to honor the unique status he had ordained for them in the created order.

This principle is the rationale underlying other enigmatic passages as well – for example, 1 Corinthians 11:3-15 – the whole question of "head coverings"...

1 Cor. 11:3	But I would have you know, that the head of every man is Christ; and the head of the woman is the man; and the head of Christ is God.
1 Cor. 11:4	Every man praying or prophesying, having his head covered, dishonors his head.
1 Cor. 11:5	But every woman that prays or prophesies with her head uncovered dishonors her head: for that is even all one as if she were shaven.
1 Cor. 11:6	For if the woman be not covered, let her also be shorn: but if it be a shame for a woman to be shorn or shaven, let her be covered.
1 Cor. 11:7	For a man indeed ought not to cover his head, forasmuch as he is the image and glory of God: but the woman is the glory of the man.
1 Cor. 11:8	For the man is not of the woman; but the woman of the man.
1 Cor. 11:9	Neither was the man created for the woman; but the woman for the man.
1 Cor. 11:10	For this cause ought the woman to have power on her head because of the angels.
1 Cor. 11:11	Nevertheless neither is the man without the woman, neither the woman without the man, in the Lord.
1 Cor. 11:12	For as the woman is of the man, even so is the man also by the woman; but all things of God.
1 Cor. 11:13	Judge in yourselves: is it comely that a woman pray unto God uncovered?
1 Cor. 11:14	Doth not even nature itself teach you, that, if a man have long hair, it is a shame unto him?
1 Cor. 11:15	But if a woman have long hair, it is a glory to her: for her hair is given her for a covering.

Once again, the issue here is telos – which is why the meaning of 1 Corinthians 11:3-15 is so puzzling for most Christians – never having been attuned to the significance of telos and, consequently, unable conform their thinking to

Paul's. What Paul is doing here is really quite straightforward and wholly in keeping with a premodern mind-set: he's insisting on maintaining the distinction between men and women – knowing that a violation of that distinction lies at the heart of sin.

Some commentators make authority the issue here; but authority is only a secondary issue and is relevant only because headship is incorporated into a man's telos and submission into a woman's telos. Others make the complementary nature of men and women the issue here – and, indeed, Paul is careful to underscore that truth; but it too is a secondary issue – and, like authority, is relevant only because a man and woman's complementary nature is imbedded in their respective "teloi."

Telos is the foundational principle underlying God's creation. It's a principle spelled out and highlighted in the very first chapter of Genesis, for example Genesis 1:11 and Genesis 1:21....

Gen. 1:11 And God said, Let the earth bring forth grass, the herb yielding seed, and the fruit tree yielding fruit ***after his kind, whose seed is in itself,*** upon the earth: and it was so.

Gen. 1:21 And God created great whales, and every living creature that moves, which the waters brought forth abundantly, ***after their kind, and every winged fowl after his kind:*** and God saw that it was good.

The word "seed" in verse 11 does not depict merely a mechanism for reproduction; it's a shorthand expression for "telos." Each fruit tree, each herb, has been assigned a specific telos and is designed to reproduce that telos in its offspring. Honoring that principle lies at the very heart of holiness – which is the sense conveyed in the phrase *"and God saw that it was good."*

Throughout Genesis Chapter One, creation is depicted as an on-going process of ***separation and distinction*** – a process that begins with Genesis 1:3...

Gen. 1:3 And God said, Let there be light: and there was light.
Gen. 1:4 And God saw the light, that it was good: and God ***divided*** the light from the darkness.

...and continues with Genesis 1:6-7...

Gen. 1:6 And God said, Let there be a firmament in the midst of the waters, and let it ***divide*** the waters from the waters.
Gen. 1:7 And God made the firmament, and ***divided*** the waters which were under the firmament from the waters which were above the firmament: and it was so.

...until its climax is reached at the end of Genesis One. In short, creation is built around the principle of *separation* and *distinction* – which God calls "good" (e.g., Genesis 1:10, 12, 18, etc.) – and which, therefore, defines holiness.

That brings us to the word "destruction" in 2 Thessalonians 1:7-9...

2 Thess. 1:7 ... when the Lord Jesus shall be revealed from heaven with his mighty angels,
2 Thess. 1:8 In flaming fire taking vengeance on them who know not God, and who obey not the gospel of our Lord Jesus Christ:
2 Thess. 1:9 Who shall be punished with everlasting ***destruction*** from the presence of the Lord, and from the glory of his power...

The word "destruction" in verse 9 does not mean "annihilation." Both the word itself (ὄλεθρος) and its context tell otherwise. Anyone undergoing destruction is *ruined* - meaning he is eternally kept from living out the telos that lies at the heart of his very being. He is left without significance and purpose - adrift in a sea of cosmic meaninglessness. That's what Paul is getting at in 2 Thessalonians 1:7-9. Man is *meant* to enjoy fellowship with God. That's his telos and anything less leaves him "in ruins."

– ***Paul's Use of Deductive Logic and Syllogisms***
Romans is sprinkled throughout with deductive logic and syllogistic reasoning. For example, Romans 2:1 is cast in the form of a syllogism – and knowing that helps us to identify the person

to whom Paul's speaking there – and so enables us to accurately "connect the dots." Romans 2:24 – 27, on the other hand, is a classic study in the use of deductive logic – and can be analyzed using Aristotle's "Categorical Language." Knowing that enables us to feel the full weight of Paul's sarcasm in Romans 2:27 – and, in so doing, keeps us from misconstruing Paul's real intentions.

- ***Links to Romans 9-11***
  Romans 9-11 comprise three of the most difficult chapters in the Bible – regardless of training and perspicacity[24]. I'm convinced, however, that in many respects it's the hub around which the entire Book of Romans revolves. Understanding it, therefore, is vital. One of the keys to unraveling its meaning lies in paying very close attention to the various "lead-ins" Paul sprinkles throughout Romans 1-8. Consequently, I've taken special pains to highlight those "lead-ins" and explain their significance – beginning on pages 15, 17, 18, 19, etc. And because Romans 8:29-30 is so clearly linked to Romans 9-11, I've also highlighted lead-ins to that passage of scripture as well.

  Moreover, it's these very lead-ins that underscore the fallacies and inconsistencies that plague Calvinism; therefore, paying close attention to them serves also to put the lie to Calvinism and dismantle its imposing - shall I say intimidating - edifice.

- ***Highlighting Personal Relevance***
  The Book of Romans is filled with tools for personal use – tools we can use to transform our lives; and I've tried to lay out a format that facilitates that. For example, from Romans 1:18b through Romans 3:20, Paul sketches out in detail the dynamics of human psychology – what, in short, makes us all tick. He spells out the compulsive nature of sin – the addictions that plague us and the fears that haunt us. In Romans Five and Six, he reveals the means God has provided to bring healing and restoration. In Romans Seven he discloses the debilitating nature of guilt – and so on and so forth. Anyone who has thoroughly studied the Book of Romans should be equipped to both understand himself better and profitably counsel others.

- ***Special Attention Given to the Human Psyche***
  Paul devotes special attention to spelling out the dynamics of the human psyche - and much of what he tells us is based on principles drawn from the Old Testament; therefore, I've chosen to delineate those principles in some detail using the Book of Leviticus to do so.

- ***Highlighting Cultural Relevance***
  The topics Paul raises in Romans are universal themes – and the conclusions he reaches and the nuances he underscores are part of the fabric of Western culture[25]. In short, the Book of Romans is *culturally* relevant. To point that out, I've drawn upon plays and novels written by a whole array of authors – from Sophocles and Aeschylus to Arthur Miller and Tennessee Williams.

- ***Use of Excurses to Elaborate on Important Topics***
  I've included a series of excurses directly touching upon issues Paul takes up in Romans. Some of them are drawn from sermons I've preached over the years. It's my hope that they will serve to enrich your understanding of those issues.

- ***Personal Devotion***
  Finally, I believe that an expository study can and should be devotional in nature. And I've tried to provide for that also in the format I've developed.

There's so much more that might be done to help gen-Xers and gen-Yers…

- connect the dots in Romans,
- spot its overarching themes, and
- grasp its personal and cultural relevance.

And perhaps in later editions I might expand my repertoire of tools – or perhaps you might have some suggestions of your own. But for the moment, we have a start. May God bless you richly as you embark upon the study of Romans; and, most especially, may it help you become a blessing to others so that when you stand before the Judgment Seat of Christ, you'll hear, *"Well done, good and faithful servant. Enter into the joy of your Lord."*

Further Observations Concerning the Premodern Teleological Thought Found in Scripture - An Excursus -

Two Kinds of Teleological Thought

For Aristotle, "manness," an example of a teleological "archetype," is inserted into every concrete, existential man and woman. For the unsaved, it's "Adam's manness" - leading to sin and death. For the saved, it's "Christ's manness" - leading to righteousness and a splendor which fully matches the splendor of Christ's very own humanity. Romans 5:12-21 reflects this form of teleological thinking.

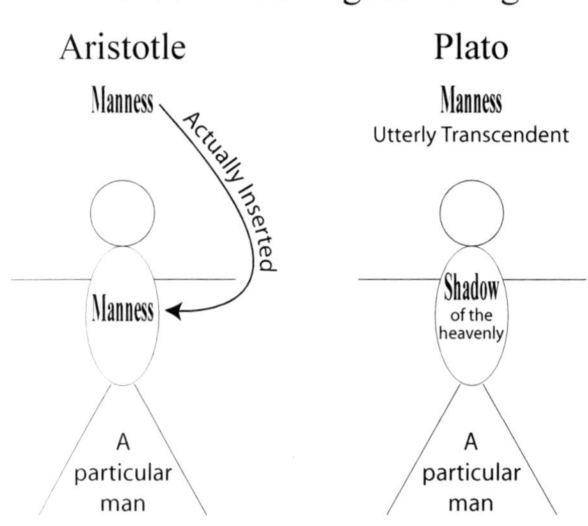

On the other hand, for Plato, "manness" exists only as a transcendent reality - and concrete, existential men and women are only shadows of that reality, unable ever to fully match its splendor. Nowhere in scripture, however, is Platonic teleology found applied to men and women. It is, however, applied to the true "Sanctuary of God" found only in heaven - with the concrete, existential sanctuary built by Moses only a shadow of the heavenly sanctuary - Hebrews 8:1-5.

****

For the most part, the premodern teleological thought found in scripture is cast in an *Aristotelian* guise - meaning it's dynamic and fully imbedded in existential phenomena. Once again, Romans 5:12-21 is a good example: there, anyone possessed of Adam's telos is destined to sin and death whereas anyone possessed of Christ's telos is destined to righteousness and life. However, the static and utterly transcendent *Platonic* teleology is also found in scripture. A good example is Hebrews 8:1-5...

Heb. 8:1 Now the main point in what we are saying is this: we have such a high priest, one who is seated at the right hand of the throne of the Majesty in the heavens,

Heb. 8:2 *a minister in the sanctuary and the true tent that the Lord and not any mortal, has set up.*

Heb. 8:3 For every high priest is appointed to offer gifts and sacrifices; hence it is necessary for this priest also to have something to offer.

Heb. 8:4 Now if he were on earth, he would not be a priest at all, since there are priests who offer gifts according to the law.

Heb. 8:5 *They offer worship in a sanctuary that is a sketch and shadow of the heavenly one; for Moses, when he was about to erect the tent, was warned, "See that you make everything according to the pattern that was shown you on the mountain."*

What we have here looks as if it were pulled straight out of Book VII of Plato's *Republic*: the true sanctuary is fully transcendent, not subject to change, and entirely static. Its existential counterpart on the earth is, therefore, only a sketch and shadow of the heavenly and can never match its splendor. And the same can be said of Hebrews 10:1...

> Heb. 10:1 For the law having a *shadow* of good things to come, and *not the very image of the things*, can never with those sacrifices which they offered year by year continually make the comers thereunto perfect.

Here again we have a contrast between "the shadow on earth of the perfect in heaven" - teleology cast in a Platonic guise, not an Aristotelian guise.

The point here, once again, is not to suggest that Paul or any of the other New Testament authors was either a Platonist or an Aristotelian, but that teleology - whatever its form - was the paradigm governing all premodern intellectual discourse - whether Semetic, Hellenic, or otherwise.

God's Plan - a Truth That Has Fallen on Hard Times - An Excursus -

That God has a plan is a notion that has fallen on hard times. A plan embraced by faith, and implying design, purpose, and comprising a set of mutually consistent propositions put off limits to challenge and criticism. That very possibility is under attack - not from just one protagonist, but two.

The first protagonist is, of course, the rationalism that arose during the Renaissance and which the Enlightenment "philosophe's" further crystallized and hardened. What stands behind "rationalism" is "doubt" – meaning an unwillingness to allow any proposition to be clothed in the guise of absolute "truth." The epistemological underpinnings of that doubt were spelled out early on by both David Hume and Immanuel Kant.

More recently, it has been summed up in Karl Popper's renowned treatise *The Logic of Scientific Discovery*, published in 1934. Science, Popper claimed, is, by its very nature, "irreducibly conjectural" – meaning whatever knowledge science produces can never be pressed beyond the "merely possible." In short, science can only spin out theory – and each step forward in the acquisition of "scientific knowledge" is predicated on "falsifying" existing theory. Doubt, then, is the engine propelling science – which is the form "rationalism" has assumed here in the West.

Thomas Kuhn, building on Popper's thesis, has suggested that science undergoes periodic crises – during which one theory is replaced by another that provides a simpler yet more complete explanation of the data under investigation. The crisis is followed by a prolonged quiescence - during which the new theory is leafed out, meaning its claims are clarified and its implications are fully developed, That, in turn, is followed by a period of growing doubt – prompted by discoveries which can't be satisfactorily subsumed under the existing theory – and a new crisis is spawned, leading to the fabrication of a still more encompassing theory that is often radically different from the one it replaces; and so on and so forth; e.g., Ptolemaic cosmology is replaced by Copernican cosmology; Newtonian physics is replaced by quantum mechanics, creation is replaced by Darwinian evolution, etc. Kuhn spelled out his insights in a book he entitled *The Structure of Scientific Revolutions*, published in 1962. Like Popper, Kuhn made it clear that doubt is the engine driving the acquisition of rational – meaning empirically based – knowledge.

So pervasive has science become in the West, especially here in America, that the doubt propelling it has become a cultural mind-set, making it very difficult for most Americans to hold onto "absolutist beliefs" – beliefs put off limits to criticism and challenge. We've been taught that it's "unreasonable" to accord any belief that kind of privileged status. Creation, the flood, the virgin birth, the Resurrection, the infallibility of scripture, heaven and hell, the inherent sinfulness of mankind, an afterlife – it's all subject to criticism and challenge, and to suggest otherwise is "irrational" – indeed, its very definition. That's a tough accusation to bear up under; consequently, most evangelicals have begun to shy away from doctrinal pronouncements of any kind. Doctrine is becoming less and less important among evangelicals – not because they're lazy and undisciplined, but because they don't want to be labeled "hayseed fundamentalists" – *they don't want to swim against the prevailing cultural tide that makes criticism and doubt the mark of intellectual respectability.* Any kind of doctrine that suggests a hard and fast definition of salvation or lays out a grand design guiding human history is becoming ever more distasteful. *So much for God's Plan.*

The second protagonist is what currently passes under the general rubric of "postmodernism." To some extent, postmodernism is both an outgrowth of and reaction to science. It builds upon many of the themes existentialists highlighted during the first half of the 20th Century.

Science is, by its very nature, geared toward the discovery of "universals" – and its effectiveness can be measured by how well it strips away the "abnormalities" and "peculiarities" that get in the way of identifying those universals. That's fine for science; but if that mind-set is carried over into every-day life, it can be pernicious. Why? Because it's those very "peculiarities" or "differences" that give rise to a sense of self. Personal identity, for example, is rooted not in what we share in common with all other men, the universals that make up human nature, but in what distinguishes us from all other men. It's the focus on differences and peculiarities that lies at the heart of postmodernism – just as it did for existentialism some thirty years earlier. Postmodernists repudiate universals – and cleave instead to heterogeneity – the belief that no one "truth" is valid.

Postmodernism first surfaced in architecture – and was a reaction against the "International Style," fostered by Le Corbusier, Mies van der Rohe, and Walter Gropius in Europe and Louis Sullivan in the United States. Charles Eames carried it over into the design of furniture. Its mantra was *"form follows function"* – meaning the essence of good design consists of eliminating whatever features don't serve the intended purpose of the building. Ornament for its own sake was deemed "a crime." In short, *less is beautiful*.

Inevitably, The International Style produced buildings that reflected a stultifying sameness. There was nothing that really distinguished one from the other. There was "no personality." The towering, glass enclosed office buildings that rise over Los Angeles and Houston, the featureless housing projects that blight Chicago – all of it reflects the deadening impact of The International Style. Nothing but dull monotony. In 1972, Robert Venturi, Denise Scott Brown, and Steven Izenour published a ground breaking book entitled *Learning from Las Vegas*. Its basic premise was *"less is a bore."* Yes, they conceded, the buildings along the Las Vegas strip are garish and ostentatious – and adorned with superfluous decoration serving no functional purpose; but for all that, they boast full-blooded personalities that proponents of The International Style have never produced and can never hope to produce.

Postmodernists assert that the quest for unifying principles and grand designs drains not only architecture but life itself of its meaning – of what Suzi Gablik calls its "enchantment."

Jean-François Lyotard, a seminal postmodernist, takes it further - insisting that life, by its very nature, is chaotic - filled with complexities and nuances most of which lie hidden in the backwaters of the subconscious - if even there. It's impossible, he claims, to reduce life to a single all encompassing story – what he calls a "metanarrative" – with a clearly defined plot featuring a beginning, a middle, and an ending. Any and all such attempts are futile - and not just futile, but inherently dishonest. Why? Because, in the end, a metanarrative reflects nothing more than the biases of the persons who fabricate it or the cultures that give rise to it. Unquestionably, Lyotard is following up on the "stream of consciousness" insights that James Joyce, Virginia Woolf, Joseph Conrad, etc. wove into their novels at the turn of the last century.

There is no grand design, only a hodge-podge of "highly localized" paradigms that often defy description, that are constantly undergoing change, and that frequently bump into each other. The key, then, is to embrace difference – even to celebrate difference; but, above all, to keep it from erupting into conflict and mayhem. Ultimately, so claim postmodernists, it was the clash of cultural metanarratives that led to World Wars I and II – a clash of ideologies arising from a refusal to embrace different notions of the truth. And that, postmodernists insist, has got to be stopped. "Truth" is relative only to the culture that has given rise to it – and should never be foisted on cultures built around competing "truths." Cultural sensitivity is, therefore, another of postmodernism's linchpins – and its violation is considered not just misguided, but profoundly immoral. The Christian Faith is certainly to be respected, but no more so than Buddhism or Islam. Its claims are not absolute and its spread to foreign cultures is wrongheaded and dangerous.

Postmodernism, like existentialism before it, emphasizes commitment. But the commitment existentialism promoted was markedly different. Existential commitment was a lonely quest undertaken by solitary "heroes;" moreover, it was never devoid of content. Existentialists went out of their way to delineate the nature of their commitment - its purpose - its intent: e.g., Sartre - Marxism, Kierkegaard - Christianity, Ezra Pound - Fascism, etc. The commitment pursued by postmodernists, on the other hand, is much more communal in nature - and is largely bereft of content - assuming more the form of a life-style than a body of propositional truths. It's precisely this feature that characterizes so many of the "emerging churches" - and helps to explain why they stress ambiance and mood and play down teaching and preaching.

That God has a plan for all mankind - a plan that's woven into the fabric of history and reflects transcendent truth – it's a notion that has indeed fallen on hard times! And its neglect and often its blatant repudiation has taken root in many evangelical churches - again, most especially among many of the so-called "emerging churches."

The Impact of Individualism on Western Art and Design - An Excursus -

Almost 80 years ago, Robert Frost intoned, "The family's where you go when no one else wants you." What prompted Frost's observation - as much a plaintive cry as an observation - were the changes then taking place in Western culture. Family was a sanctuary; a haven; a refuge. All other social institutions were fast becoming impersonal bureaucracies staffed by experts - and pointed toward well defined, rationally calculated goals. Management technique was based upon "cost effectiveness." Organizational linkages were intentionally stripped of affection and reduced instead to a mere "cash nexus." Neither management nor labor stressed personal loyalty based upon a sense of mutual respect and organic attachment. The bottom line for both was the "almighty dollar." Employees were mere ciphers, moveable parts, ***modular units*** - to be shifted around or discarded at will.

Modular Units: A New Way of Thinking Produces a New Art From

Modular units, moved about at will - perhaps the best single concrete reflection of alienation. It has been carried over onto every level of human consciousness - even onto the level of artistic consciousness. Picasso's art reflects it. His human figures are composed of "modular units" moved about at random - not bound by any thought of the whole. A nose is haphazardly attached here, an ear there, etc. The parts are all present, but not fit together according to any holistic principle. The integrating significance of the whole has been intentionally discarded – leaving many of his paintings looking like shards of broken glass.

Picasso perfectly reflected the alienation that was tightening its grip on western culture at the beginning of the Twentieth Century. That was his genius. Picasso, though, never quite captured the horror of that alienation. That was left to Edward Munch. His painting "The Scream" sends shudders through the soul of every man, woman, and child born since 1900. Each of us resonates to the dread it portrays. And what it so dramatically portrays is the insanity that alienation leads to - the horrifying solipsism it produces. Likewise, the absurdity produced by alienation is the subject of the surrealists - who transformed even space and time into "modular units." The whole flow of "modern" art is easily discerned when set against the backdrop of the individualism that's so predominant in the West - and most especially here in America.

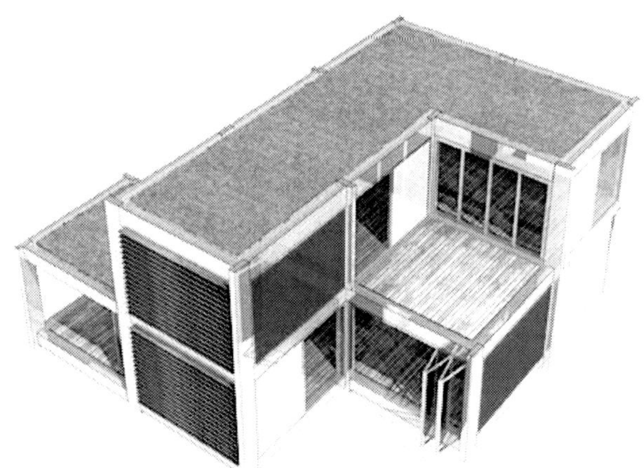

A Modular Home

A STUDY OF ROMANS

CHAPTER TWO

Verses for Chapter Two

Rom. 1:16	...the gospel...is the power of God unto salvation to everyone who believes, to the Jew first and also to the Greek.
Rom. 1:17	For in it the righteousness of God is revealed from faith to faith; as it is written, the just shall live by faith.
Rom. 1:18*a*	For the wrath of God is revealed from heaven against all ungodliness and unrighteousness of men...

Verse:

Rom. 1:16	...the gospel...is the power of God unto salvation to everyone who believes, to the Jew first and also to the Greek.

Specific words or phrases found in verse 16

"gospel"
Simply put, the word "gospel" means "good news." The gospel is *good news* for mankind. This, then, sets the theme for the entire Book of Romans: *good news*.

Key Concept

The Gospel is God's cure for all that's wrong with mankind. It's "God's power unto salvation."

"the power of God unto"
The Greek word "εις" – here translated *"unto"* – often incorporates a teleologic[26] connotation – a sense of design or purpose. What Paul is saying here, then, is that the *power* of God has been marshaled and, with painstaking care, orchestrated *to save everyone who "believes"* ("πιστιστευοντι" - from the word "πιστις," "faith") - who relies upon God - who casts himself on his mercy and trusts in his loving kindness.

Think about it

What does the use of power on God's part tell us about the foe we're up against?

"Power," ("δυναμις") should not be confused with "authority, ("εξουσια").

- Authority imposes a *moral* obligation to obey – an obligation that the person subject to it both acknowledges and reveres. Consequently, the obedience he renders is *willing*.
- Power, on the other hand, does not rely upon a willing submission grounded in a moral obligation to obey. The submission it secures is grounded only in raw, brute force and intimidation.

You're at War! Get used to it!

Christians have a hard time wrapping their minds around the stubborn truth that here on earth, peace is elusive. Peace in Christ – Yes! *But **not circumstantial** peace*. That's because we're at war. The earth is a battlefield.

The use of the word "power" here in Romans1:16 hints at the kind of struggle mankind is up against: sin acknowledges no moral obligation to submit – not even to God; it acknowledges no moral constraints whatsoever. It can't be won over; it can't be converted.

- It never yields on its own.
- It's not amenable to reason or persuasion.
- It never willingly backs off.
- It must be conquered and subjugated.[27]

The Apostle Paul puts it well in his epistle to the Philippians:

> That at the name of Jesus every knee should bow, of things in heaven, and things in earth, and things under the earth;
> And that every tongue should confess that Jesus Christ is Lord, to the glory of God the Father.
> Philippians 2:10-11

Every knee! Some, prompted by authority ("εξουσια"), will bow – acknowledging their moral obligation to do so - hearts filled with thanksgiving and gratitude. Others, however, prompted only by raw power ("δυναμις"), will do so – stubbornly refusing up to the very end to acknowledge their moral obligation to do so – hearts filled with bitterness and hatred. *Nevertheless, every knee will bow!*

"salvation"
The basic meaning of "salvation" is "rescue." We'll find that God's salvation is three-fold. In the first instance, God rescues us from his wrath[28] – the verdict of guilt and the sentence of death pronounced against us in God's heavenly assize. (See Romans 1:18*a*). In the second instance, God rescues us from the power of sin (Romans 5-7); and, finally, God rescues us from the very presence of sin (Romans 8:22-23).

Think about it

Too many Christian counselors fail to take either sin or guilt seriously – to acknowledge their stubborn refusal to yield to reason or persuasion. It's not sufficient to point out to a "counselee" that his feelings of guilt are paralyzing or that his sinful behavior is self-destructive – that it inflicts pain on those he loves the most or that it invites the judgment of God. That's an appeal to reason – to common sense; and, ordinarily, it won't work! Guilt and sin can only be conquered. They won't be backed down by force of a good argument. Nevertheless, counselors make this mistake again and again.

"power of God unto salvation"
Now, let's put it all together – meaning, not just *"power of God unto,"* or *"salvation,"* but *"power of God unto salvation."*

Connection to Romans 9-11

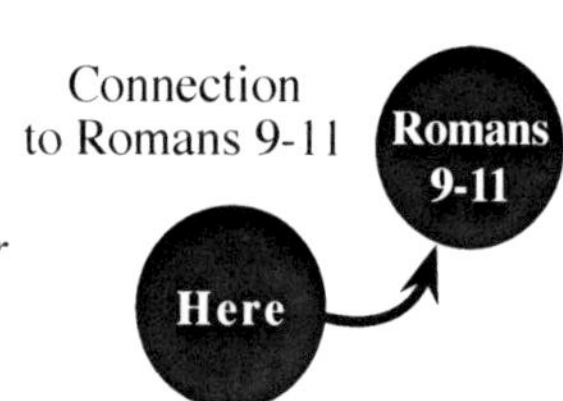

It's important to note carefully that the power Paul has in mind here – and throughout the Book of Romans – is not God's power per se, his intrinsic power, but his *power to save.*[29] And that distinction is of fundamental importance – and bears a significant impact on the interpretation of other key verses in Romans. Let's jump ahead, for example, to Chapter Nine, verses twenty-two and twenty-three – a passage of scripture that has spawned a great deal of controversy...

Romans 9:22	What if God, wanting to show His wrath and to make known His power, endured with much longsuffering the vessels of wrath fitted for destruction,
Romans 9:23	...that He might make known the riches of His glory on the vessels of mercy...

Both Boice and Piper insist that verse 22 revolves around the issue of God's sovereign power and that Paul uses it as a foil to highlight God's mercy in verse 23. As Boice puts it, "...reprobation (God's wrath) displays (God's) power in order that his powerful or sovereign name might be proclaimed throughout the whole earth." In short...

- God predestines some men to destruction (reprobation), and, in so doing, displays his wrath *to make known his power;* and, against that backdrop,
- predestines others to salvation (election) *to make known his mercy.*

Put a little differently...

- God's power is revealed in his wrath (reprobation);
- and the revelation of that power preconditions the revelation of his mercy (election).[30]

On the very face of it, however, that seems a bit implausible...

1. Nowhere else in scripture does the revelation of God's intrinsic power, *necessarily* precondition the revelation of his mercy; indeed, the Incarnation, a central doctrine of the Christian Faith, reveals God's *mercy against the backdrop of his humility – hardly his intrinsic power – a humility so profound that it led him to the Cross.*

Phil. 2:5	Let this mind be in you which was also in Christ Jesus,
Phil. 2:6	who, being in the form of God, did not consider it robbery to be equal with God,

Classic Calvinist Interpretation of Romans 9:22-23

God preordains certain persons unto wrath to display his power

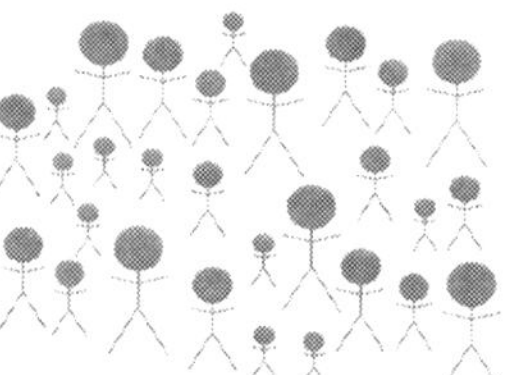

Vessels of Wrath

God preordains others unto salvation to display his mercy

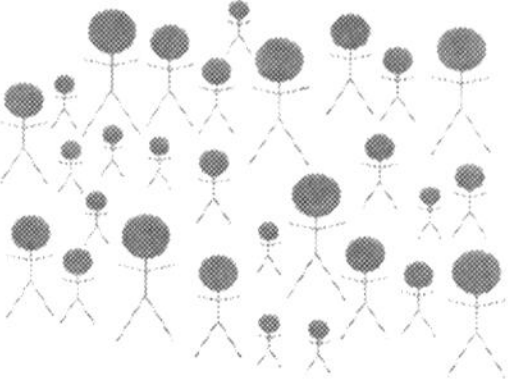

Vessels of Mercy

Phil. 2:7 but made Himself of no reputation, taking the form of a bondservant, and coming in the likeness of men.
Phil. 2:8 And being found in appearance as a man, He ***humbled*** Himself and became obedient to the point of death, even the death of the cross.

2. Moreover, it's the Resurrection, not God's wrath, that most dramatically reveals God's power.

Eph. 1:9-10 ...and what is the exceeding greatness of His power toward us who believe, according to the working of His mighty power which He wrought in Christ when He raised Him from the dead and seated Him at His right hand in the heavenly places..."

3. Finally, scripture clearly tells us it's the Cross – a single event occurring at a single moment in time – that most vividly displays God's wrath and God's mercy ...
   - God's wrath poured out on Christ; and
   - God's mercy poured out on mankind.

In short, the revelation of God's wrath and God's mercy finds its ultimate consummation in *Christ on the Cross, not as Boice and Piper would have it, in reprobation and election.*

What's especially intriguing about Boice and Piper is that time and time again they both underscore the significance of the Cross. Their comments concerning the Cross are deeply touching. Nevertheless, in the end, they - and other Calvinists as well - inadvertently subvert its importance. For them, it's not the Cross that most dramatically displays God's wrath and God's mercy; it's ...

- *reprobation*, reflecting God's wrath, and
- *election*, reflecting God's mercy.

Two Different Interpretations

Christ Crucified

The Revelation of God's wrath and God's mercy

Christ on the Cross

God's wrath poured out on Christ.
God's mercy poured out on mankind

Double Predestination

The Revelation of God's wrath and God's mercy

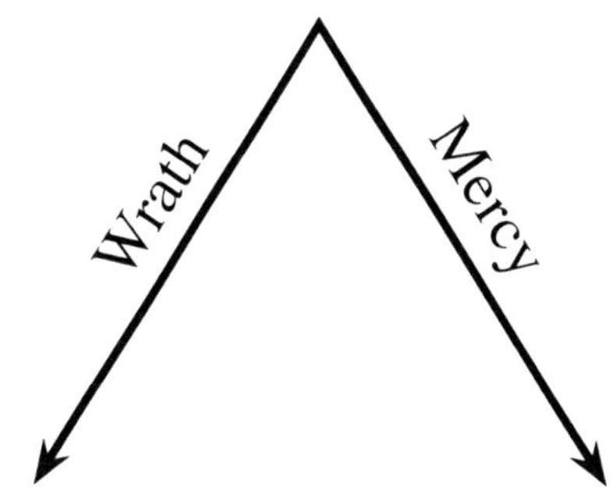

Reprobation

Some men predestined to hell

Election

Some men predestined to salvation

Their misguided interpretation arises in part from their failure to carry over to Romans 9:22 the meaning Paul gives the word "power" in Romans 1:16 – which, of course, is the theme statement of the entire book. When we do carry over that meaning, what we have is…

Romans 9:22	What if God, wanting to show His wrath and to make known His *power (to save)*[31], endured with much longsuffering the vessels of wrath fitted for destruction…
Romans 9:23	…that He might make known the riches of His glory on the vessels of mercy…

In one fell swoop, the whole meaning of Romans 9:22-23 is completely changed: verse 22 does not revolve around the issue of God's sovereign power. Nor is God's power – revealed in his wrath – the foil against which God displays his mercy. God's mercy is the single issue that dominates both verses: in verse 23, it's explicit; and in verse 22, the implied term "God's power to save" clearly suggests it.

"believes"
The word "believe" ("πιστιστευοντι") is derived from the same Greek word we translate "faith" ("πιστις"). Basically, it means "to rely upon," "to trust." "To believe God," here in this verse, amounts to a kind of surrender - both to God's assessment of mankind's sinful condition and to his unmerited favor.

"Jews and Greeks"
Here we have the first hint that God has chosen to divide mankind into two general groups for the purpose of working out his program of salvation: *Jew and Gentile*. Occasionally, "Greek" is substituted for "Gentile;" but the division still holds. The term "Greek" is meant to signify the Gentile in his most "cultured" and "sophisticated" state. This distinction will be elaborated upon at length - culminating in Chapters Nine through Eleven.

"to the Jews first and also to the Greek"
But there's more implied here in this clause than merely the division of mankind into two groups, Jew and Gentile. There's also the issue of ***priority***: clearly God has assigned priority to the Jew, not to the Gentile.

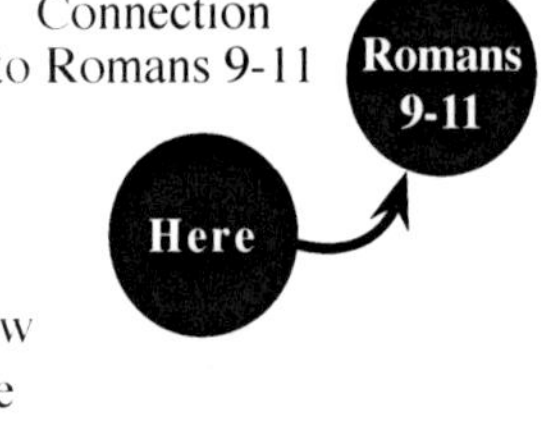

Romans 1:16	For I am not ashamed of the gospel of Christ, for it is the power of God unto salvation for everyone who believes, *for the Jew **first** and also for the Greek.*

There's simply no way of either circumventing that priority or softening it – though many have tried. But what exactly does that priority turn upon – meaning, in what sense have the Jews been assigned priority? Or, put a little differently,
– Why did God choose Israel?
– What underlies that choice?
– What purpose does it serve?

The answer is found in God's call to Abraham in Genesis 12:1-3 – and, not surprisingly, it turns upon the whole issue of mercy.

Genesis 12:1	Now the Lord had said unto Abram, Depart from your country, and from your kindred, and from your father's house, unto a land that I will show you:
Genesis 12:2	And I will make of you a great nation, and I will bless you, and make your name great; and you shall be a blessing:
Genesis 12:3	And I will bless them who bless you, and curse him who curses you: and in you shall all families of the earth be blessed.

Note carefully verse 3…

Genesis 12:3	And I will bless them who bless you, and curse him who curses you: ***and in you shall all families of the earth be blessed.***

It's what might be called the *purpose statement* of Genesis 12:1-3. It tells us ***why*** God chose Israel. *He chose her to be a blessing to all the families of the earth – meaning the Gentile nations.* Simply put…
- the Jewish people - and Israel, the collective expression of the Jewish people - were not chosen to stand above the Gentiles,
- but to bless them.
- In choosing the Jewish people and, once again, Israel, their collective expression, God was not

casting the Gentiles beyond the pale of his love;
- *quite the contrary: God was preparing a blessing for them.*

Genesis 12:3 *...and in you (the Jewish people) shall all families of the earth be blessed.*

We will learn that...
- though the Gentiles were shut out of Israel's "chosenness," *they were never shut out of God's love;*
- that, indeed, Israel's chosenness arises out of God's love for the Gentiles.
- It *proves* God's love for the Gentiles.

We will learn that...
- though Ishmael was shut out of God's chosenness (Romans 9:7), *he was not thereby shut out of God's love.*
- Likewise, we will learn that though Esau was also excluded - and emphatically so - from the circle of chosenness (Romans 9:10-13), *he was not thereby cast beyond the circle of God's love. It remained still within his reach – and was his to seize should he choose to do so.*

In short, we will learn that anyone shut out of God's chosenness is not thereby shut out of God's love***; that, indeed, the one chosen is more often than not meant to bless the one rejected:***
- We will learn Isaac was meant to bless Ishmael.
- And, likewise, Jacob was meant to bless Esau.

That's the very lesson God sought to teach the Jews in the Book of Jonah - that his love extends to the Gentiles regardless of how undeserving they might be; and should be ministered by the Jews: *Jonah, an Israelite, sent to preach God's love to Israel's most ferocious enemy - the cruel and oppressive citizens of Nineveh, capital of the Assyrian Nation!*

It's also the story of Joseph and his eleven brothers: Joseph's "chosenness" did not shut out his brothers from God's blessing; quite the contrary, God's choice of Joseph eventually redounded to their salvation, notwithstanding the cruelty Joseph suffered at their hands. Once again, the one chosen is more often than not meant to bless the one rejected. That's the underlying meaning of "chosenness" throughout the Book of Romans and, indeed, throughout the Bible: rejection is not the end of the story, as Boice and Piper and their fellow Calvinists would have it. Quite the contrary, in that very rejection God's love is often found.

We will learn that...
- Israel is God's gift to the Gentile nations...
- that in Israel God has deposited riches for the Gentiles – riches beyond measure,
- which is why Paul tells us in Romans 11:15 that when Israel is restored to God, the blessing she will heap upon the Gentiles can only be compared to the Resurrection.

Romans 11:15 For if when Israel was set aside, the gentiles were reconciled to God, what will Israel's restoration be like but life from the dead?

Israel
Meant to be a Channel of Blessing to the Gentiles

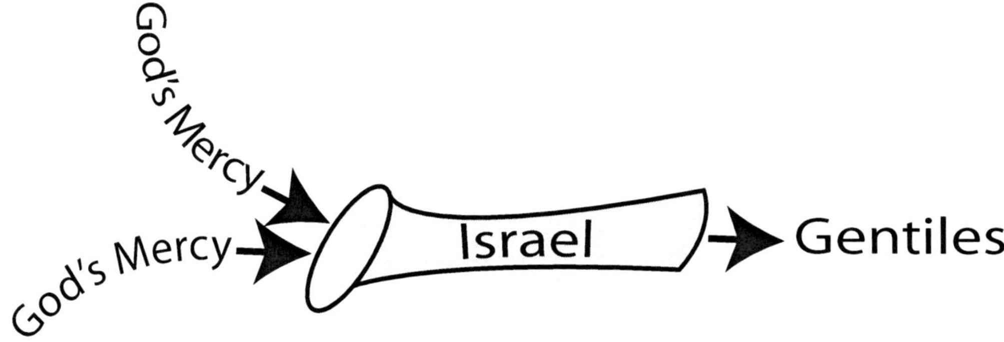

Tragically, however, we will also learn that...

- the Jews, instead of using their privileges to bless the Gentiles - privileges arising from their chosenness and delineated in Romans 2:18-20 and Romans 9:4-5 -
- used them instead to boast against the Gentiles;
- to gloat over the Gentiles;
- even to ridicule and curse the Gentiles.

We will learn that the Jews misconceived their chosenness - believing that it...

- highlighted their "deserved-ness;"
- guaranteed their personal salvation; and,
- implied God's rejection of the Gentiles.

We will learn too that the church stands in jeopardy of making that same tragic mistake – believing that God's "mission to the Gentiles" during the church age implies that he has ***"cast away"*** both the Jewish people and Israel.

Romans 11:1 I say then, has God cast away His people (i.e., the Jewish people and Israel)?

Quite the contrary...

...just as God chose Israel before the dawn of the church age to be a channel of blessing to the Gentiles and to the Gentile nations, so God has chosen the Gentiles during the church age to be a channel of blessing to the Jewish people and to the nation of Israel - that the Jewish people and Israel might be recovered.

Church

Meant to be a Channel of Blessing to Israel

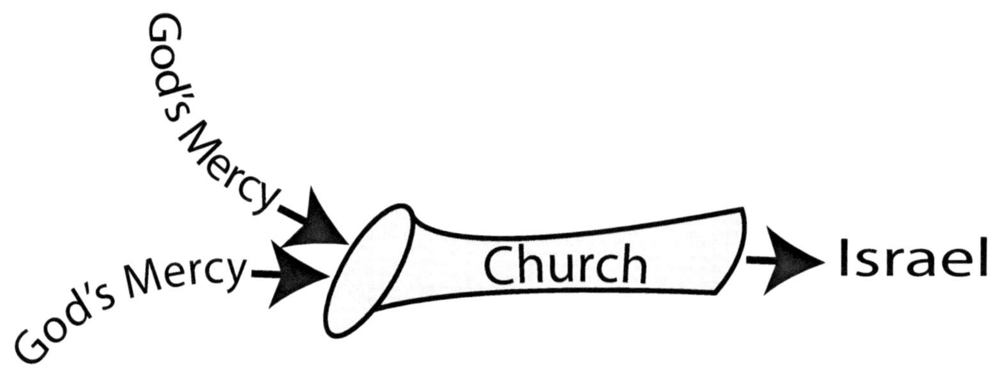

For I do not desire, my dear gentile brothers and sisters, that you should remain ignorant of this mystery...***that through the mercy God has shown you, the Jewish people might also obtain mercy.***

Romans 11:25a and 31

Verse:

Rom. 1:17 For in it the righteousness of God is revealed from faith to faith; as it is written, "But the righteous man shall live by faith."

Specific words or phrases found in verse 17

"For in it..."
The "it" here is the gospel - which is the "power of God unto salvation."[32]

"the righteousness of God"
Grammatically, the term "righteousness of God" ("δικαιουσυνη Θεου") is quite probably a "genitive of origin,"[33] not a "subjective genitive" - meaning that what the Gospel is intended to reveal isn't God's righteousness as such, an attribute, but a *righteous standing* which entitles the claimant to escape the wrath of God. In short, it's not a trait of God that the Gospel reveals; it's a kind of commodity; specifically, a *status*[34] *that justifies* the person who, *in simple faith,* lays hold of it. That's what the Gospel, the Good News, is meant to reveal.[35]

> **Key Concept**
>
> How does God save man? He confers upon him a standing in righteouness! And how is that standing conferred? By means of faith.

The meaning of the whole sentence, then, is fairly straightforward: "For in the gospel *a righteous status,* which is God's unspeakable gift to mankind, is being revealed and tendered - a righteous status which is attained altogether by faith."

"faith"[36]
The words "faith," "believe," and "trust" are, quite often, all translations of the same Greek word "πιστις." For example...

- faith a noun pistis Matt. 8:10
- I believe a verb pisteuo Mark 9:24
- I trust a verb pisteuo 2 Cor. 13:6

That, therefore, gives us the sense of what faith means. It means...
- to trust;
- to count on;
- to rely upon;
- to depend upon.

Clearly, then, the word "faith" conveys more than merely an intellectual assent[37] – though, of course, that's an important aspect of its meaning.

"faith to faith"
Here Paul is rather freely quoting Habakkuk 2:4 – and applying it to individuals rather than a corporate body of people – which was, no doubt, Habakkuk's intention. Paul's meaning is quite clear: faith is what puts a man in a right relationship with God – it's what confers upon believers the righteous status Paul has just introduced. It's faith *from beginning to end* that sustains a believer before God. In short, faith not only gets us into God's presence (i.e., "justifies"[38] us), faith *upholds* us there as well (i.e., "sanctifies"[39] us).

Faith is like our lungs: we don't simply draw one breath of oxygen and then hold it – expecting that one breath of oxygen to sustain us the rest of our lives. Likewise, we don't *"breathe in"* God's grace just once – expecting that to sustain our walk with God forever. One breath of God's grace will indeed justify us; but one breath of God's grace won't sanctify us. That's what the term *"faith to faith"* is meant to indicate.

> **Key Concept**
>
> Faith is like our lungs: it enables a Christian to "breathe" God's grace. Faith enables him to "gain access" to it. Romans 5:2 is especially explicit in this regard. There we're told quite unambiguously that it's faith that enables us, as Christians, to avail ourselves of God's grace.

"the righteous man shall live by faith"
The phrase, *"the righteous man shall live by faith,"* is merely a follow-up clause conveying essentially the same meaning: faith not only gets us into God's presence, it sustains us there as well.

I was once asked by a young man I was discipling, "Is the faith that justifies us – that gets us into the presence of God – the same faith that sanctifies us – that sustains us in his presence? Is there a difference?" The answer, I told him, is "Yes" and "No." Yes, it's the same faith; after all, the word "faith" simply means "trust." But, though it's the same faith, the level of faith – or trust – is markedly different. Again and again I've witnessed men and women trust God for the forgiveness of their sins and eternal life, but fail to trust God in their daily walk. *The one justifies them; the other sanctifies them.*

- When I believe God for the forgiveness of my sins, I'm justified – once and for all.
- When I believe God in my every day walk, I'm sanctified. Day by day I'm changed into Christ's image (2 Corinthians 3:18).

Let me put it slightly differently:
- I'm *justified* when I trust God to deliver me from

the penalty of my sins.

- I'm *sanctified* – meaning delivered from the power of sin – when I trust God for my marriage – when I trust God for my job – when I trust God for my children – etc. Ultimately, what trust – or faith – boils down to is obedience; e.g.,
    - Instead of cheating on my income tax, I pay the full amount I'm required to under the law – trusting that in my obedience to do so, I won't be "left in the lurch."
    - Instead of lying, I tell the truth – trusting that in my obedience to do so, God will sustain me.
    - Instead of holding on to anger, I let it go – trusting that in my obedience to do so, God will vindicate me.
    - Instead of giving in to a fear, I face it – trusting that in my obedience to do so, God will enable me to overcome it.

Tough Question

How willing are you to "live on the edge"? Have you fully bought into the truth that "living by faith" will inevitably propel you out of your "comfort zones"? That "walking with God" will lead you into realms where your own personal resources are wholly insufficient?

Think about it: the kind of faith that *sanctifies* us inevitably puts us "on the edge," doesn't it? It propels us out of our "comfort zones" – into realms where we know our own resources are wholly insufficient.

The pages of scripture are filled with accounts of shortcuts that reflect a lack of *sanctifying* faith.[40] A good example is found in First Samuel Thirteen - the story of Saul's disobedient sacrifice. Samuel had commanded Saul to wait for him at Gilgal before engaging the Philistines in battle - that there he would offer burnt offerings and peace offerings to consecrate the battle to the Lord. But the wait was too much for Saul's followers - and they began to desert him. Saul, instead of trusting God's prophet and remaining obedient, became fearful - and *driven by his fear, he "took matters into his own hands."* He sacrificed the burnt offerings and peace offerings himself - a ritual only Samuel was authorized to oversee - and in so doing tried to rally his deserting troops. Saul's disobedience cost him the kingdom - and God raised up David to replace him - a man who *did* trust God in his *daily walk* - whose faith in God had been nourished over many long years on the backside of the desert tending his father's flock.

Verse:

Rom. 1:18a For the wrath of God is revealed from heaven against all ungodliness and unrighteousness of men..."

Introduction to its exegesis:

Verses 16 and 17 together comprise a single passage of scripture that introduces us to the theme of Romans:

- it tells us that the Gospel is God's good news to mankind;
- that the Gospel is the power God has marshaled and expressly orchestrated to save us;
- next, it tells us *how* God saves us; specifically, by providing us with a *righteous standing* before him;
- then, it makes clear *how* that unspeakable gift is appropriated: *it's by faith;*
- finally, we're told in verse 17 that faith is not only what enables us to achieve a *righteous standing*, it also enables us to *live* in God's presence – it enables us to maintain a *walk* with God. *It's from faith to faith. The just shall live by faith.*

Now, in verse 18, Paul tells us why we need to be saved – why we need to be rescued. *It's because our sins have aroused God's wrath.*

Specific words or phrases found in verse 18a

"For"

The word *"for"* introduces an adverbial clause – and that tells us verse 18*a* is meant to explain verses 16 and 17 – which is what an adverbial clause beginning with a subordinate conjunction is intended to do – *explain whatever clause or clauses it follows*. The gist, then, of Romans 1:16 – 18*a* is quite simple and straightforward:

- Verses 16 and 17 introduce the basic gospel message...
    - that God has mercifully decided to save us;
    - that his salvation consists of a *standing in righteousness* he confers upon anyone who, in simple faith, requests it.
- Verse 18*a* now tells us *why* we need to be saved – why we need the *pardon* the gospel message reveals: *it's because our sins have aroused God's wrath.*

The bottom line here is that verse 18*a* looks *back* to

verses 16 and 17, *not forward* to verse 19 and the verses which follow. Once again, it's intended to explain verses 16 and 17 - specifically, *why* a pardon is needed - *why* God is mounting a rescue plan.

Verse 18*b*, on the other hand, looks forward to verse 19 and the verses which follow. It's a relative clause which will introduce us to the nature and consequences of *suppressing the truth* – and will carry the flow of Paul's thought through to Romans 3:20.

"the wrath of God"
God's wrath is not petulant; it's not the result of a peevish temper tantrum. That truth is especially emphasized here in verse 18*a* - where we're told that it's *our sins* that have aroused God's wrath; that, therefore, God's wrath is neither capricious nor arbitrary.[41] The term "wrath," therefore, is simply another way of saying "judgment," *but with a special emphasis placed upon God's* ***personal*** *hatred of sin*.

A Biblical Psychology of Man

Romans 1:18a
Man is *inherently* frightened of God. He knows intuitively that his sins have aroused God's wrath. He instinctively shrinks back in terror from God and hides himself. Genesis 3:7-10 illustrates this truth graphically.

Gen. 3:7	Then the eyes of both of them were opened, and *they knew that they were naked;* and they sewed fig leaves together and *made themselves coverings*.
Gen. 3:8	And they heard the sound of the Lord God walking in the garden in the cool of the day, and *Adam and his wife hid themselves from the presence of the Lord God* among the trees of the garden.
Gen. 3:9	Then the Lord God called to Adam and said to him, "Where are you?"
Gen. 3:10	So he said, "I heard Your voice in the garden, and *I was afraid* because I was naked; *and I hid myself.*"

Fear and flight – that's the primordial response God arouses among men and women everywhere – notwithstanding our fervent and indignant protests to the contrary.

Genesis 4:12 is another graphic illustration of the kind of response God's presence arouses among men and women. In point of fact, *it's a good summary description of mankind's basic psychology.*

> ... A *fugitive* and a *vagabond* you shall be on the earth.
> *Genesis 4:12*

Man's innate fear of God turns him into a ***fugitive*** and a ***vagabond***.

- A fugitive is forever looking over his shoulder – always running from justice – ridden with anxiety and the dread of impending doom;
- a vagabond is always on the move, forever restless, forever rootless, forever homeless – unable to settle down and wrap his mind and heart around a sense of enduring peace.

Think about it

Guilt and fear of impending judgment are ingrained in the human psyche – an insight acknowledged by both Christians and non-Christians. Franz Kafka's *"The Trial"* reflects this insight with uncanny perspicacity. Guilt was a major theme taken up by all the existentialist philosophers and playwrights of the early and mid 20th Century. The truth they sought to point out was quite simple and straight forward: a sense of guilt – often vague and amorphous – hangs over man and haunts him with its dread.

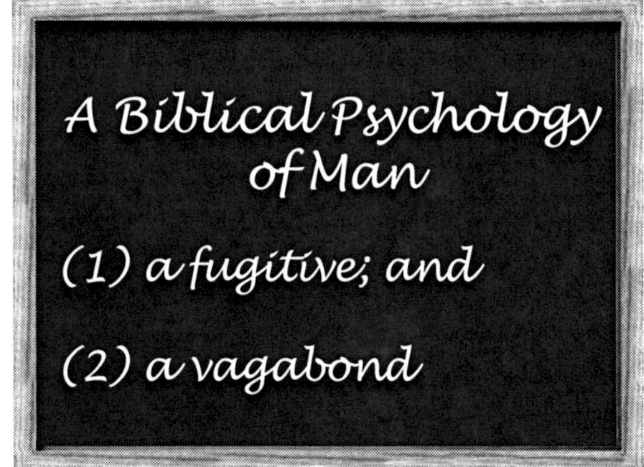

Guilt and fear of impending judgment are ingrained in the human psyche – an insight acknowledged by both Christians and non-Christians alike. Franz Kafka's *The Trial* reflects this insight with uncanny perspicacity. Guilt was a major theme taken up by all the existentialist philosophers and playwrights of the early and mid 20th Century. The truth they sought to point out was quite simple and straight forward: a sense of guilt – often vague and amorphous, but nonetheless relentless and inescapable – hangs over man and haunts him with its dread.

"revealed"
The word "reveal" here in verse 1:18*a* conveys the sense of "promulgate," "pronounce," "proclaim." And what's being proclaimed is...

- the awful truth that man is *guilty* of unrighteousness; and
- God's wrath has been aroused against him.

"from heaven"
"Heaven" here is the seat of divine authority; it's the heavenly assize - the throne room of God - where a trial has just been held and a verdict rendered. Standing in the docket was mankind - accused of ungodliness and unrighteousness - rebellion against the universal authority of the King of kings. The verdict rendered was "guilty" and the sentence pronounced was "death."[42]

- The results of the trial are now being promulgated throughout the vast reaches of the cosmos – to all the angelic hosts – along with a solemn warning that the sentence is soon to be carried out.
- Moreover, an intuitive awareness of that verdict and sentence has been injected into man's spiritual and emotional DNA – and is now the fundamental dynamic underlying his basic psychological makeup.

We're often led to believe that judgment lies in the future - at the conclusion of our lives. And that's true if by "judgment" we mean "execution of the sentence pronounced against us." But if by "judgment" we mean "trial" and "verdict," it's not true. Because, once again, the trial has *already* been held and the verdict has *already* been rendered – which is why Paul, in Ephesians 2:3, declares that all men are ***"by nature children of wrath."***

Ephesians 2:3	...among whom also *we all* once conducted ourselves in the lusts of our flesh, fulfilling the desires of the flesh and of the mind, and *were by nature children of wrath, just as the others.*

We all stand condemned – awaiting execution.

Key Concept

Mankind's only hope is a pardon grounded in God's mercy.

Mankind's only hope, then, is ***a pardon.*** And, like all pardons***, it's wholly a matter of mercy.*** A pardon is never based on a miscarriage of justice. That's a mistrial – which, if declared, warrants not a pardon, but a new trial. But here there has been no miscarriage of justice. The trial was wholly fair and righteous – and both the verdict and accompanying sentence were altogether in keeping with the facts of the case.[43]

Connection to Romans 9-11

Here → Romans 9-11

It all boils down to mercy, then, doesn't it? But an appeal based on mercy leaves mankind without any leverage whatsoever.[44] Why? Because no one ever *deserves* mercy. *That's a non-sequitur.* There are no "rights" grounded in mercy, only in justice. That means mercy lies *wholly* in the hands of God; he can either grant it or withhold it – without ever being accused of moral turpitude – without ever being indicted for wrongdoing. And that's exactly the point Paul is making in Romans 9:15-16...

Romans 9:15	For He says to Moses, "I will have mercy on whomever I will have mercy, and I will have compassion on whomever I will have compassion."
Romans 9:16	So then it is not of him who wills, nor of him who runs, but of God who shows mercy.

God, when he told Moses *"I will have mercy on whomever I will have mercy, and I will have compassion on whomever I will have compassion,"* wasn't declaring his *intention* to withhold mercy, as both Boice and Piper would have us believe; he was only asserting his *right* to do so. In short, mercy is *"God's call"* – and man can do nothing to force God's hand; or, put figuratively, *"... it's not of him who wills, nor of him who runs, but of God who shows mercy."*

Calvin on the Ropes

Paul is driving us into a corner – a corner where we're compelled to face our most disquieting fears – fears that lie at the very core of our sin-ridden psyches. He's making it very clear that mercy alone is our refuge; that there is no other refuge – no other sanctuary.

But can we rest in a hope that's grounded in God's mercy alone – a hope that leaves us with no leverage we can use against him? Only that he loves us?

- Is their no *right* we can assert?
- No *obligation* we can adduce?
- No appeal we can make that's grounded in justice – that *earns* us God's favor – that *requires* God to open heaven's gates to us?

It's a stomach churning challenge that none of us finds too palatable. The footing it secures for us seems too slippery – too unstable. And though they'd be loathe to admit it, Boice and Piper, along with their fellow Calvinists, manage to avoid that challenge by grounding their hope *not* in God's mercy, but in God's sovereign choice. Boice writes, "...because God chooses me, I can know that I'm secure..." And why? He goes on to say, "...because (his choice is grounded in) his eternal and sovereign determination."[45]

There's no doubt that Boice's interpretation assigns a role to God's mercy – that mercy isn't excluded from the drama altogether; but there's simply no way of getting around the stubborn, nettlesome truth that it's a *secondary* role – that it's not cast in the featured role. *That's reserved for God's sovereign choice.* Once again, for Boice...

- it's not *"... I can know for sure I'm secure because God is merciful;"*
- instead, it's *"... I can know for sure I'm secure because of God's sovereign choice."*

Why is mercy so pivotal for Paul*? **It's that God makes mercy the very definition of genuine love.*** The point Paul is making – indeed, an overarching theme of Romans – is quite simple: ***love that's got to be earned isn't love at all***[46] – which is precisely the point Jesus makes in his Sermon on the Mount.

Matthew 5:43	You have heard it has been said, you shall love your neighbor, and hate your enemy.
Matthew 5:44	But I say unto you, Love your enemies, bless them who curse you, do good to them who hate you, and pray for them who spitefully use you, and persecute you;
Matthew 5:45	That you may be the children of your Father who is in heaven: for he makes his sun to rise on the evil and on the good, and sends rain on the just and on the unjust.
Matthew 5:46	*For if you love them who love you, what reward have you? do not even the publicans the same?*

Love is not grounded in justice – in an "I owe you/ you owe me" formula that conditions my favor on yours and your favor on mine. Love isn't a carefully contrived balance sheet that measures expenditures against receipts. Mercy alone establishes love – kindness that's free and unconditional.

The truth Jesus is underscoring here in Matthew is made even more blatant and straightforward in Luke's version of the Sermon on the Mount.

Luke 6:27	But I say unto you who hear, love your enemies, do good to them who hate you,
Luke 6:28	Bless them who curse you, and pray for them who spitefully use you.
Luke 6:29	And unto him who smites you on the one cheek offer also the other; and him who takes away your cloak forbid not to take your coat also.
Luke 6:30	Give to every man who asks of you; and of him who takes away your goods ask for them not again.
Luke 6:31	And as you would that men should do to you, do you also to them likewise.
Luke 6:32	*For if you love them who love you, what credit is that to you? for sinners also love those who love them.*
Luke 6:33	*And if you do good to them who do good to you, what credit is that to you? for sinners also do even the same.*
Luke 6:34	*And if you lend to them of whom you hope to receive, what credit is that to you? for sinners also lend to sinners, to receive as much again.*
Luke 6:35	*But love your enemies, and do good, and lend, hoping for nothing again; and your reward shall be great, and you shall be the children of the Highest: for he is kind unto the*

unthankful and to the evil.

Luke 6:36 *Be you therefore merciful, as your Father also is merciful.*

Once again, a self-centered sinner finds no rest in mercy. He can't bring himself to rely on it – to count on it. He feels so much more secure when he's able to hedge himself about with rights and obligations – quid-pro-quo equations that impose a duty upon others to "love" him. "After all," he invariably thinks, "what if God decides to rescind his mercy? I've got no 'say' in the matter. It's all up to him; I've lost all control – and I don't like that."

That love isn't deserved!
That it isn't grounded in justice!
That it isn't grounded in rights and obligations!

It's not simply that we can't get our minds and hearts around it or that it's frightening; there's more to it than even that: *it angers us.* One of Jesus' last parables underscores just how much it's apt to anger us, *"The Parable of the Laborers in the Vineyard"* found in Matthew 20:1-15. The whole point of the parable is not God's sovereignty – as Boice and Piper would have us believe[47] – but just how much God's generosity cuts against the grain of our sin-ridden psyches.

Matt. 20:1 For the kingdom of heaven is like a landowner who went out early in the morning to hire laborers for his vineyard.

Matt. 20:2 Now when he had agreed with the laborers for a denarius a day, he sent them into his vineyard.

Matt. 20:3 And he went out about the third hour and saw others standing idle in the marketplace,

Matt. 20:4 and said to them, You also go into the vineyard, and whatever is right I will give you. So they went.

Matt. 20:5 Again he went out about the sixth and the ninth hour, and did likewise.

Matt. 20:6 And about the eleventh hour he went out and found others standing idle, and said to them, Why have you been standing here idle all day?

Matt. 20:7 They said to him, Because no one hired us. He said to them, You also go into the vineyard, and whatever is right you will receive.

Matt. 20:8 So when evening had come, the owner of the vineyard said to his steward, Call the laborers and give them their wages, beginning with the last to the first.

Matt. 20:9 And when those came who were hired about the eleventh hour, they each received a denarius.

Matt. 20:10 But when the first came, they supposed that they would receive more; and they likewise received each a denarius.

Matt. 20:11 And when they had received it, they complained against the landowner,

Matt. 20:12 saying, These last men have worked only one hour, and you made them equal to us who have borne the burden and the heat of the day.

Matt. 20:13 But he answered one of them and said, Friend, I am doing you no wrong. Did you not agree with me for a denarius?

Matt. 20:14 Take what is yours and go your way. I wish to give to this last man the same as to you.

Matt. 20:15 Is it not lawful for me to do what I wish with my own things? ***Or is your eye evil because I am good?***

The parable tells us we should be rejoicing when God extends mercy to others; but, instead, more often than not, it angers us; we grumble at it; it upsets us; it embitters us. *"That's not what they deserve,"* we think to ourselves – even if we don't say it out loud. *"It just isn't right. They haven't earned it."* We cry out in anger when God is looking for us to cry out in joy – joy at the mercy he has lavished on them.

How Calvinists could possibly suggest this parable turns on God's sovereignty (e.g., Millard Erickson) is quite beyond me. They insist that it proves God can do anything he wants - even change the "rules" when he sees fit to do so; and that he's answerable to no one - presumably not even to his own word. But that's blatantly untrue - not just because it ignores other tenets of systematic theology, but because it so clearly violates the meaning of the text itself - specifically, Jesus goes out of his way in the parable to underscore the reliability of the owner's word: "Friend, I am doing you no wrong. Did you not agree with me for a denarius?" The key sentence is the last: "Is your eye evil because I'm good?" - meaning, "Does my generosity offend you? Because if it does, it proves you're evil."

Jesus underscores the same truth in the "Parable of the Prodigal Son" – instead of rejoicing in the mercy God lavishes on others, we're often angered by it. We pick up the story at Luke 15:20.

Luke 15:20	And he (the prodigal son) arose, and came to his father. But when he was yet a great way off, his father saw him, and had compassion, and ran, and fell on his neck, and kissed him.
Luke 15:21	And the son said unto him, Father, I have sinned against heaven, and in your sight, and am no more worthy to be called your son.
Luke 15:22	But the father said to his servants, Bring forth the best robe, and put it on him; and put a ring on his hand, and shoes on his feet:
Luke 15:23	And bring hither the fatted calf, and kill it; and let us eat, and be merry:
Luke 15:24	For this my son was dead, and is alive again; he was lost, and is found. And they began to be merry.
Luke 15:25	Now his elder son was in the field: and as he came and drew nigh to the house, he heard music and dancing.
Luke 15:26	And he called one of the servants, and asked what these things meant.
Luke 15:27	And he said unto him, Your brother is come; and your father hath killed the fatted calf, because he has received him safe and sound.
Luke 15:28	And he was angry, and would not go in: therefore came his father out, and entreated him.
Luke 15:29	And he answering said to his father, Lo, these many years do I serve you, neither transgressed I at any time your commandment: and yet you never gave me a kid, that I might make merry with my friends:
Luke 15:30	But as soon as this your son was come, who has devoured your living with harlots, you have killed for him the fatted calf.
Luke 15:31	And he said unto him, Son, you are ever with me, and all that I have is yours.
Luke 15:32	***It was meet that we should make merry, and be glad: for this your brother was dead, and is alive again; and was lost, and is found.***

Here again, the issue is not God's sovereignty – that God can do whatever he wants. What's at issue is God's mercy when it's lavished on others; specifically, just how hard it is for us to reconcile ourselves to it. It grates against our sensitivities. Notice carefully the elder son's response to the generosity his father heaped on his younger brother: *"... he was angry..."*

In both parables, Matthew 20:1-15 and Luke 15:20-32, it's our sin-ridden temperament that Jesus is pointing to and censoring – the anger we find ourselves wrestling with whenever God lavishes his mercy on others.

In the Old Testament, the same lesson is underscored in the Book of Jonah – when instead of rejoicing that God was offering the Ninevites a chance to repent and be forgiven, Jonah became angry.

That's why Romans 9-11 is so terribly important. There Paul formulates a definition of love built around not simply a parable, but a specific object lesson rooted in actual on-going history: Jewish unbelief – Israel's inexcusable, perfidious rejection of Messiah. Justice cries out for God to reject Israel in turn. But, no, God won't shut the door; he holds it open still.

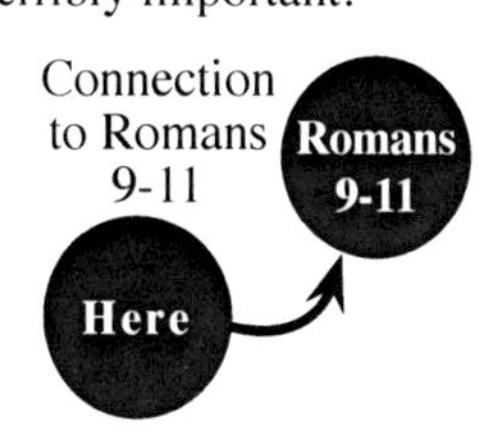

The long history of Israel tells the story of a love grounded in infinite mercy – the kind of love God was at pains to explain in the Book of Hosea, a lesson so few of us grasp.

Hosea 3:1	Then the Lord said to me, "Go again, love a woman who is loved by a lover and is committing adultery, just like the love of the Lord for the children of Israel..."

And in that definition, God warns the church, *"What about your love? Is it grounded in justice or in mercy?* What tells the truth is how we respond to the continuing mercy God lavishes on Israel.

LOVE AND MERCY: LET'S MAKE SURE WE GET IT RIGHT!

"Love isn't love that's got to be earned." That's the lesson Jesus teaches in his Sermon on the Mount.

If that's true, then love and mercy are pretty much synonymous. Why? Because that's the definition of mercy: *mercy is love that's not deserved.*

Anything short of mercy, then, isn't really love – at least as Jesus defines it.

Specific words or phrases used in verse 16

"…against all ungodliness and unrighteousness of men"

Once again, God's wrath is well grounded. It is not petulant, arbitrary, or self-serving. It's *"against all ungodliness and unrighteousness."*

Cultural Connections: The Bible and Western Thought

Franz Kafka's

THE TRIAL

Franz Kafka's *The Trial* is a genuine classic in Western literature. Not because its ideas are fresh and challenging, but because it so captures the mood of European civilization at the beginning of the 20th Century - a mood that has carried over into the 21st Century as well. Millions of persons who have never read *The Trial* are nevertheless vaguely aware of its plot.

Kafka himself is a venerated giant among European intellectuals; indeed, his name has been transformed into an adjective, "Kafkaesque" - and has become "common coin" circulating not only on the elevated pinnacles of academia, but within "popular" culture as well.

At the turn of the 20th Century, European Christianity was completely bankrupt. It's vigor was long spent. It had ceased being a source of passion; it was no longer the hub around which European thought revolved; it was no longer the lodestar of European intellectuals. It's demise is usually traced back to the French Revolution in 1789; but the seedbed of its demise is found in the Enlightenment at least fifty to seventy five years earlier - and back still further to the horrifying disillusionment spawned by the Thirty Years War fought between Catholics and Protestants during the early to mid-17th Century - a war that wrought almost as much devastation throughout Europe as did World War II - and all in the name of Christ. Christianity never recovered its credibility among European intellectuals following the Thirty Years War; and though it thrived in America, in Europe it degenerated into a pathetic caricature of the robust faith of the 16th and 17th Centuries - when whole armies would march to battle singing Christian hymns.

Soren Kierkegaard was probably the only first-rank European intellectual during the entire 19th Century who found himself seriously challenged by Christianity - and who found in Christianity the *sole* source of his intellectual fervor. None emerged in the 20th Century - with the one possible exception of Jacques Maritain who in some respects is more a product of the 19th Century than the 20th - and who casts a pale shadow alongside Kierkegaard.

At the end of the 19th Century - standing on the cusp of the 20th - European intellectuals were taking for granted the collapse of Christianity; still, very few were willing to write its epitaph - to openly acknowledge that it no longer commanded their respect - that it was no longer the engine driving their quest for knowledge and truth. Finally, Nietzsche did - declaring that *"God was dead"*[48] - meaning that God was *no longer relevant*.

It's against this backdrop that Franz Kafka - the son of a respectable middle-class Jewish shopkeeper living in Prague - frail, suffering from tuberculosis, and terribly introverted - wrote *The Trial*. It is not easy reading; it's disconcerting, opaque, and relentlessly depressing. Why? Because the truth it explores is ***guilt*** - but without any hope of forgiveness - without any hope of God's intervening grace. In short, though Kafka and his contemporaries consciously banished God from their discourse, from their journals, from their art, and from their literature, *they still found themselves fixated on the very truths listed in any basic Christian or Jewish catechism - sin, guilt, condemnation, and the fear of impending judgment.*

The Trial's central figure is a mid-level bank supervisor whose name is Josef K. His last name is never revealed - and that, no doubt, to stress the totally nondescript nature of his life - its complete anonymity.

K.'s life is distressingly routine - and its meaning is found only in whatever meager significance a bland routine of any kind can furnish.

One spring day, just before breakfast, two "warders" knock on K.'s door. They inform him that he's under arrest. K., of course, demands to know why, but the warders retort, *"We're not authorized to tell you that."*

The warders then introduce K. to an inspector - who has accompanied them to K.'s apartment and is waiting in the next room to conduct an interrogation. The interrogation, however, is a farce - because the inspector himself has not been made privy to the cause of K.'s arrest - only that it has been duly sanctioned by the proper authority - the identity of which, like the reason for the arrest, is never revealed. Following the interrogation, the inspector asks K. if he's planning on getting to work on time. K. is dumb-struck: *"How can I go to work, if I'm under arrest?"*

"Ah, I see," replies the Inspector, *"You have misunderstood me. You are under arrest, certainly, but that need not hinder you from going about your business. Nor will you be prevented from leading your ordinary life."* K is simply told to report to "The Court" periodically - without being told the exact location of the Court or the appropriate time to

The Truth of Mankind's Condition

The Past

Mankind has been declared guilty of transgressing God's authority - and the moral order underlying that authority; he stands helplessly condemned. The trial assessing mankind's guilt was altogether just and wholly in keeping with the facts of the case. There's no escaping the verdict rendered against him

The Present

The present is merely an interval between a judgment already rendered and an execution about to take place. Earth, therefore, is nothing more than a holding cell housing the condemned. Man is intuitively aware of his guilt and condemnation. That awareness – and the fear it arouses – constitutes the basic dynamic governing his psychological makeup.

The Future

Mankind's execution is scheduled to soon take place – a truth, which like his guilt and condemnation, man intuitively realizes. It's a truth that fills his mind and heart with a gnawing sense of futility. Why? Because death renders life meaningless. The execution is inevitable unless God grants a wholly undeserved pardon. Mankind's fate, therefore, turns upon an appeal to God's mercy.

schedule a hearing.

At first K. finds himself wrestling with the apparent absurdity of his arrest - and isn't able to ascribe much significance to it. Eventually, however, K. realizes that his arrest is fraught with serious consequences - and that he needs to begin preparing an effective defense. But that's impossible - because, of course, he has never been told the reason for his arrest. How can he prepare a defense against charges that have never been disclosed to him?

Gradually, the specific cause of his arrest becomes less and less important to K. It's not that he's guilty of some specific offense, it's that he *is* guilty - cosmically guilty. Guilt is part of his DNA. Eventually, K. surrenders to his guilt and helps to facilitate his own execution.

The Trial, as it turns out, is not about K.'s guilt or innocence; that has already been decided. *It's about his execution.*

- That's why the charges against K. are never revealed: *they're no longer germane*.
- That's why K.'s arrest seems so irrational - why, though he's under arrest, he's still permitted to carry on with his life - with little or no hindrance: K. is already imprisoned: *life is a holding cell housing the condemned – a mere interval between a sentence already pronounced and an execution about to be carried out* - the very truth found in Romans 1:18a; and, so Kafka insists, what we do during that interval is quite meaningless; we can do whatever we want with it; it makes no difference.
- That's also why the judicial system seems so irrational: K. is expecting a judicial system that's designed to guarantee him a fair trial, not a judicial system that presumes his guilt and that's designed instead to help him embrace that guilt and facilitate his own execution.

Franz Kafka's *The Trial* is a wholly Biblical account of mankind's plight - only minus God and the forgiveness God provides in Jesus Christ. Life is indeed an interval lying between a verdict of guilt already rendered and a sentence of death about to be executed. But Romans 1:16 and 17 tell us that the interval, contrary to Kafka's contention, is *not* meaningless: it's the time God has set aside to call us to our senses, to get us to confess our guilt and to seize the pardon he's graciously offering. Kafka's truth is Biblical truth; but, absent God's mercy, it's a bitter, depressing truth. It's Romans 1:18a without the hope of Romans 1:16-17.

Let's take some time, grab a cup of coffee, and think all this through

Connection to Romans 9-11

Here → Romans 9-11

A little thought should prompt us to ask ourselves, "Why has the human race, in light of its condemnation, been permitted to perpetuate itself? Shouldn't God have immediately followed through with the sentence of death he pronounced against Adam and Eve after their betrayal?

Genesis 3:19 ...for dust you are, and to dust you shall return.

- Hadn't God clearly warned them that eating of the Tree of Knowledge of Good and Evil transgressed his sovereign intention?
- Hadn't God clearly warned them that death was the certain punishment for its violation?

And, yes, of course, Adam and Eve did eventually die.
- But their death wasn't immediate and, even more significantly,
- they were allowed to produce children – offspring who continued the race they'd corrupted.

Let's be more specific: when Adam and Eve sinned,
- it's not just that they sinned, it's that they *became sinners:*
- it's that sin worked its way into the very fabric of their being – their spiritual, emotional, and physical DNA – making inevitable the corruption of their progeny.

But it's not simply that successive generations have inherited Adam's corruption; they've also inherited Adam's condemnation and the sentence of death pronounced against him. His fate is their fate!

Corruption, guilt, and death! Is it any wonder, then, that anguish, suffering, and heartache have been mankind's on-going lot? (cf. "A Common Fallacy" on page 54) But God has patiently endured all that corruption and guilt because there was no other way for him to "get to us" – to you and me – with his pardon.

Put a little differentely, God saw in his corrupted prototype billions of men and women – including you and me – vessels of wrath he yearned to transform into vessels of mercy. There it is: one of the most profound mysteries of scripture: *lying behind all the suffering and torment that afflicts the human race is God's mercy.* Here we've unraveled more of Paul's meaning in Romans 9:22-23.

Adam passed along to his offspring ***both*** (1) his corruption and (2) the condemnation and sentence of death pronounced against him.

Adam

Adam's Offspring

"Among whom also we all had our conversation in times past in the lusts of our flesh, fulfilling the desires of the flesh and of the mind; and were ***by nature the children of wrath, even as others."***
Ephesians 2:3

Romans 9:22 What if God, wanting to show His wrath and to make known His power (to save), endured with much longsuffering the vessels of wrath prepared for (condemned to) destruction…

The meaning is fairly straightforward – and, when carried over to verse 23, is clearly meant to highlight God's mercy…

Romans 9:23 … that He might make known the riches of His glory on the vessels of mercy, which He had prepared beforehand (see discussion of "predestination" on pages 19 -20) for glory…

1. God has patiently endured the sinfulness of all men, all of them vessels of wrath fitted for destruction – meaning sentenced to hell and death,
2. so that he *by the Cross* might make known in a single event occurring at a single moment in time both his wrath, meaning his *personal* hatred of sin, and his power to save, meaning his mercy; and
3. *through the Cross,* might grant a pardon to anyone who asks for it (Romans 1:16; cf, John 1:12, etc.), transforming him from a vessel of wrath into a vessel of mercy,
4. thereby glorifying himself - whose very nature is love, (1 John 4:8 and 4:16)
5. (once again, mercy is the definition Jesus himself gives of God's love; cf, Matthew 5:43-46, Luke 6:27-36, etc.),

Echoes of Micah 7:18…

> Who is a God like unto you, who pardons iniquity, and passes by the transgression of the remnant of his heritage? He retains not his anger for ever, *because he delights in mercy.*
>
> *Micah 7:18*

God has patiently endured Adam's offspring, all of them vessels of wrath, sinners causing endless grief, heartache, pain, and suffering...

...so that by the cross, some might be saved - as many as seize the pardon the cross provides (c.f. Romans 1:16; John 1:12) - becoming thereby vessels of mercy.

A Common Fallacy

God is often accused of permitting suffering to run unchecked and unchallenged throughout the world – starvation, war, disease, injustice, brutality. "How could a loving God permit those kinds of horrors?"

But all that terrible misery springs from man's perverted psyche´- from the corruption that's so much a part of his "DNA." God could, of course, stop it in a moment – in the twinkling of an eye. But that would entail destroying its source – and that's you and me. God's mercy cannot reach us without passing through the horrifying, sin-stained grid we've created - that surrounds *and envelopes us – that, at bottom, is actually composed of you and me*. That's the awful truth. Put a little differently: to get to us with his mercy, God holds judgment of sin at bay; but that makes the misery and suffering sin produces inevitable. *Once again, lying behind all human misery is God's mercy.*

EXCURSUS ON FAITH

Faith is an issue around which much of the Book of Romans revolves. Romans 1:16-18a, the theme statement of the entire book, turns upon it. It has been made the subject of much heated debate over the last two thousand years and that debate has not lessened in recent years. It, therefore, behooves us to press into its meaning with as much thoroughness as we can muster.

Introduction

Just recently I attended a conference hosted by the "Grace Evangelical Society." One of the featured speakers,[49] Dr. Zane Hodges, shocked many of us with an insight that evidently he's been mulling over in his mind for quite some time; specifically, that anyone who doesn't wholly embrace the doctrine of eternal security isn't saved. *Grace in Focus*, the society's flagship magazine, reports that an informal survey, conducted shortly after Dr. Hodges spoke, revealed that between one third and one half of the conferees disagreed with him. I count myself among those who disagreed with him.

The crux of Dr. Hodges' assertion is simple and straightforward: the doctrine of eternal security is at the very heart of the gospel message; therefore, disbelief in it is tantamount to disbelief in the gospel – and anyone who disbelieves the gospel can't possibly be saved. The long and the short of it is put well by Dr. Wilkin, a colleague of Dr. Hodges: *"We do not base assurance (of salvation) on feelings or life-style. We base (it) on faith* ***in the saving message."***

In other words, it's faith ***in the saving message*** that regenerates us.

Elsewhere in the same article, Dr. Wilkin writes: "A person who has never been sure he is eternally secure by faith alone in Christ alone has not yet believed the saving message. And there is no other way to be born again except by believing the saving message."

But that's not quite true to the Biblical text. The word "faith" is used hundreds of times in the New Testament; and although several passages do indeed directly or indirectly imply "faith in the message," the primary focus is clearly Christ himself. Indeed, in the Gospel of John, a book Dr. Hodges uses extensively to make his point, Jesus himself, not the message he preaches, is *always* the object of faith.[50] For example, John 11:26[51]...

John 11:26 And whoever lives and ***believes*** (πιστευον) ***in Me*** shall never die...

No doubt, however, Dr. Hodges would be quick to point out that it's not possible to believe in Christ without believing what Christ says; that *who* Christ is can't be divorced from what *he says and teaches*. Sounds good; and, unquestionably, there's more than a modicum of truth in what he asserts. But he has clearly overreached the truth that's there. It's a common mistake that anyone who builds "systems" is prone to make.

During the early part of the Twentieth Century, English philosophy was dominated by Idealism – rooted for the most part in German Hegelianism. F. H. Bradley, J. H. Muirhead, J. E. McTaggart, and Bernard Bosanquet carried the torch for the British Idealists.

Idealism – whatever its ultimate form – always begins with a series of a priori assumptions that, when spun completely out, prompt its proponents to fabricate a philosophical system that produces extravagant claims *that fly in the face of common sense*. Nevertheless, the claims are very difficult to attack because the system that gives rise to them is self-contained and internally consistent. Moreover, those claims are normally clothed in the garb of a rich and ponderous rhetoric that's often quite intimidating.

By the second decade of the Twentieth Century, the British idealists were championing claims that were clearly "off the wall." McTaggart, for example, insisted that time is unreal – a claim that, paradoxically, lined up well with the "self-evident" premises that produced it. G. E. Moore, however, refused to "play by the rules" the idealists had laid down. In short, rather than attacking McTaggart's claim from within the system he'd constructed, he simply exposed how absurd it was – how contrary to common sense. "If time is unreal," Moore asked, "ought we not to deny that we have breakfast *before* we have lunch?"

The idealists were also in the habit of rejecting the common sense observation that reality is material; that, instead, it's wholly spiritual – to which Moore responded, "If reality is spiritual, does it not follow that chairs and tables are far more like us than we think? Can it really be doubted that material objects exist, since it's certain that here is one hand, and here is another?"

Hodges' claim, like McTaggart's, lines up well with the premises underlying it; but it flies in the face of common sense – and so warrants very close scrutiny – mingled, I might add, with a touch of skepticism.

That I don't understand the doctrine of eternal security, and so fail to embrace it, does not necessarily prove that I lack faith in Christ. While I certainly acknowledge a link between, on the one hand, faith in Christ and, on the other, faith in what he teaches, common sense tells me that it's possible to *overburden* that link. For example, I reposed trust in my father long before I understood all he was trying to teach me. It's not that I *disbelieved outright* what he was teaching me; it's that quite often I didn't even know he was teaching it - meaning I didn't "see" it. Did that mean my faith in him was any less? Of course not! Had I "seen" what he was trying to teach me, I would have fully embraced it. Why? Because I'd grown to trust him – I'd learned that he was worthy of my trust – that I could rely on him. ***And so it is with faith in Christ.***

Faith and understanding do not always travel along precisely the same trajectory. Understanding usually lags a little behind and a little below. There's no doubt that some understanding of what Christ teaches is basic to faith in him; *but it's also beyond doubt that for most of us*, ***our faith in Christ was confirmed long before our understanding of him and his message was complete.***

Dr. Hodges would have us surmount obstacles that not even Peter, James, and John were required to surmount – at least not initially. Their faith in Christ was nourished not simply by his teaching, *but by their walk with him.* Indeed, it was ***because*** they reposed faith in *him* that they were able to eventually believe what he taught them though much of it they initially resisted – *quite often making what they learned from Christ a function of their faith in him, not the other way around.*

The claim Dr. Hodges makes produces very bizarre conclusions – conclusions that should prompt all of us to handle it with the utmost caution despite his well deserved reputation for outstanding scholarship. That John and Charles Wesley weren't saved is a claim that not only looks and feels "off the wall," common sense tells me it *is* "off the wall." And not only that, it threatens to divide our community at the very moment other far more challenging doctrinal controversies have arisen: the resurgence of Open Theism, denigration of the Atonement,[52] etc.

Hebrews Chapter Eleven – a Good Starting Point

Hebrews Chapter Eleven provides one of the very best Scriptural definitions of faith. And that's where I think an examination of faith should begin. What I propose doing is exploring the meaning of faith laid out from Hebrews 11:1 through Hebrews 11:27.

Let's begin, though, with Hebrews 10:39. Hebrews 10:39 has just declared that we're of faith, not of apostasy – meaning we don't "draw back."

Heb. 10:39	But we are not of them who draw back unto perdition; but of them that believe to the saving of the soul.

Chapter Eleven now begins to illustrate this truth - with both (1) a propositional definition of faith and (2) a whole array of specific examples drawn from the Old Testament. The examples serve not only to motivate and inspire us, but, in addition, to further define the meaning of faith - *but existentially.*

Propositional Definition of Faith

We begin first with a propositional definition of faith given in verse one.

Heb. 11:1	Now faith is the substance (hypostaseos - υποστασεος) of things hoped for, the evidence of things not seen.

"Hypostasis" (υποστασις) is a very common word in koiné Greek - from Alexander on; it's derived from "hypo," meaning "under," and "histêmi," meaning "what stands under an entity and supports it" (a footing, a contract, a promise). It means "to cause" or "make to stand;" "to place, put, or set;" "to establish truth in the presence of others, in their midst, before, on occasion, judges"); a "substructure;" a "foundation." It conveys the sense of "being firm;" it's the underlying essence of any phenomenon.

A philosophical use of it is found in Hebrews 1:3...

Heb. 1:3 Who being the brightness of his glory, and the express image of his ***person*** (hypostasis - υποστασεος), and upholding all things by the word of his power, when he had by himself purged our sins, sat down on the right hand of the Majesty on high...

The word "person" is actually the word "hypostasis." The meaning here is that Christ is the very image of God's being. The same sense is given in 2 Corinthians 4:6. What underlies the image and gives it meaning is the Godhead itself.

2 Cor. 4:6 For God, who commanded the light to shine out of darkness, has shined in our hearts, to give the light of the knowledge of the glory of God in the ***face*** of Jesus Christ.

The word "face" in 2 Corinthians 4:6 is a metaphor for "image" – meaning Christ reveals the essence of God. In short, anyone who has seen Christ has seen God – which is exactly what Jesus tells Philip in John 14:9.

John 14:9 Jesus said unto him, Have I been so long time with you, and yet have you not known me, Philip? He who has seen me has seen the Father; and how say you then, Show us the Father?

A slightly different and less philosophical sense of the word is found in Hebrews 3:14...

Heb. 3:14 For we are made partakers of Christ, if we hold the beginning of our ***confidence*** (hypostasis - υποστασεος) – steadfast unto the end...

The same sense is found in 2 Corinthians 9:4 – a steadiness of mind that holds a person firm in his convictions.

2 Cor. 9:4 Lest haply if they of Macedonia come with me, and find you unprepared, (and, consequently) we...should be ashamed in this same confident (hypostasis - υποστασεος) boasting.

It's commonly used in business documents to denote the ***basis*** or ***guarantee*** of transactions. And because this is its essential meaning in Hebrews 11:1, we might translate it:

Heb. 11:1 Faith is the title-deed, the guarantee, of things hoped for - the proving of things not seen.

In short, it's our faith that provides us the assurance that all God's promises will surely come to pass.

"Proving" is the Greek word "elegchos" - and is often translated "reproof," or "evidence." It frequently conveys the sense of a proof, a test, or a conviction.

2 Timothy 3:16 translates "elegchos" as "reproof."

2 Tim. 3:16 All scripture is given by inspiration of God, and is profitable for doctrine, for *reproof (elegmon),* for correction, for instruction in righteousness:

Matthew 18:15 conveys the same sense - where *"tell him his fault"* is better translated *"reprove him."*

Mt. 18:15 Moreover if thy brother shall trespass against thee, go and *tell him his fault* (i.e., reprove him) between thee and him alone: if he shall hear thee, thou hast gained thy brother.

The whole issue of *"evidence"* is further explained in verse 3. There we're told that faith provides *"evidence"* that, though not empirically based, is nevertheless cogent and compelling. *Each step of faith furnishes sufficient "**evidence**" to prompt the next - and makes inexcusable any failure on our part to take it.* That's a principle that, though not specifically taught in any one particular verse, can be clearly inferred from the passage as a whole.

The Relationship between Faith and Hope

Verse one mentions both *"faith"* and *"hope"* - and

we'll find that much of Chapter Eleven is devoted to distinguishing between the *"ground of our faith"* and the *"ground of our hope."* It's a distinction that's fundamentally important – a distinction that Dr. Hodges fails to draw. And it's that failure that gives rise to his erroneous definition of saving faith.

- *faith is grounded in God Himself;*
- *hope, however, is grounded in what God tells me – what he promises me - what he teaches me.*

Faith, therefore, turns upon a personal knowledge of God.[53] I can rely on God (i.e., repose my faith in him) only because I *know* God - or, to put it in terms common to the Book of Genesis, only because I have *walked with God.*

Gen. 5:24	And Enoch ***walked with God:*** and he was not; for God took him.
Gen. 6:9	These are the generations of Noah: Noah was a just man and perfect in his generations, and Noah ***walked with God.***

My personal, *existential* knowledge of God has led me to trust him; consequently, I can act with confidence on what he tells me to do - even though...

- he may reveal a truth to me that I initially find perplexing, or
- call upon me to step across a threshold that at first glance seems strange and foreboding.

Once again, my faith is grounded in my personal knowledge of God - *my walk with him;* my hope, however, is grounded in what God tells me, what he promises me, *what he teaches me.*

- I don't need to be convinced of the feasibility of what God's calling me to believe or to do;
- I need only be convinced of ***him*** - *that he is both able to do what he promises and is willing to do it.*

Again and again throughout the gospels Jesus grounds faith in himself. Mark 4:35-40 is a case in point.

Mark 4:35	On the same day, when evening had come, He said to them, "Let's cross over to the other side."
Mark 4:36	Now when they had left the multitude, they took Him along in the boat as He was. And other little boats were also with Him.
Mark 4:37	And a great windstorm arose, and the waves beat into the boat, so that it was already filling.
Mark 4:38	But He was in the stern, asleep on a pillow. And they awoke Him and said to Him, *"Teacher, do You not care that we are perishing?"*
Mark 4:39	Then He arose and rebuked the wind, and said to the sea, "Peace, be still!" And the wind ceased and there was a great calm.
Mark 4:40	But He said to them, *"Why are you so fearful? How is it that you have no faith?"*

Jesus' rebuke in verse 40 clearly focuses faith on himself – and, just as clearly, grounds that faith in an *existential* knowledge of himself. In short, Jesus is saying to his disciples, *"You've walked with me long enough to know that I'm trustworthy; that you can repose faith in me, and yet you don't. Here I am with you in the boat – and still you doubt that you're safe – still you doubt that I care for you (verse 38). How is it that you have no faith?"*

It's exactly the same point Paul makes in 2 Timothy 1:12.

2 Tim. 1:12	...for *I know him* whom I have believed, and I am persuaded that he is able to guard that which I have committed unto him against that day.

The word "believe" is the Greek word "pisteuo" – derived from the word "pistis" meaning "faith." In short, Paul is saying "I know him in whom I've reposed my faith."

And it's because Paul knows Christ – meaning existentially knows him – and has, therefore, reposed faith in him, that he's persuaded that God will fulfill his promise to guard what he has committed to his care. Once again, the ground of our faith is God himself; the ground of our hope is what he tells us – what he promises us.

Put in terms of Romans 5:1-2, faith puts me in a relationship with God that engulfs me in a flow of grace - and it's that grace that brings to pass the promises he has made to me.

Rom. 5:1	Therefore being justified by faith, we have peace with God through our Lord Jesus Christ:

Rom. 5:2 By whom also ***we have access by faith into this grace*** wherein we stand, and rejoice in hope of the glory of God.

Hebrews 4:16 conveys the same principle - except that here I'm put before a *"throne of grace."* The argument begins back in verse 1. Hebrews 4:1-2 speaks of faith - and warns that all the promises of God are brought to pass only through faith.

Heb. 4:1 Let us therefore fear, lest, a ***promise*** being left us of entering into his rest, any of you should seem to come short of it.

Heb. 4:2 For unto us was the gospel preached, as well as unto them: but the word preached did not profit them, ***not being mixed with faith*** in them that heard it.

And from verse 3 through verse 15 that principle is further elaborated. Then verse 16 summarizes the teaching:

Heb. 4:16 Let us therefore come boldly unto the ***throne of grace,*** that we may obtain mercy, and ***find grace*** to help in time of need.

Faith stands us before a throne of grace - and it's grace that brings to pass the promises of God. The key, then, is faith – faith in God himself and hope in his promises – in what he tells me.

Faith Is Not Unreasonable and Its Impact Is Convincing

We continue now to Hebrews 11, verse 2

Heb. 11:2 For by it the elders obtained a good report.

The antecedent of "it" is "faith." The word "elders" is simply a general term pointing to the various heroes of faith specifically enumerated in Chapter Eleven. The phrase "obtained a good report" is better translated *"had witness borne to them."* And what was that witness? *That they were men and women of faith and, hence, as verse six points out, they pleased God!*

Let's move on to verse 3.

Heb. 11:3 Through faith we understand that the worlds were framed by the word of God, so that things which are seen were not made of things which do appear.

Verse 3 seems clearly to hearken back to Romans 1 - indicating that in all probability the author of Hebrews was familiar with the Pauline epistles – or even, perhaps, that the author of Hebrews is Paul himself.

Rom. 1:19 ...because that which is known of God is manifest in them; for God manifested it unto them.

Rom. 1:20 For the invisible things of him since the creation of the world are clearly seen, being perceived through the things that are made, even his everlasting power and divinity; that they may be without excuse...

Verse 3 is designed to underscore the rational nature of faith; *that faith is not unreasonable*. Still, faith does indeed project us *beyond our senses* - to what underlies creation itself; specifically, God.

God lies beyond our senses; nevertheless, *our senses point us to God* - suggesting, without empirically proving, his existence. *What carries us beyond the limit of our senses is faith*. That's the basic meaning of verse three.

Furthermore, the conviction that faith generates is clear and unambiguous. Like Romans 1:19-20, verse 3 tells us plainly that faith produces a conviction so persuasive that unbelief is inexcusable.

Faith Pleases God - and Is Linked to Righteousness

Heb. 11:4 By faith Abel offered unto God a more excellent sacrifice than Cain, by which he obtained witness that he was righteous, God testifying of his gifts: and by it he being dead yet speaks.

Verse 4 begins a whole litany of examples - starting with Abel. It's not the nature of Abel's sacrifice that pleased God, it's that it was offered in faith. The clear implication is that Cain's sacrifice was not offered in faith. Note that verse 4 clearly links faith to righteousness - and simply restates the truth Paul makes later on in Romans 4:5.

Rom. 4:5 ...faith is reckoned for righteousness.

It's the same truth that we'll encounter once again in Hebrews 11:6

Heb. 11:6 And without faith it is impossible to be well-pleasing unto him; for he that cometh to God must believe that he is, and that he is a rewarder of them that seek after him.

Let's continue now with verse five.

Faith and Its Relationship to Knowing God

Heb. 11:5 By faith Enoch was translated that he should not see death; and was not found, because God had translated him: for before his translation he had this testimony, that he pleased God.

Genesis twice tells us that Enoch *walked with God* - and it's *that* fact that pleased God.

Gen. 5:22 And Enoch ***walked with God*** after he begat Methuselah three hundred years, and begat sons and daughters:

Gen. 5:24 And Enoch ***walked with God:*** and he was not; for God took him.

The point here is that *faith is grounded in a personal knowledge of God* - in the sense of ***existential knowledge*** - not simply knowing *about* God – but knowing him personally.[54] *It springs to life on the basis of that knowledge and none else*. Why is faith so important to God – so pleasing to God? Because it brings us into his presence. It establishes a walk with him.

Verse six simply puts in doctrinal form the meaning of verse five.

Heb. 11:6 But without faith it is impossible to please him: for he that cometh to God must believe that he is, and that he is a rewarder of them that diligently seek him.

Faith and the Word of God - God's Word alone Is a Sufficient Basis for Obedience

Verse 7 begins to spell out the implications of what it means *that faith is grounded in a personal, existential knowledge of God*.

Heb. 11:7 By faith Noah, ***being warned of God of things not seen as yet,*** moved with fear, prepared an ark to the saving of his house; by the which he condemned the world, and became heir of the righteousness which is by faith.

The first point that needs to be noted about Noah is that the Bible records that he too *"walked with God"* - just as Enoch did.

Gen. 6:9 ...Noah walked with God.

In other words, Noah, like Enoch, knew God personally, existentially. It's not that Noah knew only *about* God; it's that *what* Noah knew *about* God he had found in knowing God - in walking with him and spending time in his presence. No doubt many who perished in the flood knew *about* God, but none *knew God*. (The same sense is given in Matthew 25:12)

Verse 7, then, builds upon verses 5 and 6. What's new about verse 7 is that it links *faith in God* to *God's word* - in this case God's warning to Noah of the impending flood. The new truth that verse 7 introduces is that God's word establishes faith's *realm of activity*. Faith is grounded in God, but its *realm of activity* is established by his word. It was only when God warned Noah of the impending flood that Noah's *faith was put to work*. Faith must be put *to work*. ***And it's God's Word that puts faith to work.***

A faith that's never put to work is "dead;" it's "barren." That's the whole point of James 2:14-20.

James 2:14 What doth it profit, my brethren, if a man say he hath faith, but have not works? can that faith save him?
James 2:15 If a brother or sister be naked and in lack of daily food,
James 2:16 and one of you say unto them, Go in peace, be ye warmed and filled; and yet ye give them not the things needful to the body; what doth it profit?
James 2:17 ***Even so faith, if it have not works, is dead in itself.***
James 2:18 Yea, a man will say, Thou hast faith, and I have works: show me thy faith

	apart from thy works, ***and I by my works will show thee my faith.***
James 2:19	Thou believest that God is one; thou doest well: the demons also believe, and shudder.
James 2:20	But wilt thou know, O vain man, that ***faith apart from works is barren?***

Noah listened to God - and then acted on what God told him to do. His faith was built on a personal knowledge of God; but his faith was *proven* in his obedience to God's word – once again, *God's word put Noah's faith to work.*

Note carefully that Noah's obedience was based solely upon God's word - and required nothing else. There was no further explanation. Faith doesn't demand an explanation. Why? ***Because it's grounded not in the word spoken, but in the person speaking it*** – a truth Dr. Hodges clearly overlooks. And that brings me back to 2 Timothy 1:12.

2 Tim. 1:12	... I know whom I have believed, and am persuaded that he is able to keep that which I have committed unto him against that day.

If God provides an explanation, it's not the basis for any subsequent obedience. That's the difference between Zacharias and Mary. Zacharias sought to make the angel's explanation the basis for his obedience. God's word wasn't sufficient.

Luke 1:18	And Zacharias said unto the angel, ***Whereby shall I know this?*** for I am an old man, and my wife well stricken in years.

"Whereby shall I know this?" Zacharias, is, in effect, seeking to ground his faith not in God alone, but in a sign. His faith isn't up to the task. It can't do the job it has been assigned. It cries out for help! It wants a sign! Mary, on the other hand, while she sought an explanation, never made it the basis for her obedience.

Luke 1:34	And Mary said unto the angel, How shall this be, seeing I know not a man?

She knew God well enough to know that he's *trustworthy;* that he will sustain her in whatever task she's given - and that his love for her will never fail.

Luke 1:38	And Mary said, Behold, the handmaid of the Lord; be it unto me according to thy word. And the angel departed from her.

Zacharias was seeking to ground his obedience in a sign. Not so Mary. She was only asking how it would come to pass - and was prepared to obey with or without the explanation.

Likewise, Noah's obedience was grounded in his knowledge of God alone. The phrase *"things not seen as yet"* is tantamount to saying God's word alone was sufficient.

Faith Always Breaks the Routine

We're ready now for Hebrews 11:8 - and that brings us to Abraham.

Heb. 11:8	By faith Abraham, when he was called to go out into a place which he should after receive for an inheritance, obeyed; and he went out, not knowing whither he went.

Abraham heard God; and, in hearing, he obeyed - asking nothing more - not even insisting on knowing his destination - knowing only that God had promised to bless him, to raise up from his offspring a mighty nation, and to lead him to a land his progeny would eventually possess.

Gen. 12:2	And I will make of thee a great nation, and I will bless thee, and make thy name great; and thou shalt be a blessing:
Gen. 12:3	And I will bless them that bless thee, and curse him that curseth thee: and in thee shall all families of the earth be blessed.

And that was good enough! Only a simple promise!

It's important to note carefully that God called on Abraham to *leave* the country of his birth - *to depart from the steady routine of his life.* And Abraham's faith enabled him to do so. God often requires us to break away from our day to day habits and customs - to renounce the familiar. And that's not easy! Routine may be boring; but it provides comfort and solace. It protects us from the unknown and the uncertain; and breaking from it can arouse a profound angst. What's around the next corner? We don't know. What can we expect tomorrow? We don't know. But faith *in God* empowers us to move forward ***without*** knowing.

What about Your Own Routine?

What about your own habits and customs? Are you prepared to break from them - to lay them aside and move forward into the unknown? Your life has probably acquired a steady beat. It may not be victorious, but you know what to expect. And that alone generates a profound inertia. There are innumerable case studies of prisoners incarcerated for years who, upon learning of their impending release from prison, become depressed and afflicted with anxiety. They've spent years dreaming of release - yearning for it - talking about it with other prisoners; but when the time for their actual release finally draws near, fear closes its fingers around their minds and hearts. What's the reason? For all the misery prison inevitably entails, it affords at the very least a routine. Prison life is built around routine. There's little about daily prison life that's unexpected. Each part of the day is carefully spelled out and defined. Very little is unknown. And the inertia that produces is extreme and far-reaching. Breaking from it isn't easy. Case studies abound of prisoners who upon release commit crimes for the sole purpose of being reincarcerated.

Is that how it is for you? For all the turmoil and animosity that permeate your life, you, at the very least, know what to expect. Behavioral patterns have become deeply entrenched. Some of those habits have etched themselves into your personality - so much so that in many respects they help to define who you are. And you're now being challenged to lay them aside. You're being called, just as God called Abraham, to *"go out, not knowing whither you go."* (Hebrews 11:8). Will you go? Only if your faith is up to it. Is your faith up to it? Or do you still find yourself clinging to the routine - the expected. If your faith cannot sustain the task it's being assigned, don't despair. The solution is not that difficult. *Get into the presence of God. Let God nourish your faith - strengthen it - and it will get the job done.*

God himself will accompany you on your journey. He won't leave you to face it alone. His presence will never depart from you. Your journey may be filled with the unknown*; but it's not the journey that needs to be known, it's God alone whom you must know.*

You need nothing else. Leave! Depart! Listen to the words God spoke to Abraham. They're the same words he's speaking to you.

Gen. 12:1 — Depart from your country...unto a land that I will show you...

A land of triumph! A land of rest!

Faith Sustains Us in Our Wait

Heb. 11:9 — By faith he became ***a sojourner in the land of promise,*** as in a land not his own, dwelling in tents, with Isaac and Jacob, the heirs with him of the same promise...

Verse 9 tells us that when Abraham finally caught sight of the Promised Land, possession didn't instantly pass to him. He found himself a "sojourner" - a *stranger* in the very land God had promised him. And that will prove true for you as well. Old attitudes and habits die hard; new attitudes and habits, on the other hand - however acknowledged in principle - will seem unfamiliar and alien; and that sense of strangeness will cling to you for a long time. You won't find that you're able to shake free of it right away. You'll feel wobbly and unsettled; and, inevitably, you'll feel the tug of "old ways." They're so well known; so well tried; and produce such expected results - whatever misery they produce in the long run.

Here again faith is the answer. Faith alone can sustain us as strangers and sojourners. It's not easy to stay put and hold steady - *while the old gives way to the new.* What's not mentioned here in Hebrews, but what constitutes the backdrop of Abraham's entire journey of faith, is the many altars he built during his sojourn as a stranger in the Land of Promise. Again and again Abraham built an altar – meaning again and again Abraham sought the presence of God. And God's presence upheld and nourished Abraham's faith - so much so that Abraham was called the *"friend of God."*

Jas. 2:23 — And the scripture was fulfilled which says, Abraham believed God, and it was imputed unto him for righteousness: and he was called the *Friend of God.*

You won't be able to *"**tell** yourself to stay put and*

hold steady" and expect *that alone* to sustain you. Knowing *what to do* and *doing it* are vastly different. Yes, of course, you need to remind your soul to hold steady; but to actually do so, you'll need to resort again and again to God's presence - and seek refuge at the throne of his grace. Then your faith will prove sufficient to get the job done.

Verse 10 carries forward the same thought - and adds to it.

Heb. 11:10 ...for he looked for a city which has the foundations, whose builder and maker is God.

Verse 9 tells us that Abraham *"abode in tents"* - which is a figure of speech; it's meant to indicate that possession of the land was not yet Abraham's; that he was an alien. But he looked forward to the day when full possession would be his - figuratively expressed in the phrase *"a city which has foundations."* Strangers reside in tents; owners, however - actual possessors - reside in cities - cities securely established on firm foundations. Abraham was an *alien* - and he knew it; but he was convinced that God himself would build him a city – meaning make him *possessor*. After all, God himself had guaranteed him possession of the land; and because of that he knew it was a settled issue. *Abraham's faith was secured in his knowledge of God.* Here we have the same constellation of principles we've already examined:

1. Abraham's hope consisted of God's *promise that he would eventually inherit the land*
2. his faith, however, was grounded in *God himself* – and,
3. was sustained and strengthened in *God's presence,*

But there's more! Verse 10 introduces a new truth - a new principle. Abraham's faith also nourished his hope and energized it - *to the point that it gave his life purpose*. That's the meaning of the phrase *"he **looked** for a city..."* Not only does faith *"get the job done,"* but, in addition, it invigorates our hope to the point that our lives are given *direction and purpose*. When faith touches any one of God's promises, it transforms that promise into a *living* hope.

Once again note carefully the phrase *"whose builder and maker is God."* It drives home a truth we're all so prone to overlook and which, consequently, bears repeating again and again:

- *it's **God's job** to build the city;*
- *it's **our job** to abide in his presence and, in so doing, keep our faith strengthened and supple - and our hope alive.*

We now add a fourth principle to our constellation...

1. Abraham's hope consisted of God's *promise that he would eventually inherit the land*
2. his faith, however, was grounded in *God himself* – and,
3. was sustained and strengthened in *God's presence,*
4. which, in turn, nourished his hope that he would indeed inherit the land.

And that holds true for Christians – a truth that Dr. Hodges overlooks...

1. Our hope, *not our faith,* consists of God's promise that we will live eternally in his presence – and that nothing can separate us from his love.
2. Our faith, however, is grounded in God himself, in knowing him existentially; and,
3. is sustained and strengthened in God's presence,
4. which, in turn, nourishes our hope that we will live eternally in God's presence – and that nothing can separate us from his love.

Faith Is Based upon Knowing God - Not upon Knowing How God Works

Let's move on now to verse 11. All too often we insist upon knowing what God's plan consists of - and how it works. *But faith is built upon judging God to be trustworthy - that alone, nothing else.*

Heb. 11:11 Through faith also Sara herself received strength to conceive seed, and was delivered of a child when she was past age, *because she judged him faithful who had promised.*

The promise seemed so futile - so hollow; all ordinary means of securing its fulfillment were precluded. Romans 4:19 makes clear that it wasn't simply that Sarah had reached menopause; *it's that she was long past it.* In short, her womb was "dead," meaning it could no longer produce life.

The Bible records that at one point Sarah laughed at God's promise; it seemed so impossible.

Gen. 18:12 And Sarah laughed within herself, saying, After I am waxed old shall I have pleasure, my lord being old also?

But Genesis 18:12 doesn't tell the whole story. Clearly, after having first found belief hard to grasp, she later repented and believed - and in her belief she found grace - and that grace awakened her womb and brought it back to life - and she conceived Isaac. And what underlay the change? The last half of Hebrews 11:11 gives the answer: ***"she counted him faithful who had promised."***

Is your hope dead? God promises you that your life can be restored; that you *can* change. But is that promise lifeless? If it is, you won't give yourself wholeheartedly to the pursuit of a changed life. The hope of genuine change should cast its glow over your whole life - and give it direction and purpose. Remember Sarah! She too found hope hard to grasp. Her womb was dead! Do as Sarah did: *repent - and let your repentance turn you back to God - bathe yourself in his presence - and hear him speak...*

Gen. 18:14	Is any thing too hard for the Lord?

How foolish it must have appeared to Sarah to once again give herself sexually to Abraham. That's the meaning of her question: *"After I am waxed old shall I have pleasure, my lord being old also?"* Pregnancy requires more than belief; it requires sexual intercourse. And advanced age had made that impossible. How foolish to even try! Often, it's not just the promise itself that seems absurd; it's what God requires of us to bring it to pass. That seems absurd as well. And, frequently, it exposes us to ridicule: *Noah building an ark! Abraham and Sara attempting sexual intercourse and expecting a pregnancy to result from it!* What will my friends think? It's ridiculous! And often not just that, but embarrassing as well!

Here too faith is the answer. Faith will see you through all the ridicule. Let everyone laugh! Because beyond the laughter, beyond the ridicule, there's victory - a changed life - awash in God's grace:

1. the ark floating above the floodwaters; safe from God's wrath;
2. Sarah conceiving - and from her "dead" womb a nation of millions emerges - a nation destined to bless the whole earth.

That's the power of faith!

Faith Keeps Us from Returning to Our Erstwhile Bondages

Heb. 11:13	These all died in faith, not having received the promises, but having seen them afar off, and were persuaded of them, and embraced them, and confessed that they were strangers and pilgrims on the earth.

Verse 13 tells us that fulfillment is often projected far into the future. But it constitutes the ground of our hope; and *that* hope is sustained by faith - knowing God personally - that he is faithful to his promises; that he is trustworthy. We can believe him.

Heb. 11:14	For they that say such things make it manifest that they are seeking after a country of their own.
Heb. 11:15	And if indeed they had been mindful of that country from which they went out, they would have had opportunity to return.

Verses 14 and 15 merely continue that thought, but build upon it - adding a new feature: if our hope isn't daily nourished by our faith, we'll return to the very bondages that our faith enabled us to repudiate. ***Whenever our faith fails, we turn back to whatever we left.***

Faith Keeps Us from Shaming God

Heb. 11:16	But now they desire a better country, that is, a heavenly: wherefore ***God is not ashamed of them,*** to be called their God; for he hath prepared for them a city.

This verse takes us back to verse 6 - which declares that without faith it's impossible to please God. Faith makes us "pleasing to God" - just as the lack of faith on our part shames God.

Faith Sustains Us in Total Confusion

Heb. 11:17	By faith Abraham, being tried, offered up Isaac: yea, he that had gladly received the promises was offering up his only begotten son;
Heb. 11:18	even he to whom it was said, In Isaac shall thy seed be called:
Heb. 11:19	accounting that God is able to raise up, even from the dead; from whence he did also in a figure receive him back.

This passage is akin to verse 11 - which tells us that Sarah's dead womb did not cast her into despair - because in knowing God she had learned to trust him - believing that having made her a promise he would surely fulfill it.

- She ceased considering the state of her womb - making it the ground of her belief - and, instead,
- looked to God - making ***him*** the ground of her belief – of her faith.

Verses 17 through 19 build upon this truth - and add to it. Again and again Hebrews warns us to ground our faith in God; to know him, and in knowing him, to find him worthy of our trust. We're admonished to keep our gaze riveted upon God and nothing else - whatever it might be - including a dead womb. The question that Hebrews poses to us is: *"Is any thing too hard for the Lord?"*

But here in verses 17 through 19 it's God himself - his own demand - that becomes the stumblingblock. What if God apparently reneges on his promise? The questions that must have flooded Abraham's mind - any one of which could have sent him reeling into a desperate hopelessness! It's these very questions that Soren Kierkegaard so carefully explores in his classic study *Fear and Trembling* - a book that has caught the imagination of not just generations of Christians, but secular intellectuals as well - who, notwithstanding their hesitation to embrace the gospel message, have nevertheless accorded Kierkegaard their profound respect and adminration for having so boldly layed out the meaning of what it takes to walk by faith - especially when faced by demands which so frequently seem to call into question God's very goodness.

Is God merely toying with me? Is that what I am - just an amusing distraction for God? What if there's no moral purpose underlying God's relationship with us? What if he's capricious? What if God traffics only in his sovereignty - and doesn't bind himself to his own word?

There are moments when all of us feel that God *himself* is pulling the rug out from under our feet; that he's "setting us up to take a fall;" that God is "snookering us." A dead womb is bad enough; but God himself! It's the very fear that plagued the children of Israel in the Wilderness: *"Has he led us into the Wilderness to die?"*

Exodus. 14:11 And they said unto Moses, Because there were no graves in Egypt, have you taken us away to die in the wilderness? Why have you dealt thus with us, to carry us forth out of Egypt?

How can we keep our faith alive when God himself seems to be challenging it? It's a terrible test; but one that each of us must eventually face. The thoughts that must have raced through Abraham's mind! They're the same thoughts that often race through our minds as well.

- God gave me Isaac merely to take him away; he set me up to let me down.
- God gave me my husband to crush my spirit.
- God gave me my wife to destroy me.
- God gave me children to cause me endless grief.

How well do you know God? How long have you been his friend? How convinced have you become of his goodness and justice - his love and his mercy?

Deut. 32:4 The Rock, his work is perfect; for all his ways are justice: a God of faithfulness and without iniquity, just and right is he.

It's not the kind of knowledge that comes quickly; it grows slowly - over many years - one day at a time. And it's certainly not the result of "book-learning" only. Yes, study "feeds" into it; but there's an existential, personal component that simply can't be overlooked. It's the kind of knowledge that marks out God's finest servants - and leads them to their most sublime victories.

Abraham didn't second guess God. His faith stood firm. God was his friend! And he knew it! Does God want to take Isaac? I don't understand it, but I know God. I know that he's good; that he's not capricious; that he's altogether holy and just. Once again, we're brought back to 2 Timothy 1:12.

2 Tim. 1:12 ...for I know him whom I have believed, and I am persuaded that he is able to guard that which I have committed unto him against that day.

Let's now examine verse twenty through twenty two.

Heb. 11:20 By faith Isaac blessed Jacob and Esau, even concerning things to come.

Heb. 11:21 By faith Jacob, when he was dying, blessed each of the sons of Joseph; and worshipped, leaning upon the top of his staff.

Heb. 11:22 By faith Joseph, when his end was nigh, made mention of the departure of the children of Israel; and gave commandment concerning his bones.

Each verse depicts a hero of faith at the end of his life - Isaac blessing Jacob and Esau; Jacob blessing Joseph's sons; Joseph looking forward to Israel's deliverance from Egypt. Faith has become the hallmark of their lives. It sustained them during life - and now ennobles them at death. For each of them, their faith becomes a bridge to the next generation.

Verses 24 through 27 highlight three additional features:

- faith leads us occasionally to step away from blessings;
- faith leads us occasionally to step into want and deprivation;
- faith leads us occasionally to expose ourselves to personal danger.

Stepping away from Blessings

Heb. 11:24 By faith Moses, when he was grown up, refused to be called the son of Pharaoh's daughter;

Moses, the son of Pharaoh's daughter! By faith, Moses stepped away from the status and privilege it afforded him.

Stepping into Suffering

Heb. 11:25 ...choosing rather to share ill treatment with the people of God, than to enjoy the pleasures of sin for a season...

Not only did Moses step away from the blessings his privileged status accorded him, but, in addition, faith led him into suffering and deprivation. Even early on, before he was exiled to Median, Moses had cultivated a walk with God - and that existential, personal knowledge is what underlay his faith to do so.

Heb. 11:26 ...accounting the reproach of Christ greater riches than the treasures of Egypt: for he looked unto the recompense of reward.

God chose Median, at the southern tip of the Arabian peninsula, to deepen Moses' faith. God knew that whatever faith Moses had cultivated in Egypt while at Pharaoh's court, it was insufficient for the mission he had chosen for him. There, on the backside of the desert, for forty years, God drew Moses ever closer to himself – deepening his faith for the severe challenges that lay ahead.

Years later, David underwent the same training – away on the backside of the desert tending his father's sheep. And it was that training that enabled David, as it did for Moses, to cultivate the faith he needed – in David's case the faith he needed to lead the nation of Israel to the pinnacle of her glory.

Has God apparently consigned you to a desert? Are you being kept out of "the spotlight"? If so, have you considered the possibility that it's for the purpose of deepening the faith you'll need for a ministry God has in mind for you? What distinguishes Saul from David is nothing more than faith. Saul's faith failed him; David's faith – having been nourished on the backside of the desert – was sufficiently deep to sustain him.

Stepping into Personal Danger

Finally, we have verse 27 - which shows Moses exposing himself to personal danger - led by God's clear word to do so - and finding himself upheld by his faith to walk it out.

Heb. 11:27 By faith he forsook Egypt, not fearing the wrath of the king: for he endured, as seeing him who is invisible.

Any truly effective man of God will eventually find himself exposed to personal danger. Has your faith been sufficiently strengthened to undergo that kind of trial? If so, God can use you to build his kingdom; if not, your usefulness will always be limited. May God grant you the grace to deepen your walk with him – and, in so doing, deepen your faith – so that whatever task God's word assigns you, you'll undertake it with a confidence rooted in your personal knowledge that God is altogether trustworthy; that his love will never depart from you; that you're the very apple of his eye.

Summary

Hopefully, this brief excursus on faith will provide a clearer understanding of what faith means – of what it means to repose trust in Christ. I'm especially hopeful that I've made clear an important distinction that Dr. Hodges, outstanding scholar that he is, has clearly overlooked: the distinction between the ground of our faith, God himself, and the ground of our hope, what God tells us, i.e., his teaching, his promises; that, furthermore, the key to increasing our faith is not trying harder to believe what God tells us, but drawing closer to him. How's your walk? It's a question I'm not only posing to you, I ask it of myself every day.

CHAPTER THREE

WHAT IT MEANS TO BE A FUGITIVE AND A VAGABOND - A FURTHER EXAMINATION - - DEVELOPING A BIBLICAL PSYCHOLOGY OF MAN -

In the last chapter we learned that God has openly revealed his wrath against all unrighteousness[55] – not only to the angelic hosts throughout the vast stretches of the universe, but also to mankind. It's a revelation he has woven into the fabric of our basic psychological makeup; he has injected it into our spiritual and emotional DNA. And the fear that revelation arouses transforms us into *fugitives* and *vagabonds*.

- We're forever looking over our shoulders – running from justice – defensive and unsure of ourselves. *Angst* - a word carried over from German and popularized by existentialists during the 1950s and 1960s - gives the sense of how it *feels* to be a fugitive.
- We're homeless and rootless; forever haunted by a sense of alienation. *Anomie* - a word carried over from French and popularized by Emile Durkheim, a renowned French sociologist, gives the sense of how it *feels* to be a vagabond.

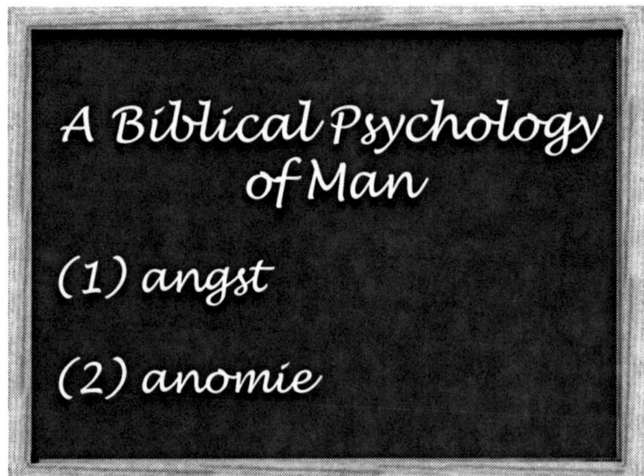

A more detailed account of just what it means to be a fugitive and vagabond – of what it means to suffer from angst and anomie – of what it means to harbor a basic psychology that's driven by angst and anomie - is found, of all places, in the Book of Leviticus. The Book of Leviticus reveals five basic sacrifices[56] for sin:

- The Whole Burnt Offering;
- The Grain Offering;
- The Peace Offering;
- The Purification Offering (sometimes called the Sin Offering); and, finally,
- The Reparation Offering (sometimes called the Trespass Offering).

We know, of course, that all *five* offerings are consummated in Christ's *one* offering on the Cross. Put somewhat differently: we know that Christ's *one* offering incorporates the meaning of all *five* offerings described in Leviticus. But what is the meaning of those offerings? And why five? Simply put: each of the offerings described in Leviticus points to a *wound* that sin inflicts – and then goes on to reveal how God intends to heal that wound in Christ. Thus, what Leviticus provides us with is the *basic, underlying psychology of a sinner and – since all men are sinners – of mankind generally*. Let's take a careful look:

The Whole Burnt Offering[57]

The Whole Burnt Offering is entirely consumed[58] on the altar - that's its unique feature. The meaning is rather obvious, isn't it? The Whole Burnt Offering displays God's wrath poured out in horrifying judgment.

The Whole Burnt Offering is the primary atoning sacrifice[59] – meaning it, more than any of the others, displays "propitiation;" i.e., it shows that God's wrath has been appeased – appeased at Calvary – with Christ on the Cross.

If that's its meaning, the wound it points to is just as obvious: sin inflicts a sense of guilt – and guilt, in turn, generates a fear of impending judgment. It's that wound the Whole Burnt Offering is meant to call our attention to – so that we can know for sure that we've been healed of it in the Cross of Christ. The Cross releases us from guilt and the fear of judgment.

The Grain Offering
The Grain Offering is the only non-blood-shedding sacrifice – and it's based on a ritual common to many premodern cultures. Most premodern societies lacked an organized central government able to provide effective day-to-day protection for its subjects – especially its weaker ones. Consequently, a weaker subject would often bind himself contractually to a stronger subject in a lord-vassal relationship. The "lord" would afford the "vassal" his protection; and the vassal, in turn, would provide for his lord's daily sustenance – a specified amount of his produce – normally a "tithe," but occasionally more. That was his "service." The relationship was frequently confirmed in a simple ritual undertaken at the beginning of each year: the vassal would bring his lord a token of his promised service – often in the form of a few grains of wheat or barley – and lay it at his lord's feet – and then swear his loyalty for the upcoming year. The lord, in turn, would swear his protection to the vassal for the upcoming year. If the vassal failed to serve his lord faithfully, the contract was broken and the vassal could no longer expect his lord to protect him. He was on his own – left to fend for himself - to use whatever meager resources he might be able to muster on his own without his lord's help.

Think about it

Do you still suffer from an amorphous sense of guilt? Do you still feel condemned - that you don't quite measure up? Are you still haunted by a fear of impending doom?

Christ has borne the wrath of God in your place. You are free from condemnation - the fear of not measuring up. You will never suffer the wrath of Almighty God. You may be chastened; but you'll never be disowned by God or suffer his rage. Wrap your heart around this truth.

That, then, is the meaning of the Grain Offering. It symbolizes a contractual relationship between God and man.
- God affords man his protection; and
- man, in turn, affords God his loyalty and faithful service.

The contract is valid only so long as a man faithfully serves God. And therein lies the dilemma: sin voids the contract – leaving man to fend for himself – cut off from God's protection. Sin leaves man haunted with
- the fear of being unprotected –
- the fear of being defenseless –
- the fear of being unguarded and vulnerable.

The sacrifice of Christ on the Cross restores the contract – and reestablishes God's protection. It releases a sinner from the fear of being left defenseless, unprotected, unguarded, and vulnerable. It releases him from the fear that God isn't watching over him – the fear that God doesn't care.[60]

Think about it

Do you feel uncovered and unprotected? Do you feel uncared for - that nobody is watching out for you? Do you feel that you have no "champion" to take up your cause?

Christ has taken up your cause. He stands guard over you. He is watching out for you. He is your "champion." He "wears your colors." You are engraved on the palms of his hands. You are the apple of his eye. Wrap your heart around this truth!

The Peace Offering
The Peace Offering is essentially a shared meal. That's its unique feature.
- God shares in the meal – he is the guest of honor;[61]
- The supplicant shares in the meal.
- The supplicant's family and friends share in the meal.
- And the officiating priest shares in the meal.

It's certainly true that three of the other offerings tender a portion of the sacrifice to the priest, but more in the form of payment than a shared meal. Here it's strictly a matter of a shared meal, not a payment for service rendered or a token of loyalty.

In almost all premodern cultures, a meal is far more than merely a matter of sustenance. It's encrusted with symbolic meaning – and what it most symbolizes is fellowship, peace, and family. A meal, therefore, is a celebration. *It celebrates a sense of belonging.* Anyone invited to share a meal is being invited to share "family" – to, in a sense, become family. He's made party to all that the family provides – especially companionship, love, and joy.

Clearly, the Peace Offering points to the wound it's meant to heal: ***alienation***. Sin disrupts the bonds of love that unite

- man and God;
- husband and wife;
- parents and children;
- siblings;
- friends;
- etc.

Sin scars mankind with a terrible sense of loneliness and estrangement. It afflicts him with a sense of "not belonging." Sin leaves a person feeling that...

- he's "not invited;"
- he's not wanted;
- he's "odd man out;"
- he doesn't fit.

Eugene O'Neill is probably America's preeminent playwright – noted especially for his haunting, unforgettable tragedies. And, of all his tragedies, the one that has most captured the American imagination is *Long Day's Journey into Night*. It's an autobiographical sketch of O'Neill's own family. Its theme is alienation – and its most memorable lines are spoken by the youngest of the Tyrone family's sons, Edmund – no doubt O'Neill himself: *"It was a great mistake, my being born a man. I would have been much more successful as a sea gull or a fish. As it is, I will always be a stranger who never feels at home, who does not really want and is not really wanted, who can never belong, who must always be a little in love with death."*

How deeply is alienation etched into the American character? Those lines tell us*: deeply, profoundly, powerfully!*

Christ on the Cross heals that wound – and restores to mankind a sense of belonging, a sense of family – a sense of love, peace, and fellowship.

The Purification Offering (The Sin Offering)

The unique feature that characterizes the Purification Offering is *cleansing*. The blood of the Purification Offering is used to cleanse the bronze altar, to cleanse the utensils used in the temple rituals, to cleanse the supplicant, to cleanse the golden altar, and, on the Day of Atonement, to cleanse the Mercy Seat itself. The wound, then, that the Purification Offering calls our attention to is obvious, isn't it? Sin leaves man feeling filthy; it leaves him feeling stained; but there's more to it than just that. Whatever sin touches is not just filthy and stained, it's also defiled – *meaning it's useless to God* – whether animate or inanimate – it doesn't matter. Sin breeds a sense of futility and vanity – a haunting feeling of ennui – an all consuming emptiness.

Further Explanation of the Purification of Offering: Filth

The 20th Century western mind is apt to overlook what the pre-modern mind couldn't possibly fail to notice: that sin leaves behind an indelible stain - a stain that reminds the sinner of his heinous crime. Act 5, Scene 1 of Shakespeare's *Macbeth* is a telling witness...

MacBeth

Attendant, noticing that Lady Macbeth, guilty of murder, but yet undiscovered, is forever washing her hands...	It is an accustomed action with her, to seem thus washing her hands. I have known her to continue in this a quarter of an hour.
Lady Macbeth – looking at her hand...	Yet here's another spot.
An attending doctor...	Hark, she speaks. I will set down what comes from her to satisfy my remembrances.
Lady Macbeth looking down at her hands again...	Out, damned spot! out, I say! ...who would have thought the old man to have had so much blood in him?

For Shakespeare, the "stain" is visual – Lady Macbeth trying desperately to expunge the stain of sin from her hands; but for Poe, whose mind clearly reflected a medieval, pre-modern cast, it's auditory – the sound of a beating heart – the heart of a murdered man buried under the planks of his killer's living room floor. The climactic lines of the story are unforgettable. "Yet the sound increased – and what could I do? It was a low, dull, quick sound – much like the sound a watch makes when enveloped in cotton – and yet the officers heard it not. ... again! hark! louder! louder! louder! louder! I admit the deed! Tear up the planks! here, here! It is the beating of his hideous heart!"

- Lady Macbeth – trying desperately to wash away the stain her vile crime has left behind on her hands!
- A murderer – apparently unperturbed by his hideous crime – a classic sociopath unable to "feel" his victim's pain – nevertheless haunted by the "beating heart" of a corpse he has cleverly buried under the planks of his living room floor!

Dramatic witness to the "stain" sin leaves behind!

Defilement

The defilement that sin breeds – the loss of purpose and the enervating sense of futility it causes - is reflected brilliantly in the opening and closing lines of T. S. Eliot's well-known poem *The Hollow Men*.

We are the hollow men
We are the stuffed men
Leaning together
Headpiece filled with straw. Alas!
Our dried voices, when
We whisper together
Are quiet and meaningless
As wind in dry grass
Or rats' feet over broken glass
In our dry cellar.

Shape without form, shade without color,
Paralyzed force, gesture without motion...
This is the way the world ends,
This is the way the world ends,
This is the way the world ends,
Not with a bang, but with a whimper.

Shortly after *The Hollow Men* was published in 1925, Eliot noted despondently that he meant it to reflect not just a state of mind afflicting a few sensitive, self-absorbed men and women recoiling in horror from the slaughter of World War I, but all mankind. He meant it to be a universal indictment of the human condition. It's the same sense that Solomon describes in Ecclesiastes:

Vanity of vanities, says the Preacher;
Vanity of vanities, all is vanity.
What profit has a man from his labor
In which he toils under the sun?

All things are full of labor;
Man cannot express it.
The eye is not satisfied with seeing,
Nor the ear filled with hearing.

The Cross of Christ heals that terrible wound. It washes away the otherwise indelible mark that sin leaves behind. It restores to man a sense of innocence and moral purity. It also reestablishes his sense of usefulness – and leaves him once again feeling that his life counts – that his life is meaningful. Once again, he can feel God's hand drawing him back into his purposes – and filling him with a sense of significance.

The Reparation Offering (The Trespass Offering)

The unique feature characterizing the Reparation Offering is the restitution that accompanies it. What that signifies is pretty clear: *sin is theft. It's robbery.*

- Murder *robs* a man of his life;
- burglary *robs* a man of his property;
- adultery *robs* a man of his wife;
- slander *robs* man of his reputation.
- etc.

Robbery offends our sense of justice – whether we're the perpetrator or the victim – and, if unchecked, it can arouse a pervasive sense of insecurity – which leaves us feeling that the world is amiss – that it's "off kilter."

"Off kilter" – the sense that Shakespeare means to convey in the line he gives Marcellus to speak in scene 4, Act 1 of Hamlet: *"Something is rotten in Denmark"* - a phrase we're all familiar with, but the significance of which we often miss. Marcellus suspects that a grave injustice has been committed, but he's not yet sure what it might be. And that sense produces a gnawing, stomach-churning feeling that the world is "out of kilter."

And that's what injustice produces – both when it's merely suspected and when it's known but not made right.

We're left feeling disoriented, contingent, shaky, and nauseous - a sense that was carefully and thoughtfully probed by the post-World War II French existentialists emerging from the trauma of France's defeat in 1940 and the humiliation of Vichy's[62] collaboration with the German Nazis. Jean Paul Sartre's short novel *Nausea* is a good example of their efforts.

But the Bible provides even better examples – especially in the Book of Job, in the Psalms, and in the Prophets. A good illustration is found in Psalm 73 – where Asaph complains that the wicked go unpunished; that injustice is not reproved; that wrongs aren't made right; that what's upside down isn't turned right side up again:

> But as for me, my feet had almost stumbled; my steps had nearly slipped.
> For I was envious of the boastful, when I saw the prosperity of the wicked.
> For there are no pangs in their death, but their strength is firm.
> They are not in trouble as other men, nor are they plagued like other men.
> Therefore pride serves as their necklace; violence covers them like a garment.
> Their eyes bulge with abundance; they have more than heart could wish.
> They scoff and speak wickedly concerning oppression; they speak loftily.
> They set their mouth against the heavens, and their tongue walks through the earth.
> Therefore his people return here, and waters of a full cup are drained by them.
> And they say, how does God know? And is there knowledge in the Most High?
> Behold, these are the ungodly, who are always at ease; they increase in riches.
> Surely I have cleansed my heart in vain, and washed my hands in innocence.

What's stolen must be returned; what's wrongfully seized must be recovered;

- otherwise we feel our feet slipping from under us – and a debilitating vertigo spinning us out of control;
- otherwise, anger and resentment begin to boil up inside us – twisting our psyche and poisoning our heart.

The Cross of Christ proves that God *is* concerned about justice. The Cross *confirms* God's justice. Therefore, it heals us of the nausea and bewilderment that sin inflicts – the sense of contingency it arouses. It quiets the anger that poisons our minds and hearts. It calms us with the quiet assurance that God will not permit injustice to continue forever; that wrongs *will be* righted. That what's upside down *will be* turned right side up again.

Summary

The Five wounds described in Leviticus – when taken together – delineate a biblical

Think about it

Do you feel that justice is an empty promise? That iniquity runs rampant? That life is upside down - and nobody can put it right side up again?

Do you feel angry at all the injustice that apparently goes unchallenged and unchecked?

Christ on the Cross proves that God is concerned about justice - that injustice has not gone unchallenged and unchecked - that justice will be a hallmark of the coming kingdom. It will cover the whole earth. Wrap your heart around this truth!

psychology of man. An updated sketch of man's basic psychology is provided below; and a graphic depicting those wounds and the healing God the Father provides in his Son Jesus Christ is found on pages 74 and 75.

A Biblical Psychology of Man

(1) guilt and fear of impending judgment;
(2) unprotected and vulnerable;
(3) alienated, uninvited, unwanted;
(4) unclean, stained, aimless, futile
(5) bewildered, disoriented, bitter.

The Offering Each of the five offerings listed here reflects a specific aspect of sin.	What's at Issue	Behavior Susan Cook, MA. M.F.C.C., and Elizabeth Shearer, MS. Clinical Psychology, sketched out the following behavioral patterns.
Whole Burnt Offering	*Guilt and Judgment* **I'm guilty. Judgment is right around the next corner. I'm bad! I'm worthless!** The Whole Burnt Offering reveals Christ bearing the ***penalty*** of sin in our place. Christ has become the sinner's substitute on the Cross. It shows God's provision in Christ for relieving a sinner of his sense of guilt and his fear of impending judgment.	A sense of guilt, worthlessness, and imminent judgment is apt to induce the following in persons so affected: (1) refuse forgiveness; sin in order to confirm a guilt ridden conscience; (2) act out the role of "saint" or "martyr;" feign altruism; (3) become self-righteous and legalistic; become critical and intolerant; become a "moral crusader;" (4) engage in addictive behavior in order to dampen guilt and deaden emotions.
Grain Offering (Cereal Offering)	*Rebellion* **I'm unprotected. I'm uncared for.** Sin is an act of ***rebellion*** on the part of a servant against his lord; and, as such, it voids the lord's obligation to provide protection and care. The Grain Offering shows how Christ's sacrifice on Calvary entitles us once again to God's protection and care. It renews in us a sense of being guarded and defended by a powerful, utterly good, and infinitely loving father.	A sense of being unprotected and uncared for is apt to induce the following in persons so affected: (1) Allows himself to be exploited – allows himself to be victimized - which often leads to self-degradation. (2) Exploits others in order to feel powerful; persecutes others to feel powerful. (3) Substitutes addictions for genuinely intimate relationships. (4) Develops self-protective mechanisms; e.g., physical strength, financial self-sufficiency, etc.
Fellowship Offering (Peace Offering)	*Fellowship* **I've been excluded from God's presence! No one wants me around! I'm all alone! I can never seem to "break in" with others.** Sin ***alienates*** us from God and from our fellow man. The Fellowship Offering reveals God in Christ inviting us into his presence and into the presence of his people. It both restores fellowship and celebrates it.	A sense of being excluded is apt to induce the following in persons so affected: (1) Becomes a loner, independent; inordinately self-reliant. (2) Seeks attention. (3) Becomes manipulative and superficially social. (4) Seeks to "buy" friendships. (5) Pursues the development of self-empowerment techniques. (6) Substitutes addictions (e.g., gambling, sexual perversions, etc.) for genuinely intimate relationships.
Purification Offering (Sin Offering)	*Pollution and Uselessness* **I'm unclean! I'm dirty! I make everyone I touch dirty as well. Not only that, but my life is meaningless.** Sin ***stains*** and ***pollutes*** both the person who commits it and the person against whom it's committed. The Purification Offering reveals God in Christ washing us of all the stains sin has caused and, in addition, drawing us back into His purpose and infusing our life with meaning.	A sense of being polluted and defiled is apt to induce the following in persons so affected: (1) Engages in shameful behavior; e.g., sexual perversions; provocative behavior; "coarse talk." (2) Becomes legalistic and self-righteous. (3) Gravitates toward "self-help;" e.g., education. (4) Overemphasizes physical beauty. (5) Becomes a perfectionist. (6) Prone to certain addictions; e.g., food, drugs, alcohol, sex, exercise.
Reparation Offering (Trespass Offering)	*Theft* **I've been robbed! There's no justice!** Sin is an act of ***theft***; it deprives God and others of what is rightfully theirs. The Reparation Offering reveals God in Christ restoring what sin has stolen. It renews in us a sense of justice - and relieves us of the anger that a sense of being wronged always generates.	A sense of having been robbed or cheated is apt to induce the following in persons so affected: (1) Co-dependent. Apt to be excessively generous and easily exploited. (2) Exploits others' generosity and goodwill; opportunistic; cheap; selfish; prone to hoarding. (3) Distrustful; self-reliant; controlling; ascetic; (4) Resentful - especially of the rich. (5) Materialistic. (6) Substitutes addictions for intimate relationships.

Summary Drawn from Matrix on Previous Page

Developed by

Susan Cook, MA. M.F.C.C.

The Distorted Self-Image Sin Produces	I'm guilty. God is going to judge me because I'm so bad. I'm worthless. I'm unprotected. I'm uncared for. I can't trust anyone. I'm all alone. Nobody wants me around. I'm unclean. I'm dirty. I've been robbed. I've been wronged. Justice is an empty promise; it's merely a device the strong use to exploit the weak. I need to "get" others before they "get" me.
The Behavior a Distorted Self-image Often Produces	(1) *Confirms the distortion* by living out the distorted role. (2) *contradicts the distortion* by engaging in behavior that is its "polar opposite." (3) *Corrects the distortion* through the exclusive use of one's own carnal resources. (4) *Conceals the distortion* by avoiding both intimacy and emotional depth. Common example: a woman who has suffered sexual abuse as a child might feel unclean, powerless, or unworthy of love; consequently, she might: (1) *confirm the distortion* by becoming a prostitute or by allowing others to exploit her sexually; (2) *contradict the distortion* by becoming sexually aggressive and acting out the role of a powerful seductress; or she might "turn her sexuality off" and become celibate; and urge others to remain unmarried and celibate as well; (3) *correct the distortion* by eventually marrying a "sex addict" and becoming locked into co-dependent behavior designed to "fix" or control her husband. (4) *Conceal the distortion* - perhaps by becoming obese in order to hide her sexuality from men.

Cultural Connections: The Bible and Western Thought

Jean Paul Satre's

Nausea

Jean Paul Sartre, a French Jew, was born in Paris in 1905. He was just nine years old when the First World War broke out and was thirteen years old when the armistice was signed in 1918 ending the war. He finished his secondary education during the early 1920s and went on to study philosophy at the École Normale during the mid to late 1920s - where he met his lifelong friend and confidant, Simone de Beauvoir, herself a noted existentialist and author of one of the most influential books of the 20th Century, *The Second Sex*.

The First World War and its aftermath generated a powerful impact on Sartre. France, though victorious, had suffered terribly during the war. A whole generation of young Frenchmen had been slaughtered in the trenches that ran for over three hundred miles from the English Channel to Alsace near Basel, Switzerland. Northern France, occupied by the Germans for almost five years, lay in ruins.

The war had left France a lifeless hulk. Her confidence had been drained. Her will to resist had been shattered. And when the Germans began to rearm shortly after Hitler was appointed Chancellor in 1933, the French sought refuge in collective denial.

Had France struck boldly and decisively against Germany anytime between 1933 and 1938, she could have stopped Hitler dead in his tracks and averted the disaster that fell upon her in 1940. But she vacillated. She wavered. She equivocated. And her moment passed. Sartre's whole philosophy - indeed, his whole personality - crystallized around this failure - the failure to be decisive; the failure to choose; the failure to acknowledge evil and confront it head-on.

Nausea was Sartre's first attempt to articulate his philosophy. It was published in Paris in 1938 - ironically at the very moment Hitler was swallowing up Czechoslovakia - with the French standing aside, paralyzed with fear.

Nausea is cast in the guise of a diary - detailing the life of Antoine Roquentin, a writer who has settled in Normandy to complete a research project he has taken up. Roquentin shuffles back and forth between café and public library, meditates on many of the conversations he strikes up, and jots down notes to himself in his journal. The whole tenor of the book is terribly self-reflective - to the point of lapsing into a kind of schizophrenia. It's very tedious reading - and requires a truckload of patience to complete.

Sartre's philosophy is not that terribly complicated - especially when we strip away all its muddled esoterica. Simply put, evil is a very real presence in the world;[63] but most of us choose to ignore it. Why? Because evil provokes a sense of injustice - which reminds us of mankind's terrifying contingency - and that contingency - the sense that our feet are slipping out from under us, that there's nothing we can rely upon - produces a sickening nausea. Anyone willing to acknowledge the presence of evil must accustom himself to the feeling of nausea. It becomes a constant fixture in his life. "Nausea is not inside me," Sartre declares early on in the book, "I feel it out there in the wall, in the suspenders that hold up my trousers, everywhere around me. It makes itself one with the café I'm sitting in, I am the one who is within it."

Only the most courageous of humans, Sartre pessimistically maintains, can live with nausea - can force themselves to adjust to its stomach-turning presence. Most persons refuse to muster the necessary courage, and, instead, deny the evil that surrounds them - or, at the very least, try to appease it - try to accommodate themselves to it - in short, try to "strike a pact with the devil."

Sartre, like Kafka, is not that far off the mark. What we have with Sartre is exactly what we found with Kafka: *Biblical truth minus God.* Once again, though Western intellectuals have expunged the Christian faith from their discourse, they can't avoid the truths it highlights: in the case of Sartre, it's the presence of evil and mankind's unwillingness to confront it - especially when the evil seems overwhelming. The injustice that evil produces spawns a sickening nausea - a terrifying sense of vertigo that leaves us feeling that we're losing our balance - that the world is out of kilter. In short, the Biblical truth of man's condition absent God's mercy is almost unbearable.

CHAPTER FOUR

Verses for Lesson Four:

Rom. 1:18b ...who suppress the truth in unrighteousness
Rom. 1:19 because what may be known of God is manifest in them, for God has shown it to them.
Rom. 1:20 For since the creation of the world His invisible attributes are clearly seen, being understood by the things that are made, even His eternal power and Godhead, so that they are without excuse,
Rom. 1:21 because, although they knew God, they did not glorify Him as God, nor were thankful, but became futile in their thoughts, and their foolish hearts were darkened.
Rom. 1:22 Professing to be wise, they became fools,
Rom. 1:23 and changed the glory of the incorruptible God into an image made like corruptible man—and birds and four-footed animals and creeping things.
Rom. 1:24 Therefore God also gave them up to uncleanness, in the lusts of their hearts, to dishonor their bodies among themselves,
Rom. 1:25 who exchanged the truth of God for the lie, and worshiped and served the creature rather than the Creator, who is blessed forever. Amen.
Rom. 1:26 For this reason God gave them up to vile passions. For even their women exchanged the natural use for what is against nature.
Rom. 1:27 Likewise also the men, leaving the natural use of the woman, burned in their lust for one another, men with men committing what is shameful, and receiving in themselves the penalty of their error which was due.
Rom. 1:28 And even as they did not like to retain God in their knowledge, God gave them over to a debased mind, to do those things which are not fitting;
Rom. 1:29 being filled with all unrighteousness, sexual immorality, wickedness, covetousness, maliciousness; full of envy, murder, strife, deceit, evil-mindedness; they are whisperers,
Rom. 1:30 backbiters, haters of God, violent, proud, boasters, inventors of evil things, disobedient to parents,
Rom. 1:31 undiscerning, untrustworthy, unloving, unforgiving, unmerciful;
Rom. 1:32 who, knowing the righteous judgment of God, that those who practice such things are deserving of death, not only do the same but also approve of those who practice them.

Introduction:

In Romans 1:16 – 18a, Paul has summed up the gospel message - and, in doing so, has revealed the theme of the epistle:

- Man is a sinner.
- A verdict of guilt has already been rendered against him and a sentence of death has already been pronounced.
- All that remains is execution of that sentence.
- However, God, in his infinite mercy, has provided a pardon for anyone who in simple faith asks for it.

The next step is obvious: ***ask for the pardon.***

However, it's not quite that simple: ***man suppresses the truth of his own sinfulness and, therefore, is unaware of his need for a pardon – unaware of the terrible danger stalking him.*** It's a frightful dilemma that calls for drastic measures. But what? Paul's solution is a carefully crafted, hard-hitting polemic that extends from Romans 1:18b all the way to Romans 3:20 – ending with a ringing declaration that no one can sustain his own righteousness before God – that we're all guilty – that without God's forgiveness, hell is mankind's inevitable destiny.

It's easy to lose sight of the purpose Paul gives his polemic: he wants...

- to bring us to our senses.

- to shake us out of our stupor.
- to awaken us to our need.

And lose sight of it is exactly what Boice and Piper, along with their fellow Calvinists, do. Romans 3:10-11, which stands a little before the end of Paul's long polemic, is a case in point.

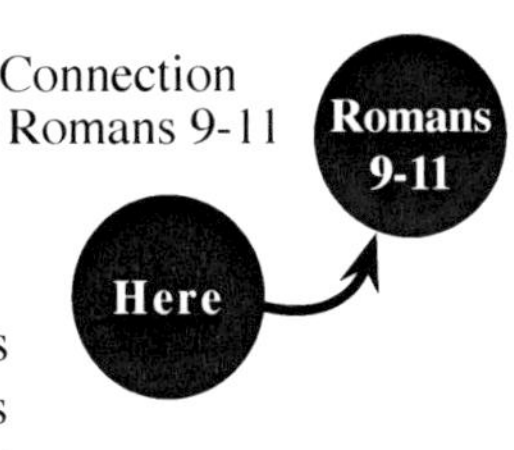

Rom. 3:10	As it is written: There is none righteous, no, not one;
Rom. 3:11	There is none who understands; There is none who seeks after God.

Boice and Piper insist that Romans 3:10-11 proves that man is incapable of sensing his need for a pardon – that he's too morally depraved. It's one of their primary proof texts. ***But the whole purpose of the polemic is to wake us up, not to prove that doing so is impossible.***

Moreover, the conclusion of Paul's polemic – its summary – isn't found in Romans 3:10-11; it's found in Romans 3:19-20 – *and there the focus is mankind guilt, not his depravity.*

Rom. 3:19	Now we know that whatever the law says, it says to those who are under the law, that every mouth may be stopped, *and all the world may become **guilty** before God.*
Rom. 3:20	Therefore by the deeds of the law no flesh will be justified in His sight, for by the law is the knowledge of sin.

Clearly, Romans 3:10-11 is merely a way-station along the track leading to Paul's conclusion in Romans 3:19-20. In short, Boice and Piper have jumped off the train too soon – before it has reached the end of the line.

Why, then, the supercharged language of Romans 3:10-11 and, of course, the language that follows? *Because it's a polemic! That's why!* Paul's language here is no different from what we find in any other polemic. A polemic is developed using overwrought language – sound and fury – "sturm und drang" – words, terms, and phrases designed to break down our defenses and prepare us for a conclusion that ordinarily we'd resist – regardless of how logical it might be or how well grounded. The ultimate

Total Depravity in Light of Romans 1:18b - 3:20

Clearly, Romans 1:18b – 3:20 is not first and foremost a description of mankind's inherent sinfulness; it's a polemic designed to turn sinners back to the truth they instinctively suppress. But that presumes sinners ***can*** be turned back to the truth; that their intellect is not so impaired that they're unable to acknowledge their plight and cry out to God for his forgiveness. In short, Calvinists press the description Paul gives of mankind's sinfulness in Romans 1:18b – 3:20 beyond the parameters Paul's *purpose* logically implies: *to turn sinners back to the truth, not to prove that doing so is impossible.*

Put a little differently: a polemic is, by its very nature, an appeal to reason; and its use takes for granted that those to whom the appeal is being made are indeed amenable to reason – and, of course, the purpose the appeal is designed to effect, specifically, in the case of Romans 1:18b – 3:20, salvation through faith in Christ; that it's not, as Calvinists insist, a hopeless undertaking. How Calvinists can possibly suggest otherwise is puzzling to say the very least – especially in light of formidable scriptural evidence to the contrary; for example Isaiah 1:18...

Isaiah 1:18	Come now, and *let us **reason** together,* says the Lord: though your sins be as scarlet, they shall be as white as snow; though they be red like crimson, they shall be as wool (italics mine).

meaning of a polemic, then, isn't found at the three quarter point. The three quarter point of a polemic is precisely where the assault against our defenses is being ratcheted up and the sound and fury begins to build toward a crescendo.

Boice and Piper must certainly know that. They ignore it only because they have trapped themselves in the strictures of a self-contained, internally consistent theology that argues in favor of Calvinist conclusions drawn from Calvinist premises.

If Boice and Piper are wrong about Romans 3:10-11 – and it's apparent that they are – the doctrine of "total depravity" is stripped of one of its primary proof texts. And that, in turn, undermines the doctrine of double predestination – a doctrine that guides and governs the Calvinist interpretation of Romans 9-11.

No, Romans 9-11 is not about God's sovereignty; it's about the unfettered nature of God's mercy.

Romans 3:20 marks the end of Paul's polemic – his long digression – and Romans 3:21 marks his return to the "main trunk line" - the gospel message itself - God's Rescue Plan - what it is and how it works. How do I know? Because...

- he begins Romans 3:21 with the words *"But now"* – which clearly tell us that a parenthetical section has just been completed; and
- he once again takes up a phrase he first introduced back in Romans 1:17: *"the righteousness of God"*

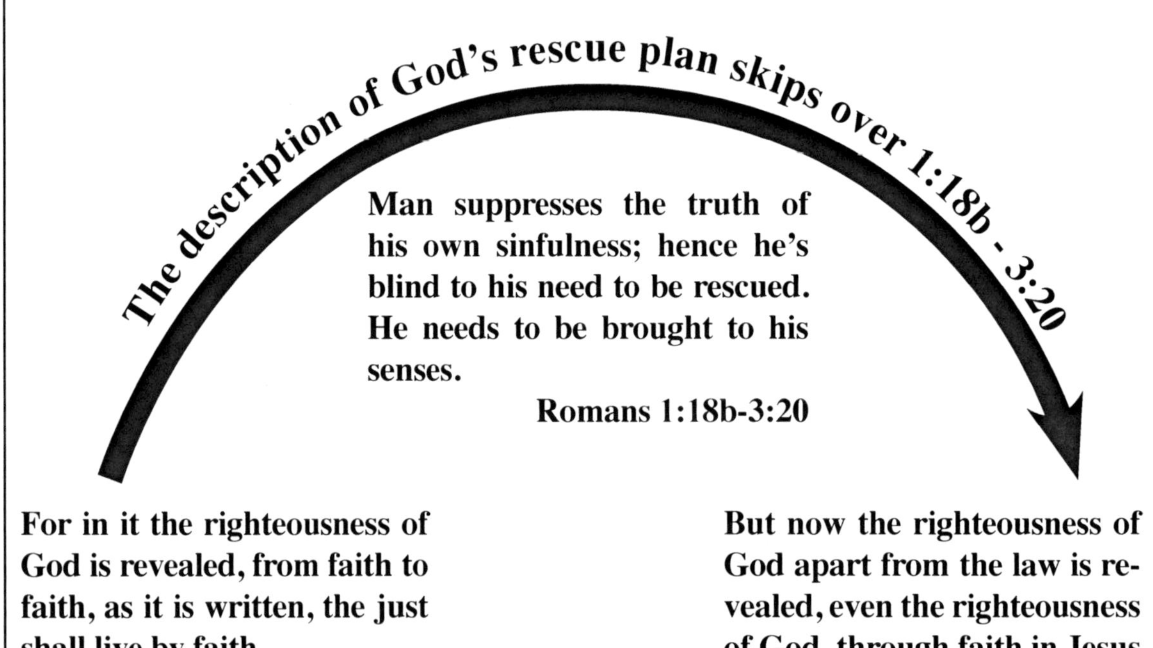

Or, put a little differently:

Paul introduces God's Rescue Plan and briefly describes it.

Scripture	The Flow of Paul's Teaching
Rom 1:16 ...gospel of Christ ... is the power of God unto salvation for everyone who believes, for the Jew first and also for the Greek. Rom 1:17 For in it ***the righteousness of God*** is revealed from faith to faith; as it is written, "The just shall live by faith." Rom 1:18a For the wrath of God is revealed from heaven against all ungodliness and unrighteousness of men...	Romans 1:16 - 18a proclaims a truth that Paul wants clearly delineated: • Man is guilty of unrighteousness and has aroused God's wrath. • A sentence of death has been pronounced against him. • His only hope is a pardon consisting of a righteous standing God confers upon anyone who in simple faith asks for it.

Paul breaks away from describing God's Rescue Plan to awaken man to his need to be rescued.

Scripture	The Flow of Paul's Teaching
Rom 1:18b ...who suppress the truth in unrighteousness,  Rom 3:20 Therefore by the deeds of the law no flesh will be justified in His sight, for by the law is the knowledge of sin.	Man suppresses the truth of his own sinfulness and is, therefore, unaware of his need for a pardon. It's this issue that Paul now takes up - extending from Romans 1:18b through Romans 3:20. Paul's purpose here is to awaken man to his need for God's forgiveness, not, as Calvinists would have us believe, to prove that doing so is impossible.

Paul once again takes up the description of God's Rescue Plan

Scripture		The Flow of Paul's Teaching
Rom 3:21	...But now ***the righteousness of God*** apart from the law is revealed, being witnessed by the Law and the Prophets... 	Romans 3:21 marks the beginning of Paul's return to the "main trunk line" of his thought - God's Rescue Plan - what it is and the dynamics underlying it. Nowhere else in scripture is the theology of God's Rescue Plan so clearly and so thoroughly described. We know that Paul has once again picked up the topic of the rescue plan because he uses a term he introduced in Romans 1:17 - the "righteousness of God" - meaning a standing in righteousness God confers upon anyone who is simple faith asks for it.
Rom 8:37	...we are more than conquerors through Him who loved us.	

The Grammatical Structure of Verses 18b and the Verses Which Follow

The grammatical structure of verse 18*b* and the verses which follow is very complex. Nevertheless, it's important to sort our way through it. We begin by taking note once again of the relationship between verses 18*a* and 18*b*:

Rom. 1:18*a*	For the wrath of God is revealed from heaven against all ungodliness and unrighteousness of men
Rom. 1:18*b*	*who* suppress the truth in unrighteousness ...

Relationship between verses 1:18a and 1:18b

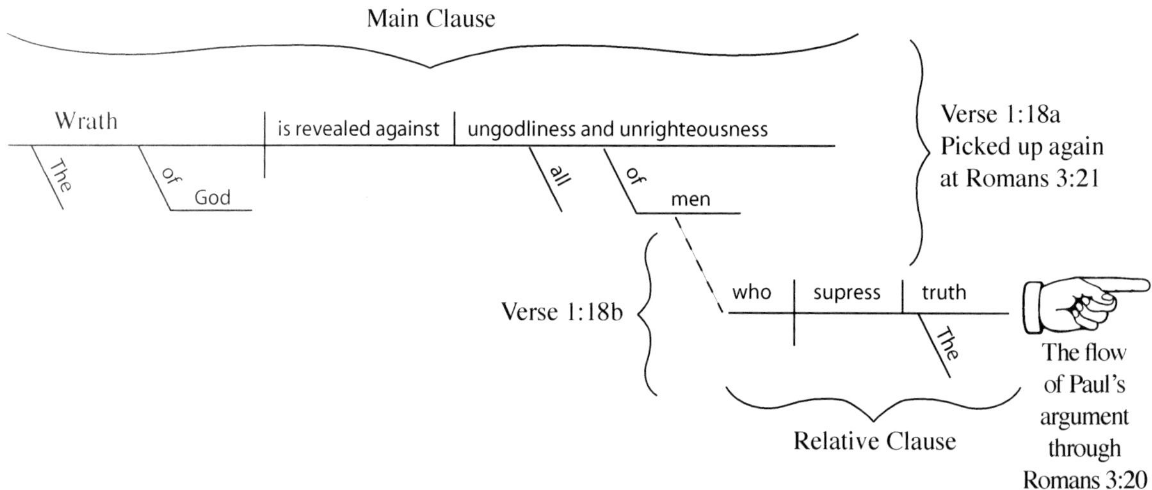

The word "who," which begins verse 18*b*, introduces *a relative clause that carries the flow of Paul's thought through, in the short run, to Romans 1:24* – where three appalling judgments of God are delineated – extending all the way through to verse 32. The antecedent of "who," is, of course, the "men" in verse 18*a* accused by Paul of ungodliness and unrighteousness. The relationship between verses 18*a* and 18*b* is sketched out on the previous page:[64]

Verse 18*b*, *"who suppress the truth in unrighteousness,"* sets up the "therefore clauses" in verses 24, 26, and 28, *"Therefore God gave them over..."* In more technical terms, verse 18*b* is what grammarians call a *"protasis"* – meaning it states a condition leading to an *"apodosis"* – meaning a consequence.

The verses that lie between 18*b* and 24, verses 19 – 23, consist of four adverbial clauses each of which is introduced by one of two subordinate conjunctions, "because" or "for." The use of the subordinate conjunctions "because" and "for" tells us that each of the adverbial clauses they introduce is meant to explain the clause that precedes it – *either a "why" or a "how."*

Since verse 18*b*, not 18*a*, is carrying the flow of Paul's thought through 3:20, we conclude that the first of the adverbial clauses is anchored to the word "suppress" in 18*b* - and is meant to explain *why* the truth can't be ignored – *why*, instead, it's got to be forcefully stifled – *"because what may be known of God is manifest in them (verse 19)."* That's why.

A close look at verses 21 – 23 reveals that they comprise a secondary protasis/apodosis...

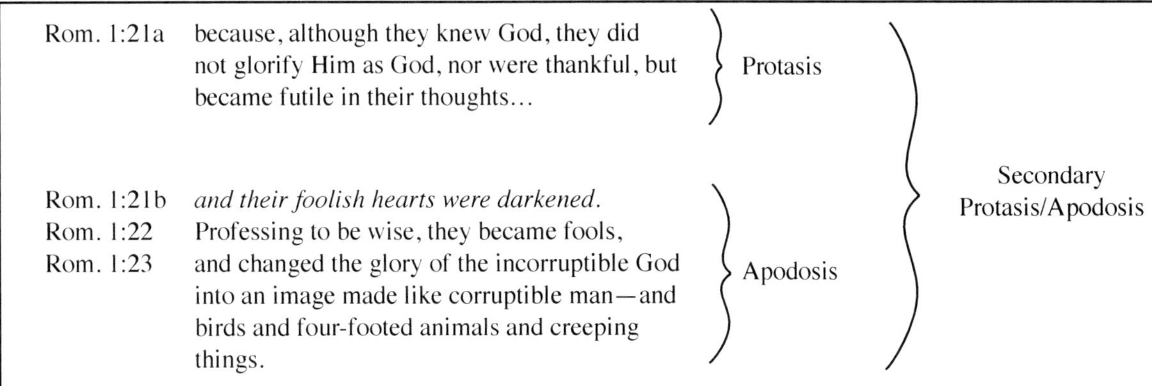

.... imbedded within the primary protasis/apodosis ...

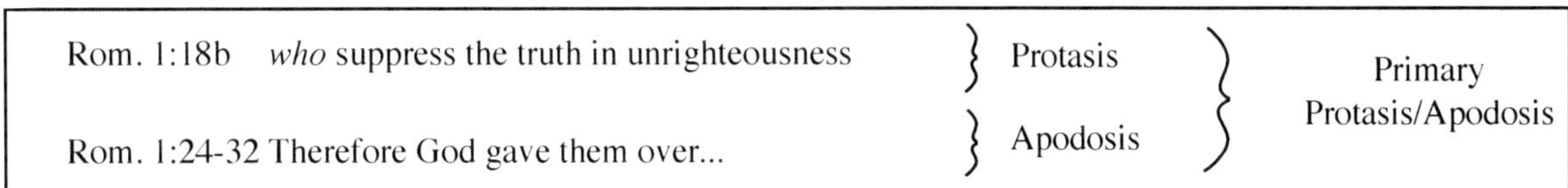

Connection to Romans 9-11

Romans 9-11

Here

The secondary protasis/apodosis is *not* a judicial consequence personally orchestrated by God himself*; it's what rationalizing the truth inevitably leads to: a darkened heart – meaning a hardened heart;* and man bears responsibility for that, not God. *Obviously, then, it's only after man has first hardened his own heart (verses 21a-23) that God judicially hardens it even further* (verses 24-32).

And that throws light on Romans 9:18.

Rom 9:18 ... and whom He wills He hardens.

Boice and Piper, along with their fellow Calvinists, insist that the hardening described here in Romans 9:18 is...

- undertaken by God alone;

- with no role whatsoever assigned to man.

However that's at odds with the pattern Paul's at pains to explain in Romans 1:21-23: *God hardens man only after man has first hardened himself.* We conclude, therefore, that it was only after Pharaoh (Romans 9:17) first hardened his own heart - a tragedy for which he bears sole responsibility - that God hardened it still further.

I have sketched out below a diagram of verses 18*b* – 23.[65]

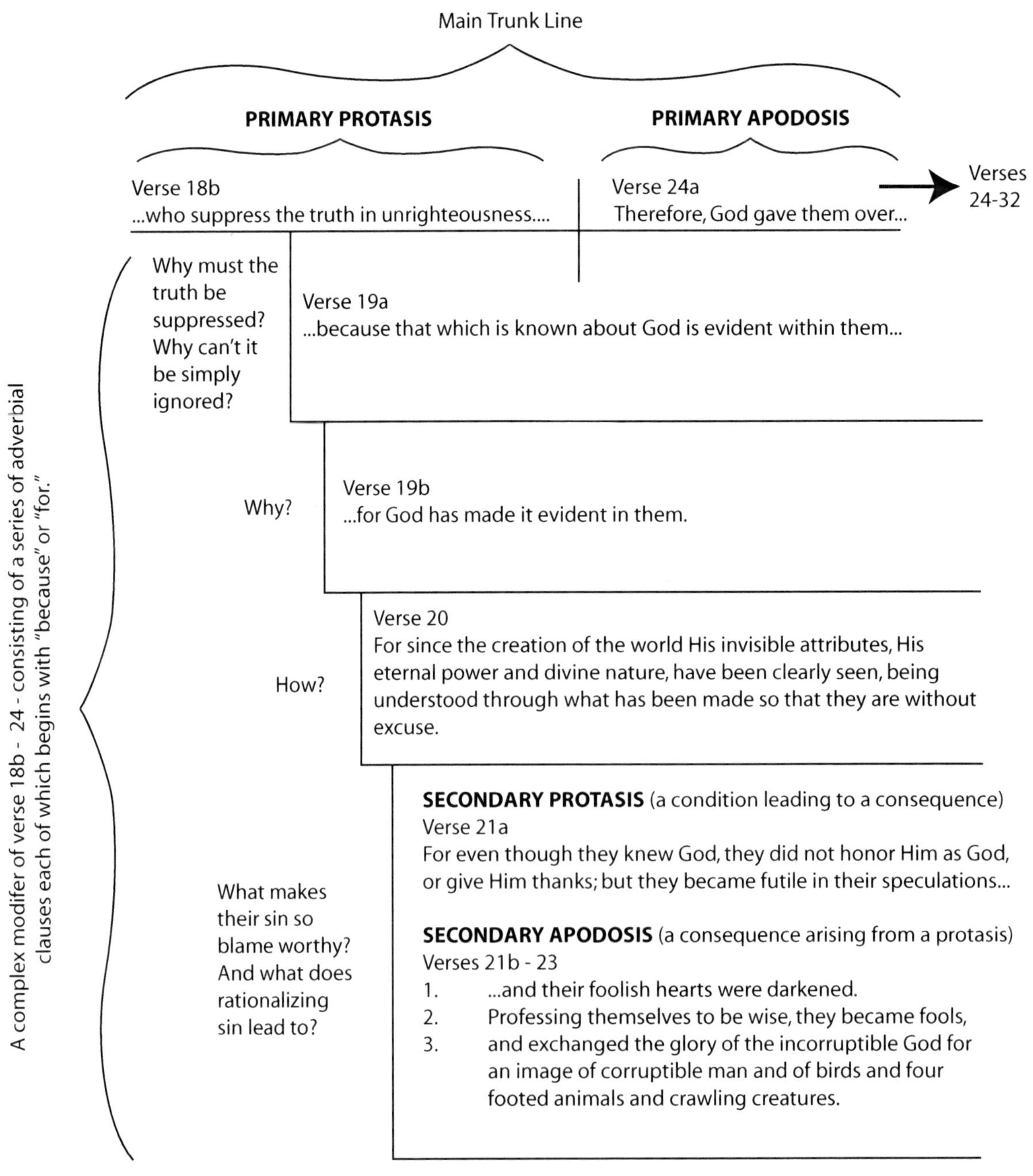

The Primary Protasis – a condition leading to an apodosis, meaning a consequence - consequences that are found in verses 24, 26, and 28

Verse:

Rom. 1:18*b* ...who suppress the truth in unrighteousness

Specific words or phrases found in verse 18b:

"suppress"

The word "suppress" means to "hold down."[66] The truth about God and his hatred of unrighteousness is inherent - and to avoid facing it requires effort; it's not easily done. The truth has got to be *held down.* It's not possible to simply walk around it - to ignore it.

Connection to Romans 9-11

Here → Romans 9-11

"the truth"

What truth? The truth sketched out in Romans 1:16 – 18*a*.

- Man is a sinner – he's guilty of unrighteousness;
- his only hope is to throw himself on God's mercy.

The phrase *"suppress the truth"* doesn't necessarily imply that the *whole* truth is being "suppressed." In the case of a hypocrite (Romans 2:1 and 2:17), it's his own sinfulness that's being suppressed, not the sinfulness of mankind generally.

- That alone, however, is enough to prompt the rationalizing Paul describes in verse 21a,
- which, in turn, leads inevitably to the hardening he describes in verses 21b-23 – a hardening which is entirely of his own making.
- That, in turn, may, though not necessarily, lead to the still further hardening described in verses 24-32. Whether or not it does is up to God. Some men God hardens; others, he doesn't. It's his call – which is the meaning of Romans 9:18...

Rom 9:18 ... and whom *He wills* He hardens.

Suppressing the truth and the intellectual, moral, and spiritual hardening that results therefrom is universal; in short, it afflicts the Jews – who presume to be mankind's judges – every bit as much as the Gentiles; i.e., it's not unique to the Gentiles only - which, after all, is a rather silly suggestion on the face of it – especially in light of the history of Israel sketched out in the Old Testament.[67]

"in unrighteousness"

Any attempt to suppress the truth is inherently unrighteous – because it's *God's* truth; its suppression reflects mankind's basic sinfulness.

Verse:

Rom. 1:19 because that which is known about God is evident within them, for God has shown it to them.

1st Adverbial Clause – meant to explain the protasis

"because that which is known about God is evident within them..."

This is the first of four adverbial clauses – each of which is meant to explain the clause it follows. Paul is saying that the evidence pointing to the truth[68] is so compelling that it can't be ignored – that no one can simply walk on by it - *which is why verse 18b tells us that the truth has got to be suppressed – forcefully stifled.*

But why, then, doesn't Romans 1:19 read "...because that which is known *about the truth* is evident within them..." rather than "...because that which is known *about God* is evident within them..."? It's because the one implies the other: anyone who refuses to acknowledge his own sinfulness, ipso facto, suppresses the knowledge of God. It's exactly what Jesus tells us in John 3:19-20.

John 3:19 And this is the condemnation, that the light has come into the world, and men loved darkness rather than light, because their deeds were evil.

John 3:20 For everyone practicing evil hates the light and does not come to the light, lest his deeds should be exposed.

Anyone who won't acknowledge he's a sinner runs from the light into the darkness - away from the presence of God - away from the knowledge of God. Likewise, anyone who is brought into the presence of God is, ipso facto, convicted of sin - convicted of his own unrighteousness. Isaiah 6:1 - 5 provides a graphic illustration:

Isaiah 6:1 In the year that King Uzziah died, ***I saw the Lord sitting on a throne,*** high and lifted up, and the train of His robe filled the temple.

Isaiah 6:2	Above it stood seraphim; each one had six wings: with two he covered his face, with two he covered his feet, and with two he flew.
Isaiah 6:3	And one cried to another and said: Holy, holy, holy is the Lord of hosts; The whole earth is full of His glory!
Isaiah 6:4	And the posts of the door were shaken by the voice of him who cried out, and the house was filled with smoke.
Isaiah 6:5	***So I said: Woe is me, for I am undone! Because I am a man of unclean lips, And I dwell in the midst of a people of unclean lips; For my eyes have seen the King, The Lord of hosts.***

2nd Adverbial Clause – meant to explain the 1st adverbial clause

"for God has shown it to them..."

Here we have the second adverbial clause – answering the question posed by the first: *The truth is obvious! Why? Because God himself has made it so.* It's God who has made the truth so compelling that we can't possibly ignore it! We can only suppress it!

Verse:

Rom. 1:20	For since the creation of the world His invisible attributes, his eternal power and divine nature, are clearly seen, being understood by the things that are made, even His eternal power and Godhead, so that they are without excuse...

3rd Adverbial Clause – meant to explain the 2nd adverbial clause

"for since the creation of the world his invisible attributes, his eternal power and divine nature, have been clearly seen, being understood through what has been made..."

Here we have the third adverbial clause – answering the question posed by the second: *How has God made the truth so obvious – so compelling? The answer: nature is God's witness.* Notice that what we have here is a deliberate non-sequitur: *"His invisible attributes...have been clearly seen..."* How can invisible attributes be clearly seen? A deliberate non-sequitur is sometimes used to convey a sense of mystery and wonder – which is why Paul is using one here. He wants to preserve the sense of God's transcendent wonder – to make it clear that whatever knowledge of himself God conveys, it's never sufficient to overcome that wonder. Still, the meaning is clear: God's creation brings to light his invisible attributes. Psalm 19:1 is a good example of Paul's meaning:

Psalm 19:1	The heavens declare the glory of God; and the earth shows his handiwork.

So convincing is the witness of nature that the Psalms frequently give nature a human voice – indicating that man must actually stop up his ears to avoid hearing it.

Psalm 148:3	Praise him, sun and moon; praise him, all stars of light!
Psalm 148:4	Praise him, highest heavens, and the waters that are above the heavens!

Moreover, it's not merely some transcendent truth that has been disclosed; it's the truth about God himself - *him personally* - which is what's implied in the phrase "His invisible attributes, His eternal power and divine nature." Paul is not a "Jewish Plato" emerging from the shadows of a half-lit cave into the sun-bathed world of *impersonal* archetypes.[69]

Paul, however, is certainly not positing here a "natural theology." He is not saying that nature so reveals God that scripture is unnecessary or superfluous. That would run totally contrary to Paul's assertion in Romans 1:16-17 - that the gospel (i.e., scripture, the written word), not nature, reveals God's plan of salvation. It would also run totally contrary to Romans 3:21. What Paul is saying, however, is that nature reveals *enough* of God to make inexcusable our attempts to suppress the truth of his existence, his righteousness, and his hatred of sin. The intricate design of nature - its exquisite beauty[70] - is a more than sufficient testimony.

"so that they are without excuse"

The whole point of verses 19 and 20 is to underscore the truth that the denial of God's existence is wholly without excuse; God has clearly revealed himself to mankind.

Verse:

Rom. 1:21a	For even though they knew God, they

did not glorify Him as God, nor were thankful, but became futile in their speculations...

4th Adverbial Clause – meant to explain the 3rd adverbial clause – and leading to a Secondary Protasis/Apodosis

4th Adverbial Clause - Secondary Protasis

"For even though they knew God they did not honor him as God or give him thanks,
Here we have the fourth adverbial clause answering the question posed by the third and leading into a secondary protasis: *"Why are their excuses so terribly egregious?" Because, though knowing God, they have failed either to honor him or thank him.* Against the backdrop of ancient Middle Eastern culture, this failure is especially culpable. A monarch's presence was never a matter of pedestrian indifference; it customarily elicited an elaborate display of honor and gratitude. And if not, judgment was instant – most frequently death.[71]

> **Think about it**
>
> Man knows God exists. He can't escape that knowledge. No one is truly an agonstic or an atheist. It's not possible.

Notice too that no one can truly claim to be either an atheist or an agnostic. Everyone has at one time "known God." Every person has, at some point in his past, *personally* encountered God and has acknowledged his existence.

"...but became futile in their speculations..."
The Greek word translated "speculations" is "διαλογισμοις." Its meaning throughout the New Testament is more akin to *excuse making* than to logical thought; that's what makes its use here so interesting.
In other words, the Greeks were well aware that our mind is more a servant to our emotional predispositions than most of us care to admit; in short, we tend to rationalize; we tend to use our vaunted intellect not to "reason our way to the truth," but to excuse the "bent of our sinful inclinations."

> **Think about it**
>
> Our vaunted human intellect is more often used to rationalize than to reason.

And that inevitably leads to a darkened heart – meaning a hardened heart; and that's precisely Paul's point in the next clause, *"and their foolish hearts were darkened."*

4th Adverbial clause - Secondary Apodosis

"and their foolish hearts were darkened"
The word "foolish" translates the Greek word "ασυνετος" – and it means "uncomprehending," "void of understanding." The Greek word "καρδια" conveys far more than the English word "heart." It denotes the inner self – including the intellect, the emotions, and the will. And because it's modified by the adjective "ασυνετος" – meaning "uncomprehending" – what Paul probably has most in mind is the intellect. Therefore, we may conclude that when a man turns his back on God it's the intellect that's first affected.

> **Think about it**
>
> It's the mind - the intellect - that's first affected when a man turns away from God.

When our immoral "bents" - our corrupt proclivities - are sufficiently rationalized, our hearts become "darkened." That's because "rationalizations" encrust falsehood with a thin coat of respectability. Paul is saying precisely what Christ said in Matthew 6:22-23.

Matt. 6:22	The lamp of the body is the eye: if therefore your eye be single, thy whole body shall be full of light.
Matt. 6:23	But if your eye be evil, thy whole body shall be full of darkness. If therefore the light that is in thee be darkness, how great is the darkness!

***Verse*:**

Rom. 1:22	Professing to be wise, they became fools...

A fool is anyone who denies the obvious; but a quintessential fool is someone who not only denies the obvious, but then wraps his denial in pedantic sophistries.

Verse:

Rom. 1:23	and changed the glory of the incorruptible God into an image made like corruptible man—and birds and four-footed animals and creeping things...

The word "changed" conveys the sense of "exchanged."[72] The point here, then, is rather straightforward and simple: in refusing to honor God or cultivate a grateful "spirit," man has, in effect, consented to a tragically foolish "exchange." He has exchanged the unspeakable glory of the Creator for the infinitely lesser glory of creation – and a sin-tainted creation at that. It's an exchange that has *cheapened* and *degraded* him. He has exchanged "incorruption" for "corruption." And he is now doomed to "live out" the consequences of that exchange - of the degradation it entails - in his attitudes and behavior.

There's an underlying truth here that's very easy to overlook: *ontologically,*[73] *man is a mirror* - meaning he reflects whatever he points himself toward – never actually becoming it sui generis,[74] but assuming its shape and form – displaying all its essential qualities.

> **Think about it**
>
> Worshp is an act of "turning toward" God; of staying turned toward him; and, in so doing, reflecting God.

It's one of the first truths elucidated in the scriptures: Genesis Chapter One makes it clear that mankind was made in the *image* of God – meaning we were meant to reflect God – to bear his *likeness* – to, in effect, stand in his stead – to represent him.

Gen. 1:26	And God said, let us make man in our image, after our likeness...

But man turned himself away from God – and, therefore, he no longer reflects God's glory – he no longer bears his likeness[75] - which is precisely the truth underscored in both Psalm 106:20 and Jeremiah 2:11.

Ps. 106:20	Thus they changed their glory into the image of an ox that eats grass.
Jer. 2:11	Has a nation changed its gods, which are not gods? But my people have changed their Glory for what does not profit.

2 Corinthians 3:18 tells us that the whole point of salvation is to bring us back into the presence of God - where, as we turn ourselves back toward him and keep ourselves turned toward him, we will once again reflect his glory and assume his likeness.[76] *And isn't this a definition of worship?*

> **Think about it**
>
> Man is, in essence, a mirror. He is designed to reflect whatever he's pointed toward.

> "But we all, with unveiled face beholding as a mirror the glory of the Lord, are being transformed into the same image from glory to glory, even as from the Lord the Spirit."
>
> *2 Cor. 3:18*

If in turning away from God we lose his likeness, in turning back to God, we regain his likeness. Overcoming the power of sin, therefore, is not so much a matter of trying harder; it's more a matter of turning back to God and staying in his presence; it's a matter of...

- keeping ourselves pointed toward God;
- delighting ourselves in him;
- learning how to rest in him.

"into an image"
It's unlikely that Paul has "full blown" idolatry in mind here – notwithstanding the use of the words "ομοιωματι εικονος" ("likeness of an image") - which, if they stood alone, certainly might give rise to that conclusion. However, the "exchange" he's describing here does not necessarily require it;[77] and, indeed, the context, which is the "queen rule" of hermeneutics, seems to suggest otherwise; specifically, in verses 21 through 28 Paul is

> **Think about it**
>
> Consider the deadly peril a fixation poses. If you are, in essence, a mirror - reflecting whatever you're turned toward, and, what's more, in a sense, becoming whatever you're turned toward, what does that tell you about the danger a fixation poses. For example, anyone who becomes fixated on an injustice, regardless of how egregious it might be, and who, consequently harbors anger and bitterness in his heart, will, in time, become a bitter, angry person.

describing a progression – and idolatry, as such, isn't "fitted" into that progression until further on: first, man suppresses the truth (verse 18). That leads to rationalizing our denial of the truth – "putting a spin" on what we've done – excusing it – which, inevitably, hardens our heart. That, in turn, may, though not always, lead to the first of God's "judgments" (verse 24): *man is given over to impurity – primarily sexual impurity.* Impurity, then, often leads to idolatry (verse 25 – where the word "worship" is used – indicating the presence of "full blown" idolatry) – which, then, may, though not always, lead to a second judgment: *man is given over to "degrading passions."* And so on through the third judgment – leading to a *debased mind.*

The Primary Apodosis – a series of consequences arising from the protasis found in verse 18b

Verse:

Rom. 1:24 Therefore God also gave them over to uncleanness, in the lusts of their hearts, to dishonor their bodies among themselves…

1st Punishment

"Therefore God also gave them over to uncleanness"

This is a judicial act on God's part. It's the first of three *"giving overs."* The others are found in verses 26 and 28. Each one is a punishment - not merely a consequence of sin, but an actual punishment for sin. Verse 27 makes this point especially clear.

Hebrews 11:25 acknowledges that there's "pleasure in sin for a season." But here Paul makes it plain that eventually the sin we find so exhilarating, so titillating – that very sin becomes wormwood and gall. Sin is like a baited trap; the bait lures us into a trap - which eventually snaps shut - catching us in a prison of anguish and misery.

The first "giving over" is to ("εις"[78]) "impurity" - primarily *sexual impurity.* The Greek word is "ακαθαρσια." Impurity arises from out of the "lusts of the heart" ("επιθυμιαις των καρδιον αυτον") which are ordinarily held in check by God's grace. But here God withdraws his grace (the judicial act of "giving over"), and the lusts are left uncontrolled and unchecked. The end result is "impurity" - which is often linked to greed ("πλεονεξια"), which denotes a terrifying state of emptiness - a condition that drives its victims relentlessly; and the more that's gained, the greater the sense of emptiness and the sharper the pangs. There's never any rest - never any sense of satisfaction - only a momentary reprieve followed invariably by another cycle of frenzied sinfulness - more gripping than before. Impurity is far more than a particular lust ("επιθυμια"); it's an inordinate craving - a gripping, mind-numbing compulsion.

Think about it

Clearly, anyone "given over" to a sin has been delivered into bondage. The sin has become compulsive.

Are you caught fast in the bondage of a compulsive sin? Isn't it possible that God has given you over to it in order to bring you to your senses?

What's the first step in overcoming a compulsive sin? Isn't it acknowledging the truth? If suppressing the truth leads to bondage, doesn't acknowledging the truth lead toward freedom?

"gave them over"

Think about what it means to be *"given over."* Clearly, it implies domination and bondage. We're made the *prisoners* of sin. Again, what we have here, then, is a "compulsion" - usually a sexual compulsion, which is what the Greek word "ακαθαρσια" implies.

Verses:

Rom. 1:25 who exchanged the truth of God for the lie, and worshiped and served the creature rather than the Creator, who is blessed forever. Amen.

Rom. 1:26 For this reason God gave them over to vile passions. For even their women exchanged the natural use for what is against nature.

Rom. 1:27 Likewise also the men, leaving the natural use of the woman, burned in their lust for one another, men with men committing what is shameful, and receiving in themselves the penalty of their error which was due.

Rom. 1:28 And even as they did not like to retain God in their knowledge, God gave them over to a debased mind, to do those things which are not fitting;

"who exchanged the truth of God for the lie, and

worshiped and served the creature rather than the Creator, who is blessed forever. Amen."

Sexual impurity almost always leads to idolatry Why? The dynamic is simple and straightforward: *fornication profanes sex* - meaning it *makes common* what God intended to be sacred - reserved *exclusively* for the marriage bond. *Likewise, idolatry profanes worship*. It profanes what God intended to be sacred - reserved *exclusively* for him. That's why fornication and idolatry are so closely linked throughout the Bible and why one leads almost inevitably to the other: *profanity cannot be contained; profanity at one level spills over to all levels. Fornication almost always leads to idolatry.*[79]

It's this very insight that underlay Balaam's advice to Balak, King of Moab. Balaam knew that if Israel could be seduced into committing fornication with the women of Moab that would inevitably prompt Israel to commit idolatry; and it did.

2nd Punishment

"For this reason God gave them over to vile passions. For even their women exchanged the natural use for what is against nature. Likewise also the men, leaving the natural use of the woman, burned in their lust for one another, men with men committing what is shameful, and receiving in themselves the penalty of their error which was due."

Idolatry prompts the second of God's judgments – men and women are given over to "dishonoring passions." The Greek words are "παθη ατιμιας." "ατιμιας" means "without honor." Here another line is crossed along the descent into human depravity. It's not merely that nature is pushed to its limits (e.g., gluttony, heterosexual excesses and impurities, etc.); it's that nature ("φυσιν" – "nature") is violated ("παρα φυσιν" – "against nature"); e.g., homosexuality, bestiality, pedophilia, etc. Such sins are "παθη ατιμιας" – meaning by their vary nature, they dishonor, humiliate, and disgrace the person afflicted.

Think about it

What do "gay activists" most desperately want? Is it what they claim it is - tolerance? No. It's respect. Their insistence on tolerance is secondary - meant only to establish the groundwork for their primary objective - respect.

Think about it. What's the name of one of their most prominent organization? It's "Dignity." That speaks volumes, doesn't it? Dignity is exactly what their sin has stripped them of - and it's what they're trying frantially to recover.

Homosexuality, by its very nature, is a "dishonoring sin." That's what it does: it dishonors! In short, their quarrel isn't with "Bible thumpers" and "rednecks," it's with the sin itself.

3rd Punishment

"And even as they did not like to retain God in their knowledge, God gave them over to a debased mind, to do those things which are not fitting"

Finally, the mind itself ("νους") is "given over." This is the third "giving over." There's more at issue here than the translation suggests. The kind of behavior that's being described here does not "fit" human nature ("μη καθηκοντα"). Why? Because man is fundamentally – meaning essentially – a moral being[80] - and, therefore, his rejection of all moral constraints leaves him *less than human*. What he has made of himself is completely at odds with God's intention.

Think about it

A "closet" homosexual is ashamed of his sin and tries desperately to conceal it. Inevitably, then, he leads a double life. A flagrant homosexual, on the other hand, makes no attempt whatsoever to conceal his homosexuality; instead, he flaunts it.

Two homosexuals: both profoundly dishonored by their sin; but one is acutely ashamed of his sin, while the other renounces his shame - projecting it onto those he believes are condemning him and his life-style. Why the difference? The one has undergone the second of God's judgments, described in Romans 1:26-27; the other has undergone the third of God's judgments, described in Romans 1:28-32. That's the difference!

Once again, it should be carefully noted that the Greek word "νους" is not exactly synonymous with the English word "mind." For the Greeks, the mind was not just the intellectual dimension of man's self; it was also the seat of moral integrity and spiritual perception. Indeed, it more closely corresponds to what the Keswick pietists called "the human spirit." Here – at this third level – a person's total intellectual, moral, and spiritual identity is lost. He is left with a "depraved humanity" - a "νους αδοκιμος" - a "humanity that doesn't measure up" – a psyche that can hardly be called "human" – wholly indifferent to shame and dishonor[81] – incapable of even a modicum of genuine empathy. These kinds of individuals are the Ted Bundys and Joseph Mengelers of the world. They're what psychologists call "sociopaths."

The descent corresponds to the following pattern: we begin with the lusts of the heart held in check by God's grace.

- The first "giving over" is to "impurity" – compulsive excesses – especially of a sexual nature.
- The second "giving over" is to "degrading passions" - an immoral condition that goes beyond mere excess - that, instead, violates nature itself; e.g., homosexuality, bestiality, pedophilia.
- The third "giving over" is to a "failed humanity" - an intellectual, moral, and spiritual condition that's no longer truly "human" – that can assume the form of terrible cruelty and heartless indifference. I'm personally convinced that whole nations,[82] not just individuals, can be turned over to a depraved mind; e.g., Nazi Germany.

At each of the three descending levels, the person undergoing judgment *suffers a profound loss* – meant both to bring him to his senses and to display the horrifying consequences that result from turning away from God – *from suppressing the truth.*

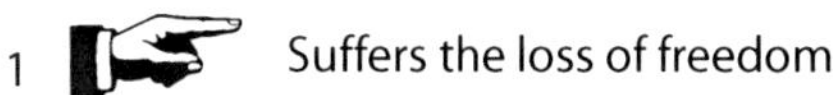

1 Suffers the loss of freedom

2 Suffers the loss of honor and dignity

3 Suffers the loss of basic humanity

Verses:

Rom. 1:29	being filled with all unrighteousness, sexual immorality, wickedness, covetousness, maliciousness; full of envy, murder, strife, deceit, evil-mindedness; they are whisperers,
Rom. 1:30	backbiters, haters of God, violent, proud, boasters, inventors of evil things, disobedient to parents,
Rom. 1:31	undiscerning, untrustworthy,

Paul's Typology of Sin

Sinners

Romans 1:28-32

Romans 1:21-27

Flagrant Sinners

Hypocrites
Sinners who conceal their sinfulness

unloving, unforgiving, unmerciful...

Verse 29 begins a relative clause which modifies verse 28. Normally, a relative clause is introduced by a relative pronoun - most frequently the word "who." However, here in verse 29 the word "who" has been omitted, though, grammatically, it's assumed. The technical term for an omitted pronoun is a "zero relative pronoun." The relative clause that verse 29 begins extends through verse 31, making verses 28 - 31 a single grammatical unit. But verse 32 is also a relative clause - which means that it too is a part of that single grammatical unit. *The bottom line is simple: Paul is making a clear distinction between the persons described in verses 21 - 27 and those described in verses 28 - 32.* In short, the flow of Paul's thought corresponds to a typology of sin that he's developing (see graphic on page 91). Paul elaborates on this distinction in Romans Chapter Two when he takes up the issue of hypocrisy.

Verses 29 – 31 provide a horrifying description of persons who have been given over to a "debased mind" – a psyche devoid of basic human decency – persons hardly worth calling human. It's almost a carbon copy of Paul's description of the Last Days

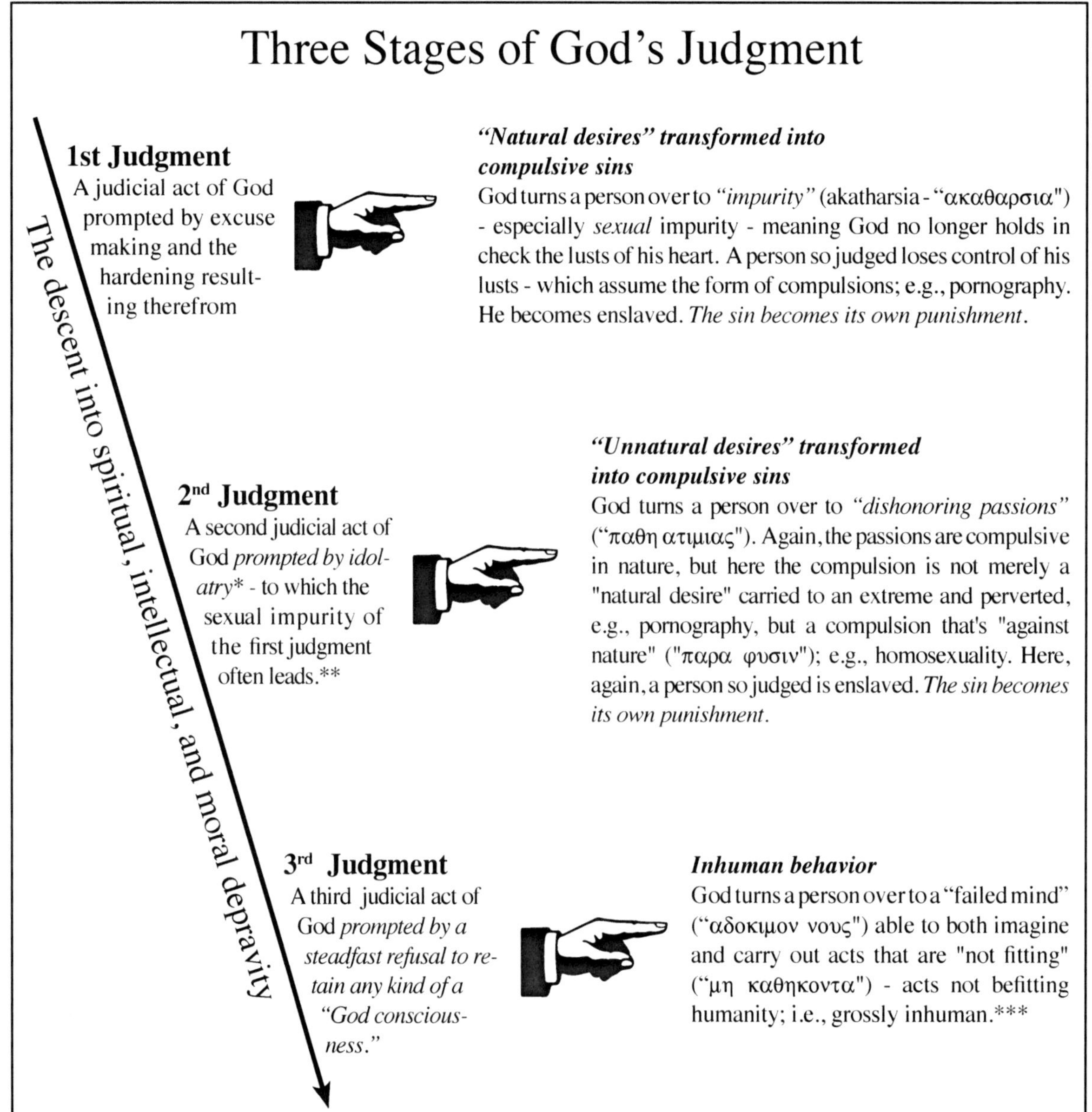

Terms Used in "Three Stages of God's Judgment"

Idolatry • Sexual Impurity • Gross Inhumanity

* Idolatry reflects a mind-set that holds nothing sacred. That's its underlying essence. The transcendent nature of God is lost almost completely. There's little sense of the holy. For example, none of the Greek gods is fundamentally concerned with righteousness and personal integrity. The entire pantheon of Greek gods is devoid of a single illustration of unbending moral purity. And the same holds true for any other pantheon - whether Egyptian, Hittite, Canaanite, Amorite, Hindu, "New Age," or whatever.

** Fornication *profanes* sex - meaning it makes common what God intended to be sacred - reserved *exclusively* for the marriage bond. Likewise, idolatry *profanes* worship. It profanes what God intended to be sacred - reserved *exclusively* for Him. That's why fornication and idolatry are so closely linked and why one leads almost inevitably to the other: *profanity cannot be contained; profanity at one level spills over to all levels. Fornication almost always leads to idolatry (see Appendix I).*

*** Romans 1:29-31 describes the inhumanity to which such persons are given over. These persons are especially dangerous - they can be hideously cruel and malicious. They are the Ted Bundys of the world, the Joseph Mengelers, the Adolph Eichmans, etc.

generation found in 2 Timothy 3:1-5.

2 Tim. 3:1	But know this, that in the last days perilous times will come:
2 Tim. 3:2	For men will be lovers of themselves, lovers of money, boasters, proud, blasphemers, disobedient to parents, unthankful, unholy,
2 Tim. 3:3	unloving, unforgiving, slanderers, without self-control, brutal, despisers of good,
2 Tim. 3:4	traitors, headstrong, haughty, lovers of pleasure rather than lovers of God,
2 Tim. 3:5	having a form of godliness but denying its power.

A word of caution:
We shouldn't conclude that any of the three "giving overs" is irremediable.[83] 1 Corinthians 6:9-11 proves otherwise.

1 Cor. 6:9	Know you not that the unrighteous shall not inherit the kingdom of God? Be not deceived: neither fornicators, nor idolaters, nor adulterers, nor effeminate, nor abusers of themselves with mankind,
1 Cor. 6:10	Nor thieves, nor covetous, nor drunkards, nor revilers, nor extortionists, shall inherit the kingdom of God.
1 Cor. 6:11	*And such were some of you: but you are washed, but you are sanctified, but you are justified in the name of the Lord Jesus, and by the Spirit of our God.*

In other words, many of the redeemed are drawn from the same cesspool Paul describes here in Romans 1:29-31.

Verses:

Rom. 1:32	who, knowing the righteous judgment of God, that those who practice such things are deserving of death, not only do the same but also approve of those who practice them.

Romans 1:32 tells us that the persons described in verses 29 – 31 make no excuses for their sinfulness – they make no attempt to hide it; in fact, they not only sin themselves, but actually endorse and encourage the sinfulness of others. That's the extent to which their rebellion has carried them. They consciously and quite willfully resist any kind of moral constraints – no doubt clothing their defiance in righteous indignation – claiming ...

- that their civil liberties are being violated;
- that their artistic imagination is being thwarted;
- that civilization itself is being threatened by narrow minded bigots and "bourgeois philistines."

The On-Going Mercy of God:
It's hard to be dogmatic about the passage of scripture we've been examining – beginning with 18b and extending through 32; but there's evidently a pattern here that Paul is sketching out ...

- The hardening Paul describes in Romans 1:21b-23 appears to be the unavoidable consequence of rationalizing our sinfulness (Romans 1:18b-21a). It's not prompted by God – at least not directly; it's simply "the way our psyches are wired": they're hardened whenever we excuse or justify our sinful proclivities.
- The hardening may reach a point at which a person's conscience can no longer generate sufficient conviction to hold his lusts in check.
- If that occurs, God intervenes. He, so to speak, "shoves our face" in the sin we've been "toying with" – the sin we've found so titillating – so tempting. He turns us over to it – to the anguish and misery which is always its bottom line. That's what Paul is describing in Romans 1:24-32.
- If indeed we are brought back to our senses, it's not simply because shame has drawn us back – though shame may continue to play a diminished role;[84] it's because anguish and misery have drawn us back. It's no different from what my friend's father did when as a teen-ager he caught him smoking a cigarette. He made him smoke a whole pack. It wasn't the shame of smoking that brought him back to his senses – he was largely beyond that; it was the misery caused by smoking an entire pack. he was sick for a week – and resolved never to smoke again.
- In any case, God never hardens us until we've first hardened ourselves; and then the hardening he prompts – though certainly justly deserved – is ultimately meant to bring us to our senses – to see sin for what it is – to feel its horror and to be crushed under its tyranny – not just our own lives, but the lives of those we love the most – our parents, our wives and husbands, our sons and daughters, our friends, our colleagues. In short, lying behind the terrible judgments God inflicts on sinners – the judgments spelled out in Romans 1:24-32 – is God's mercy. Once again, we hear echoes of Micah 7:18.

Micah 7:18	Who is a God like unto you, who pardons iniquity, and passes by the transgression of the remnant of his heritage? He retains not his anger for ever, *because he delights in mercy.*

A Biblical Psychology of Man - Continued
At the end of Chapter One, we began to develop a Biblical psychology of man. We based it on insights gleaned from Romans 1:18*a*. We concluded that man is a *fugitive* and a *vagabond* - meaning that...

- he's forever looking over his shoulder – running from justice – defensive and unsure of himself;
- he's homeless and rootless; forever haunted by a sense of alienation.

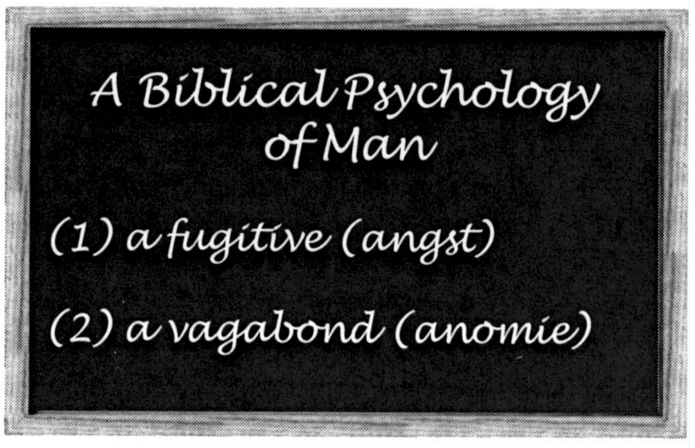

In Chapter Two, we elaborated on that basic definition somewhat. We employed two descriptive terms coined by 20th Century existentialists and social psychologists to describe what it *feels* like to be a fugitive and a vagabond: *angst* and *anomie*.

Then, we turned to the first six chapters of Leviticus to complete our sketch. Those six chapters describe the five basic sacrifices for sin incorporated in the Mosaic order:

- The Whole Burnt Offering;
- The Grain Offering;
- The Peace Offering;
- The Purification Offering (sometimes called the Sin Offering); and, finally,
- The Reparation Offering (sometimes called the Trespass Offering).

We suggested that each of the five sacrifices described in Chapters One through Six points to a wound sin inflicts - and when those five wounds are added together we have a still further elaboration of what it means to be a fugitive and a vagabond - of what it means to suffer from angst and anomie.

It's obvious, however, that further elaboration is required. Why? Because the punishments God inflicts on man for *suppressing the truth* also generate a profound impact upon his psyche. And that impact needs to be added to the insights gleaned from Romans 1:18*a*. What we have, then, is depicted on the next page.

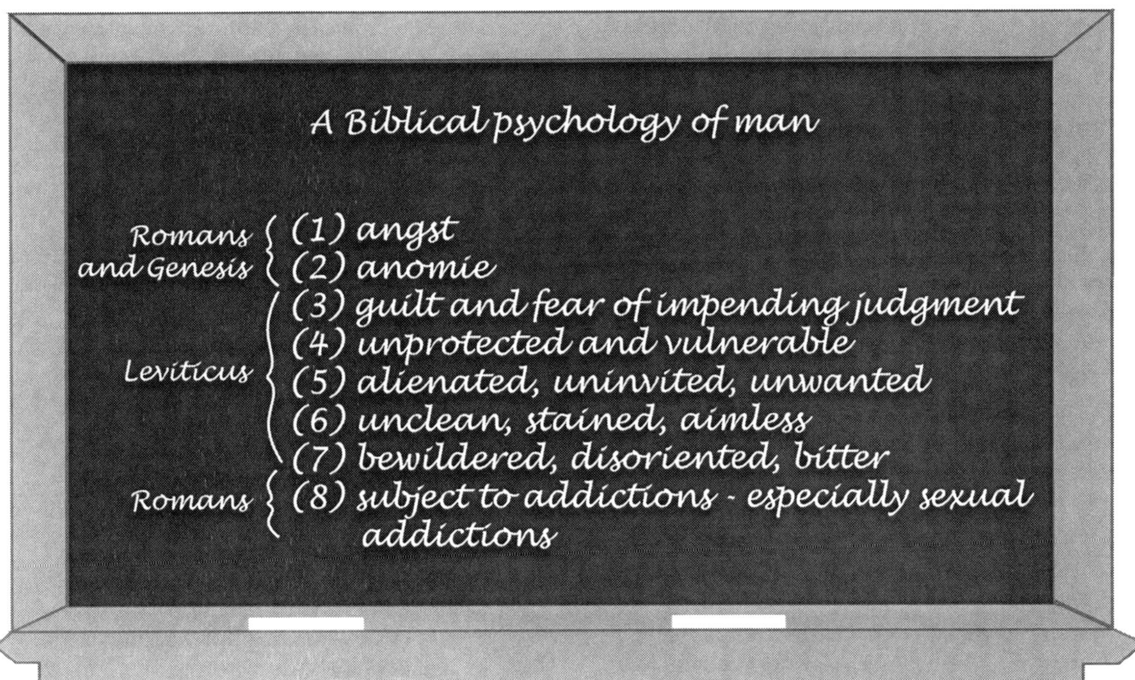

Let's take some time, grab a cup of coffee, and think all this through

Before we move on to Romans 2:1, let's examine the impact of Romans 1:18b–32 on our interpretation of Romans 9–11.

Connection to Romans 9-11

Here → **Romans 9-11**

1. We've learned that, notwithstanding the Fall, man is basically a moral being – that, more specifically, it's only when God finally turns man over to a "disapproved mind"[85] (αδοκιμον νουν) that he actually becomes *less than human* - meaning his humanity is "no longer fitting" (μη καθηκοντα)" – and so loses, I believe, the "image of God" – the "imago dei."
   - It's only then that he becomes shameless;
   - it's only then that he flaunts his sinfulness rather than concealing it;
   - it's only then that he no longer denounces the sinfulness of others, but instead endorses and actually encourages it.

   More pointedly still, in Romans Chapter Two, which we'll get to shortly, Paul insists that the gentiles – to whom God's Law was never imparted and who represent the vast majority of mankind – are indeed morally sensitive;[86] e.g.,

Rom. 2:14	For when the Gentiles, which have not the law, do by nature the things contained in the law, these, having not the law, are a law unto themselves:
Rom. 2:15	Who show the work of the law written in their hearts, their

> conscience also bearing witness, and their thoughts the meanwhile accusing or else excusing one another.

Notice the phrase *"do by nature the law"* ("φυσει τα του νομου ποιωσιν") in verse 14. In other words, God has inserted a moral compass into the very heart of fallen man's psyche´- it's there *by nature*. It's part of man's – fallen man's – intellectual, moral, and spiritual DNA. And verse 15 confirms its potent impact*: "who show the work of the law written in their hearts... their thoughts the meanwhile accusing or else excusing one another.."*[87]

Clearly, then, gentile behavior is held in check[88] by very real moral constraints – constraints *rooted in their minds and hearts* – constraints they not only acknowledge *but actually try to enforce.* Moreover, those constraints reflect a moral order that is sufficiently close to the "Torah truth" God vouchsafed to the Jews[89] that it provides a wholly legitimate basis for justifying their condemnation.

2. We've also learned that all men know intuitively that God exists. Romans 1:19-21 makes it clear that no one can truly claim to be either an atheist or an agnostic. Everyone has at one time or another "known God." Everyone has, at some point in his past, personally encountered God and acknowledged his existence. Yes, mankind suppresses the knowledge of God, but not to the point that God's existence is invariably called into question. In point of fact, that's quite rare – and is by and large limited to the sociopaths described in Romans 1:28-31.

Rom. 1:28	And even as *they did not like to retain God in their knowledge, God gave them over to a debased mind,* to do those things which are not fitting;
Rom. 1:29	being filled with all unrighteousness, sexual immorality, wickedness, covetousness, maliciousness; full of envy, murder, strife, deceit, evil-mindedness; they are whisperers,
Rom. 1:30	backbiters, haters of God, violent, proud, boasters, inventors of evil things, disobedient to parents,
Rom. 1:31	undiscerning, untrustworthy, unloving, unforgiving, unmerciful...

What we're left with, then, is inarguable: *most men and women do indeed harbor both...*

- *a conscience, and*
- *a God consciousness;*

... which means that they're not totally depraved – as James Boice, John Piper, and the Calvinists would have us believe[90].

- Are they under the bondage of sin? *Most certainly.*
- Are they condemned? *Most certainly.*

But they're not totally depraved – at least...

- ***not*** in the sense that they're left devoid of a conscience;
- ***not*** in the sense that they no longer suffer the pangs of guilt;
- ***not*** in the sense that they fail altogether to acknowledge God.

And that alone is sufficient to call into question the Calvinist doctrine of "double predestination[91] – the doctrine which guides and informs Boice's interpretation of Romans 9-11. Why? Because "total depravity" is one of the supporting pillars[92] underlying "double predestination."[93]

Once again, Boice suggests that Romans 3:10-11 supports his argument[94] – that mankind is so radically depraved that *he's incapable of "choosing God."*[95] I've already pointed that out (see pages 79-80).

Rom. 3:10	As it is written: There is none righteous, no, not one;
Rom. 3:11	There is none who understands; There is none who seeks after God.

Boice writes, "...there is not a portion of our being that has not been ruined by sin. Sin pervades all our actions and darkens all our natural understanding..."[96] He goes on to ask rhetorically: "How could a creature as depraved as that possibly come to God unless God should first set his saving choice upon him...?"[97] But, as we've already noted, that tears Romans 3:10-11 from its context. Romans 3:10-11 is part of a long polemic orchestrated by Paul to prove...

- that man can't justify himself;
- that his plight is hopeless apart from God's mercy;
- that, in short, he's totally condemned, but not

that he's totally depraved – so depraved that he's incapable of acknowledging his need for mercy and seizing it when tendered to him.

Once again, the point of the polemic is not to prove that man is incapable of opting for God's mercy – which is the interpretation Calvinists give it – but that his condemnation puts him in desperate need of crying out for it.[98] That and only that is what Paul has been driving at since verse 1:18b. Boice and Piper have clearly overreached themselves.

What we have, then, is...

- God *freely chooses* to tender man an offer of mercy – meaning he's not constrained to do so; and
- man, in turn, either...
  - *freely chooses* to seize that offer – meaning he's not constrained to do so; or
  - *freely chooses* to spurn it – meaning he's not constrained to do so.

The loss of mankind's freedom does not extend to his freedom to perceive his own sinfulness or opt for God's mercy. That freedom remains wholly intact.

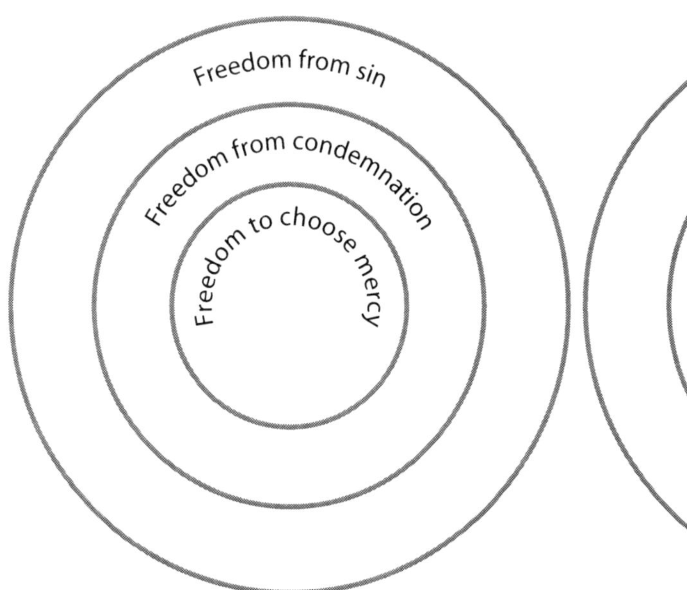

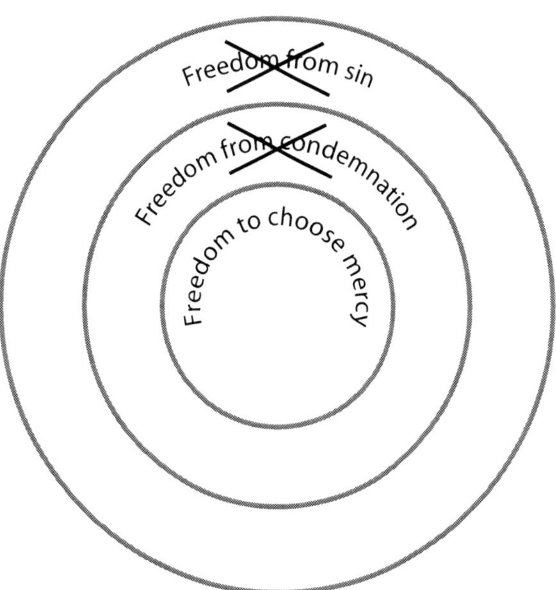

The implications are profound:

- since all men – within the limited scope[99] of freedom their sin and condemnation have left them – *can indeed choose to acknowledge their sins and seize God's mercy when tendered to them*,
- Calvin's dark world[100] of double predestination[101] collapses...

...and what we're left with is a God who delights in mercy[102].

Micah 7:18	Who is a God like unto you, who pardons iniquity, and passes by the transgression of the remnant of his heritage? He retains not his anger for ever, *because he delights in mercy.*

And if that's true, and so it seems to me, additional

light is shed upon Paul's otherwise enigmatic statement found in Romans 9:6, "*For they are not all Israel, who are of Israel...*"

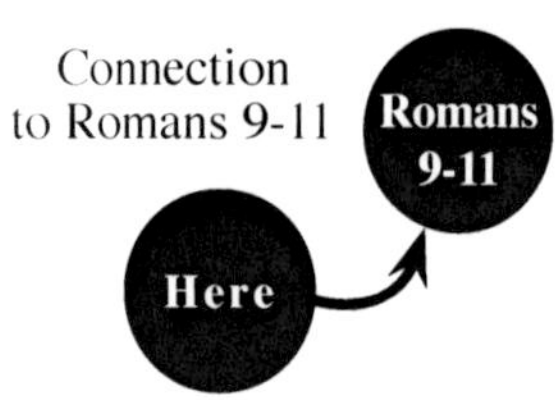

Romans 9:6	Not as though the word of God has taken none effect. *For they are not all Israel, who are of Israel...*

The meaning is quite simple: God has graciously revealed himself to Israel – and within the scope of that revelation has tendered her an offer of mercy. The offer was wholly free of any moral constraints – meaning God was not bound by his holy justice to do so. But Israel was equally free to either seize the offer or reject it.

- Those who have chosen (their choice, not God's choice) to reject the offer are still "of Israel," meaning they're still Jews," but they *don't* comprise the "Israel of God." (Galatians 6:16).
- Only those, themselves also Jews, who have chosen (their choice, not God's choice) to seize it comprise "the Israel of God" (Galatians 6:16) – and for them the Word of God has indeed "taken effect."

Note carefully that it's not a matter of God sovereignly electing some Jews to salvation and consigning others to damnation; God has left that choice to each individual Jew. Put a little differently, God has elected the Jewish People[103] – meaning he has tendered them an offer of mercy – all of them; but that election must be, in a sense, "ratified" by each Jew.

- Those who choose to ratify it "consummate" their election and so become the "Israel of God" (Galatians 6:16).
- Those who don't, fail to consummate their election – and, while remaining "Israel," are left outside the "Israel of God" (Galatians 6:16).

In short, it's not, as John Murray[104] - or for that matter, Steven Ger, an associate of Dr. Arnold Fruchtenbaum and a committed premillennialist - would have us believe, that within God's election of Israel, there's a "second election" – with that second election comprising the "Israel of God." No. *There's only one election which must be ratified to be consummated.*

Let's continue to examine the impact of Romans 1:18b-32 on our interpretation of Romans 9-11 – focusing on a passage of scripture Calvinists camp out on – making it a proof-text for double predestination.[105]

Rom. 9:10	And not only this, but when Rebecca also had conceived by one man, even by our father Isaac
Rom. 9:11	(for the children not yet being born, nor having done any good or evil, that the purpose of God according to election might stand, not of works but of Him who calls),
Rom. 9:12	it was said to her, "The older shall serve the younger."
Rom. 9:13	As it is written, "Jacob I have loved, but Esau I have hated."

Romans 9:10-13 is part of a larger passage of scripture[106] establishing the line of God's election from Abraham, through Isaac, to Jacob – bypassing both Ishmael and Esau. Verses 10-13 focus on Jacob and Esau.

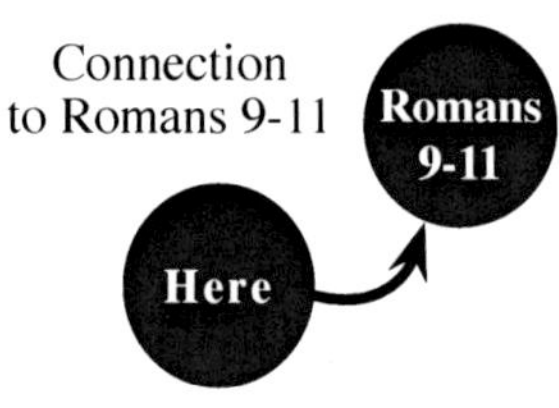

Calvinists refuse to limit the meaning they find in Romans 9:10-13 to Israel, but, instead, transform it into a general paradigm for salvation. And though that's not true to the text, let's grant them their error – and see if indeed it can be used as a paradigm for salvation.

Calvinists insist that verse 11 is pivotal; that...

- because it so obviously dismisses out of hand any criterion based on merit, Jacob's salvation[107] cannot possibly lie in his own hands;
- it must, therefore, be grounded in God's sovereign will;
- likewise, Esau's damnation.[108]
- They contend that no other reasonable conclusion is left us. It's either merit or God's sovereign will. One or the other.

But verse 11 does not force that conclusion upon us. Only if merit were Jacob and Esau's *sole* recourse would they...

- be deprived of any role whatsoever to play in their own salvation;
- leaving *God's sovereign will* the lone remaining explanation for the mercy God affords Jacob[109] and, correspondingly, the damnation he consigns Esau to suffer.

But that's not the case. Merit is not their sole recourse. ***What about faith?*** How could Boice and Piper possibly have overlooked faith – or, for that matter John Murray, or Robert Haldane, or any other of a whole army of Calvinists? But overlook it is exactly what they, in effect, do.

- James Boice writes:

  "...the words ("love" and "hate") must involve a double predestination in which, on the one hand, Jacob was destined to salvation and, on the other hand, Esau was destined to be passed over and thus to perish."[110]

  No mention is made of faith. For Boice, it's either merit or God's sovereign will. One or the other.

- Likewise, John Murray writes:

  "...the definitive actions denoted by "loved" and "hated" are represented as actuated not by any character differences in the two children but solely by the sovereign will of God..."[111]

  Once again, no mention is made of faith. God's sovereign will is apparently all that's left us.

- In the same vein, Robert Haldane writes:

  "When the Savior was first announced, Genesis 3:15, mankind was divided into two classes – the one to be saved and the other to be lost..."[112]

  Again, no mention is made of faith, leaving for Haldane no other recourse but God's sovereign will.

The reason Calvinists overlook faith is not that difficult to pinpoint. For Calvinists, faith is merely a spin-off of God's sovereignty. It's reserved exclusively for those whom God has elected and is beyond the reach of anyone else. In short, though, of course, Calvinists are loathe to admit it, faith, like mercy (cf. pages 45-48), is assigned only a bit part in the drama of salvation. The featured role belongs to God's sovereignty.

Furthermore, Boice and Piper, along with their fellow Calvinists, usually[113] ***start with*** (1) God loving Jacob, and (2) hating Esau. And that too is clearly off base. Why? Because both Jacob and Esau are Adam's offspring – meaning ***both begin*** as "children of God's wrath." ***That's their starting point*** – not just Esau's, ***but Jacob's as well.***

Eph. 2:3	...among whom also *we all* once conducted ourselves in the lusts of our flesh, fulfilling the desires of the flesh and of the mind, and *were by nature children of wrath, just as the others.*

It's not that Jacob was eternally predestined to God's love and Esau eternally predestined to God's hatred – meaning his wrath. It's that Jacob, unlike Esau, *believed* God; and, like Abraham before him, that belief altered wholly and completely his standing before God; that is, it transformed him...

- from a "vessel of wrath" (Romans 9:22)
- into a "vessel of mercy" (Romans 9:23).

It's elegantly simple: *what was true of Abraham...*

Romans 4:3	... Abraham believed God, and it was accounted to him for righteousness.

...became true for Jacob as well.

Moreover, it's exactly what Paul tells us in Romans 1:16-17...

Rom. 1:16	... the gospel ... is the power of God unto salvation for ***everyone who believes,*** for the Jew first and also for the Greek.
Rom. 1:17	For in it, the righteousness of God is revealed from faith to faith...

What could be clearer? The gospel reveals the "righteousness of God" – meaning a "right standing before God" – which God ***mercifully*** bestows upon ***anyone who in simple faith asks for it***.

- Jacob asked for it in faith;
- Esau didn't.

That's what underlies verse 13...

Rom. 9:13	As it is written, "Jacob I have loved, but Esau I have hated."

- ***not*** God's sovereign will,
- but Jacob's faith and Esau's lack of faith.

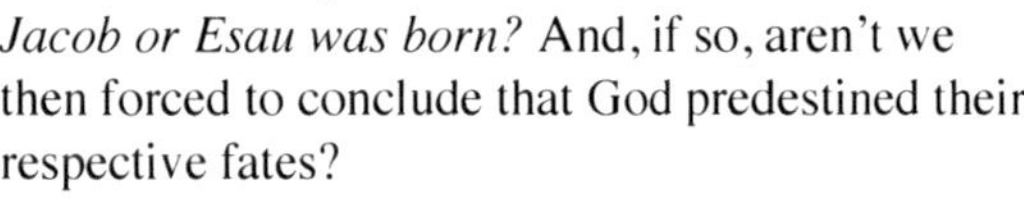

But doesn't verse 11 cast God's love of Jacob and, correspondingly, his hatred of Esau *back before either Jacob or Esau was born?* And, if so, aren't we then forced to conclude that God predestined their respective fates?

Not at all. God's foreknowledge does not determine the fate of specific individuals;[114] it simply lifts awareness of their fate – a fate arising from their own choices – from the temporal realm into the eternal realm – a realm that lies beyond time and space. Calvinists are forever conflating foreknowledge and predestination. *In short, for Calvinists foreknowledge doesn't really stand on its own.* That's because they commit one of two subtle intellectual errors - either (1) they make foreknowledge nothing more than an effect of predestination - a derivative of predestination, or (2) they make foreknowledge itself causal.

Foreknowledge an Effect of Predestination - Its Derivative

Some Calvinists make foreknowledge merely an effect of predestination: *God knows because he predestines*. But that's an obviously truncated definition of foreknowledge – or, more accurately, omniscience; and reflects limitations that constrain man, not God. The truth is far more profound and sublimely mysterious than that...

- God doesn't know merely because he predestines;
- God knows because he's God.

Foreknowledge Is Itself Causal

For other Calvinists – however they try to conceal it – foreknowledge is itself causal. But that makes foreknowledge little more than predestination cast in a different guise – little more than its clone.

Four Links or Five Links?

What we have here is not just a theological conundrum - which is what scholars ordinarily make of it and then attempt to resolve, but a linguistic/ grammatical conundrum. When Calvinists conflate foreknowledge and predestination - either making foreknowledge an effect of predestination or making foreknowledge itself causal - they inadvertently strip foreknowledge of any genuine meaning, thereby transforming Romans 8:29-30 from a five link chain into a four link chain...

Foreknowledge is not a derivative of predestination. In other words, it's not that God knows simply because he predestines; he knows because he's God; he knows because he knows. In short, foreknowledge stands on its own.

For whom he did (1) *predestine*, he also did (1) *predestine* to be conformed to the image of his Son, that he might be the firstborn among many brethren.
Moreover whom he did predestine, them he also (2) called: and whom he called, them he also (3) justified: and whom he justified, them he also (4) glorified.

...rather than the five link chain it actually is...

For whom he did (1) ***foreknow***, he also did (2) ***predestine*** to be conformed to the image of his Son, that he might be the firstborn among many brethren.
Moreover whom he did predestine (in accordance with his foreknowledge), them he also (3) called: and whom he called, them he also (4) justified: and whom he justified, them he also (5) glorified.

Many Calvinists care not one whit that they've transformed Romans 8:29-30 into a four link chain. For them it doesn't matter. Other Calvinists, however, do their best to make foreknowledge stand on its own, thereby recovering the fifth link in Paul's "golden chain." Yes, they concede, "foreknowledge" means exactly that: *God looks down the corridor of time*. It's just that there's no one there – at least no one who has chosen to avail himself of God's mercy. Why? Because, so they argue, fallen man is incapable of making that choice. His enmity against God is too deeply entrenched. His "depravity" is too profound - a conclusion that Romans Chapters One and Two prove is fallacious; nevertheless, even if we overlook that mistake, their conclusion still begs the question: if God's "foreknowledge" serves no meaningful purpose, in that looking down the corridor of time he sees no one who has availed himself of his mercy, what actual contribution does the word "foreknowledge" make in Romans 8:29-30? The answer is obvious: ***Nothing!*** In the end, notwithstanding their attempts to stand foreknowledge on its own, they too are forced back to a four-link chain rather than the five link chain they'd prefer and intuitively know it is – meaning for them as well "foreknowledge" is essentially equivalent to "predestination." The Calvinist doctrine of "total depravity" leaves them with no other option.[114]

That, however, begs a still further question:

- Would Paul use a word, "foreknowledge," that's empty of any real meaning – empty of any real significance?
- Or, put a little differently, if "foreknowledge" is essentially equivalent to "predestination," why did Paul tack on to his chain what amounts to a superfluous link?

It's one more conundrum that Calvinists are unable to

Foreknowledge and predestination occur on the eternal plane; however, calling, justification, and glorification all occur on the existential, temporal plane - the plane of time and space.

resolve. The interpretation we give to Romans 8:29-30 is radically changed when we stand foreknowledge on its own. Why should we be surprised that God can look down the corridor of time and know...

- that Jacob will choose to ground his relationship with God in faith – Jacob's choice, not God's – thereby putting him in right relationship with God and transforming him from a "vessel of wrath" into a "vessel of mercy,"
- whereas Esau will choose to spurn faith – Esau's choice, not God's – thereby rejecting God's offer of forgiveness, thus leaving unaltered his status before God: a child of wrath?

Once again, why should that surprise us?

We will learn later that foreknowledge and predestination occur on the "eternal plane" whereas calling, justification, and glorification occur on the existential plane – a plane of time and space – meaning those whom God foreknows will gratefully and thankfully seize the opportunity to be forgiven through faith in Christ (their choice, not God's), he predestines to be conformed to the image of Christ (the nature of which is God's choice, not man's), and, then, on the existential plane, within the realm of time and space, he calls them, then justifies them, and, finally, glorifies them – transforming them from "vessels of wrath" into "vessels of mercy."

Acts 13:48 provides a good illustration of how Romans 8:29-30 works itself out on both the eternal and existential planes...

Acts 13:48	And when the Gentiles heard this, they were glad, and glorified the word of the Lord: and as many as were ordained to eternal life believed.

God, on the ***eternal plane***, looking down the corridor of time and...

1. ***knowing*** who in 1st Century Pisidian Antioch will acknowledge their sins and cry out to him for his forgiveness – their choice, not his –
2. ***predestines*** them to eternal life – the nature of which is his choice not theirs[115];

...and, then, on the ***existential plane***...

3. sends Paul and Barnabas to preach the gospel to them, ***calling*** them to belief,
4. which, then, leads inexorably to ***justification*** and eventually
5. to ***glorification*** – meaning they're conformed to the image of Christ and stood holy and blameless before God in love, (Ephesians 1:4)...
6. transforming them from "vessels of wrath" into "vessels of mercy."

Likewise, there's John 6:44...

John 6:44	No one can come to me unless the Father who sent me draws him; and I will raise him up at the last day.

What we have here in John 6:44 is exactly what we found in Acts 13:48...

God the Father, on the ***eternal plane***, looking down the corridor of time, and...

1. ***knowing*** what persons will ground their relationship with him in faith (faith, not virtue; their choice, not his),
2. ***predestines*** them to be conformed to the image of Christ (the nature of which is his choice, not theirs).

Accordingly, on the ***existential plane***,

3. Christ ***draws*** them – meaning he ***calls*** them to belief, thereby...
4. ***justifying*** them, and eventually
5. ***glorifying*** them...
6. transforming them from "vessels of wrath" into "vessels of mercy."

Again, what we have here is predestination grounded in God's foreknowledge of how each individual will respond to him - whether...

- in faith, as was the case with Jacob; or
- spurning faith, as in the case of Esau.

Godet, in his well known and highly regarded *Commentary on the Epistle to the Romans,* reaches a conclusion that's not much different. He writes, "In what respect did God thus foreknow them? ...There is but one answer: foreknown as sure to fulfil the condition of salvation, viz. faith; so: foreknown as His *by faith*." (italics his).

Boice, Murray, and Haldane, are brilliant scholars whose contributions to the church are much appreciated and whose labor for the kingdom is well established. How they could have overlooked faith

– which is exactly what they, in effect, do – is mind-boggling! Faith is so key – and the role it's assigned in the drama of salvation is so obvious.

> Hebrews 11:6 But without faith it is impossible to please Him...

I can only conclude that they rely too much on systematic theology – meaning they begin with the first principles a self-contained, internally consistent Calvinism enforces on them – and spin out corollaries from those principles without always checking their conclusions against the Biblical text – not because they aren't first class scholars, but because their Calvinist predispositions bias them against the clear meaning of the biblical text.

But what about the phrase in verse 11 *"...that the purpose of God according to election might stand..."?* Isn't "election" a code-word for predestination? Certainly that's what most Calvinists make of it. However, even if we grant them that, still it's not the fate of specific individuals that Biblical predestination turns upon (pages 19-20); it's God's eternal plan and the purposes that plan reflects. Put a little differently, it's not that God has foreordained specific individuals to be saved,

- it's that fellowship with God grounded in holiness is the telos God has predestined for mankind – precisely what salvation restores to man. That's God's choice, not man's. That's where God has anchored his sovereignty;
- whether or not specific individuals conform their lives to that telos – God has made that their choice, not his.

Forgiveness – accessible to anyone who in simple faith asks for it! Once again, the focus is where the scriptures so clearly put it: God's mercy, not God's sovereignty.

Mercy, Not Sovereignty: Let's go over it once again...

For Paul, God's sovereignty is not an issue that requires much elaboration. It's a "given" so clearly delineated in the Hebrew scriptures that it doesn't often draw Paul's attention; for the most part, he relegates it to the backdrop of his theology, not the forefront. What does draw Paul's attention, though, is God's mercy – which, of course, Jesus himself in the "Sermon on the Mount" makes the very definition of God's love.[116] Nevertheless, the way Paul describes mercy – the way he defines it and spells out its implications – leads Boice and Piper, along with their fellow Calvinists, to think it's God's sovereignty he's describing, not his mercy. And that has led to much needless confusion.

Once again, Romans 9:15-16 is a case in point...

> Romans 9:15 For he says to Moses, "I will have mercy on whomever I will have mercy, and I will have compassion on whomever I will have compassion."
> Romans 9:16 So then it is not of him who wills, nor of him who runs, but of God who shows mercy.

Boice and Piper would have us believe that the issue Paul's raising here is God's sovereignty – that, more specifically, God sovereignly "elects" some men to salvation and consigns others to damnation.[117] But that's not at all the truth Paul's eliciting here. It's that...

- God's mercy is the recourse of those who *acknowledge* they're sinners;
- who *acknowledge* that their appeal cannot be grounded in justice; that justice is actually served in sending them to hell;
- who *acknowledge* that the sentence of death pronounced against them is altogether righteous;
- who *acknowledge* that God is under no obligation to tender the mercy they're crying out for.

Simply put, Paul is saying that God's mercy lies beyond the scope of man's control; that it lies wholly in God's hands; that no one can ground his appeal for God's favor in a right that backs God into a corner and requires him to grant it. Man, therefore, stands before God in abject helplessness.[118] That alone is the point Paul's making in Romans 9:15-16. It's not that God will actually withhold his mercy from someone who cries out for it; only that the decision to be merciful is God's alone.

Boice and Piper's mistake leads to a whole series of consequences that in my opinion are genuinely tragic – the most grievous of which is the portrait it sketches of God[119] – a portrait which Boice's honesty compels him to admit "seems monstrous" – a doctrine that casts God into the image of an "indifferent deity who sits in heaven arbitrarily assigning human destinies, saying, as it were, 'This one to heaven and I don't care; and this one to hell and I don't care.'"[120]

And, yes indeed, if that's where our exegesis were

to lead us, then that's the portrait we'd be forced to live with – no matter how much it might repulse us. But it's not! Calvinists have failed to grasp the meaning Paul ascribes to mercy and the implications he draws therefrom; consequently, when they read a passage like Romans 9:15-16 what they see is God's sovereignty, not the unfettered nature of God's mercy – that mankind cannot obligate God to tender it.

St. Augustine: Foreknowledge and Predestination

Let's take a close look

The relationship between foreknowledge and predestination boasts a history that is both long and convoluted - involving many of the most renowned theologians of the church. On theological grounds, it has never been satisfactorily resolved; and no consensus has ever truly emerged. St. Augustine's treatment sums up many of the complex issues that are at stake. Augustine denied that foreknowledge is causal - meaning God knows the future because he predestines it. Whatever God foreknows, Augustine insisted, will indeed occur, but not because God causes it. How exactly that works itself out Augustine never quite said. He delineated his thesis in a book he entitled *The Free Choice of the Will.*

Augustine knew that quite possibly the mystery of God's foreknowledge would remain just that - a mystery. That it would never be fully understood! Accordingly, he was fond of falling back on Romans 11:33, *"O the depth of the riches both of the wisdom and the knowledge of God! how unsearchable are his judgments, and his ways past tracing out!"*

Later, however, while still insisting that foreknowledge is not causal, Augustine drifted away from "free choice" and "bought into" predestination - again, not because he believed God's foreknowledge is causal, but because he decided that man is much too depraved to, on his own, acknowledge his sinfulness, turn to God, and cry out to be forgiven. His own personal experience of salvation prompted his decision - an experience he recorded in one of the most famous books of antiquity, *The Confessions of St. Augustine,* a classic of Western Literature. *The Predestination of the Saints* spells out Augustine's conclusion that free will is nothing but a chimera.

The controversy surrounding the relationship between foreknowledge and predestination was carried over into the Medieval Era and became a major preoccupation of medieval theologians - including St. Thomas Acquinas, Duns Scotus, William of Ockham, and the Jewish philosopher Baruch Spinoza. The solutions they suggested were fraught with difficulties - and, in the end, for the most part, made foreknowledge itself causal - little more than a derivative of predestination. In short, their solution, though they were loath to admit it, was to transform Romans 8:29-30 from a five link chain into a four link chain - a solution Augustine never opted for. It's the very same solution proffered by most Calvinists, including Boice and Piper.

Contemporary theologians, no doubt affected by postmodern influences, are tending toward a redefinition of omniscience: *omniscience is not the knowledge of all, but the knowledge of all that can be known.* In short, they're truncating the classic definition of omniscience. To me, what that reflects is an overweening arrogance. It amounts to little more than a disguised, though poorly disguised, attempt to "cut God down to size" - to make him fit within the limits of our human intellect. Augustine was far too humble to fall into that trap. Again, he acknowledged that a solution might not be possible - that the relationship between foreknowledge and predestination might be "too big" for theologians to ever get their minds around.

It seems to me that the far better approach to Romans 8:29-30 is to treat it as a linguistic/grammatical problem rather than a theological problem. There's no doubt that from a linguistic/grammatical standpoint Romans 8:29-30 describes a five link chain, not a four link chain; and for that to be true, foreknowledge must stand on its own, necessarily making predestination a function of foreknowledge - however many imponderables that spawns.

****

Faulty Translation • Faulty Reasoning Faulty Exegesis

Calvin's Faulty Translation:

Calvin, as might be expected, makes the word "foreknow" ("προεγνω") here in Romans 8:29 mean "adopt" - implying "pre-election." In short, for Calvin foreknowledge and predestination are essentially synonymous. A few lexicologists (e.g., Arndt and Gingrich) have agreed with his translation, but just a few. The overwhelming majority refute it. Meyer, for example, points out that the early church fathers (e.g., Origin, Chrysostom, Augustine, Jerome) translated it to mean "prescience," not "pre-election." He then goes on to say - with an obvious touch of irritation - that the meaning of "foreknow" in Romans 8:29 *"is not to be decided by dogmatic presuppositions, but simply by usage of the language, in accordance with which "προεγνω" never in the New Testament [not even in Romans 11:2 or 1 Peter 1:20 (parenthesis his)] means anything else than to know beforehand... That in classical language it ever means anything else cannot be at all proved."*

Vincent is equally as emphatic: "'*προεγνω' does not mean 'foreordain.' It signifies 'prescience,' not 'pre-election.*'" He goes on to add in a footnote that, like Myer's comment, is tinged with exasperaton: *"This is the simple common-sense meaning. The attempt to attach to it the sense of 'pre-election,' to make it include the divine decree, has grown out of dogmatic considerations in the interest of a rigid predestinarianism. The scope of this work does not admit a discussion of the infinitesimal hair splitting which has been applied to this passage, and which is as profitless as it is unsatisfactory."*

Calvin's Faulty Reasoning:

Paul has carefully arranged his "golden chain" (Romans 8:29-30) such that each of its "events" - foreknowledge, predestination, calling, justification, and glorification - is prompted by the "event" it follows; *necessarily, then, each "event" is different from the others* - because a "cause" and the "effect" it prompts are, perforce, *always* different. The conclusion is obvious: Paul never meant justification to be synonymous with glorification; nor calling with justification; nor predestination with calling; *nor, finally, foreknowledge with predestination.* Furthermore, it's not just that predestination is *necessarily* different from foreknowledge, it's that predestination *is actually grounded in* foreknowledge.

Clearly, then, Calvin's reasoning is faulty on two accounts: (1) he fails to come to terms with the logic that makes each of the "events" in Paul's "golden chain" *necessarily* different from the others; and (2) he fails to come to terms with the logic that *necessarily* denies to predestination the seminal role he casts for it, but, instead, makes it merely a function of another "event," specifically, foreknowledge - meaning predestination is not, as Calvin would have it, the all-important hub around which Romans 8:29-30 revolves.

Faulty Exegesis

Some Calvinists argue that the word "foreknow" means "love," or "marked out for a special purpose." Murray, for example, contends that... "(the) word 'know' has a pregnant meaning which goes beyond ... mere cognition. It is used in a sense practically synonymous with 'love,' 'to set regard upon,' 'to know with peculiar interest, delight, affection'..." Likewise, Haldane comments, "All the called of God, are foreknown by him...that is, they are the objects of his eternal love..." So too Millard Erickson: "...the (Hebrew) word "yada" which seems to lie behind Paul's use of "proginosko" signifies more than advance knowledge or precognition. It carries the connotation of a very positive and intimate relationship. It suggests looking with favor upon or loving someone..." In short, God, from eternity, loves some sinners – tendering them an offer of forgiveness they're predestined to avail themselves of, while, at the same time, passing over others – thereby consigning them to hell. It's the doctrine of limited atonement.

But that argument, as we shall soon discover, runs afoul of the truth Paul delineates in Romans 3:29. There Paul asks pointedly, "Is God the God of the Jews only? Is he not the God of the Gentiles as well?" To which he responds, "Yes, of the Gentiles also..." The meaning here is simple and straightforward: the Jews never doubted that God is the God of the gentiles – in the sense that he's their Creator and Judge. But, by and large, they limited his mercy to themselves – that though he is indeed the God of the gentiles, his mercy is restricted to the Jews only. Clearly, what we have here is a Jewish version of limited atonement.

Paul, however, discloses in Romans 3:29 just how erroneous that notion is. The Cross reveals that God is as merciful as he is righteous and holy – that he's *ontologically* merciful – meaning mercy, no less than righteousness and holiness, arises from God's very nature. Therefore, if the consequences arising from God's righteousness, that is, moral accountability and justice, extend to all mankind – because righteousness and holiness originate in God's nature – so also does his mercy – because mercy likewise originates in his nature. Or, put a little differently: because mercy lies at the very core of God's being, he can't be merciful to the Jews without at the same time being merciful to the gentiles as well. The implication is obvious: God can't tender an offer of mercy to some sinners without tendering that very same offer to all sinners? *It's an imperative grounded in the oneness of God* – a truth Paul makes explicit in the next verse, Romans 3:30: "...since indeed *God who will justify the circumcised by faith and the uncircumcised by faith is one.*"

There's nothing novel about the doctrine of limited atonement. It caused the Jews to stumble in the First Century, and it's causing Calvinists to stumble today, notwithstanding their well deserved reputation for outstanding scholarship – and, indeed, it is well deserved.

****

Calvin Himself
Foreknowledge and Predestination

Calvin himself insists that election is not derived from foreknowledge. A single quote drawn from Calvin's massive tome, *The Institutes of the Christian Relgion* underscores that fact:

> "We, indeed, ascribe both prescience (i.e., foreknowledge) and predestination to God; but we say that it is absurd to make the latter subordinate to the former." (Taken from Beveridge's translation, Eerdman's publication, Book Three, page 206)

The reason Calvin insists on the priority of predestination is not that difficult to pinpoint? For Calvin, nothing is more urgent – nothing more pressing – than protecting the Godhead from any doctrine that might, in his estimation, lessen its matchless dignity; and for him that means highlighting the supreme preeminence of God's sovereignty – that none of God's other attributes can measure up to its importance; and sovereignty means nothing if it doesn't mean predestination.

The importance Calvin ascribes to God's sovereignty – and, hence, to predestination – is reflected in the interpretation he gives other doctrines – often reducing them to little more than corollaries of God's sovereignty. The Fall of Man is a good example:

> "Nor ought it to seem absurd when I say that God not only foresaw the fall of the first

> man, and in him the ruin of his posterity; but also at his own pleasure arranged it." (Taken from Beveridge's translation, Eerdman's publication, Book Three, page 232)

Righteousness too, like The Fall, is cast in terms that seem to make it little more than a by-product of God's sovereignty.

> "The will of God is the supreme rule of righteousness, so that everything which he wills must be held to be righteous by the mere fact of his willing it." (Taken from Beveridge's translation, Eerdman's publication, Book Three, page 227)

Likewise, faith amounts to nothing more than an offshoot of predestination – and plays only a bit role in the drama of salvation. It can boast no real identity of its own.

> "And, indeed, faith is aptly conjoined with election, provided it hold second place." (Taken from Beveridge's translation, Eerdman's publication, Book Three, page 223)

****

CHAPTER FIVE

It's important to grasp the *flow* of Paul's thought – and that's not always easy to do because there are so many important *"spurs"* he spins off from his *"main trunk line."* And those spurs are fascinating and intriguing in and of themselves; as a result, it's easy to get lost out among them – and lose sight of the "main trunk line." Consequently, I want to begin Chapter Five with a brief review of *"where Paul has taken us thus far."* It will help keep us oriented.

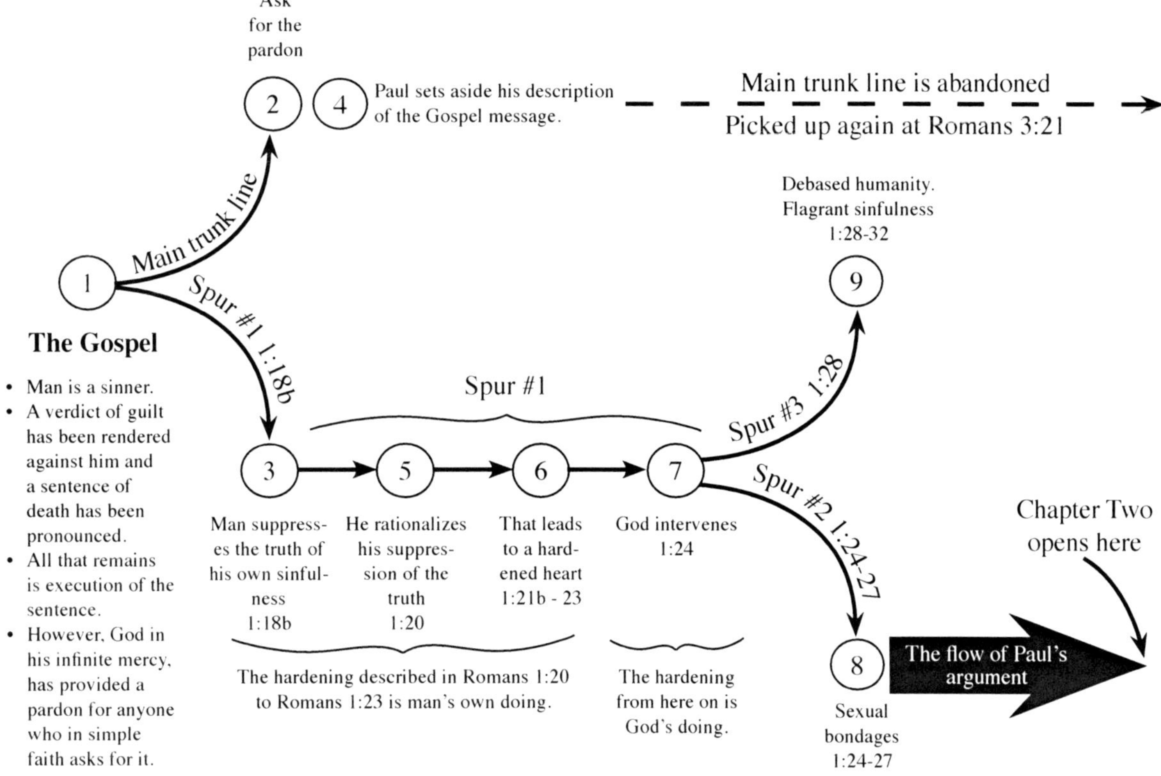

1. In Romans 1:16 – 18a, Paul sums up the gospel message (Point #1 on the graphic) - and, in doing so, reveals the theme of the epistle:
    - man is a sinner;
    - a verdict of guilt has already been rendered against him and a sentence of death has already been pronounced;
    - all that remains is execution of the sentence;
    - however, God, in his infinite mercy, has provided a pardon for anyone who in simple faith asks for it.
2. The next step should be obvious: *ask for the pardon* (Point #2 on the graphic).
3. However, it's not quite that simple: man suppresses the truth of his own sinfulness (Point #3) and is, therefore, blind to his need for a pardon.
4. Paul, therefore, sets aside his description of the Gospel message (Point #4) and doesn't pick it up again until Romans 3:21,
5. and takes up instead the issue of man's sinfulness - what it means to suppress the truth - its nature and consequences. ***We've now left the "main trunk line" and are on "spur #1."***
6. Suppressing the truth leads us to rationalize our sinfulness (Point #5) - which, in turn, hardens our

heart (Point #6) - meaning our conscience can no longer generate sufficient conviction to hold lust at bay. The hardening here is man's own doing, not God's.

7. That prompts God to personally intervene with three judgments (Point #7) – each of which is designed not merely to inflict punishment, but to bring the person undergoing judgment back to his senses. God is "shoving man's face into the sin" he has been toying with – to make him feel the full weight of its horror. If he's brought back, it's because of the anguish and suffering he undergoes, not because of conviction. Each judgment is listed in order of its severity – with the first the least severe and the last the most severe (Points #8 and #9). The hardening here (what Paul calls "turning over,") is God's doing, not man's.
8. The first judgment leads to the loss of freedom (Point 8); the second judgment leads to the loss of dignity (also Point #8). ***That puts us on Spur #2.*** We will learn here in Lesson Five that the persons suffering these two judgments are *not* flagrant sinners - meaning they're ashamed of their sinfulness and try to hide it - which makes them faultfinding hypocrites - an insight Paul elaborates on beginning with Romans 2:1.
9. Paul now turns his attention to the third judgment (Point #9). ***That puts us on spur #3.*** Persons who undergo this judgment reject all moral constraints; they acknowledge no norms of human decency; and since man is by nature a moral being, they thereby suffer the loss of their humanity. They sin openly and flagrantly – with no attempt to hide their sinfulness; furthermore, they endorse the sinfulness of others and encourage them to sin still further.
10. At this juncture, Paul turns his attention back to persons who don't sin flagrantly – who, instead, try to hide their sins. Obviously, they're hypocrites.[121] ***That backs us out of spur #3 and puts us back on spur #2.***
11. It's at this point that Romans Chapter Two begins.

We're now ready to take up Chapter Two of Romans.

Romans Chapter Two General Introduction

Romans Chapter Two is well stocked with intimidating challenges.

1. ***The Question of Identity?***
   To whom is Paul speaking in Romans 2:1?

   Rom. 2:1 Therefore ***you*** are inexcusable, Oh man, whoever you are who judges...

   Who is the "you"? Is he one of the flagrant sinners Paul describes in Romans 1:29 - 32? Is he a Gentile? Is he a Jew? Does it matter? Commentators are badly divided.

2. ***The Question of Theme?***
   What's the theme of Romans Chapter Two? Salvation? Rewards? Faith? Hypocrisy? Self-deception? Judgment? It's difficult to get a fix on it.

3. ***The Question of Merit or Faith?***
   And, most importantly, a straightforward reading of Romans 2:6 - 10 seems to make salvation a matter of merit, not faith. And that's also true of verses 12 - 16 and verses 25 - 29. Is Paul undermining his own theology? Commentators have fallen over one another trying to explain it away. Cranfield alone lists ten possible resolutions - and, though he finally settles on one, he doesn't seem fully persuaded. He seems almost to throw up his hands and say, "This is my pick. What's yours?"

Verse

Rom. 2:1 Therefore you are inexcusable, Oh man, whoever you are who judges, for in whatever you judge another you condemn yourself; for you who judge do the same things.

"you" and "Oh man"

To whom is Paul speaking here in Romans 2:1? From Romans 2:17 through the end of Chapter Two, there's little doubt that Paul is speaking to the Jews. How do we know? He tells us that straight-out. There's no ambiguity whatsoever:

Rom. 2:17 Indeed ***you are called a Jew***, and rest on the law, and make your boast in God...

What could be clearer? But that's not true of Romans 2:1 - 16. The "you" in Romans 2:1 is steeped in ambiguity. Some commentators suggest that the "you" is a carry-over from Romans 1:29 - 32 - that he's one of the flagrant sinners described there. Some insist that he's a Gentile and still others that he's a Jew. Let's take a look.

The word "therefore," which begins Romans 2:1, seems to be an adverbial conjunction indicating a causal connection. At first glance, it appears to be connected to verse 1:32, making Romans 2:1 a conclusion derived from verses 1:29 – 32 - thereby linking the "you" of Romans 2:1 with the flagrant sinners described there. But that's impossible. Think about it: the "you" here in verse 1 can't be one of the persons described in Romans 1:29 – 32. Why? Because, whoever the "you" might be, *he condemns sins*, if not the sin he himself commits, at least the sins of others...

> Rom. 2:1 Therefore you are inexcusable, Oh man, ***whoever you are who judges***, for in whatever ***you judge another*** you condemn yourself; for ***you who judge*** do the same things.

...and that's precisely what the persons described in verses 29 - 32 refuse to do. Instead,

- rather than concealing their sins, they flaunt their sins; and,
- rather than condemning the sinfulness of others, they commend it and actually encourage it.

> Rom. 1:32 ...who, knowing the righteous judgment of God, that those who practice such things are deserving of death, ***not only do the same but also approve of those who practice them***.

We conclude, then, that the "you" in Romans 2:1 isn't one of the flagrant sinners described in Romans 1:29 - 32; that, consequently, Romans 2:1 is not a conclusion drawn from Romans 1:29 - 32.

What, then, is the purpose of the word "therefore" here in Romans 2:1? Why is Paul using it here? Put a little differently: what is the word "therefore" *"thereforing"?* The answer is found in the grammatical structure of Romans 2:1.

The word "you" is the subject of the sentence; while the verb "are" and the subject complement "inexcusable" constitute the predicate. This, then, is the main clause of Romans 2:1. The next clause *"Oh man, whoever you are who judges"* doesn't actually affect the grammatical structure of verse 2:1. It's what grammarians call a "direct address" - and in sentence diagramming a direct address is always set off to one side apart from the diagram itself. The rest of the sentence is composed of two adverbial clauses each of which begins with the subordinate conjunction "for." That tells us that the first adverbial clause, *"for in whatever you judge another you condemn yourself,"* is meant to explain the main clause, *"you are inexcusable;"* while the second adverbial clause, *"for you who judge practice the same things,"* is meant to explain the first adverbial clause. The abbreviated diagram is, then, simple and straightforward.

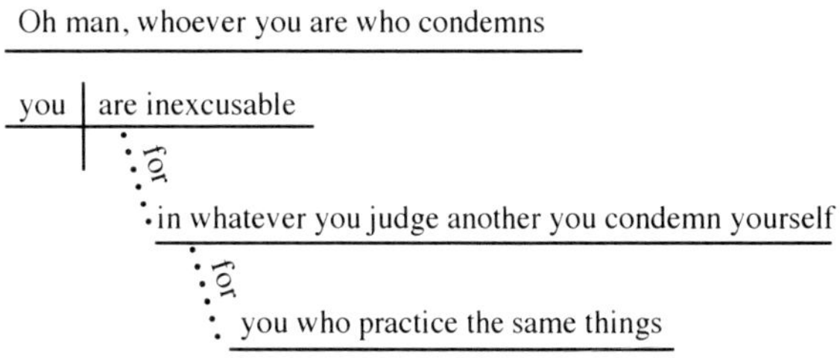

Oh man, whoever you are who condemns

you | are inexcusable

for

in whatever you judge another you condemn yourself

for

you who practice the same things

What we have here is fairly obvious:

- you are inexcusable.
- *Why? Because* in judging others for their immoral behavior, you're condemning yourself.
- *Why? Because* you're guilty of the same immoral behavior.

Look closely. It's a syllogism, isn't it? A syllogism consists of a major premise, a minor premise, and a logical inference. For example,

- major premise — All men die.
- minor premise — Socrates is a man.
- logical inference — *Therefore*, Socrates will die.

The logical inference of any syllogism is always prefaced with an adverbial conjunction - usually *"therefore"* or *"hence."* That, then, explains the word *"therefore"* in Romans 2:1. It's not being used to indicate a conclusion drawn from Romans 1:32; it's used here because Romans 2:1 is a syllogism - and the word "therefore" prefaces the second half of a two-part logical inference drawn from the major and minor premises found in the two adverbial clauses.

- You condemn (judge) others for their immoral behavior;
- you are guilty of the same immoral behavior;
- hence,
  - you condemn yourself, and

– are ***therefore*** without excuse.

The phrase *"you are without excuse"* might at first glance seem to convey the sense *"your behavior is reprehensible;"* but that's not what it means here. What it means is *"you have no basis for an appeal."* Why? Because, though you're unaware of it, in condemning others for the same behavior you yourself have committed, you've just condemned yourself. And your self-condemnation is tantamount to a confession - and a freely tendered confession can't be appealed.

Finally, it should be noted that Paul gives his syllogism a slight twist: he introduces it using the second half of his logical inference: *"You are therefore without excuse."*

So, then, who is the "you" of Romans 2:1? We know now that he isn't one of the flagrant sinners described in Romans 1:29 - 32. But who is he?

- We know that he's a faultfinder - because that's how he's described in the "direct address" itself: *"whoever you are who judges (i.e., condemns)..."*
- We know that though he's not a *flagrant* sinner, he's nevertheless a sinner - because we're clearly told "for you who judge *practice the same things."*
- We know that he's suppressing the truth of his own sinfulness – and, therefore, his heart has been hardened; consequently, it's entirely possible that he has undergone one or both of the judgments described in verses 24 and 26.
- We know that he's a hypocrite – because he commits the very sins he condemns in others.

What else do we know about him? We know that his ethnicity is not specific - meaning that Paul is probably speaking to *both* Gentiles and Jews. Why?

- *Because* the direct address *"Oh man"* ("ω ανθροπε"), to which the pronoun "you" is linked here in verse one, is a very general term – almost always indicating *both* Jew and Gentile. It's not the specific term *"you, a Jew"* ("ιδε συ ιουδαιο") that we find in verse 17 – where the issue of the Jew is clearly and unambiguously raised. Perhaps, however, Paul is simply being "sly;" that from Romans 2:1 through 2:16, he's "sneaking up on the Jew" - and, then, in verse 17, he springs his trap - accusing the Jew directly of faultfinding and hypocrisy. But that's certainly a "stretch." Paul is ordinarily more straightforward than that.
- *Also because* the phrase *"of the Jew first and also of the Greek"* is used twice in verses 1–16, and not once in verses 17–29, the passage of scripture which is introduced by the direct address *"...you, a Jew..."* It seems apparent that Paul consciously chose that phrase *to distinguish between the two passages,* verses 1–16 on the one hand and verses 17–29 on the other; *that the one, verses 1–16, includes all hypocrites regardless of ethnicity, and the other, verses 17–29, Jewish hypocrites only.*
- *Finally,* it's clear that Paul is addressing two related but different issues: specifically, (1) in Romans 2:1-16, he is taking up the challenge of spelling out the dynamics of God's sovereign jurisprudence; i.e., *how God judges*; whereas (2) in Romans 2:17-29, he is applying those very principles to the *specific case of the Jew* – who harbors two grave misconceptions which threaten his salvation, to wit...
  - he believes that mere possession of the Mosaic Law entitles him to special consideration before the bar of God's holy justice; and, in addition,
  - he believes that circumcision proves his justification.

"...whoever you are who judges, for in whatever you judge another you condemn yourself; for you who judge do the same things."

There's little question that much of Romans Two revolves around the theme of ***faultfinding and hypocrisy***. Why? Because the syllogism Paul constructs in Romans 2:1 - which sets the direction of the chapter - revolves around faultfinding and hypocrisy; that, and, of course, the self-condemnation which follows in its wake.

- You condemn others for their immoral behavior;
- you are guilty of the same immoral behavior;
- hence, you condemn yourself.

Faultfinding and hypocrisy are endemic. Mankind suffers from both; indeed, the two seem to go hand-in-hand. Faultfinders are inveterate hypocrites. Likewise, hypocrites are inveterate faultfinders.

Faultfinding

Faultfinding is a common psychological device: we hate the sin we commit; but rather than bearing the guilt ourselves, we project it onto others – and then heap condemnation on them.

- It momentarily appeases our own aggrieved sense of justice; and

- it helps to placate our own sense of guilt.

Our own self-loathing and self-hatred are cast upon others – who then become the targets of our censure and denunciation. Back in the early 1980s I was invited to attend a conference the focus of which was "overcoming sin." The speaker was a well known pastor from the Midwest. The sin he most singled out was homosexuality. He dwelt on that sin almost exclusively – describing just how shameful it is, the terrible betrayal of trust it reflects, etc. Six months later word got back to me that he was himself a homosexual – that he had been caught in the very act.

Hypocrisy

Hypocrisy is an American preoccupation - dramatically and powerfully reflected in American literature, especially among American playwrights. One of the best examples is Arthur Miller's *Death of a Salesman*. It provides an in-depth study of hypocrisy cast within the framework of American culture. It's well worth a brief examination.

Cultural Connections: The Bible and Western Thought

Arthur Miller

Death of a Salesman

Arthur Miller's *Death of a Salesman* is an American classic. It was first produced in 1949, shortly after the Second World War. The war had produced untold heartache and sacrifice – and the returning American servicemen were eager to put it behind them. They wanted to get back to "the good life" – new homes, new cars, a good education, a fulfilling career; in short, they wanted to resume their pursuit of the American Dream.

That's the backdrop against which Arthur Miller wrote *Death of a Salesman*.

What makes *Death of a Salesman* so intriguing is its focus on hypocrisy – which, according to Miller, is what's required of anyone pursuing the American Dream. Hypocrisy fosters a double life that absorbs more and more intellectual and emotional capital to keep it going – eventually consuming the lives of everyone touched by it.

Like so many novels and plays of the 20th Century, there is no simple, straightforward plot. Instead, there's a series of vignettes and flashbacks that provide a glimpse of each of the characters – their strengths and weaknesses – their dreams and failures – and, of course, their relationship to one another.

Willy Loman is the central figure – and the play revolves around him. Willy is a salesman who's determined to be successful – determined to make a name for himself. He's convinced that material wealth is the key to achieving happiness – and that it's within the grasp of anyone willing to work hard for it. Hard work and determination – that's all a man needs.

However, Willy, as it turns out, is only a mediocre salesman – and that despite all the hard work and determination he can muster. The formula he so fervently believes in and which he so doggedly pursues isn't panning out. But he won't abandon it; it's too much a part of the warp and weft of his life. And, so, the inevitable occurs: Willy's growing sense of failure forces him into a double life – he becomes a hypocrite: he pretends to be what he isn't.

The truth, however, can't be concealed – at least not in the long run. It surfaces first with his wife, Linda, who knows that he's not "bringing home the bacon." Next it surfaces with his neighbor, Charlie, who offers Willy a less demanding job more in keeping with his abilities – an offer which Willy contemptuously spurns because he feels it's insulting. Finally, it surfaces with his oldest son Biff, who possesses all the charm and talent Willy so abysmally lacks and which no amount of grit and determination can ever make up for. He surprises his father with a visit to his Boston hotel room and catches him in a tryst with another woman. Willy tries to explain it away, but Biff storms out of the room calling him a "phony little fake." Willy's double life is unraveling – and, with it, all that's left of his self-respect.

Still, Willy tries to "carry on." He won't abandon his charade. Instead, he becomes ever more critical of his family and friends – especially of Biff. Willy complains that Biff hasn't lived up to his expectations – exactly what Willy himself has failed to do. Biff, on the other hand, complains that Willy is a fraud. And on it goes – with no letup. That, of course, only worsens Willy's alienation – which, in turn, exacerbates his growing sense of failure.

The cost of sustaining a double life – the fraud and deceit it entails, the growing isolation, the mounting exposure that inevitably occurs – all of it begins to eat away at Willy's nerves – and he starts to come unglued.

In the end, Biff breaks away from his father's emotional tyranny; Willy commits suicide; and Linda, his longsuffering wife, is left sobbing at the grave site, "I'm free." It's not a pretty story. There's no happy ending. But that's what hypocrisy is like – that's its inevitable outcome – it leads always to suicide – if not an actual suicide, an isolation and loneliness that's tantamount to suicide.

Death of Salesman explores several facets of hypocrisy:

- Anyone who refuses to confront his own failure is *driven* to hypocrisy – meaning he's forced into a double life; the one leads inevitably to the other. Willy's refusal to confront his own mediocrity and to take a job that demands less of him is what leads to his undoing. That's exactly what Paul is pointing out in Romans Two; anyone who refuses to acknowledge his own spiritual and moral bankruptcy is forced into hypocrisy. He's forced into a double life – and all that a double life entails - pain, deceit, anguish, etc.
- *Death of a Salesman* also points out the enormous expenditure of intellectual, emotional, and spiritual capital required of a person to sustain his hypocrisy – especially among family and friends – persons intimately familiar with him. That's precisely the point that Paul is getting at in Romans Two. Exposure is a constant threat; it's always close at hand; it's a permanent fixture imbedded in the life of every hypocrite. Hypocrisy may begin in a backroom, tucked away in some corner; but, sooner or later, it fills the whole house. *It takes over.* Hypocrisy is enervating; it's draining; it's debilitating; it's consuming; it's exhausting.
- *Death of a Salesman* underscores too the correlation between hypocrisy on the one hand and faultfinding on the other – especially once the double life begins to unravel. Biff becomes the target of Willy's destructive criticism *after* Biff discovers Willy's infidelity. That's when it begins. Paul himself makes "no bones" about that correlation; it's the very first truth he underscores in his examination of hypocrisy: *hypocrisy and faultfinding are flip sides of the same coin.*
- *Death of a Salesman* underscores as well the truth that the constant criticism hypocrisy always produces leads inevitably to alienation and loneliness. The once affectionate relationship between Willy and his two sons – especially Biff – is destroyed by Willy's never ending denunciation of Biff's failure to live up to his potential. It's a truth that Paul only hints at in Romans Two, but is easily inferred.

Death of a Salesman is the story of every hypocrite.

Hypocrisy is also explored in Tennessee Williams' epic play *A Streetcar Named Desire*. Here another important aspect of hypocrisy is highlighted.

Cultural Connections: The Bible and Western Thought

Tennessee Williams

A Streetcar Named Desire

Tennessee Williams' play *A Streetcar Named Desire* opened on Broadway in 1947, two years before *Death of a Salesman*. It was directed by Elia Kazan and starred Marlon Brando as the raw, brutish Stanley Kowalski. That year it won a Pulitzer Prize in literature. In 1951, it was adapted to the screen – with, once again, Elia Kazan directing it and Marlon Brando playing Stanley Kowalski. Vivien Leigh played Blanche DuBois and Kim Hunter played Stella, Stanley's wife and Blanche's sister.

The play revolves around the relationship between Blanche DuBois and Stanley Kowalski. Blanche is an aging beauty born to a once wealthy family from Laurel, Mississippi. She has just arrived in New Orleans for a visit with her younger sister Stella, who is married to Stanley. The family home back in Laurel, an elegant plantation manor, has been recently sold to pay off debts – and Blanche has no other recourse.

Stanley and Stella live in a rundown section of the French Quarter. Stella makes no bones about her loss of status and has adapted well to her new "station in life" with the uncouth and animalistic Stanley. She enjoys his raw virility and harbors no pretensions that she will regain her family's past "glory." But Blanche lives in a fantasy world – pretending that she hasn't suffered any loss of status – at least not permanently. She won't face facts – which, of course, keeps her from adapting. She refuses to face up even to her encroaching middle age – living instead indoors in dimly lit rooms that don't show off her wrinkles and fading skin tone. One of Blanche's lines tells her whole story: "I don't want realism. I want magic! Yes, yes, magic. I try to give that to people. I do misrepresent things. I don't tell the truth. I tell what ought to be truth."

But Stanley will have nothing to do with Blanche's pretensions. Stella is willing to play along, but not Stanley. He doesn't hide who he is; and he's disgusted with anyone who does. Stanley is the glaring light-bulb that reveals all of Blanche's fantasies – and tears the "magic" away from them.

Stanley checks out Blanche's claims of virtue and genteel aristocracy – and finds that while back in Laurel, Mississippi, she had resorted to prostitution to "make ends meet." Her denunciation of his coarse, immoral behavior rings hollow in light of her own compromises – and Stanley, armed now with the truth of Blanche's hypocrisy, begins to destroy her dream castles.

In the end, Blanche – unable to live without the web of deception she has spun for herself - descends into insanity. She, too, like Willy Loman in *Death of a Salesman*, commits a kind of suicide.

Blanche is the hypocrite described in Romans 1:21 - 27 and elaborated on in 2:1 – 16; and Stanley is the flagrant sinner described in Romans 1:28 – 32. And the one, the hypocrite, is defenseless against the other, the flagrant sinner: Blanche is unable to defend herself against Stanley's ruthless onslaught. Why?

- *Because* a hypocrite spends too much of his emotional and intellectual "capital" on keeping his charade going; there isn't enough left over to use against a Stanley Kowalski.
- *Because* fantasy – which is what hypocrisy amounts to – makes realistic adaptation impossible. That's why *inordinate* hypocrites are so dysfunctional…
  - why they so often fail at holding down a job;
  - why they so often fail to move forward in life;
  - why they almost always fail when pitted against a Stanley Kowalski.

Stanley and Blanche Fitted to Paul's Typology of Sin

(See page 92)

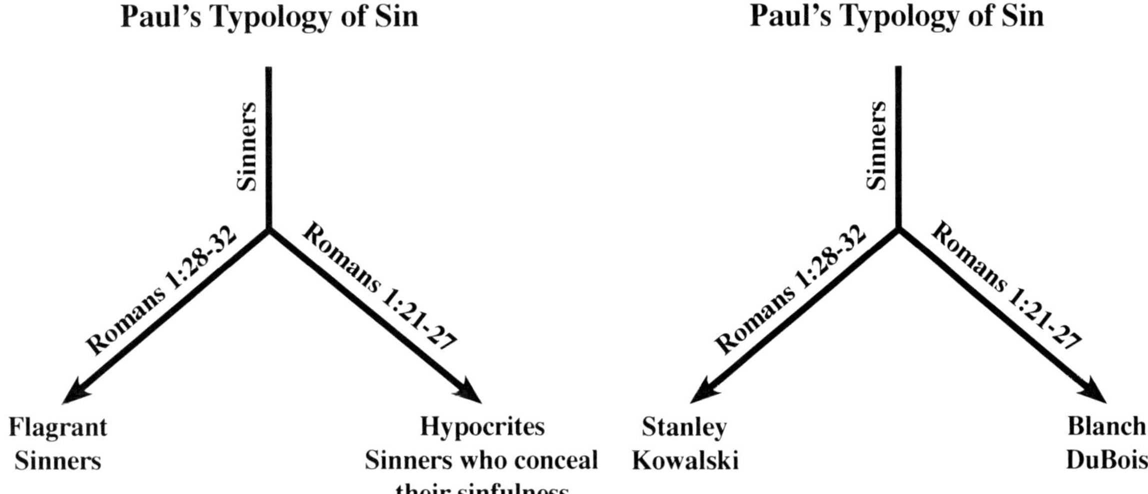

All Sinners - Except for Flagrant Sinners – Are Faultfinding Hypocrites

Some expositors insist that hypocrisy afflicts only *some* sinners - *only* the self-righteous "moralists" lurking among us - only the "Pharisees" who have insinuated themselves into our midst - suggesting that not all sinners are faultfinding hypocrites; that, instead, some of us are *just* sinners - whatever that means. And the wording of Romans 2:1 seems to confirm their interpretation.

Rom. 2:1 Therefore you are inexcusable, Oh man, *whoever you are who judges*, for in whatever you judge another you condemn yourself; for you who judge do the same things.

The phrase *"whoever you are who judges..."* seems to make hypocrites a subset of all sinners; that, therefore, not all sinners are hypocrites. But that's clearly not true. Romans Two is part of Paul's extended examination of the nature and consequences of *suppressing the truth* - which began with Romans 1:18b and continues through Romans 3:20 (See the graphic on page 109). Therefore, everyone included within the scope of that examination is guilty of *suppressing the truth*. No one is excluded. That means - *with the exception of the flagrant sinners Paul describes in Romans 1:29 – 32,*

- we *all* try to conceal our sins;
- we're *all* self-righteous;
- we *all*, to some extent, lead double lives;
- therefore, we're *all* hypocritical - and, if hypocritical,
- then, inevitably, we're *all* faultfinders as well.

Why, then, is the word *"whoever"* used in verse 1? Actually, the answer is very simple and straightforward. Quite frequently, the word *"whoever"* is intended for *rhetorical* effect only. It's not meant to indicate a subset. An obvious example is Jesus' reply to the Pharisees in John 8:7.

John 8:7 So when they continued asking him, he lifted up himself, and said unto them, *Whoever* is without sin among you, let him first cast a stone at her.

Clearly, Jesus is using the word *"whoever"* for rhetorical effect only. He does not mean to imply that there might actually be a *sinless* person standing there in the crowd with a stone in his hand. The word "whoever" *personalizes* the crime that's about to occur - meaning it prompts each person to examine himself. It "pops" the *crowd mentality* that has taken over. And that's precisely what Paul is doing here in Romans 2:1. He's drawing each of us into his argument - making it a personal matter. He's not just speaking to others, he's speaking to you and me.

Rom. 2:1 Therefore you are inexcusable, Oh man, ***whoever*** you are who judges...

Once again, the word "whoever" is meant for rhetorical effect only. It's not intended to indicate a subset. Paul is prompting us to examine ourselves and confess *our* own hypocrisy.

The conclusion Paul forces us to acknowledge is profoundly simple: faultfinding is a built-in inclination - a knee-jerk reaction - a kind of "Pavlovian response" *all of us* resort to...

- whenever our backs are up against the wall;
- whenever we feel ourselves threatened with censure or denunciation;
- whenever we feel our "covers are being pulled;"
- whenever we feel our sins are about to be exposed;
- whenever we feel our moral integrity is being called into question.

Anyone who feels that he's being condemned or that he's about to be condemned, condemns others - *especially the person he feels is condemning him.* It's that simple and straightforward.

Mistaking Criticism and Counseling for Condemnation

The correlation can become so ingrained, so deeply entrenched that all criticism - even when lovingly and sensitively given - is spurned. Why? Because the person being criticized mistakes criticism - even simple counseling - for condemnation - that's how acutely sensitive he is - thereby triggering the knee-jerk "condemned/ condemn response." And what's important to bear in mind is that it's not some consciously contrived strategy to ward off the criticism. It's a second nature reaction. No thought is given to it. The person being criticized instinctively condemns the person criticizing him; he either spots some obvious fault his "critic" is "guilty" of or he imagines a fault - often betrayal - and starts "pounding on it." He then writes off the criticism leveled at him - because when the messenger is renounced, his message is renounced along with him.

- "Who are you to criticize me? You're the pot calling the kettle black!"
- "Clean up your own life before you try cleaning up mine!"
- "You're no better than I am; so get off my back!"

Think about it

Obviously, in counseling, one of the first obstacles that needs to be overcome is the Condemned/Condemn Response. Yes, a sense of safety needs to be cultivated, but that alone isn't sufficient. It's the actual fear of criticism - the knee-jerk "Condemned Condemn Response" itself that needs to be dealt with.

Think about it

Obviously, a mature Christian is able to master the *"Condemned/ Condemn Response"* that's so built into human nature; but even for him it can prove to be very difficult and challenging. Overcoming it - mastering it - is a mark of real Christian maturity - an indication that sanctification is truly taking hold. And, correspondingly, a Christian who is not able to master it is not mature. His failure is proof of his lack of maturity - though he may "huff and puff" otherwise.

Some persons are so severely traumatized that they suffer from a *generalized sense* of condemnation. For them, it's beyond simply mistaking criticism for condemnation. For them, condemnation is a pervasive mind-set. They simply *feel* condemned - that they don't measure up. It's their "steady state." No specific incident is required to trigger the *"Condemned/Condemn Response."*

The "Condemned/Condemn Response" - the Danger It Poses to Christian Maturity

Paul has put his finger on a very real obstacle hindering Christian maturity here in Romans 2:1. Christians cannot afford to be hardened to criticism - inured to it - impervious to it. Why? Because criticism - what Hebrews 12:5 - 11 calls "chastening," "rebuke," "correction," even "scourging" - is the sine-qua-non of Christian maturity. It's the engine that propels sanctification.

> And you have forgotten the exhortation which speaks to you as to sons: My son, do not despise the *chastening* of the Lord, nor be discouraged when you are *rebuked* by Him;
> For whom the Lord loves He *chastens*, and

scourges every son whom He receives."

If you endure *chastening*, God deals with you as with sons; for what son is there whom a father does not chasten?

But if you are without *chastening*, of which all have become partakers, then you are illegitimate and not sons.

Furthermore, we have had human fathers who *corrected* us, and we paid them respect. Shall we not much more readily be in subjection to the Father of spirits and live?

For they indeed for a few days *chastened* us as seemed best to them, but He for our profit, that we may be partakers of His holiness.

Now no *chastening* seems to be joyful for the present, but painful; nevertheless, afterward it yields the peaceable fruit of righteousness to those who have been trained by it.

Hebrews 12:5-11

The Biblical Psychology of Man - Continued

Once again, we need to revise our biblical psychology of man - to accommodate the new insight revealed here in Romans 2:1 - that all sinners, with the exception of flagrant sinners, are faultfinding hypocrites - though, certainly, some more than others. There are now nine basic constituents we've identified that characterize mankind's psyche.

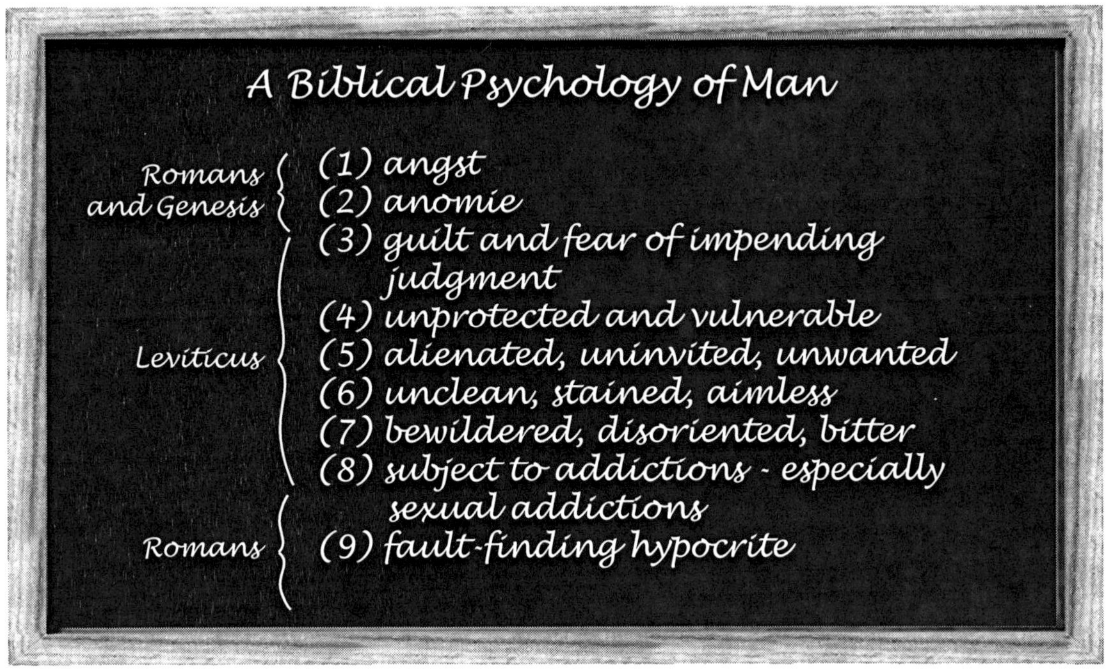

Counselors Beware

Anyone who has been severely traumatized - and, consequently, suffers from a generalized sense of condemnation - is terribly difficult to counsel. Great patience is required. The "starts" and "stops" are interminable. Very often, when the counseling first begins, the counselor is cast in the guise of a hero. He's almost adulated. But as the counseling continues and troubling issues are raised - especially issues that engender a sense of condemnation, a sense of not measuring up - the counselor is cast in the guise of an enemy. It's what I call the *"Crown the King, Kill the King Syndrome."*

Still, such individuals can be helped - with lots of love - especially when the counseling occurs against the backdrop of a larger church community that's committed to helping such persons.

The counseling should always begin with some kind of warning concerning the likely series of responses the counselee is going to be grappling with - so that when it occurs a certain amount of objectivity can be retained.

CHAPTER SIX

Verses for Chapter Six

Rom. 2:2	But we know that the judgment of God is according to truth against those who do such things.
Rom. 2:3	And do you think this, Oh man, you who judge those practicing such things, and doing the same, that you will escape the judgment of God?
Rom. 2:4	Or do you despise the riches of His goodness, forbearance, and longsuffering, not knowing that the goodness of God leads you to repentance?
Rom. 2:5	But in accordance with your hardness and your impenitent heart you are treasuring up for yourself wrath in the day of wrath and revelation of the righteous judgment of God,
Rom. 2:6	who will render to each one according to his deeds:
Rom. 2:7	eternal life to those who by patient continuance in doing good seek for glory, honor, and immortality;
Rom. 2:8	but to those who are self-seeking and do not obey the truth, but obey unrighteousness—indignation and wrath,
Rom. 2:9	tribulation and anguish, on every soul of man who does evil, of the Jew first and also of the Greek;
Rom. 2:10	but glory, honor, and peace to everyone who works what is good, to the Jew first and also to the Greek.
Rom. 2:11	For there is no partiality with God.
Rom. 2:12	For as many as have sinned without law will also perish without law, and as many as have sinned in the law will be judged by the law
Rom. 2:13	(for not the hearers of the law are just in the sight of God, but the doers of the law will be justified;
Rom. 2:14	for when Gentiles, who do not have the law, by nature do the things in the law, these, although not having the law, are a law to themselves,
Rom. 2:15	who show the work of the law written in their hearts, their conscience also bearing witness, and between themselves their thoughts accusing or else excusing them)
Rom. 2:16	in the day when God will judge the secrets of men by Jesus Christ, according to my gospel.

– Exegesis –

Let's pick up where we left off – with Romans 2:1 – because it lays the foundation for Romans 2:2 – 2:16.

Verse:

Rom. 2:1	Therefore you are inexcusable, Oh man, whoever you are who judges, for in whatever you judge another you condemn yourself; for you who judge do the same things.

Specific words or phrases found in verse 1

"judgment" and "condemn"
Verse 1 obviously raises the issue of judgment. The word "krino" (κρινο), translated in verse 1 "to judge," means

- to evaluate moral integrity;
- to determine right and wrong.

Whenever judgment (krino - κρινο) is rendered, it leads to a "recompense" - either

- *approbation* leading to reward or
- *condemnation* leading to punishment.

Here, of course, in Romans 2:1, there's no question that the judgment (krino - κρινο) leads to condemnation, not reward, because that's exactly what we're told - that's the word Paul uses: "condemn" (katakrino - κατακρινο).

Rom. 2:1	Therefore you are inexcusable, Oh man, whoever you are who judges (krino - κρινο), for in whatever you judge (krino - κρινο) another you condemn (katakrino - κατακρινο) yourself; for you who judge (krino -

κριvo) do the same things.

The judgment here in Romans 2:1 is, of course, rendered by hypocrites; but it's judgment nonetheless. And that provides Paul an occasion to take up the issue of *God's* judgment in verse 2 - and to set it in contrast to the flawed judgment sinners exact.

Nowhere else in scripture can we find a better description...

- of God's sovereign jurisprudence,
- of how God adjudicates the issue of *"just deserts..."*

****

Romans 2:2-10 - God's Jurisprudence

Showing Both the Evaluation Phase and the Recompense Phase and How the Issue of "Just Deserts" Is Adjudicated at the Bar of God's Holy Justice

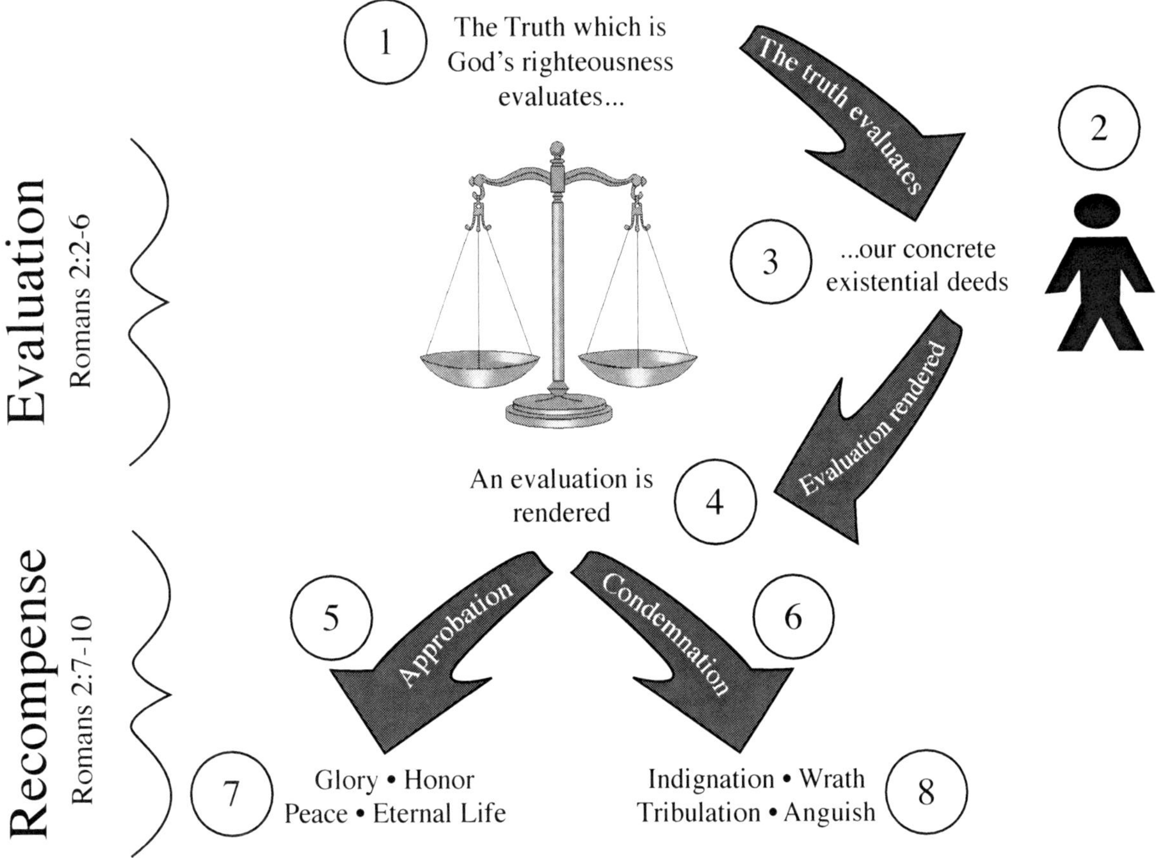

The truth (1) – which is God's righteousness – is the criterion God uses for evaluating mankind's (2) moral integrity. The focus of God's evaluation is our concrete deeds, (3). That's his exclusive focus. No other factor (e.g., reputation, social status, ethnicity, office, etc.) is considered. Nothing avails to put anyone beyond its pale. An evaluation is rendered, (4); whether good and deserving of approbation, (5); or evil and deserving of condemnation, (6). A recompense is then administered – if good, glory, honor, peace, and eternal life, (7); if evil, indignation, wrath, tribulation, and anguish, (8).

...than here in Romans 2:2-10. It's here that we're provided the judicial backdrop against which Romans 1:18a was written...

Rom. 1:18a For the wrath of God is revealed from heaven against all ungodliness and unrighteousness of men...

Basically, Romans 2:2-10 tells us that God's judgment, like the judgment depicted in Romans 1:18a, is two phased. It consists of an *evaluation* and a *recompense*. Romans 2:2-6 describes the *evaluation*

****

Romans 2:2-10 - God's Jurisprudence

Showing the Adjudication Process Leading to Mankind's Condemnation before the Bar of God's Holy Justice

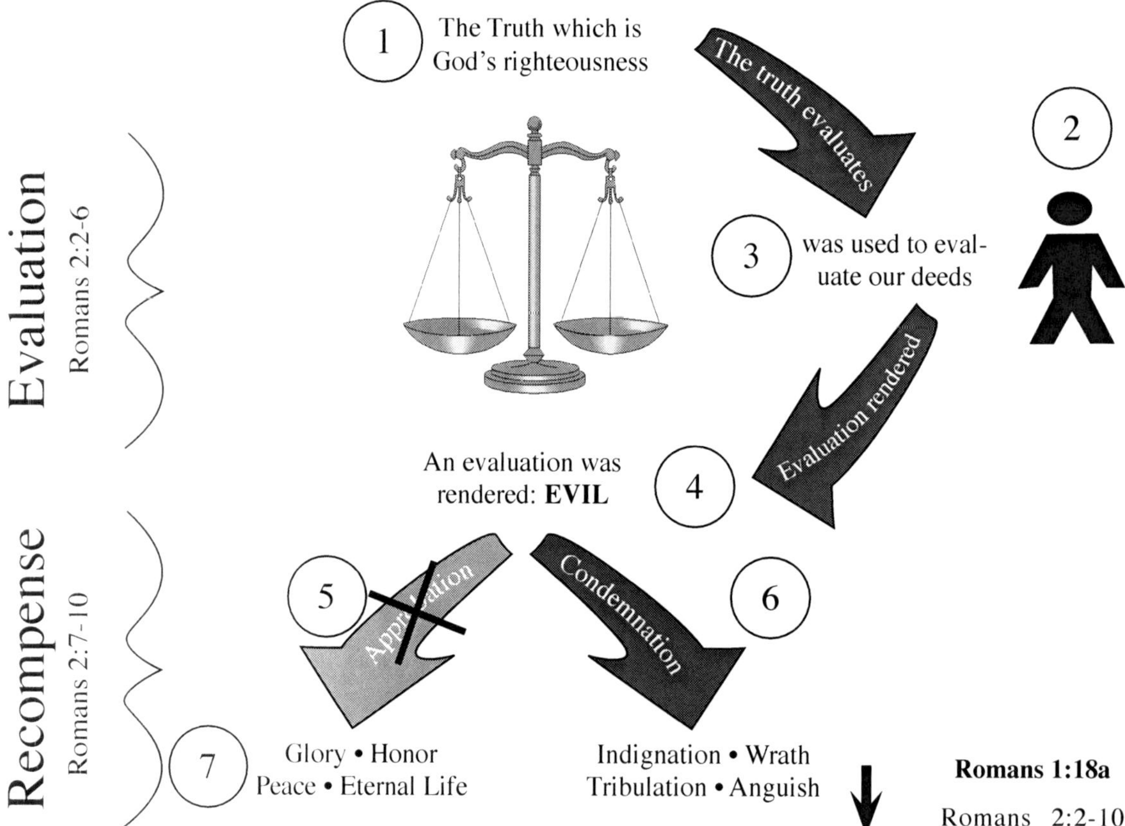

Romans 1:18a

Romans 2:2-10 describes the judicial process that led to the condemnation described in Romans 1:18a – and the wrath that's due to follow in its wake.

The truth (1), which is God's righteousness, was the criterion God used for evaluating mankind's (2) righteousness. The focus of God's evaluation was our concrete deeds, (3). That was his exclusive focus. No other factor (e.g., reputation, social status, ethnicity, office, etc.) was considered. Nothing availed to put anyone beyond its pale. The evaluation rendered was ***evil,*** (4) – deserving of condemnation, (6). A recompense is soon to be administered: indignation, wrath, tribulation, and anguish, (8) The trial is over – the verdict has been rendered. Man's only hope at this juncture is a pardon.

phase and Romans 2:7-10 describes the *recompense phase*.

- Evaluation Phase
  - Romans 2:2 introduces us to the ***criterion*** of God's evaluation: ***the truth***.
  - Romans 2:2 also reveals the ***object*** of God's evaluation: ***our concrete, existential deeds*** - and that's confirmed in Romans 2:3.
  - Romans 2:3-5 discloses both the inevitability and the severity of God's judgment -
    - that no can escape it –
    - there is no way any of us can put ourselves beyond its pale –
    - that no one should misconstrue God's forbearance - that it's meant only to lead us to repentance and neither indicates God's approval of our sins nor his indifference.
  - Romans 2:6 stresses once again that the focus of God's evaluation is our concrete deeds.
- Recompense Phase
  - Finally, Romans 2:7-10 tells us the ***recompense*** of God's judgment:
    - glory, honor, peace, and eternal life to those who "do good;" and
    - indignation, wrath, tribulation, and anguish to those who "do evil."

Verse:

Rom. 2:2	But we know that the judgment of God is according to truth against those who do such things

Specific words or phrases in verse 2

"*truth*"

Judgment never occurs within a vacuum. It requires a benchmark of some kind - a standard - a norm - a ***criterion.*** Otherwise, the judgment is *baseless*. And that's precisely what verse 2 provides. Verse 2 tells us that the ***criterion*** God uses is the ***truth.*** But why the truth? Why not righteousness? Wouldn't that correlate better with the issue of judgment? The answer is "no." Why? Because Hebrew scripture draws very little, if any, distinction between the two. God's truth is his righteousness; likewise, God's righteousness is truth. A good illustration is the synonymous parallelism[122] of Hebrew poetry found in the Book of Psalms: it consistently equates the two - especially Psalm 96:13.

Ps. 96:13	For He is coming, for He is coming to *judge* the earth. He shall *judge* the world with *righteousness*, And the peoples with His *truth*.

But other examples abound.

Ps. 15:2	He who walks uprightly, And works *righteousness*, And speaks the *truth* in his heart...
Ps. 40:10	I have not hidden Your *righteousness* within my heart; I have declared Your faithfulness and Your salvation; I have not concealed Your lovingkindness and Your *truth* from the great assembly.
Ps. 85:11	*Truth* shall spring out of the earth, And *righteousness* shall look down from heaven.
Ps. 119:142	Your *righteousness* is an everlasting righteousness, And Your law is *truth*.

The concept of "truth" was far more dynamic for the ancient Greeks and Hebrews than it is for us - living in the 21st century. For them, truth was not simply an *inert* standard of righteousness;

- it was living;
- it was animate;
- it was probing;
- it was intrusive.

Cultural Connections to Western Thought

Aeschylus, Sophocles, and Euripides - the three greatest playwrights of ancient Greek tragedy - all presumed a *dynamic, personified* sense of the truth: in Sophocles' Oedipus trilogy, the furies, guardians and enforcers of the truth, hunt down Oedipus with unwavering perseverance. Likewise, in Aeschylus' Oresteia trilogy, Agamemnon is hunted down by the truth, personified in Clytemnestra, Agamemnon's wife, for having sacrificed his daughter

Iphigenia to calm the winds Artemis had sent against his fleet; so too, Clytemnestra is stalked by Orestes, Agamemnon's son, who, in the hands of Aeschylus, becomes the personification of truth and, of course, its handmaiden, justice.

Much of Greek tragedy revolves around justice - more specifically, the often conflicting claims of justice - claims that can't be reconciled. The Orestes Triology is perhaps the finest example. Let's look at it a little more closely.

Paris, a Trojan prince visiting Agamenon's court, abducts Helen. Justice requires that Agamemnon pursue Paris to Troy, rescue Helen, and avenge his honor.

But Artemis, Zeus' daughter and goddess of the hunt, sends a wind against the Greek fleet carrying Agamemnon's army. She requires that he sacrifice his daughter Iphigenia before she calms the wind and allows his fleet safe passage to Troy. Grief-stricken, Agamemnon complies; but, in so doing, he incurs the guilt of his daughter's murder.

Justice requires that Agamemnon be punished - and Clytemnestra, Agamemnon's wife and Iphigenia's mother, is the chosen instrument. But in slaying Agamemnon, she becomes guilty of murdering her husband.

Justice then requires that Clytemnestra be punished - and Orestes, her son, is the chosen instrument. But in slaying Clytemnestra, Orestes becomes guilty of matricide. The conflicting claims of justice can't be reconciled - and therein lies the key principle underlying the Oresteia trilogy - and, for that matter, all Greek tragedy.

On the other hand, Shakespearean tragedy, the mold from which all modern tragedies in the West have been cast, does not revolve around justice and its often contradictory claims; it revolves around character - more specifically, the "tragic flaw" – the classic examples of which are Hamlet's indecisiveness and King Lear's inability to "let go."

The difference highlights the importance justice played among the ancient Greeks and Hebrews - and suggests why both the Greeks and the Jews cast justice in such a dynamic light and why it's so much more inert and passive for us.

Throughout the scirptures, it's the Greek/Hebraic sense of truth and justice, not the Western Shakespearean sense, that's highlighted; for example, Hebrews 4:12 - where, quite clearly, the "word of God" can be equated with "the truth."

Heb. 4:12 For the word of God (i.e., the truth) is living, and powerful, and sharper than any twoedged sword, piercing even to the dividing asunder of soul and spirit, and of the joints and marrow, and is a discerner of the thoughts and intents of the heart.

Here, the truth is dynamic, not some inert ethical norm. It probes, it cuts, it divides. And that's precisely what Paul has in mind here in Romans 2:2. The criterion of God's judgment is not just the truth, but the *living* truth - probing, searching, intrusive, relentless.

- The truth tears away at our rationalizations and excuses;
- it exposes our lies and kicks over the sand-castles we've erected to protect them;
- nothing escapes its gaze;
- nothing can be concealed.

And, of course, we shouldn't be surprised. Why? *Because Jesus himself is the truth.* He is its *living* embodiment. He explicitly declares that in John 14:6.

John 14:6 Jesus said to him, I am the way, ***the truth,*** and the life. No one comes to the Father except through Me.

It's Jesus himself who won't let us conceal the truth; it's Jesus himself who tears away at our rationalizations and excuses; it's Jesus himself who kicks over the sand-castles we've erected. It's Jesus himself who awakens us at night in a cold-sweat.

Personal Testimony

Twenty five years ago, I encouraged an old friend of mine to invest $5,000.00 into a project I persuaded him would earn back more than twice that amount. The project turned sour - and all the money he invested was lost. I convinced myself that I wasn't responsible for his loss - that, after all, it was an investment - and occasionally investments don't pan out.

But though my intellect was easily convinced, my conscience wouldn't let me off the hook quite so readily; nevertheless, over time I managed to pretty much stifle it - though never completely. Every once in a while, I would sense God's truth prodding me - picking at me - troubling my peace. But I'd hold steady - refusing to pay it much heed.

For twenty years I fought God's nudging - hoping that he'd tire of his efforts - that my excuses and rationalizations would finally prevail with him. But that never occurred. Finally, just a few weeks before I was to preach an important sermon on worship, God broke through to me: *"How can you preach on worship when you haven't yet resolved your sin? First resolve your sin; then I'll release you to preach with power."*

I wasn't even sure that I could locate my friend. It had been almost fifteen years since I'd seen him. But after several days of searching, I finally tracked him down and made arrangements to pay him back.

I'd carried a burden of sin on my shoulders for years - and had actually grown accustomed to it - so much so that I'd lost all awareness of it. It was only when I finally confessed it and made restitution that I could feel its onerous weight as it was lifted from off my shoulders. The lesson I learned I've never forgotten. Our sins do indeed grieve the Holy Spirit - and that grief can't be washed away by pathetic excuses.

Too often we sugarcoat Jesus - as if he's not distressed by our hypocrisy; as if our wretched excuses cut any mustard with him. We convince ourselves that Jesus won't continue pushing and prodding us if we cry out in pain - that he'll back off if we shed enough tears. *But to get to the Father, we must pass through Jesus...*

> John 14:6 — ***...No one comes to the Father except through Me.***

...and that means we've got to pass through The Truth - confessing our sins and acknowledging our hypocrisy. That's a meaning of John 14:6 too few of us ever seriously grapple with - and why so often our sanctification is hindered.

"such things"[123]
The ***focus*** of God's judgment falls exclusively upon our ***concrete, existential deeds*** - that's the clear sense conveyed by the phrase "such things." And the implications of that are profound: *it means that status - whether social, ethnic, or whatever - does not buffer God's judgment.* Judgment is not passed through a grid composed of special considerations. It's not mediated by position, rank, reputation, or even past achievements.

What we have here is not novel. It wholly conforms to the stipulations delineated in the Mosaic Covenant.

> Lev. 19:15 — You shall do no injustice in judgment. You shall not be partial to the poor, nor honor the person of the mighty. In righteousness you shall judge your neighbor.

Note that Leviticus 19:15 "cuts both ways." Traditionally, it's the rich and the socially well-positioned who are accorded special consideration; but Leviticus 19:15 tells us that special consideration is not to be accorded to the poor either. And that's especially important for *Americans* to fathom. American culture is wedded to egalitarian principles; consequently there's a very pronounced tendency among Americans to accord a privileged standing to the poor at the bar of justice. We frequently excuse their sinfulness - citing the *very real* deprivations that have plagued them: childhood abuse, both physical and emotional, ruptured family structure, inadequate education, etc. And that too must be resisted. Whether rich or poor, whether black or white, whatever - *all that matters is the deed itself. That's the focus of God's judgment.*

> Prov. 24:12 — If you say, Surely we did not know this, Does not He who weighs the hearts consider it? He who keeps your soul, does He not know it? *And will He not render to each man according to his deeds?*

> Isa. 3:10 — Say to the righteous that it shall be well with them, *For they shall eat the fruit of their doings.*
> Isa. 3:11 — Woe to the wicked! It shall be ill with him, *For the reward of his hands shall be given him.*

> Jer. 17:10 — I, the Lord, search the heart, I test the mind, *Even to give every man according to his ways, According to the fruit of his doings.*

"I Can't Take It Anymore; God Understands; Surely God Won't Judge Me."

Not long ago a woman burst into my office without having made an appointment. There was a look on her face that reflected far more than mere frustration. She was angry and filled with a deep-seated indignation. "I can't take it anymore," she blurted out.

"What can't you take anymore?" I asked.

"My husband," she replied. "I've been married to him for over twenty five years - and there's no love; no sensitivity; no willingness to partner with me. Nothing! Our marriage is a sham. It's a living hell. I deserve more. And because he can't provide more, I've decided to file for divorce. Life is too short. And I've wasted too much of it on this man."

I'd known Sally for many years. She was an apparently mature Christian woman who had served faithfully in church ministry. But she was plagued with a marriage that was, putting it euphemistically, less than fulfilling. Frank, her husband, was a hard man - not given to much tenderness. He worked late hours - often not returning home until 10:00 or 11:00 in the evening. He was more married to his job than to Sally. Whatever companionship they might once have enjoyed had long ago disappeared. Still, he provided a good income for his family; he'd never been physically abusive; and he was not an alcoholic. It's just that he was an insensitive clod who didn't know how to love his wife - and didn't seem to care much about rectifying his deficiencies.

I looked Sally square in the eye and asked her, "Do you have Biblical grounds for a divorce? Has he been unfaithful?"

"No. Not that I know of," she shot back at me - knowing where I was going. "But it's beyond that kind of technicality. He's unkind; he's unloving; he's incapable of providing for my emotional needs."

"But, Sally," I said, "even though I grant you all that, the divorce you're contemplating isn't sanctioned Biblically. God hates divorce - and provides no grounds for it except in the case of infidelity - and then only because of the hardness of our hearts."

"I expected more from you than this," Sally retorted angrily. "I was hoping for some understanding. God knows I've tried for twenty five years. I've given it my best shot. I've reached the end of my rope. God understands even if you don't. I know divorce is wrong; but God knows I've reached my limit - and what you won't permit, Pastor, I know God will."

How does that work? She knows it's wrong; but she says God understands - and is wholly convinced that he will turn a blind eye to her sinful deed. How exactly does that work?

We're forever trying to introduce mitigating circumstances that put us beyond the pale of God's judgment; but God's gaze can't be deflected; it's fastened on the deed itself - and is unmoved by the excuses we marshal to justify it. It's the deed itself - naked and standing alone - that's the object of God's judgment. Once again,

- God's truth tears away at our rationalizations and excuses;
- it exposes our lies and kicks over the sand-castles we've erected.
- nothing escapes its gaze;
- nothing can be concealed.

Verse:

Rom. 2:3	And do you think this, Oh man, you who judge those practicing such things, and doing the same, that you will escape the judgment of God?

This is not merely a rhetorical question - with an assumed answer of "no." Quite the contrary: the whole thrust of Paul's argument assumes a reply of "yes," *not* "no." Why? Because that's precisely the folly Paul is attempting to refute - and what he continues to refute through to the end of Chapter Two. An answer of "no" at this point in Paul's argument is far too premature.

Moreover, any pastor will tell you that the answer is "yes," not "no." His experience in counseling convinces him of that. Again and again he has witnessed his congregants - notwithstanding their obvious sinfulness - place themselves beyond the pale of God's judgment. But how? There are, generally, four strategies that I've taken note of over the years:

One Strategy

The role of a judge is a kind of prophylaxis.

It's not merely that faultfinding is the flip-side of hypocrisy - that the two go hand in hand - though that, of course, is certainly true. There's more to it. A faultfinder - however unconsciously - is casting himself in the role of a judge - and, in so doing, he's keeping himself from playing the role of the accused.

He can't play both roles simultaneously. He can't think of himself as *both* the judge and the accused. He's either one or the other. The role of a judge, therefore, is a kind of prophylaxis. It protects him from *feeling his own guilt.*

A Second Strategy
He casts his own behavior in a different light.

He judges himself using one benchmark - one criterion of sinful behavior; but he judges others using another benchmark - far more stringent, far more severe, far harsher.

What I call it when you do it	What I call it when I do it
You stole it	I borrowed it
You procrastinate	I'm cautious
You lost your temper	I laid down the law
You're a tyrant	I'm decisive
You can't make up your mind	I'm keeping my options open
You committed adultery	I was seduced

A Third Strategy
Another strategy is to cease identifying himself with his sinful behavior.

The double life a hypocrite is inevitably forced into can become so pointed and so extreme that he psychologically bifurcates himself - meaning he develops two actual, well defined personas: there's the "good persona" and the "bad persona" - and ego identification is invested in the one and withdrawn from the other. It's Blanche DuBois in Tennessee William's *A Street Car Named Desire*. It's also Robert Louis Stevenson's *Dr. Jeckle and Mr. Hyde*.

Once again, many hypocrites live in a fantasy world - and the fantasies they construct are very powerful and deeply entrenched - a truth Paul underscores later in verse 5.

Rom. 2:5 But in accordance with your ***hardness and your impenitent heart***...

One of the best descriptions of the "double life" syndrome is Robert Louis Stevenson's *Dr. Jekyll and Mr. Hyde*.

Cultural Connections: The Bible and Western Thought

Robert Louis Stevenson

Dr. Jekyll and Mr. Hyde

In 1886, Robert Louis Stevenson published his classic thriller *Dr. Jekyll and Mr. Hyde*. In the first six months alone, over forty thousand copies were sold – a remarkable number for the late 19th Century. Queen Victoria herself spent days locked away in her bedroom reading it; and for the next several years it seized the imagination of millions.

Initially, it wasn't stocked in American bookstores; eventually, however, it was given a favorable revue by several well known critics and soon it became a best seller - most remarkably among Christians. Not only was it read by Christians in the quiet of their own homes, it quickly became the subject of thousands of Sunday morning sermons as well.

The novel's hero is Dr. Jekyll, a rich, well-intentioned physician. His years of scientific research have culminated in the development of an intoxicating potion - which, when he drinks it, transforms him into a hideous monster, Mr. Hyde. Dr. Jekyll is at first fascinated with his discovery; but his metamorphoses become ever more frequent and long-lasting. He tries desperately to stop drinking the potion, but its addictive power is overwhelming - and soon Mr. Hyde becomes the dominant "persona."

What's not well known is that the novel is actually based on a recurring nightmare that terrified Stevenson in his youth. He wrote it in an attempt to break its hold on his own mind and heart - and purge it forever from his psyche.

What is it that Christians - specifically Christians - find so intriguing about Dr. Jekyll and Mr. Hyde? It's that it strikes such a responsive chord in all of us! It's so true - though not always to the extent portrayed in Stevenson's novel. Why? Because we lose sight of God's grace and mercy; and instead of confessing our sins - not just to God, but to fellow believers - we conceal and rationalize them - certain that no one will be able to sympathize with our plight and provide genuine help - certain that they'll condemn us - certain that we'll lose our hard-won status among our friends and within the congregation as a whole. Slowly, inexorably, two personas begin to emerge - and Stevenson's scenario starts to play itself out:

1. one persona is carefully cultivated and promoted. It's clean and pure, the very embodiment of moral integrity;
2. the other persona is kept secret and hidden away. It's repulsive, sordid, and out of control.

The two personas are always mutually exclusive - meaning the distinguishing features which characterize one are always absent from the other; so the more I try to "clean up the one," the more disgusting and perverse the other becomes. Evil is not eradicated; it's merely transferred.

A Fourth Strategy

I'm indispensable. God can't do without me.

Used by Permission

Used with "Joe's" permission in the hopes it will help others

It was 11:00 in the evening - and off in the distance I could hear the telephone ringing. Sita and I had been asleep for over an hour - and I couldn't quite rouse myself into full consciousness. Finally, Sita gave me a push - and I tumbled out of bed. I was hoping that by the time I reached the phone, it would have stopped ringing and I could get back into bed. But no such luck! The ringing was incessant. I picked up the receiver and muttered "Hello."

The voice on the other end of the line was high-pitched and just a tad out of control, "Pastor, I've got some really bad news for you. You've got to sit down for this one."

"OK," I said, by now wide awake. "What's up?"

"Joe's been found out."

"What do you mean 'found out'?" I asked. "What's going on?"

"Joe's been 'outed,'" was the reply.

Still confused, I asked, "What the heck are trying to tell me? Stop speaking in riddles."

"Joe, our missionary to Africa - Joe's a homosexual. He's been exposed. It happened just a few days ago - though I didn't find out until this evening just a little while ago. You're the first person I called."

It was true: Joe Blankenship,[124] (not his real name) apparently a loving husband, married for over twenty years, father of three teenage children who thought the sun rose and set on him, Joe Blankenship had been arrested for soliciting a male prostitute. I was thunderstruck. Words failed me. I talked a little while longer, then hung up the phone. My heart was filled with all sorts of conflicting emotions: anger, compassion, despair, bewilderment.

The next morning I called Joe on the phone - and he confirmed that he'd been arrested for soliciting a male prostitute. I was senior pastor of his home church - and, as such, I told him to return immediately to Sacramento - and to bring his whole family with him.

Over the course of the next several months, Joe shared his nightmare with me - from beginning to end. Joe's marriage had been a sham - almost from its very inception. Within just a few short weeks following their wedding, his wife Mary had discovered his homosexuality - and it had devastated her. Nevertheless, she had kept it quiet - thinking she could help him overcome it. But there was never any victory - only momentary respites.

Notwithstanding his sin and his sham-marriage, Joe applied for admission to a well known and highly respected missionary school in Texas. Mary applied as well. Their applications were approved - and eventually the two of them graduated 1st and 2nd in their class. They were then sent to language school - where, once again, they graduated 1st and 2nd in their class. Finally, they were assigned to a country in central Africa. Over the course of the next five years, their ministry flourished. Both Joe and Mary were gifted teachers and administrators - a rare combination that usually guarantees success. Not only did their ministry thrive, but their fund raising far exceeded their own personal needs. Joe and Mary were the bright lights of the entire missionary organization - and it wasn't long before they were promoted to General Superintendents of all Central Africa - the two of them - a husband/wife team.

Joe and Mary had hoped that ministry would provide a fresh start for them - that their marriage would be re-sanctified - that Joe would be granted the grace he needed to overcome his sin. But quite the contrary was occurring. Their marriage was unraveling badly - and at the very moment their success in ministry was reaching a crescendo. Joe and Mary were leading double lives - not just Joe, but Mary as well. By now, Mary was fully complicit. Joe was slipping away at night ever more frequently - with Mary well aware that he was sneaking off to gratify his sinful lusts. Finally, the inevitable occurred: *Joe was exposed.*

I asked Joe what made him think that God wouldn't eventually "pull his covers." His reply staggered me. "Because," Joe confessed, "I thought I was indispensable - that my ministry was too important - that for the sake of my ministry, God would wink at my sin. God's forbearance led me to believe that I was exempt from judgment." I asked Mary the same question. And her reply mirrored his: their ministry was too important for God to pull Joe's covers. Joe's sin was - in light of his staggering success in ministry - a trifling matter - a minor infraction that God was willing to overlook - a mere peccadillo. When I questioned her about the sham-marriage she had suffered through over the last twenty years - the absence of any genuine intimacy - the personal humiliation she had undergone – her reply was the same: "It was my duty as a woman of God," she said, "to look beyond Joe's sin and bear it quietly." What kind of twisted scriptural logic is that! Yet what's so surprising is the number of good Christians who would agree with her - and think her a saint - when, in God's estimation, she was almost as blameworthy as her husband. It wasn't just Joe's covers that were pulled; it was hers as well.

It's a scenario that's played out again and again: Jim Bakker, Jimmy Swaggert, and Ted Haggard are names that come quickly to mind. And those are just three of the hundreds of recognizable names that could be marshaled. Furthermore, those are just three of the "big names." There are thousands of others whose names are hidden in obscurity. But the horror they've undergone and the devastation they've caused are terrible as well. And each one was seduced into believing that God was winking at his sin. It's ***"The Special Person Syndrome."***

The Bottom Line

Again, the bottom line here is simple - and we shouldn't be surprised by it: the answer to the question Paul poses in verse 3 - "And do you think this, Oh man, you who judge those practicing such things, and doing the same, that you will escape the judgment of God?" - is "yes." He does indeed think he will escape the judgment of God. And verse 4 tells us why he's apt to feel so confirmed in his folly.

Verses:

Rom. 2:4	Or do you despise the riches of His goodness, forbearance, and longsuffering, not knowing that the goodness of God leads you to repentance?
Rom. 2:5	But in accordance with your hardness and your impenitent heart you are treasuring up for yourself wrath in the day of wrath and revelation of the righteous judgment of God

A hypocrite misconstrues God's forbearance. That's the meaning of verse 4. He confuses forbearance with approval - if not approval, then at least indifference. He sins, but God, in his mercy, withholds his judgment. "Yes, indeed," he thinks to himself, "I *am* special - tucked away in a safe-zone - beyond the reach of God's judgment - and put there by God himself." A hypocrite believes that God's forbearance proves he's a "special case." It's the very rationale depicted in Psalm 94:4-11.

Psalm 94:4	They utter speech, and speak insolent things; All the workers of iniquity boast in themselves.
Psalm 94:5	They break in pieces Your people, O Lord, And afflict Your heritage.
Psalm 94:6	They slay the widow and the stranger, And murder the fatherless.
Psalm 94:7	*Yet they say, The Lord does not*

Romans 2:4 and Its Relationship to Romans 9:22

It's important to take note of exactly how Paul has "freighted" the word "longsuffering" in Romans 2:4 with a meaning that plainly calls into question the standard Calvinist interpretation of Romans 9:22.

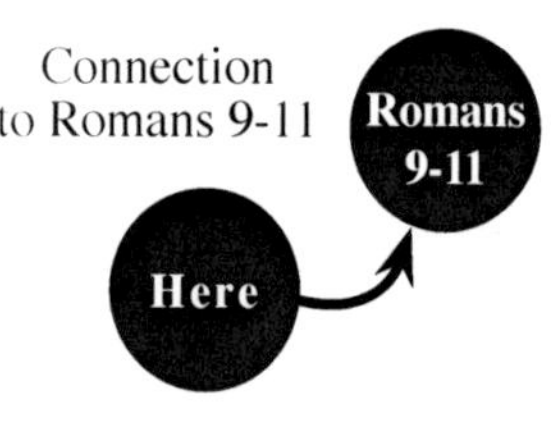

In Romans 2:4, the word "longsuffering" is clearly linked to God's kindness and, just as clearly, *is meant to lead sinners to repentance*.

Rom. 2:4 Or do you despise the riches of His goodness, forbearance, and ***longsuffering***, not knowing that the goodness of God leads you to ***repentance***?

And that's the meaning Peter gives longsuffering as well; for example...

2 Peter 3:9 The Lord is not slack concerning his promise, as some men count slackness; but is ***longsuffering*** to us-ward, not willing that any should perish, but that all should come to ***repentance***.

And just six verses further on, Peter, takes it one step further: it's not just that God's longsuffering is meant to lead sinners to repentance, it's meant to lead them to salvation.

2 Peter 3:15 And account that the ***longsuffering*** of our Lord is salvation; even as our beloved brother Paul also according to the wisdom given unto him has written unto you...

In otherwords, the meaning and purpose Paul gives to God's longsuffering in Romans 2:4 - that it's meant to lead sinners to repentance - is "standard" with Paul - and, for that matter, the whole New Testament. Therefore, to willy nilly change its meaning in Romans 9:22 is surely without foundation.

Let's take a close look

Rom. 9:22 What if God, willing to show his wrath, and to make his power known, endured with much ***longsuffering*** vessels of wrath fitted unto destruction.

Nevertheless, change its meaning is exactly what Calvinists do! For Calvinists, God "endures with much longsuffering" vessels of wrath not because he's affording them an opportunity to repent and be saved, but only because he's using them as a foil to highlight the forgiveness he bestows on vessels of mercy.

A logically consistent Calvinist will acknowledge that it's not God's longsuffering that leads sinners to repentance, it's God's soveregin will. Calvinist theology "locks" sinners into whatever status God ostensibly assigns them...

- whether a "vessel of mercy" or a "vessel of wrath;"
- whether "election" or "reprobation;"
- whether heaven or hell.

That Calvinists could so cavalierly violate the meaning Paul consistently gives to God's longsuffering - and not just Paul but the New Testament generally - is, to say the least, mystifying. It's one more intellectual snag they've failed to reckon with in any meaningful way.

	see, Nor does the God of Jacob understand."
Psalm 94:8	Understand, you senseless among the people; And you fools, when will you be wise?
Psalm 94:9	He who planted the ear, shall He not hear? He who formed the eye, shall He not see?
Psalm 94:10	He who instructs the nations, shall He not correct, He who teaches man knowledge?
Psalm 94:11	The Lord knows the thoughts of man, That they are futile.

And that's a terrible mistake. Why? Because God's goodness - assuming the form here of forbearance - is meant for only one purpose - *to call sinners to repentance*. And if that doesn't occur - if instead God's forbearance is "despised" - meaning squandered - and the only use made of it is to pile up additional sins, then all that's produced, tragically, is a wider ranging exposure and a harsher punishment. That's the meaning of the phrase "treasuring up for yourself wrath."

Put a little differently: God will not permit his dignity and majesty to be impugned indefinitely; he will not allow his righteousness to be trampled upon and his justice called into question. If a sinner refuses to acknowledge his sins and repent of them - and, in doing so, seize the pardon God has mercifully tendered, God's wrath - or, in the case of believers, his anger and harsh censure[125] - is inevitable.

Verse:

Rom. 2:6	who will render to each one according to his deeds:

Specific words or phrases in verse 6

"render"
The word "render" translates the Greek word (apodosei - αποδωσει) - and there's no question that it conveys the sense of...

- a deserved recompense;
- a due payment arising from a just obligation.

Why? Because that's the meaning of "αποδωσει" everywhere else in scripture - and there are no valid grounds for altering its meaning here - unless, of course, we *mistakenly* assume that Paul is examining the issue of salvation - either justification or sanctification; and then we're forced to alter its

Romans 2:6-10

The Recompense Phase of God's Judgment

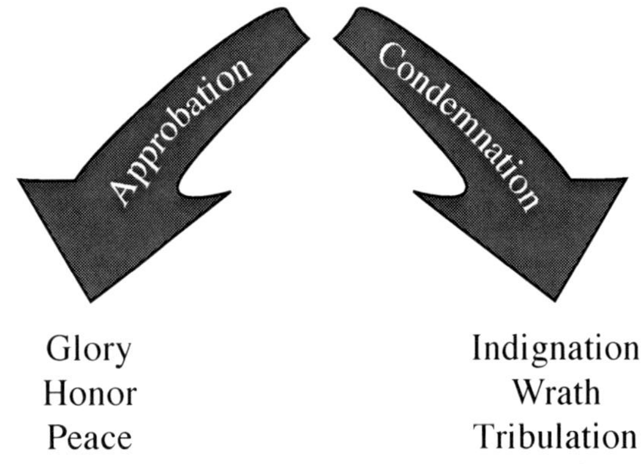

Glory	Indignation
Honor	Wrath
Peace	Tribulation
Eternal Life	Anguish

meaning to preserve what Paul has said heretofore ...

- that "eternal life" (verse 7) is not our "due;"
- that God is under no obligation to tender it;
- that salvation is a gift - freely bestowed, not earned;
- that salvation is not a matter of merit; it's a matter of grace.

But, clearly, Paul is ***not*** examining the issue of salvation here in Romans 2:6-10:

- instead, he's examining God's sovereign jurisprudence;
- instead, he's explaining how the issue of "just deserts" is adjudicated at the bar of God's holy justice;
- *instead, he's describing the dynamics of that adjudication - laying bare its details.*

"according to his deeds"
Here we have nothing more than the truth depicted in verse 2 - that the focus of God's judgment is our concrete, existential deeds. But there it was the *evaluation phase* that was at issue. Here, in verse 6, it's the *recompense phase* that's at issue. Why? Because verse 6 clearly *leads into* a remarkably detailed account of recompense (verses 7-10):

- glory, honor, peace, and eternal life to those who "do good;" and
- indignation, wrath, tribulation, and anguish to those who "do evil."

Needless Confusion
Whenever salvation has been made the subject of

God's judgment is simple You get what you deserve

A due payment arising from a just obliigation

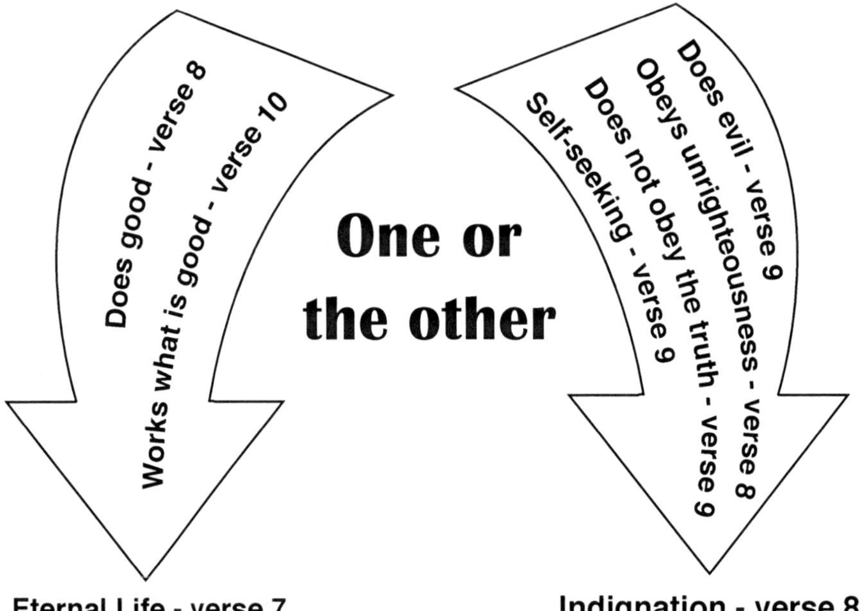

Eternal Life - verse 7
Glory - verses 7 and 10
Honor - verses 7 and 10
Immortality - verse 7
Peace - verse 10

Indignation - verse 8
Wrath - verse 8
Tribulation - verse 9
Anguish - verse 9

****

Romans 2:6-10, scholars have stumbled all over themselves trying to safeguard Paul's theology of grace. And it has led to one exegetical error after another, to wit...

- *That Paul is merely suggesting a hypothetical.* But that's not true. Every man, woman, and child has already undergone God's judgment and stands condemned before the bar of God's holy justice - no exceptions. *Hardly a hypothetical!* That's why Paul tells us in Ephesians 2:3 that we are *by nature the children of wrath.*

Eph 2:3 Among whom also we all had our conversation in times past in the lusts of our flesh, fulfilling the desires of the flesh and of the mind; and were *by nature the children of wrath, even as others.*

Their only hope is a pardon without which their plight is *utterly hopeless.*

- *That what Paul really means here in verse 6 is not simply "work" as such (εργα - erga - "work," sometimes translated "deed"), but "work of faith."*

Rom. 2:6 who will render to each one according to his *"work of faith..."*

Likewise, in verse 7, "doing good" really means *"living by faith."*

Rom. 2:7 ...eternal life to those who by patient continuance in *"living by faith"* seek for glory, honor, and immortality...

And so on and so forth throughout Romans 2:6-10. But that's obviously a stretch. It's a clear-cut example of eisegesis - meaning an interpretation forced on a passage of scripture.

- *That actual conduct is indeed at issue here in Romans 2:6-10, but conduct arising from faith, not simply conduct itself.*
  But that's also a stretch; Paul is not that obscure - that opaque. Furthermore, the emphasis here is on deeds that ***merit*** justification, not deeds that ***reflect*** justification. The word "αποδωσει" in verse 6 makes that perfectly clear.

All that kind of tortured intellectual gamesmanship can be avoided simply by keeping in mind the issue Paul is *actually* examining: ***not*** *salvation - neither justification nor sanctification, but God's jurisprudence - that and that alone.*

Verse:

Rom. 2:7 ...eternal life to those who by patient continuance in doing good seek for glory, honor, and immortality;
Rom. 2:8 but to those who are self-seeking and do not obey the truth, but obey unrighteousness—indignation and wrath,
Rom. 2:9 tribulation and anguish, on every soul of man who does evil, of the Jew first and also of the Greek;
Rom. 2:10 but glory, honor, and peace to everyone who works what is good, to the Jew first and also to the Greek.
Rom. 2:11 for there is no partiality with God.

Some expositors - who fail to grasp what's at issue here, *not salvation, but God's jurisprudence* - suggest that Paul is restating the same truth he delineates in 1 Corinthians 3:12-15 - to wit, that all believers will undergo judgment at the bema of Christ - that their *Christian service* will be evaluated there - with rewards and punishments allocated accordingly. But that can't possibly be true. Why? Because included among the "rewards" and "punishments" enumerated in Romans 2:6-10 are two that any freshman exegete knows shouldn't be there:

- "eternal life" - verse 7, and
- "wrath" - at least for the redeemed - verse 8.

Eternal life (verse 7) can't be earned; it's a gift. Moreover, the theology of rewards never makes eternal life a recompense for faithfulness, only our status in the coming kingdom - only the scope of our authority there. Likewise, *wrath* (verse 8) is never a recompense God consigns the redeemed to suffer. Rebuke - yes! Correction - yes! Scourging -yes! (Hebrews 12:5-11) *But never wrath.*

Rom. 5:9 Much more then, having now been justified by His blood, ***we shall be saved from wrath through Him.***

No! All Paul wants to prove here in verses 7-10 is that God's justice renders to every man what he deserves. It's that straight-forward. *God's justice is simple:* ***you get what you deserve*** *(see page 132).*

If what we deserve is indignation, wrath, tribulation, and anguish, but what we get is eternal life, glory, honor, immortality, and peace, it's only because God, in his infinite mercy...

- has not only pardoned us from the one,
- but has freely given us the other.

That, in a nut-shell, is what Romans 2:2-10 is all about.

"to the Jew first and also to the Greek ... for there is no partiality with God"
Once again, Paul points out that priority has been assigned to the Jew; but here, unlike Romans 1:16, the phrase *"to the Jew first and also to the Greek"* is merely a foil he uses in the next verse, verse 11, to affirm that God's judgment is utterly impartial - that whatever priority the Jew enjoys, it will not protect him from undergoing the *same judgment* facing the Gentiles.

- The *same criterion* will be used: the truth;
- the *same focus:* concrete, existential deeds; and, lastly,
- the *same recompense:*
  - eternal life, glory, honor, immortality and

peace to those whose deeds are deemed "good;" and
- indignation, wrath, tribulation, and anguish to whose deeds are deemed "evil."

It should also be noted that the phrase *"to the Jew first and also to the Greek"* once again confirms for us that while only the Jew is being addressed in verses 17-29, *both* Jew and the Gentile are being addressed in verses 1-16. Otherwise, the truth Paul's elucidating here, God's impartiality, is little more than a pedantic display of Talmudic scholarship, not the ominous warning it so obviously is - a warning Paul wants *all* mankind - *both* Jews and Gentiles - to get a grip on - *that no one can claim a privileged standing before the bar of God's holy justice.*

Verse:

Rom. 2:12	For as many as have sinned without law will also perish without law, and as many as have sinned under the law will be judged by the law...

Specific words or phrases in verse 12

"the law"

The Jew *alone* - among all the races of mankind - has been entrusted with *The Law* - God's "oracles" - his self-disclosure - his self-revelation - including...
- the revelation of his authority;
- the revelation of his covenants;
- the revelation of his plan of salvation; and, of course,
- the revelation of his holiness - *most especially his holiness.*

God's holiness - his perfect righteousness - is a theme that's sounded again and again in the Old Testament. Holiness is not just an attribute of God; it defines his very essence - *God **is** holy.* Moreover, holiness *conditions* mankind's relationship with God - not just in part, but in every whit. It's the *ground* of that relationship - its sine qua non; its unchanging, unwavering, immutable precondition.

Heb 12:14	Pursue...holiness, without which no one will see the Lord...

That truth is what the Book of Leviticus is all about - the central principle it enunciates. It's encapsulated most tellingly in a single phrase that's repeated again and again throughout the Book of Leviticus: "*You shall be holy, for I am holy.*"

Lev. 11:44	For I am the Lord your God. You shall therefore consecrate yourselves, and *you shall be holy; for I am holy.* Neither shall you defile yourselves with any creeping thing that creeps on the earth.
Lev. 11:45	For I am the Lord who brings you up out of the land of Egypt, to be your God. *You shall therefore be holy, for I am holy.*
Lev. 19:2	Speak to all the congregation of the children of Israel, and say to them: *You shall be holy, for I the Lord your God am holy.*
Lev. 20:26	And *you shall be holy to Me, for I the Lord am holy,* and have separated you from the peoples, that you should be Mine.

The same theme is clearly underscored in the New Testament

Eph. 1:4	...just as He chose us in Him before the foundation of the world, *that we should be holy and without blame before Him in love...*
1 Thes. 4:7	For God did not call us to uncleanness, *but to holiness.*
1 Pet. 1:15-16	...but as *He who called you is holy, you also be holy in all your conduct, because it is written, Be holy, for I am holy.*

Without holiness, any kind of relationship with God is fraught with deadly peril. Why? Because God's holiness is a consuming fire - meaning it devours all unrighteousness. In short, like the "truth," God's holiness is not inert;
- it's alive;
- it's dynamic
- it's active

Ex. 24:17	The sight of the glory of the Lord was like *a consuming fire* on the top of the mountain in the eyes of the children of Israel.

Deut. 4:24	*For the Lord your God is a consuming fire*, a jealous God.
Deut. 9:3	Therefore understand today that the *Lord your God is he who goes over before you as a consuming fire*. He will destroy them and bring them down before you; so you shall drive them out and destroy them quickly, as the Lord has said to you.
Heb. 12:29	For *our God is a consuming fire*.

The Law, then, speaks to the issue of holiness and tells us that holiness is the ground of mankind's relationship with God. It "codifies" the standard against which mankind's righteousness is measured - and, corresponds, therefore, to the word "truth" in Romans 2:2. "The Law," the "truth," and "righteousness" are all pretty much synonymous terms.

Specific words or phrases in verse 12
"without the law" and "under the law"
Those "without the Law" are, of course, the Gentiles; and those "under the Law" are, of course, the Jews.

It's important to note that when Paul asserts that the Gentiles are "without the Law,"

- he means only that "they are outside the pale of God's special revelation."
- he means only that they fall outside the jurisdiction of the Mosaic Law," God's *directly* mediated self-disclosure – a revelation vouchsafed only to the Jews.

In short, Paul isn't suggesting that Gentile society is anarchic - that it's lawless, only that it isn't grounded in "the Mosaic Law." Indeed, the phrase "law unto themselves" found in Romans 2:14 is merely Paul's way of saying "Gentile law."

Moreover, when Paul declares that the Gentiles who "sin without the Law will perish without the law," he means only that they will perish *outside the jurisdiction of the Mosaic Law*. He isn't suggesting that there's no moral basis upon which an objective assessment of Gentile guilt can be rendered - that the judgment of guilt and condemnation levied against them will be baseless. Indeed, the Gentiles will be judged *by their own laws* - which Romans 2:14-15 and 3:21 tell us will constitute a wholly sufficient basis for rendering an accurate judgment. Why? Because Gentile law is based on "the law written on their hearts" (Romans 2:15), i.e., their consciences; and it reflects enough of the truths incorporated in the Mosaic Law to establish an altogether adequate basis for a just verdict.

The truth Paul is underscoring here is the same truth he elucidated back in Romans 1:28 - 32 - that man, contrary to what the Calvinists claim, is essentially a moral being - and that flagrant sinfulness (indicating a "nous adokimos" - νους αδοκιμος) does not "fit" humanity (μη κατηκοντα); it's *contrary* to human nature - *even the human nature of fallen man*.

Connection to Romans 9-11

Here → Romans 9-11

Verse:

Rom. 2:13	(for not the hearers of the law are just in the sight of God, but the doers of the law will be justified...

Specific words or phrases in verse 13
"not the hearers of the law ... but the doers of the law"
Once again, Paul is highlighting a principle he has already underscored time and time again: that the focus of God's judgment is our concrete, existential deeds - not what we know, but what we do.

In addition, however, he's laying the groundwork here for rectifying a misconception that blinds the Jews to their need for a pardon - a misconception he takes up beginning with Romans 2:17...

- that there's no "rest" in the law;
- that mere possession of the law affords no protection whatsoever against God's wrath;
- that God's jurisprudence takes account of only our deeds - our concrete behavior - and waves off both possession of the law and knowledge of the law.

Specific words or phrases in verse 13
"just" and "justified"
This is Paul's first use of the word "justify" - and its meaning here in verse 13 must be assessed against the backdrop of Romans 2:2-10, the description Paul gives there of *God's jurisprudence*. In short, the "justification" here in Romans 2:13 is *not* the gift of righteousness, i.e., the pardon Paul ever so briefly

It's not the hearers of the law who are just in the sight of God, but the doers of the law ...

Romans 2:13

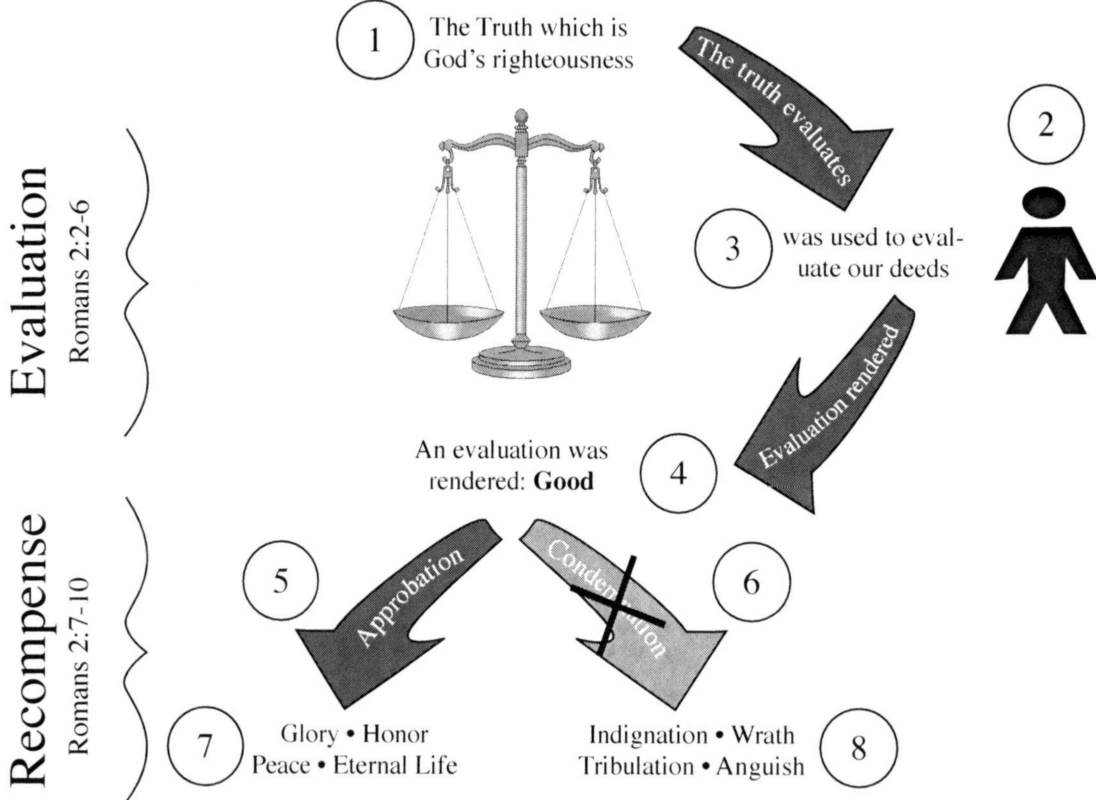

xxxxxxxxxxxxxxxxxxx

described back in Romans 1:16-17 - a description he broke off in Romans 1:18 and won't pick up again until Romans 3:21; *quite the contrary: "justification" here in Romans 2:13 is the approbation God's jurisprudence entitles me to* ***if*** *my* ***deeds*** *warrant it.*

Simply put, if I hope to be justified at the bar of God's holy justice - apart from any pardon God graciously provides - it will be my deeds that justify me. Nothing else!

- God's jurisprudence doesn't adjudicate *knowledge*; it adjudicates *deeds*.
- God's jurisprudence doesn't adjudicate *hearing*; it adjudicates *doing*.

That's why Paul tells us...

Rom. 2:13 ...(it's) not the hearers of the law who are just in the sight of God, but the doers of the law will be justified...

Calvin on the Ropes

Verse:

Rom. 2:14 — for when the Gentiles, who do not have the law, by nature do the things in the law, these, although not having the law, are a law to themselves...

Specific words or phrases in verse 14

"for when the Gentiles, who do not have the law"

Here, in verse 14, "those without the law" in verse 12 are explicitly identified - there can be no doubt whatsoever: *the Gentiles*

Specific words or phrases in verse 14

"by nature do the things in the law"

The phrase "by nature" conveys the sense of "instinctively." Once again, what we have here is the same truth Paul was underscoring back in verse 12 - that man is a moral being...

- that knowledge of God's righteousness is intrinsic;
- it's intuitive;
- it's part of mankind's spiritual and emotional DNA.

And, also once again, it's the same truth that prompted Paul in Romans 1:28-32 to assert that anyone given over to flagrant sinfulness - who not only sins openly and brazenly himself, but endorses and encourages the sinfulness of others - is less than fully human - that his "nous" (not just his "mind," but his inner being) is "adokimos" (doesn't measure up - fails the test).

Man instinctively knows right from wrong - meaning he's able to distinguish between good and evil. He, of course, is not able to live out the right and suppress the wrong; but he nevertheless establishes laws which reflect those distinctions - laws which encourage and reward the one and discourage and punish the other. A classic example is the "Code of Hammurabi" - an ancient Middle Eastern collection of laws many of which are all but carbon copies of laws found in the Jewish Torah.

Specific words or phrases in verse 14

"not having the Law"

i.e., the Law of Moses - God's special revelation - his directly mediated self-disclosure vouchsafed only to the Jews.

Specific words or phrases in verse 14

"are a law to themselves"

The translation here is unfortunate - because for most Americans the phrase *"are a law unto themselves"* conveys the sense of "lawlessness" or "anarchy;" e.g., "Jesse James was a law unto himself." And that's not at all what Paul means. How do I know? Because the phrase *"are a law to themselves"* is obviously defined by the phrase *"by nature do the things in the law;"* specifically,

The Gentiles...

- *"in doing* instinctively the things of the law"
- are a "law unto themselves."

Or, put slightly differently, the Gentiles...

- are a "law unto themselves"
- *"in that* they do instinctively the things of the law"...

Clearly, then, the phrase "law unto themselves" means *"law arising from the conscience"* - which, of course, is confirmed in verse 15. In short,

- Jewish law arises from the Torah.
- Gentile law arises from the conscience.

The one is codified; the other is instinctive. But both "register" sin (cf. verse 15) - and, in doing so, legitimize judgment and condemnation.

Verse:

Rom. 2:15 — ...in that they show the work of the Law written in their hearts, their conscience bearing witness, and their thoughts alternately accusing or else defending them...

Specific words or phrases in verse 15

"in that they show the work of the Law written in their hearts"

Paul is merely repeating himself here for further emphasis: Gentile law reflects an intrinsic awareness of God's righteousness.

But there's more: he's laying the groundwork for the truth he's about to elucidate in the next clause: Gentile law registers sin - which is the meaning of the phrase "their thoughts alternately accusing or else defending them..." That's the "work of the law" - it's purpose - what God intends it to do. It's the same truth Paul declares a bit later in Romans 3:20.

Rom. 3:20 — ...for by the law is the knowledge of sin.

Clearly, the phrase *"the law written in their hearts"*

does not convey the meaning Jeremiah gives it in Jeremiah 31:33

Jer. 31:33 ...I will put my law in their minds, and write it on their hearts...

There, the meaning is ***regeneration*** - not at all the meaning Paul gives it here in Romans 2:15.

Specific words or phrases in verse 15
"their conscience bearing witness"
Biblically, the heart is multifaceted - including the mind, the will, the emotions, and the conscience.

- The mind is the seat of human reasoning - the seat of the human intellect;
- the emotions are the seat of human empathy and passion;
- the will is the seat of human volition; and
- the conscience is where God has deposited an awareness of his righteousness.

Thus, it's perfectly consistent for Paul to tell us that "the work of the Law is written in their hearts" and, likewise, that "their conscience bears witness." The one, the conscience, is subsumed under the other, the heart.

Specific words or phrases in verse 15
"and their thoughts alternately accusing or defending them."

Gentile law - arising from the conscience - is sufficiently adequate to register sin - which is exactly the function the Torah serves (Romans 3:20). That's the meaning here.

Summing up Verses 13 - 15:

Verses 13 - 15 are clearly parenthetical - a digression Paul undertakes to explain an important principle legitimizing Gentile judgment. The gist of the matter is simple. But let's go back to verses 2-12 to lay the groundwork for it.

1. From verses 2 - 10, Paul delineates God's sovereign jurisprudence.
2. The final clause of verse 10 makes it clear that God's jurisprudence is universal - that it applies to *both* Jew and Gentile.
3. Verse 11 simply makes that truth explicit - *"there is no partiality with God"* - the same jurisprudence that condemns the Jew condemns the Gentile as well.
4. Verse 12 acknowledges, however, that the Gentile falls outside the pale of the Mosaic Law.
5. Nevertheless, the fundamental principle holds: it's not the hearers of the law who will be justified, it's the *doers of the law* who will be justified.
6. But how can the Gentiles *"do the law"* when, in point of fact, the law has never been revealed to them? Their condemnation will be baseless - meaning there's no law to adjudicate their condemnation. And doesn't that make their condemnation unfair?
7. But, no; *the law has been revealed to them.* The same basic law vouchsafed to the Jew in the Torah has been vouchsafed to the Gentile in his conscience.
8. Thus, the same law that condemns the Jew condemns the Gentile as well.

Connection to Romans 9-11
Romans 9-11
Here

Few other verses can be so decisively arrayed against Five Point Calvinism as these: Romans 2:14-15. They leave no doubt that man – *meaning fallen man* – is not devoid of a conscience – a conscience that's quite capable of discerning good from evil...

- so much so that he enacts laws that reward the one and punish the other;
- so much so that his conscience alone provides a sufficient basis for justifying his condemnation before the bar of God's holy justice.

If the doctrine of total depravity is a sine-qua-non of Five Point Calvinism – and it most assuredly is[126] – then we're certainly justified in calling Five Point Calvinism into question.[127] And, if so, the classic Calvinist interpretation of Romans 9-11 is, ipso facto, also called into question – suggesting, once again, that Romans 9-11 is not about God's sovereignty, as the Calvinists would have it; it's about God's mercy.

And that brings us to verse 16.

Verse:
Rom. 2:16 ...on the day when, according to my gospel, God will judge the secrets of men through Christ Jesus.

Specific words or phrases used in verse 16
"... on the day ..."
Clearly, the "day" here in verse 16 is the very same

day Paul has in mind in verse 5.

Rom. 2:5	But in accordance with your hardness and your impenitent heart you are treasuring up for yourself wrath *in the* ***day*** *of wrath and revelation of the righteousness judgment of God...*

Specific words or phrases used in verse 16

"according to my gospel, God will judge ..."

When we think of the gospel message, most of us think only of redemption. However, the gospel message includes not only the good news of God's redemptive mercy, but a somber warning that unless that mercy is appropriated, the execution already pronounced[128] against mankind will indeed be carried out. In short, the gospel embraces a message of judgment, condemnation, and wrath, not just a message of forgiveness and reconciliation. Indeed, Paul makes it clear that the one cannot be fathomed without the other. The two go hand in hand.

"... the secrets of men ..."

For some expositors (e.g. Cranfield), the word "secrets" (κρυπτα) is a short-hand expression for "secrets of the heart" (τα κρυπτα τη καρδια) - and, as such, points to thoughts, attitudes, intentions, sentiments, and dispositions; but that apparently runs contrary to Paul's insistence that God judges only our *concrete deeds* - a truth he underscored in verse 6.

However, there's little justification for making "secrets" synonymous with "secrets of the heart" - meaning thoughts and attitudes. Paul does not ordinarily leave us guessing: if he'd meant "secrets of the heart," there's no doubt that's what he would have penned. It's more likely that Paul means nothing more than *hidden* deeds rather than *visible* deeds - deeds subject to public scrutiny.

- Many sins are committed in complete secrecy - with no witnesses other than the single individuals committing the sins.
- Other sins are committed "behind closed doors" - with more than a single individual involved (e.g., conspiracies, secret deals, etc.) but hidden from public scrutiny. That's another possible meaning Paul might have in mind here.

And isn't that exactly what Jesus himself means in Luke 12:2-3? He isn't talking there about thoughts and attitudes; he's talking about concrete *deeds - but hidden from public scrutiny.*

Luke 12:2	For there is nothing covered, that shall not be revealed; neither hid that shall not be known.
Luke 12:3	Therefore whatsoever you have spoken in darkness shall be heard in the light; and that which you have spoken in the ear in closets shall be proclaimed upon the housetops.

Likewise, in Luke 8:17 the sense is *hidden deeds* - which though concealed are nevertheless very concrete.

Luke 8:17	For nothing is secret that shall not be made manifest; neither any thing hid, that shall not be known and come abroad.

And the same holds true for Matthew 10:26.

Mt. 10:26	...for there is nothing covered, that shall not be revealed; and hid, that shall not be known.

In short, we shouldn't feel constrained to limit our interpretation here in Romans 2:16 to thoughts, attitudes, intentions, sentiments, or dispositions. Paul is making a very simple point: though we might conceal our sins from men and, therefore, escape their judgment, we can't conceal our sins from God and, in so doing, escape his judgment.

But what about Matthew 5:28 - where Jesus does apparently call into judgment a person's thoughts?

Mt. 5:28	But I say to you that whoever looks at a woman to lust for her has already committed adultery with her in his heart.

Actually, however, that interpretation misses the whole point Jesus is making. Matthew 5:28 is part of a series of *"But I say unto you"* verses following in the wake of verse 20.

Mt. 5: 20	*For I say to you,* that unless your righteousness exceeds the righteousness of the scribes and Pharisees, you will by no means enter the kingdom of heaven.

Each one is designed to show the disciples how sin

is prompted - its origin - its seedbed. It arises, Jesus says, from within our heart.

- How does murder arise? There are two distinct steps. It arises...
    1. first, from anger and, then,
    2. from calling into question a person's basic worth - demeaning his importance; e.g., calling him "empty headed" (the meaning of "Raca") or "a fool" - and in so doing making his murder seem less reprehensible.

Mt. 5:21	You have heard that it was said to those of old, You shall not murder, and whoever murders will be in danger of the judgment.
Mt. 5:22	*But I say to you* that whoever is (1) *angry* with his brother without a cause shall be in danger of the judgment. And whoever says to his brother, (2) *'Raca!'* shall be in danger of the council. But whoever says, *'You fool!'* shall be in danger of hell fire.

- How does adultery arise? It arises from lust.

Mt. 5:27	You have heard that it was said by them of old time, You shall not commit adultery:
Mt. 5:28	*But I say unto you* that whosoever looks on a woman to lust after her has committed adultery with her already in his heart.

In short, Jesus wants the disciples to guard their hearts - to "circumcise" their hearts - exactly the warning Moses highlights in Deuteronomy 10:16 and in Deuteronomy 30:6. Why? Because that's where the war against sin is won or lost.

De 10:16	Therefore *circumcise the foreskin of your heart,* and be stiff-necked no longer.
De 30:6	And the Lord your God will *circumcise your heart* and the heart of your descendants, to love the Lord your God with all your heart and with all your soul, that you may live.

Anyone who fails to guard his heart - who allows his mind to wrap itself around the thought of sin - who permits his heart to toy with it - to coddle it - *that person makes sin - concrete, existential sin - all but inevitable.* That's the point Jesus is making in Matthew 5:28. If your mind harbors lust - if it allows lust to find a home there - eventually you'll commit adultery. It's that simple. James makes the same point in his epistle.

James 1:12	Blessed is the man who endures temptation; for when he has been approved, he will receive the crown of life which the Lord has promised to those who love Him.
James 1:13	Let no one say when he is tempted, I am tempted by God; for God cannot be tempted by evil, nor does He Himself tempt anyone.
James 1:14	*But each one is tempted when he is drawn away by his own desires and enticed.*
James 1:15	*Then, when desire has conceived, it gives birth to sin;* and sin, when it is full-grown, brings forth death.

Notice how James distinguishes between lust – obviously a thought – and sin - *how lust is made a precursor to sin – how it gives birth to sin.* Sin originates in lust, but is itself distinguished from lust.[129] Notice too how James makes sin the all but *inevitable consequence* of allowing lust to find a home in our minds and hearts. And that's the very truth Jesus is warning his disciples about: *that they will fail at righteousness - just as the Pharisees have failed - unless they first circumcise their heart - unless they guard their hearts very carefully.*

Pr 4:23	Keep your heart with all diligence, for out of it spring the issues of life.

The struggle against sin occurs in our minds and hearts. That's the simple truth Jesus is underscoring. It's a grave exegetical error to expand the meaning of Matthew 5:28 much beyond this narrowly drawn truth.

On the other hand, however, it's certainly true that the total complex of any concrete, existential sin - when it's actually committed - does indeed include thoughts and attitudes; and to *that* extent thoughts and attitudes will indeed be "factored into" God's judgment on "that day." That much can be conceded without allowing for a conflict between verses 6 and 16 - *but only that much*. The principle still holds*: it's the deed itself that determines guilt or innocence.*

Genesis 20 – the story of Abimelech, Sarah, and Abraham – casts a fascinating light on this principle. Abimelech, King of Gerar, seizes Sarah, Abraham's wife, and puts her in his harem, having been told that she is Abraham's sister. During the night, God confronts Abimelech in a dream and tells him, "...*you are a dead man because of the woman whom you have taken, for she is another man's wife.*" Abimelech protests that he didn't know Sarah was married to Abraham; that he'd been told by Abraham himself that Sarah was his sister, not his wife. And note carefully God's response: *"Yes, I know that you did this in the integrity of your heart (i.e., you seized her for yourself unaware that she was a married woman). For I also withheld you from sinning against me; therefore I did not let you touch her."* The implication here is clear: if Abimelech had in fact "touched" Sarah he would have indeed been charged with sin notwithstanding his ignorance. In short, ignorance would *not* have constituted sufficient grounds for holding him innocent. *It's the deed itself that determines guilt or innocence.* What we have here is the age-old adage: "Ignorance of the law (or of having transgressed the law unawares) is no excuse."

The same principle is at the heart of Sophocles' Oedipus Trilogy: it becomes for Sophocles the underlying meaning of tragedy. Oedipus, a heroic figure, unwittingly murders his father and marries his mother. Nevertheless, notwithstanding his personal integrity and the unwitting nature of his crime, he is driven from his kingdom and hounded mercilessly by the furies. Again, the deed itself condemns him – it and it alone.

Specific words or phrases used in verse 16
"... through Christ Jesus."
Jesus Christ is the agent of judgment. That right is reserved for him alone.

CHAPTER SEVEN

Verses for Chapter Seven

Rom. 2:17 But if you bear the name "Jew," and rely upon the Law, and boast in God,

Rom. 2:18 and know His will, and approve the things that are excellent, being instructed out of the law,

Rom. 2:19 and are confident that you yourself are a guide to the blind, a light to those who are in darkness,

Rom. 2:20 an instructor of the foolish, a teacher of babes, having the form of knowledge and truth in the law.

Rom. 2:21 You, therefore, who teach another, do you not teach yourself? You who preach that a man should not steal, do you steal?

Rom. 2:22 You who say, "Do not commit adultery," do you commit adultery? You who abhor idols, do you rob temples?

Rom. 2:23 You who make your boast in the law, do you dishonor God through breaking the law?

Rom. 2:24 For "the name of God is blasphemed among the Gentiles because of you," as it is written.

Rom. 2:25 For circumcision is indeed profitable if you keep the law; but if you are a breaker of the law, your circumcision has become uncircumcision.

Rom. 2:26 Therefore, if an uncircumcised man keeps the righteous requirements of the law, will not his uncircumcision be counted as circumcision?

Rom. 2:27 And will not the physically uncircumcised, if he fulfills the law, judge you who, even with your written code and circumcision, are a transgressor of the law?

Rom. 2:28 For he is not a Jew who is one outwardly, nor is circumcision that which is outward in the flesh;

Rom. 2:29 but he is a Jew who is one inwardly; and circumcision is that of the heart, in the Spirit, not in the letter; whose praise is not from men but from God.

Rom. 3:1 What advantage then has the Jew, or what is the profit of circumcision?

Rom. 3:2 Much in every way! Chiefly because to them were committed the oracles of God.

Rom. 3:3 For what if some did not believe? Will their unbelief make the faithfulness of God without effect?

Rom. 3:4 Certainly not! Indeed, let God be true but every man a liar. As it is written: "That You may be justified in Your words, And may overcome when You are judged."

Rom. 3:5 But if our unrighteousness demonstrates the righteousness of God, what shall we say? Is God unjust who inflicts wrath? (I speak as a man.)

Rom. 3:6 Certainly not! For then how will God judge the world?

Rom. 3:7 For if the truth of God has increased through my lie to His glory, why am I also still judged as a sinner?

Rom. 3:8 And why not say, "Let us do evil that good may come"? --as we are slanderously reported and as some affirm that we say. Their condemnation is just.

Rom. 3:9 What then? Are we better than they? Not all together.[130] For we have previously charged both Jews and Greeks that they are all under sin.

Rom. 3:10 As it is written: "There is none righteous, no, not one;

Rom. 3:11 There is none who understands; There is none who seeks after God.

Rom. 3:12 They have all turned aside; They have together become unprofitable; There is none who does good, no, not one."

Rom. 3:13 "Their throat is an open tomb; With their tongues they have practiced deceit"; "The poison of asps is under their lips";

Rom. 3:14 "Whose mouth is full of cursing and bitterness."

Rom. 3:15 "Their feet are swift to shed blood;

Rom. 3:16 Destruction and misery are in their

	ways;
Rom. 3:17	And the way of peace they have not known."
Rom. 3:18	"There is no fear of God before their eyes."
Rom. 3:19	Now we know that whatever the law says, it says to those who are under the law, that every mouth may be stopped, and all the world may become guilty before God.
Rom. 3:20	Therefore by the deeds of the law no flesh will be justified in His sight, for by the law is the knowledge of sin.

Verse:

Rom. 2:17	But if you bear the name "Jew," and rely upon the Law, and boast in God,

Specific words or phrases found in Romans 2:17
"But if you bear the name 'Jew,'"

Notice the coordinate "but." Ordinarily, it points to a *contrast* that's about to be drawn – a *disjunction* that's about to be stipulated.[131] Occasionally, however, it's used to single out a specific case for special follow-up – in which case it's translated "indeed," exactly how it's translated in the NKJV.

Rom. 2:17	***Indeed*** you are called a Jew, and rest on the law, and make your boast in God,

Paul intends to apply the principles he has just elucidated in verses 2-16 – the principles underlying God's jurisprudence – to the specific, concrete case of the Jew. *But why?*

- Hasn't he already made it clear that God doesn't "play favorites" – and that includes the Jews? *Yes!* That's the whole point of Romans 2:7-11. Romans 2:7-11 tells us that God's sovereign jurisprudence applies to all men regardless of ethnicity. God is wholly impartial.

Rom. 2:7	...eternal life to those who by patient continuance in doing good seek for glory, honor, and immortality;
Rom. 2:8	but to those who are self-seeking and do not obey the truth, but obey unrighteousness—indignation and wrath,
Rom. 2:9	*tribulation and anguish, on every soul of man who does evil, of* ***the Jew first and also of the Greek;***
Rom. 2:10	*but glory, honor, and peace to everyone who works what is good,* ***to the Jew first and also to the Greek.***[132]
Rom. 2:11	***for there is no partiality with God.***

- The *same criterion* will be used for both Jew and Gentile: the truth;
- the *same focus:* concrete, existential deeds; and, lastly,
- the *same recompense:*
    - eternal life, glory, honor, immortality and peace to those whose deeds are deemed "good;" and
    - indignation, wrath, tribulation, and anguish to those whose deeds are deemed "evil."

- Hasn't Paul also made it clear that mere possession of the law avails nothing at the bar of God's holy justice? *Yes!* That's the whole point of Romans 2:13. In Romans 2:13, Paul tells us that *mere knowledge* counts for nothing.

Rom. 2:13	...for not the hearers of the law are just in the sight of God, but the doers of the law will be justified...

- God's jurisprudence doesn't adjudicate *knowledge*; it adjudicates *deeds*.
- God's jurisprudence doesn't adjudicate *hearing*; it adjudicates *doing*.

Why, then, is Paul retracing his footsteps? *It's because the Jew can't seem to "connect the dots."* His stubbornness – his intransigence – makes that simple task all but impossible. The long and the short of it is that the Jew is *peculiarly* blind – a truth Paul underscores in Romans 10:2-3...

Romans 10:2	For I bear them (the Jews) witness that they have a zeal for God, ***but not according to knowledge.***
Romans 10:3	For ***they (the Jews) being ignorant*** of God's righteousness...

Connecting the dots for the Jews – that's what

Romans 2:17-3:20 is all about.

Specific words or phrases used in verse 17
"...and rely upon the law..."
The word that's here translated "rely upon" can also be translated "rest"[133] – and that implies complacency – which is the sense Paul wants conveyed here. But the Jew should be desperate, not complacent. He's resting on a morass of quicksand that's about to swallow him up. He's bedding down on top of a steel trap that's about to snap shut on him. He's half-asleep and feels safe and secure when he ought to be wide awake and ridden with anxiety. ***There's no rest in the Law! It's not possible!*** The law condemns anyone who doesn't measure up to its holy stipulations – anyone at all, whether Jew or Gentile.[134]

Specific words or phrases used in verse 16
"...and boast in God..."
Boasting in God isn't always bad (e.g., Romans 5:11); but here it is exactly that. Why? Because the Jew's boasting is founded on a misconception that puts him in dire jeopardy.

Verse:

Rom. 2:18	and know His will, and approve the things that are essential, being instructed out of the Law...

Verses 18-20 appear to be a straightforward delineation of both the advantages the Law has bestowed upon the Jew and the responsibilities that bestowal implies – more specifically...

- verse 18 outlines the advantages the Law confers upon the Jew; and
- verses 19-20 outline the responsibilities those advantages impose on him.

But there's more here than just that. We need to bear in mind that verses 18-20 are sandwiched between...

- verse 17, which tells us that the Jew "rests" in the law, a hopeless undertaking in light of Romans 2:2-16, *and*
- verses 21-24, which pointedly – even sarcastically – underscore the Jew's hypocrisy.

That's the backdrop against which verses 18-20 must now be interpreted. And when that's done what we have is a tragic irony – *the very privileges God has conferred upon the Jew have produced in him an overweening "hubris" – an arrogance that has not only blinded him*[135], but has left him in jeopardy of hell – which explains why Paul, in Romans 11:9, quotes Psalm 69:22-23...

Connection to Romans 9-11
Here
Romans 9-11

Rom. 11:9	And David says: *Let their table become a snare and a trap*, a stumbling block and a recompense to them.

...meaning the blessings God has lavished upon the Jews – here figuratively called "their table" – have become a snare and a trap – which is the inevitable result of any blessing that's misunderstood, mishandled, and perverted.

The Jew is boasting (verse 17) in a privilege that has never been accorded him: *a favored standing before the bar of God's holy justice*. That's a tragic misconception; in point of fact, when standing before God in judgment, Jew and Gentile are on an equal footing. Neither is favored over the other.

- There's no doubt that the Jews are a ***chosen*** people. That truth is affirmed again and again in the Book of Romans (cf. Romans 3:1-2, but especially Romans Chapters Nine through Eleven). The Jew has been ***chosen*** to bear witness to God's glory; and, accordingly, the Jew has been invited into intimate fellowship with God. It is with the Jewish nation alone that God chose to "tabernacle." It is to the Jew alone – of all the nations of the earth – that God declared: *"I will be your God; you shall be my people; and I will dwell in the midst of you."* ***However...***
- the Jew's ***"chosenness"*** does not entitle him to escape God's judgment or to be less severely judged than the Gentile.

In short, the Jew's ***"chosenness"*** is very real, but it's not what he thinks it is. It affords him no grounds for complacency.

Specific words or phrases found in Romans 2:18
"...know His will..."

"...his will" – what Paul has in mind here is far more than merely a compendium of ethical imperatives – of "do's and don'ts." It's far more than merely a call to holiness. We severely – even gravely – truncate its meaning if we cast the term in that guise only.

- It's certainly true that the Law, which spells out God's will, underscores God's holiness and, of course, reveals the moral code that necessarily flows from it.

- But that's only because holiness is *the ground of fellowship with God.* Fellowship, not holiness, is what the Law is most concerned about.

The story of the Old Testament – and the New as well – can, in large measure, be summed up in a four part formula[136] that highlights this truth:

1. I will be your God.[137]
2. You shall be my people.[138]
3. I will dwell in the midst of you.[139]
4. Therefore, be holy for I am holy.[140 141]

The first three parts of the formula comprise its heart – what it's all about. God's will is found exactly there – *fellowship*; the fourth, the command to be holy, is what brings it to pass – what makes it work. God wants man to be holy *so that he can fellowship with him.* It's that simple. Holiness is not an end in itself. It's a means to an end – or, more accurately – ***the*** means to ***the*** end.

The Law and the Prophets, which, once again, codify God's will, disclose God's *purposes* – especially highlighting fellowship with God; and knowing that reveals the majesty and nobility of mankind's creation and ***enables the Jew, therefore, to lend meaning and certainty to his life.***

Specific words or phrases found in Romans 2:18
"...approve the things that are essential..."
...meaning *"to distinguish what's important and central about life from what's inconsequential and peripheral."* In short, what the Law and the Prophets teach is "good judgment" and a balanced perspective. ***That enables the Jew to prioritize the issues of his life – and to maintain his focus.***

Specific words or phrases found in Romans 2:18
"...being instructed out of the Law."
The Gentile was left to *speculate* about ethics;[142] and not just ethics, but epistemology[143] and ontology[144] as well. Not so the Jew. He was "instructed out of the Law." That's why the Jewish people never produced a Plato or an Aristotle. That's why there were no labyrinthine musings about Prime Movers, First Causes, and a transcendent world of pure archetypes.[145 146]

The Jew was able to fall back on the Torah – God's very own self-disclosure. There was no need for him to spin out corollaries from supposed self-evident, a priori postulates – which, in the end, have always proven to be rootless and without foundation – leaving the Gentile disoriented, confused, bewildered, cynical, and despairing.

Cynicism and despair – it's a mind-set that permeated the Roman Empire at the end of 2nd Century AD – and which led to its loss of confidence and paralysis in 3rd and 4th Centuries – and to its collapse early in the 5th Century![147] And it's a mind-set that once again grips the entire Gentile world[148] – now crossing the threshold into the 21st Century.

In short, the Jew is freed from all the vacuous speculation, conjecture, and musing that has always plagued the Gentile – and the enervating uncertainty and ennui[149] that has so often followed in its wake. The meaning the Jew is able to lend to his life and the focus he's able to sustain are rooted in the certainty of God's Word.

Verses:

Rom. 2:19	and are confident that you yourself are a guide to the blind, a light to those who are in darkness,
Rom. 2:20	a corrector of the foolish, a teacher of the immature, having in the Law the embodiment of knowledge and of the truth,

Verse 18 has sketched out the advantages God's self-disclosure confers upon the Jew.

Verses 19 and 20 turn now to the responsibility that self-disclosure imposes. The Jew is called upon to be God's *witness* – and, in so doing, to bless the Gentile.

Isaiah 2:3 and Micah 4:2 convey the sense of the Jew's responsibility – the form his *witness* was meant to assume.

Isaiah 2:3	Many people (i.e., the Gentiles) shall come and say, "Come, and let us go up to the mountain of the Lord, to the house of the God of Jacob; He will teach us His ways, and we shall walk in His paths." For out of Zion shall go forth the law, and the word of the Lord from Jerusalem.
Micah 4:2	Many nations (i.e., the Gentiles) shall

> come and say, "Come, and let us go up to the mountain of the Lord, to the house of the God of Jacob; He will teach us His ways, And we shall walk in His paths." For out of Zion the law shall go forth, and the word of the Lord from Jerusalem.

More specifically, the Jew was meant to be a...

- guide to the blind
- a light to those in darkness
- a corrector of the foolish
- a teacher of the immature

Romans 2:19-20, then, defines the relationship between Jew and Gentile: *the Jew has been charged with the responsibility of compassionately ministering to the Gentile's needs.*

The Relationship between Jew and Gentile

The Gentile is blind.	The Jew has been charged with the responsibility of being his guide.
The Gentile gropes about in darkness.	The Jew has been charged with the responsibility of bringing him into the light.
The Gentile is foolish.	The Jew has been charged with the responsibility of reproving his foolishness and teaching him God's wisdom.
The Gentile is immature.	The Jew has been charged with the responsibility of leading the Gentile into maturity.

There is no suggestion here of the Jew's intrinsic superiority. Only of the Jew's responsibility in light of the undeserved advantage God's Law has conferred upon him. In fact, Moses made it a point to remind the Jew that God's choice of him was not based upon merit, but upon grace.

Deut. 7:7 The Lord did not set his love upon you, nor choose you, because you were more in number[150] than any people; for you were the fewest of all people:

Deut. 7:8 But because the Lord loved you, and because he would keep the oath which he had sworn unto your fathers, hath the Lord brought you out with a mighty hand, and redeemed you out of the house of bondmen, from the hand of Pharaoh king of Egypt.

God has graciously blessed the Jew; and the Jew is now called upon to graciously bless the Gentile.

Specific words or phrases found in Romans 2:19-20

"... guide to the blind..."

The Jew, blessed by God with the Law and the Prophets, was meant to compassionately intercede before God in behalf of the Gentile who, without the Law and the Prophets, was bereft of sight.

"... a light to those in darkness..."
And because the Gentile was bereft of sight, he was left to grope, hopelessly and helplessly, about in the darkness – a prey to the devil and his minions whose realm is that very darkness.[151] The Jew, graciously afforded the light of God's Law, was charged with the responsibility of bearing that light to the Gentile – of becoming, in a sense, that light himself.

"... a corrector of the foolish..."
The word "foolish" carries us back to Romans 1:21-22.

Rom. 1:21	...because, although they knew God, they did not glorify Him as God, nor were thankful, but became futile in their thoughts, and their *foolish* hearts were darkened.
Rom. 1:22	Professing to be wise, *they became fools...*

The Gentile's futile search for wisdom apart from God's self-disclosure – his implacable refusal to acknowledge God and glorify him - has transformed him into a fool – and not just a fool, but a quintessential fool – because he has compounded his foolishness by wrapping it in vain sophistries.

"... a teacher of the immature..."
The Greek word translated "immature" means much more than merely "childishness." Its meaning is linked to the Greek word "telos" – a word used extensively by Aristotle and transformed by him into a philosophical principle that was "common coin" throughout the Hellenic world – including Palestine[152] – at the time of both Jesus and Paul. The gist of its definition is "foreordained purpose" – and perhaps the one word in English that most closely reflects its meaning is "destiny." Mankind, like all phenomena, is possessed of a "telos"[153] – and each single individual is impregnated with it.[154] However, there's no guarantee that any single individual will manage to conform his life to it – especially if he's unaware of what it is – if he can't define it;[155] and to the extent that he fails, he's *immature*, meaning...

- he has fallen short of his purpose, i.e., his telos;
- he doesn't measure up to it; and, consequently,
- his life is pointless and futile.

That's what Paul is getting at here. The Law defines for the Jew mankind's preordained "telos" – and, in so doing, enables him to attain maturity, thereby lending his life meaning and purpose. And it's now the Jew's responsibility to convey that same knowledge to the Gentile – permitting the Gentile, like the Jew, to reach maturity, thereby lending his life meaning and purpose as well.

"... having in the Law the embodiment of knowledge and of the truth."
Paul is merely underscoring a truth he has already highlighted – that the Law is God's directly mediated self-disclosure, which, when fully comprehended, enables mankind to lend meaning and purpose to his life.

Verses:

Rom. 2:21	you, therefore, who teach another, do you not teach yourself? You who preach that one should not steal, do you steal?
Rom. 2:22	You who say that one should not commit adultery, do you commit adultery? You who abhor idols, do you rob temples?[156]

Romans 2:21-22 shouldn't catch anybody by surprise; it's merely a follow-up on what Paul has already pointed out in Romans 2:1...to wit, that all men are hypocrites[157] – with, of course, the exception of the flagrant sinners Paul describes in Romans 1:28-32.

Rom. 2:1	Therefore you are inexcusable, Oh man, whoever you are who judges, for in whatever you judge another you condemn yourself; for you who judge do the same things...

Paul is merely applying the principles he delineated in Romans 2:1-16 to the specific case of the Jew here in Romans 2:21-22. That's all; nothing more. Why? Once again, it's because the Jew can't seem to connect the dots. The very privileges God so graciously afforded him, instead of prompting humility and a resolve to share God's grace, prompted pride - and so blinded him.[158]

Verses:

Rom. 2:23	You who boast in the Law, through your breaking the Law, do you dishonor God?
Rom. 2:24	For "the name of God is blasphemed

> among the Gentiles because of you,"
> just as it is written.

Paul now goes on to construct a syllogism[159] in verses 23 and 24 arising from the hypocrisy he underscored in verses 21 and 22:

- Major Premise: Anyone who boasts in the Law, but who nevertheless transgresses the Law, dishonors God.
- Minor Premise: The Jew boasts in the Law, but nevertheless transgresses the Law.
- Logical Inference: The Jew dishonors God.

And, tragically, it's among the Gentiles that God is dishonored – the very persons to whom the Jew is meant to bear the light of God's glory.

The principle that's delineated here in verses 23 and 24 is true of all teachers. If a teacher can't walk-out the precepts he's teaching, he dishonors both

- those very precepts, and
- whomever or whatever those precepts are founded upon and are meant to reveal.

It's critically important, therefore, for teachers to be honest with themselves:

> "Am I living out the message I'm teaching? Am I a living embodiment of that message? If not, my teaching will cast ridicule and contempt on it."

It's a grave responsibility that teachers bear. And it's this very truth that underlies James' admonition in the third chapter of his epistle:

James 3:1	My brethren, let not many of you become teachers, *knowing that we shall receive a stricter judgment*.

Verse:

Rom. 2:25	For indeed circumcision is of value, if you practice the Law; but if you are a transgressor of the Law, your circumcision has become uncircumcision.
Rom. 2:26	If therefore the uncircumcised man keeps the requirements of the Law, will not his uncircumcision be regarded as circumcision?

Here in verses 25 and 26, Paul is taking up the Jew's insistent claim that his circumcision is tantamount to justification.[160] He proves that it's illogical – *and because it's illogical, it's spurious as well*. Why? Because within the framework of Romans 1:18b through Romans 3:20 it leads *necessarily* to the conclusion that *the Jew must be a lawkeeper – and obviously he's not*. The argument is simple and straightforward – and its proof is readily apparent using the simplest principles of deductive logic.[161]

- The Jew claims that circumcision secures his justification before the bar of God's holy justice; that, in short, circumcision is tantamount to justification.
- Paul, however, with painstaking care, has defined[162] the basic nature of God's sovereign jurisprudence – that was the whole thrust of his argument from Romans 2:2 through Romans 2:16. And the gist of it is very simple: anyone wishing to base his justification on his own merits – apart from God's mercy – must submit his deeds to God's evaluation and secure God's approbation. The criterion God uses for his evaluation is the truth – and that truth is both codified and embodied in the Law. Hence, anyone basing his justification on his own merits must necessarily be a "lawkeeper."
- Therefore, when the Jew insists that his circumcision is tantamount to justification, he is *necessarily* asserting that he is a lawkeeper. And if he isn't a lawkeeper, his circumcision is meaningless.[163] The proof is simple:

  - A = circumcision
  - B = justification
  - C = lawkeeping

...then

- if A = B; (the Jew's claim)
- and if B = C; (Paul's argument in Romans 2:2-16)
- then A = C meaning the Jew is necessarily a lawkeeper.

Therefore, if he's *not* a lawkeeper, his circumcision is null and void – exactly what Paul asserts in verse 25.

Rom. 2:25	... if you are a transgressor of the

Law, your circumcision has become uncircumcision.

Furthermore, if the Gentile *is* a lawkeeper, then, ipso facto, he is circumcised – which is exactly what Paul avers in verse 26.

Rom. 2:26 If therefore the uncircumcised man keeps the requirements of the Law, will not his uncircumcision be regarded as circumcision?

Why? Because the *converse* of "every circumcised person is a lawkeeper" is "every lawkeeper is circumcised." *And a converse is always implied in the case of a universal affirmative sentence the subject and predicate of which are equivalent.* Paul, as it turns out, is a stellar logician.

DRAWING OUT THE IMPLICATIONS OF THE SENTENCE "EVERY CIRCUMCISED PERSON IS A LAWKEEPER" USING THE PRINCIPLES OF DEDUCTIVE LOGIC

Definitions:

A = Circumcison
Non-A = Uncircumcision
C = Law-keeper
Non-C = Law-breaker

Sentence to be Analyzed	**Kind of Sentence**
Every circumcised person is a lawkeeper.	A universal affirmative sentence the subject and predicate of which are equivalent

The Rule* and its Application	The Artificial Language	The Specific Logical Implication
The ***converse*** – always implied in the case of a universal affirmative sentence the subject and predicate of which are equivalent.	Every C is an A	***Every lawkeeper is circumcised.*** This is the implication Paul draws out in verse 26.
The ***contrapositive*** – always implied in the case of any universal affirmative sentence.	Every non-C is a non-A	***Every lawbreaker is uncircumcised.*** This is the implication Paul draws out in verse 25.
The ***obverse*** – always implied in the case of any universal affirmative sentence.	Every A is not a non-C	***Every circumcised person is not a lawbreaker.*** This too is an implication Paul draws out in verse 25.

* Note: A "rule" in formal logic is the "operational" part of a deductive system that enables us to analyze the semantic features of a particular sentence or series of sentences; it's especially helpful in determining valid inferences.

Verse:

Rom. 2:27 And will not he who is physically uncircumcised, if he keeps the Law, will he not judge you who though having the letter of the Law and circumcision are a transgressor of the Law?

Paul has now backed the Jew into a corner; and verse 27 is his "coup de grâce" – his master stroke – which he delivers with obvious glee – pointing out that the Gentile, if he is a lawkeeper,[164] and, therefore, circumcised, will judge the Jew who is not a lawkeeper and whose circumcision is therefore null and void.[165] Why? Because the circumcised always judges the uncircumcised. Imagine! The Gentile judging the Jew! Nothing could be more humiliating and offensive to the Jew.

It's important, however, to bear in mind that verse 27 is rhetorical only. It's no more possible for the Gentile to "keep the law" than the Jew. Paul's purpose here is to awaken the Jew – to rouse him from his complacency; and he's not too concerned about the means he uses to do that – whether it's a gentle prod or the biting prick of sarcasm.

Verse:

Rom. 2:28 For he is not a Jew who is one outwardly; neither is circumcision that which is outward in the flesh.

Rom. 2:29 But he is a Jew who is one inwardly; and circumcision is that which is of the heart, by the Spirit, not by the letter; and his praise is not from men, but from God.

Here we have Paul's conclusion – and it's a truth we all need to be reminded of again and again: means shouldn't be confused with ends. Circumcision is merely a means of eliciting the Jew's attention – of pointing him toward what really matters to God – and that's a heart circumcised by the Spirit of God – a heart that has been "cut free" from sin[166] – a heart that can't be turned aside to sin. Why? Because it's within a circumcised heart that fellowship with God is established. That's the meaning underlying Deuteronomy 6:4-5 – what every observant Jew recites to himself day in and day out – the very essence of the Law.

Deut. 6:4 Hear, O Israel: The Lord our God, the Lord is one!

Deut. 6:5 You shall love the Lord your God with all your heart, with all your soul, and with all your strength.

Moses himself was well aware of the Jew's tendency to confuse means and ends[167] – of making the rite of circumcision significant in and of itself – which is why he warned the Jews to keep in mind its real meaning – that it's a matter of the heart – that its meaning is found there.

Deut. 10:16 Circumcise therefore the foreskin of your heart, and be no more stiff-necked.

Deut. 30:6 And the Lord thy God will circumcise thy heart, and the heart of thy seed, to love Jehovah thy God with all thy heart, and with all thy soul, that you may live.

And notice too that in Deuteronomy 30:6 Moses makes it clear that it's God alone who can circumcise the Jew's heart – a truth confirmed by the prophets as well.

Ezek. 36:26 A new heart also will I (i.e., God) give you, and a new spirit will I put within you: and I will take away the stony heart out of your flesh, and I will give you an heart of flesh.

Ezek. 36:27 And I will put my spirit within you, and cause you to walk in my statutes, and ye shall keep my judgments, and do them.

The question, then, concerning justification, isn't...

- "Have I undergone the rite of circumcision?" but, rather
- "Is my heart wholly turned toward God?" – which, of course, is the real meaning of circumcision.

Paul has proven that physical circumcision does not confirm justification; that it does not put the Jew at an advantage before the bar of God's holy justice. The question then arises: "Then what advantage does circumcision confer?" Or, more to the point: "What advantage does Jewish ethnicity confer?" And that's exactly the question Paul poses in Romans 3:1.

Calvin on the Ropes

Verse:

Rom. 3:1	Then what advantage has the Jew? Or what is the benefit of circumcision?

And Paul's answer is found in the very next verse, verse 2.

Verse:

Rom. 3:2	Great in every respect. First of all, that they were entrusted with the oracles of God.

The point here is that though circumcision, which is the mark of Jewish ethnicity, confers no advantage on the Jew at the Judgment Seat of God, it confers numerous other advantages – the most obvious of which are the "oracles of God" – meaning Scripture – the Law and the Prophets. And that advantage is very weighty - very substantial – very significant.

Paul doesn't spell out the nature of that advantage in the verses which follow – probably because he has already spelled it out – especially in Romans 2:18-20.

1. The Law enables the Jew to know God's will (verse 18) – making it possible for him to lend meaning and certainty to his life.

2. The Law enables the Jew to distinguish what's important and central about life from what's inconsequential and peripheral (verse 18) – making it possible for him to prioritize the issues of his life – and to maintain his focus.

3. The Law defines the relationship between Jew and Gentile (verses 19-20)...

The Gentile is blind	The Jew has been charged with the responsibility of being his guide.
The gentile grops about in darkness	The Jew has been charged with the responsibility of bringing him into the light.
The gentile is foolish	The Jew has been charged with the responsibility of reproving his foolishness and teaching him God's wisdom
The gentile is immature	The Jew has been charged with the responsibility of leading him to maturity.

... clearly establishing the Jew's priority vis-à-vis the Gentile.

In addition, the Law – meaning the entire body of Hebrew Scripture – discloses God's covenants – which reveal that the Jews are God's special treasure...

Deut. 7:6	For you are a holy people to the Lord your God; the Lord your God has chosen you to be a people for Himself, a special treasure above all the peoples on the face of the earth.
Psalm 135:4	For the Lord has chosen Jacob for Himself, Israel for His special treasure.

... the medium through which he has chosen to reveal his salvation (Romans 3:21).

It was a Jewish ethnicity that clothed Jesus Christ - and it was Jewish culture which served as the backdrop against which Christ preached the gospel.

Galatians 3:23-25 tells us that the Law is our schoolmaster assigned the task of leading us to Christ – of pointing him out – that we might be justified by faith...

Gal. 3:23	But before faith came, we were kept in ward under the law, shut up unto the faith which should afterwards be revealed.
Gal. 3:24	So that the law is become our schoolmaster to bring us unto Christ, that we might be justified by faith.
Gal. 3:25	But now faith that is come, we are no longer under a schoolmaster.

The Law is the very embodiment of knowledge and truth (verse 20). And it is a uniquely Jewish possession – a trust God has vouchsafed only to the Jew.

But the Jew, Paul declares, has not proven faithful to that trust.

Connection to Romans 9-11

Here → **Romans 9-11**

The question then arises, as it does later in Romans 9, *"Does the Jew's unfaithfulness – his infidelity – nullify the faithfulness of God?"* In short, does it void God's covenant with him, specifically, the Abrahamic Covenant which made the Jew God's special treasure – thereby conferring upon him the honor and privilege of having the "oracles of God" entrusted to his care?

And that's the very question Paul poses in verse 3...

Verse:

Rom. 3:3	What then? If some did not believe, their unbelief[168] (i.e., their unfaithfulness) will not nullify the faithfulness of God, will it?

And his answer is found in verse 4. It's the very same answer he gives later in Romans 9. *Absolutely not!*

Verse:

Rom. 3:4	May it never be! Rather, let God be found true, though every man be found a liar, as it is written, "That Thou mightest be justified in Thy words, And mightest prevail when Thou art judged."

Specific words or phrases found in Romans 3:4
"May it never be!"
The Greek words translated "May it never be!" ("μη γενοιτο") mean not only "Absolutely not!", but convey a sense of moral revulsion as well. In short, the very suggestion is irreverent and impious.

Specific words or phrases found in Romans 3:4
"Rather, let God be found true, though every man be found a liar..."
How much more pointed can Paul possibly be? God's faithfulness is not grounded in man's faithfulness. The one, man's faithfulness, does not condition the other, God's faithfulness. That's what Paul is saying here. The very suggestion, Paul tells us, is absurd – and not only absurd, but verges on blasphemy.

- Even if every man alive is found guilty of "breaking his word," God's word stands sure. God will never go back on his word.
- Even if every man alive is found guilty of violating the covenants that bind him to God, nevertheless those very covenants remain in full force and effect. God will never abrogate his covenants.

Psalm 89:30-34 is an inspiring testimony to God's faithfulness – a reminder to the Jewish people that he will never break covenant with them – that his word is immutable – that it stands sure notwithstanding their own frailties and shortcomings – their own sinfulness and the fickle, erratic, and capricious nature of their own word.

Psalm 89:30	If his sons forsake My law And do not walk in My judgments,
Psalm 89:31	If they break My statutes And do not keep My commandments,
Psalm 89:32	Then I will punish their transgression with the rod, And their iniquity with stripes.
Psalm 89:33	Nevertheless My lovingkindness I will not utterly take from him, Nor allow My faithfulness to fail.
Psalm 89:34	My covenant I will not break, Nor alter the word that has gone out of My lips.

Specific words or phrases found in Romans 3:4
That Thou mightest be justified in Thy words, and mightest prevail when Thou art judged.
The sentence here is a quote taken from Psalm 51 – and at first glance it's not at all clear why Paul is using it. How does it support Paul's contention that God's faithfulness is not affected by man's unfaithfulness?

The explanation is actually quite simple. Psalm 51 records David's confession of sin; specifically, his adultery with Bathsheba and his murder of Uriah, Bathsheba's husband.

Psalm 51:3	For I acknowledge my transgressions, and my sin is always before me.
Psalm 51:4	Against You, You only, have I sinned, And done this evil in Your sight – that You may be found just when You speak, And blameless when You judge.

David is acknowledging that God's judgment and condemnation is not only deserved, but necessary – because it upholds God's righteousness and underscores his holiness. In short, God's condemnation of sin and the punishment that follows in its wake affirms his righteousness. And that's the truth Paul is adducing here.

Paul is saying that the Jew's faithlessness (i.e., his sin) neither caught God off guard nor "put him behind the eight-ball." Indeed, it merely provided him an opportunity to display his own righteousness[169] – to render it all the more visible and obvious and its glory all the more astonishing.

Verse:

Rom. 3:5	But if our unrighteousness demonstrates the righteousness of God, what shall we say? The God who inflicts wrath is not unrighteous, is He? (I am speaking in human terms.)

Verse four tells us that the condemnation of man's sin displays God's righteousness. Verse five, however, devises a subtle twist and then slips it in through backdoor – that man's sin displays God's righteousness. Not the condemnation of man's sin, but man's sin alone! And that subtle twist – which is barely noticeable – leads to all the mischief described in verses 5 – 8 – because if man's sin displays God's righteousness, why would God want to judge it? And, in a sense, wouldn't judging it make God unrighteous?

Verse:

Rom. 3:6	May it never be! For otherwise how will God judge the world?

Once again, the exclamation "May it never be!" ("μη γενοιτο"), means more than merely "Absolutely not!;" it conveys a sense of moral revulsion as well. In other words, the principle delineated in verse five – that man's sin displays God's righteousness – is not only intellectually indefensible, it's also morally indefensible. Why? Because it leads to an infinite regress that permits sin to run rampant.

The Infinite Regress Delineated in Verse 5

Man's sin displays God's righteousness; therefore man should continue to sin in order to display more of God's righteousness – producing still more sin – that displays still more of God's righteousness – ad infinitum – or, perhaps better put, ad nauseam.

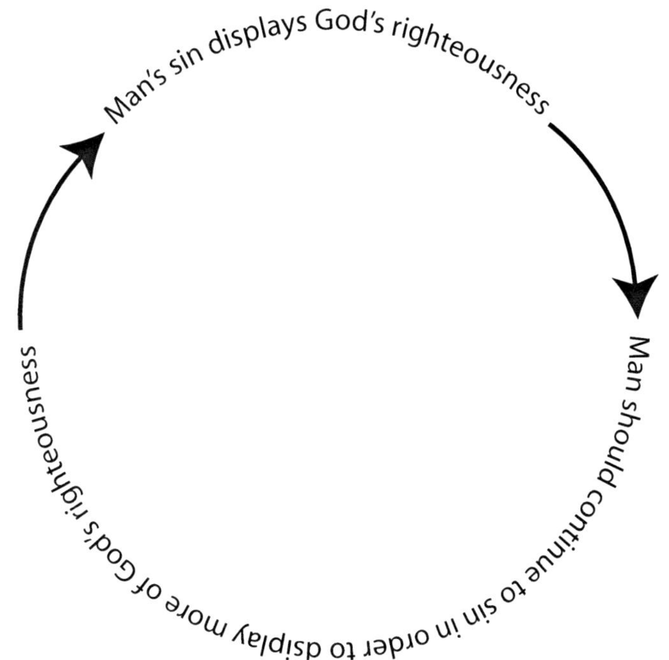

Verses:

Rom. 3:7	But if through my lie the truth of God abounded to His glory, why am I also still being judged as a sinner?

In verse five, it was God's own righteousness that was being called into question; specifically, "If man's sin displays God's righteousness, why would God want to condemn sin? And, in a sense, wouldn't its condemnation make God unrighteous?" But here in verse seven, Paul's protagonist[170] shifts the focus of his argument – to what's really on his mind:

his own condemnation. "If my own personal sins display God's righteousness, why would God want to condemn me? After all, my sins serve only to highlight God's holiness." And in verse eight, Paul delineates its ultimate form. "Let's all sin that God's righteousness might be displayed."

Rom. 3:8	And why not say (as we are slanderously reported and as some affirm that we say), Let us do evil that good may come? Their condemnation is just.

The argument is so morally repulsive that Paul simply asserts that anyone buying into it deserves whatever punishment is inflicted on him. But it's not that Paul is skirting the question – simply passing over the argument spelled out here because it's so reprehensible – which is what some expositors suggest. He has already challenged it and laid it to rest – back in verse four when he pointed out that it's not man's sin that displays God's righteousness, but the condemnation of man's sin. Again, all the mischief described in verses 5-8 arises from that subtle twist.

Verse:

Rom. 3:9	What then? Are we better than they? Not altogether;[171] for we have already charged that both Jews and Greeks are all under sin;

Specific words or phrases found in Romans 3:9
"Are we better than they"
Clearly, the "we" here in verse 9 means "we Jews." It's also clear that the word "better" means "better advantaged." Finally, the "they" are obviously the Greeks – i.e., the Gentiles.

Specific words or phrases found in Romans 3:9
"not all together"
Most English versions of the Bible, including the New King James Version, translate "Ου παντως" "Not at all." Cranfield, however, suggests that the better translation is "Not wholly" or "Not altogether" – which, he asserts, is the normal translation of "Ου παντως." "Παντως ου," not "Ου παντως" is properly rendered "Not at all." Furthermore, Cranfield insists, the context itself suggests that "Not altogether" is the better translation.

Exposition
Romans 3:3 through 3:8 is, of course, a parenthetical section that examines the issue of God's righteousness and mankind's sinfulness. Therefore, in expositing Romans 3:9, it's helpful to omit verses 3 – 8 and simply read verse 9 as if it followed verses 1 and 2.

Rom. 3:1	What advantage then has the Jew, or what is the profit of circumcision?
Rom. 3:2	Much in every way! Chiefly because to them were committed the oracles of God.
Rom. 3:9	What then? Are we (i.e., the Jews) better (i.e., better advantaged) than they (i.e., the Gentiles)? Not all together. For we have previously charged both Jews and Greeks that they are all under sin.

The question is asked in Romans 3:1, "What advantages does a Jewish ethnicity confer?" In the next verse, verse two, Paul responds emphatically; and the exact wording seems to admit of no exceptions – that every possible advantage has been bestowed – that no advantages whatsoever have been omitted:

> "Πολυ κατα παντα τροπον"
> – meaning "Much in every way."

Clearly, however, Paul does not mean to be taken literally; after all, that would be inconsistent with his argument in both...
- Romans 2:2-16 – that God's judgment is wholly impartial – and in
- Romans 2:17-29 – that Jewish ethnicity confers no advantage whatsoever at the judgment seat of God.

Romans 2:11 is especially pointed:

Rom. 2:11	...for there is no partiality with God.

meaning...
- The same criterion will be used for both Jew and Gentile: the truth;
- the same focus: concrete, existential deeds; and, lastly,
- the same recompense:
- eternal life, glory, honor, immortality and peace to those whose deeds are deemed "good;" and
- indignation, wrath, tribulation, and anguish to those whose deeds are deemed "evil."

Paul's answer in Romans 3:2 was configured for emphasis, not for technical precision. He wanted to make certain that no one might be tempted to call into question the priority of the Jews – that, in short, the gospel does not undermine that priority. Here now, in verse nine, the issue at hand is indeed technical precision. "Yes," Paul is saying, "the Jew enjoys advantages that are beyond the reach of the Gentile, but he can boast of no advantage at the judgment seat of God. There, Jew and Gentile are on an equal footing; and, what's more, both stand utterly condemned."

Paul's Long Digression Is Ending

Paul has all but completed his long digression beginning back at Romans 1:18b.

Paul's Long Digression Is Ending

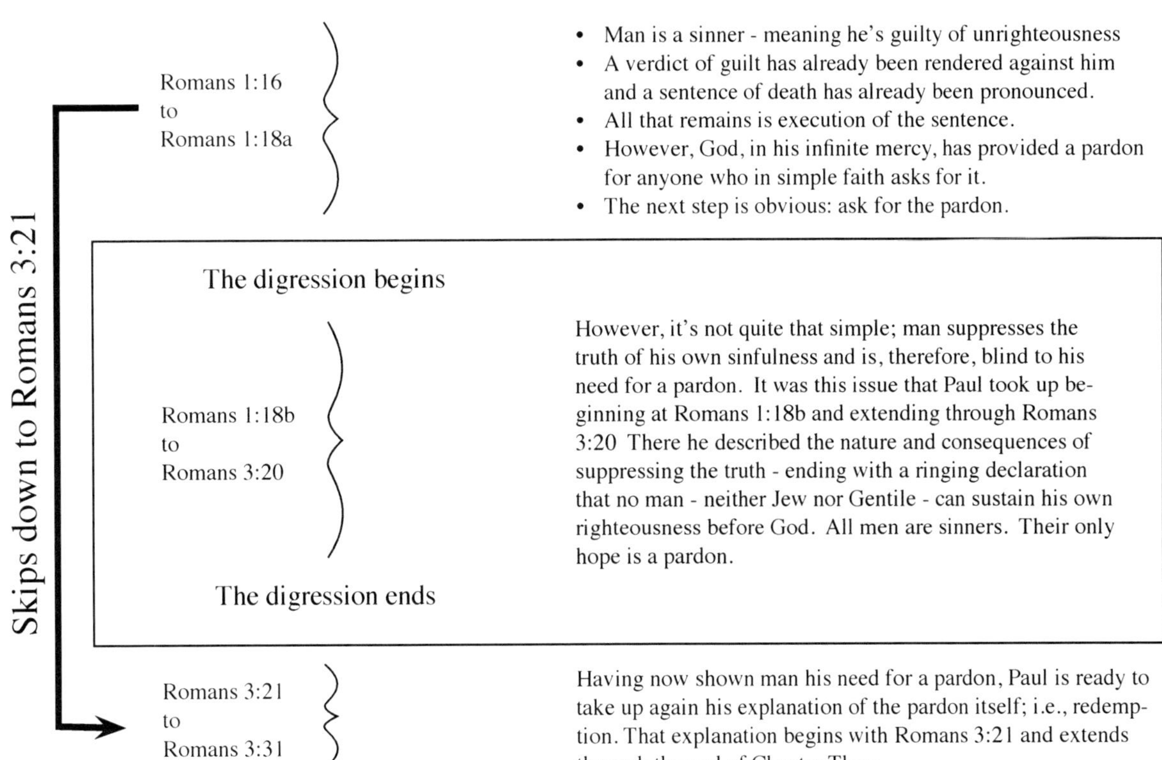

Romans 3:9, though it's the beginning of the end of Paul's long digression, is not quite the end itself. Verses 10-18 catalogue a series of Old Testament passages confirming the conclusion Paul records in verse 9; specifically, "...that both Jews and Greeks are all under sin..." And then verses 19 and 20 provide both

- a final, climatic summation; and
- a set-up for Paul's account of justification – beginning with Romans 3:21 and ending with Romans 3:31.

Verse:

Rom. 3:10	as it is written, There is none righteous, not even one;
Rom. 3:11	There is none who understands, There is none who seeks for God;
Rom. 3:12	All have turned aside, together they have become useless; There is none who does good, There is not even one.

Verses 10-12 paraphrase portions of the Septuagint's version[172] of Psalm 14:1-3.

Psalm 14:1	The fool has said in his heart, "There is no God." They are corrupt, they have done abominable works, there is none who does good.

Psalm 14:2 The Lord looks down from heaven upon the children of men, to see if there are any who understand, who seek God.
Psalm 14:3 They have all turned aside, they have together become corrupt; there is none who does good, no, not one.

Psalm 14 is frequently misunderstood. The whole psalm describes the mind-set and behavior of a fool. It's not merely that a fool denies the existence of God, which is the meaning most commonly suggested; it's that...

- he is also corrupt;
- his behavior is abominable;
- his mind is vacuous;
- he has turned aside from the pursuit of God; etc.

In short, Paul is saying that all men are fools – that's what their sinfulness proves. Only fools are drawn away into sin. It's the very same point Paul made back in Romans 1:21-22.

Romans 1:21 ...because, although they knew God, they did not glorify Him as God, nor were thankful, but became futile in their thoughts, and their foolish hearts were darkened.
Romans 1:22 Professing to be wise, they became fools...

And it's not simply that sin has transformed man into a fool, it's that it has also rendered him useless and, therefore, worthless – which is the truth Paul underscores in Romans 3:12.

Rom. 3:12 All have turned aside, together they have become useless; There is none who does good, There is not even one.

Man's life is devoid of meaning and purpose; he has lost the intrinsic value God originally imparted to him. He's fit only for the scrap heap. That's what sin has done to him. Two passages from Shakespeare – one from *Macbeth* and the other from *Richard II* – put it well. The passage taken from *Macbeth* is more general in nature – and is meant to reflect the sense of futility that pervades all mankind regardless of position or rank. The one drawn from *Richard II* tells us that even kings and potentates are plagued by a terrifying sense of mortality and ennui – that their status does not render them immune to it.

****

Macbeth

Tomorrow, and tomorrow, and tomorrow
Creeps in this petty pace from day to day
To the last syllable of recorded time,
And all our yesterdays have lighted fools
The way to dusty death. Out, out, brief candle,
Life's but a walking shadow, a poor player
That struts and frets his hour upon the stage
And then is heard no more. It is a tale
Told by an idiot, full of sound and fury,
Signifying nothing.

Shakespeare's Macbeth
Act 5, scene 5

Richard II

... For within the hollow crown
That rounds the mortal temples of a King
Keeps Death his court; and there the antic sits,
Scoffing his state and grinning at his pomp,
Allowing him a breath, a little scene,
To monarchize, be feared, and kill with looks,
Infusing him with self and vain conceit,
As if this flesh which walls about our life
Were brass impregnable; and humored thus,
Comes at the last, and with a little pin
Bores through his castle wall; and farewell king.

Shakespeare's Richard II
Act 3, scene 2

****

It's this very sense of futility and aimlessness that's depicted in the Purification Offering[173] we examined back in Chapter Three. Sin defiles a man – meaning it renders him useless – it puts him outside the pale of God's purposes.

Verse:

Rom. 3:13 Their throat is an open grave, with

	their tongues they keep deceiving, the poison of asps is under their lips;
Rom. 3:14	Whose mouth is full of cursing and bitterness;

The first two lines of Romans 3:13 paraphrase the 2nd half of Psalm 5:9.

Psalm 5:9	For there is no faithfulness in their mouth; Their inward part is destruction; Their throat is an open tomb; they flatter with their tongue.

The last line of Romans 3:13 quotes Psalm 140:3, which like Psalm 14, is a psalm attributed to David.

Psalm 140:1	Deliver me, O Lord, from evil men; preserve me from violent men,
Psalm 140:2	Who plan evil things in their hearts; they continually gather together for war.
Psalm 140:3	They sharpen their tongues like a serpent; the poison of asps is under their lips. Selah.

Romans 3:14 quotes the 1st half of Psalm 10:7.

Psalm 10:7	His mouth is full of cursing and deceit and oppression; Under his tongue is trouble and iniquity.

Paul's focus here in Romans 3:13-14 is obviously centered upon speech – which is why the lips, tongue, throat, and mouth are all depicted. And its description is horrendous: deceit, poison, cursing, and bitterness – that's what permeates all human discourse. Why? Because the mouth – which here is meant to be a composite of the lips, tongue, and throat – opens to a grave – which, of course, is always filled with death and corruption. Clearly the word "grave" is meant to be a metaphor of the human heart. The human heart is thoroughly corrupted; therefore, it's quite inevitable, Paul is saying, that human discourse reflects that corruption. The truth Paul is conveying here is no different from what Jesus himself declares in Matthew 12:34.

Mt 12:34	O generation of vipers, how can you, being evil, speak good things? for out of the abundance of the heart the mouth speaks.

Jesus is telling us that what we say springs from our heart – meaning it reflects the condition of our heart.

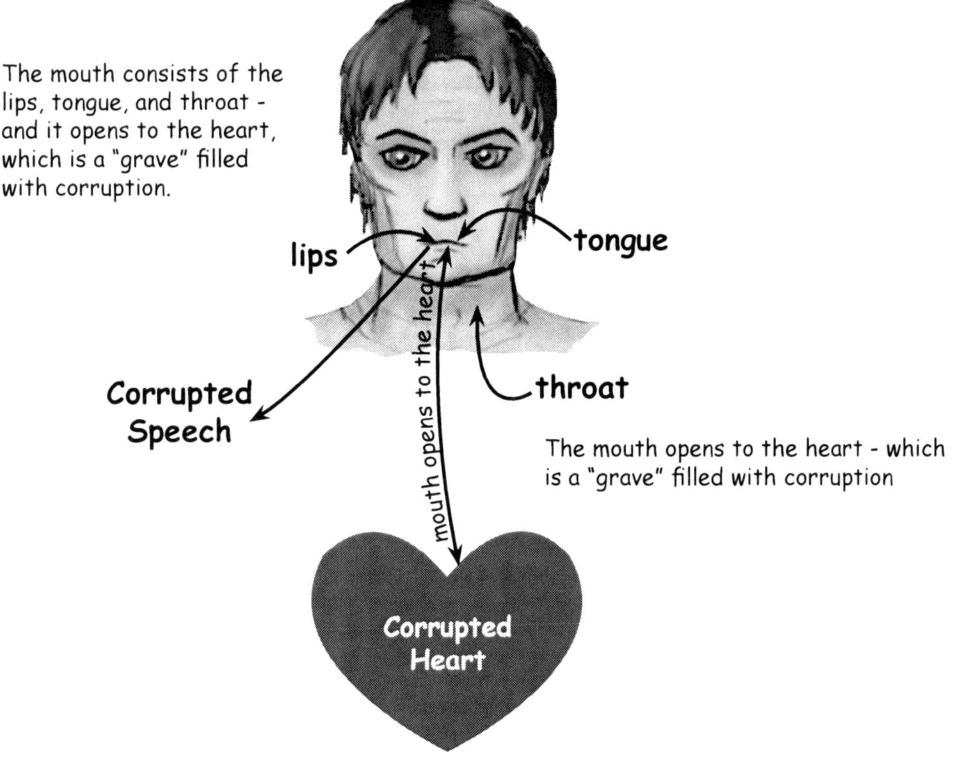

A corrupt heart produces corrupt speech.

Given the sinful condition that plagues all mankind, even apparently edifying or benign speech is, at some level, self-serving and, therefore, pervaded with deceit and wickedness.

What we hear is corrupted as well

But there's more: a little thought leads us to conclude that...

- it's not just what we say that's corrupted, it's what we hear as well;
- it's not just how we speak; it's how we listen.

Why? Because human communication is a relationship - consisting of *both* what we say and what we hear.

What we say / What we hear

The Tenuous Nature of Community

That makes community a very "iffy" proposition, doesn't it? Community, by its very definition, is built around talking and listening – meaning...

- discussion,
- dialogue,
- conversation,
- discourse.

Discourse is what connects us to one another; it's what binds us together; it's what links person to person to form friendships, marriages, families, clans, nations, etc. But if discourse has been corrupted by a sinful heart, it's just as apt to tear down community as build it up. Instead of encouraging one another, we slander one another; we're drawn into destructive gossip; we engage in rumor mongering – all of which undermine community.

And even when we try to speak the truth – even when we try to listen with an unbiased mind and heart, misunderstanding inevitably arises. We reach out for one another, momentarily touch, and then slip away.

Paul now shifts his focus from what man says to what he does.

Verse:

Rom. 3:15	Their feet are swift to shed blood,
Rom. 3:16	Destruction and misery are in their paths,
Rom. 3:17	And the path of peace have they not known.
Rom. 3:18	There is no fear of God before their eyes.

Romans 3:15-17 paraphrases Isaiah 59:7-8.

Isaiah 59:7	Their feet run to evil, And they make haste to shed innocent blood; Their thoughts are thoughts of iniquity; Wasting and destruction are in their paths.
Isaiah 59:8	The way of peace they have not known, And there is no justice in their ways; They have made themselves crooked paths; Whoever takes that way shall not know peace.

And verse 18 quotes Psalm 36:1b.

Psalm 36:1	An oracle within my heart concerning the transgression of the wicked: There is no fear of God before his eyes.

The point here is very straightforward: whatever man does leads eventually to desolation; and wherever man goes, ruin and misery follow in his wake. And why? Because the fear of God isn't set before his eyes; the fear of God doesn't govern his life. In short, when "push comes to shove," God doesn't count; God is unimportant. However much man might intellectually acknowledge God, God is ignored whenever and wherever the "rubber meets the road." Man goes...

- where his lusts direct him;
- where his ambitions direct him;
- where his greed directs him;
- where his misplaced loyalties direct him.

And it's not just obvious sin that Paul has in mind here; clearly he means to include apparently benign priorities as well – job, family, etc.

God alone is meant to be mankind's gyroscope – his lodestar. The prophet Jeremiah puts it well.

Jer. 10:23	O Lord, I know that the way of man is not in himself: it is not in man who walks to direct his steps.

In other words, only God can lead man into love, joy, and peace. Whatever else we set before our eyes – whatever else we allow to direct our lives – whatever it might be – it will inevitably shipwreck us – leaving us and everyone we touch wretched and miserable.

Matt. 6:31	Therefore take no thought, saying, What shall we eat? or, What shall we drink? or, wherewithal shall we be clothed?
Matt. 6:32	(For after all these things do the Gentiles seek:) for your heavenly Father knows that you have need of all these things.
Matt. 6:33	But seek ye first the kingdom of God, and his righteousness; and all these things shall be added unto you.

Romans 3:18 completes Paul's litany of quotations – all of which were drawn from the Old Testament and meant to confirm mankind's sinfulness. And it's altogether fitting for Paul to close with the truth: *man does not fear God.*

Rom. 3:18	There is no fear of God before their eyes.

Why? Because that's the truth Paul opened with in quoting Psalms 14:1 – the theme of which is "the fool has said in his heart, 'there is no God.'"

Psalm 14:1	The fool has said in his heart, "There is no God."

- Romans 3:10, in quoting Psalm 14, tells us that man is a fool; and, likewise,
- Romans 3:18, in declaring that "there is no fear of God before (his) eyes," tells us that man is a fool – since the fear of God is the beginning of wisdom.

Prov. 9:10	The fear of the Lord is the beginning of wisdom: and the knowledge of the holy is understanding.
Job 28:28	And unto man he said, Behold, the fear of the Lord, that is wisdom; and to depart from evil is understanding.

In short, Paul begins in Romans 3:10 with the truth that all men are fools – and, then, closes in Romans 3:18 with the same truth: all men are fools.

Taken all together, Romans 3:10-18 sums up the Old Testament's assessment of mankind's condition ...

- sin has transformed man into a fool;
- his heart is filled with death and corruption;
- what he says, therefore, is likewise permeated with evil and can produce nothing worthwhile or establish any kind of lasting community; and, finally,
- wherever he goes, desolation and gloom invariably follow.
- Why? Once again, because sin has transformed man into a fool – there is no fear of God before his eyes.

Paul is now ready for his climactic summation.

Verse:

Rom. 3:19	Now we know that whatever the Law says, it speaks to those who are under the Law, that every mouth may be closed, and all the world may become accountable to God;
Rom. 3:20	because by the works of the Law no flesh will be justified in His sight; for through the Law comes the knowledge of sin.

Specific words or phrases found in Romans 3:19-20

"Now we know"

Paul is pointing to a premise he believes should be self-evident – a truth for which his readers require no proof.

Specific words or phrases found in Romans 3:19-20

"what the law says"

Clearly what Paul has in mind here are the verses he has just quoted – all of which are drawn from the Old Testamentt.

"What the Law says..."

Rom. 3:10	as it is written, There is none righteous, not even one;
Rom. 3:11	There is none who understands, There is none who seeks for God;
Rom. 3:12	All have turned aside, together they have become useless; There is none who does good, There is not even one.
Rom. 3:13	Their throat is an open grave, with their tongues they keep deceiving, the poison of asps is under their lips;
Rom. 3:14	Whose mouth is full of cursing and bitterness;
Rom. 3:15	Their feet are swift to shed blood,
Rom. 3:16	Destruction and misery are in their paths,
Rom. 3:17	And the path of peace have they not known.
Rom. 3:18	There is no fear of God before their eyes.

Normally, the scope of the word "law" extends only to the Torah – the first five books of the Bible – Genesis, Exodus, Leviticus, Numbers, and Deuteronomy

– often called the Pentateuch. Occasionally, however, its use is intended to include the entire scope of the Old Testament – including not just the Torah, but the prophets, the histories, and the wisdom literature as well (1 Corinthians 14:21; John 10:34; etc.). Its use here, therefore, is not out of place.

Specific words or phrases found in Romans 3:19-20
"it speaks to those who are under the law"
To whom does the Law speak? Clearly, the Jews; because they alone have been made subject to its jurisdiction. It was this very truth that Paul made clear in Romans 2:12.[174]

Rom. 2:12	For as many as have sinned without law shall also perish without law: and as many as have sinned in the law shall be judged by the law;

See pages 134-141 for an exegesis of Romans 2:12-16.

Specific words or phrases found in Romans 3:19-20
"that every mouth may be closed, and all the world may become accountable to God..."
The picture Paul draws here is quite gripping: a defendant at last given an opportunity to speak up in his own defense, but so startled by the evidence the prosecution has amassed against him that he stands mute – unable to say anything, his mouth closed in shame and defeat.

At first glance we seem to have a conflict here:
- on the one hand we're told that law "speaks" only to the Jew – because they alone fall under its jurisdiction;
- on the other hand, however, we're told that all mankind stands condemned, not just the Jew.

The conflict, however, is only apparent. Paul is telling us that in proving guilty the one race that might reasonably presume itself excepted from condemnation, he has necessarily proven that all mankind stands condemned. In short, if the Jew stands condemned, so obviously does the Gentile. What we have, of course, is another one of Paul's syllogisms.

- If the Jew stands condemned, so also does all mankind.
- The Jew stands condemned.
- Therefore all mankind stands condemned.

Specific words or phrases found in Romans 3:19-20
"because by the works of the Law no flesh will be justified in His sight..."
Romans 3:20 brings us back to Romans 3:9 and restates it: all mankind – both Jew and Gentile – stands helplessly condemned before the bar of God's holy justice – every hope of earning the approbation of God utterly dashed.

In Romans 3:20 we have Paul's second use of the word "justify." His first use of it was back in Romans 2:13 – where he declared that it's not the hearers of the law who will be justified, but the doers of the law. But here Paul is telling us quite categorically that there are no doers of the law. No one can truthfully claim that he's a doer of the Law and has, consequently, escaped its condemnation; and that clearly leaves us all – both Jew and Gentile – in jeopardy of God's wrath.

Specific words or phrases found in Romans 3:19-20
"for through the Law comes the knowledge of sin."
The word "for" introduces an adverbial clause that tells us why we can't use the law to justify ourselves: because that was never its purpose. It was meant only to show man his helpless plight – that he stands utterly condemned before the bar of God's holy justice; and is, therefore, in desperate need of mercy.

Romans 5:20 declares the same truth – that the law is meant to reveal mankind's sinfulness and, therefore, his condemnation.

Rom. 5:20	And the Law came in that the transgression might increase (i.e., might be made ever more obvious)...

As does Romans 7:7...

Rom. 7:7	What shall we say then? Is the Law sin? May it never be! On the contrary, I would not have come to know sin except through the Law; for I would not have known about coveting if the Law had not said, You shall not covet.

As does Galatians 3:24...

Gal. 3:24	So that the law is become our schoolmaster to bring us unto Christ, that we might be justified by faith.	In other words, the law is meant to point us to Christ - and God's gift of forgiveness found in Christ – amazing grace, free and totally unmerited.

CHAPTER EIGHT

Verses for Chapter Eight

Rom. 3:21	But now the righteousness of God apart from the law has been manifested, being witnessed by the Law and the Prophets,
Rom. 3:22	even the righteousness of God, through faith in Jesus Christ, to all and on all who believe. For there is no difference;
Rom. 3:23	for all have sinned and fall short of the glory of God,
Rom. 3:24	being justified freely by His grace through the redemption that is in Christ Jesus,
Rom. 3:25	whom God set forth as a propitiation by His blood, through faith, to demonstrate His righteousness, because in His forbearance God had passed over the sins that were previously committed,
Rom. 3:26	to demonstrate at the present time His righteousness, that He might be just and the justifier of the one who has faith in Jesus.
Rom. 3:27	Where is boasting then? It is excluded. By what law? Of works? No, but by the law of faith.
Rom. 3:28	Therefore we conclude that a man is justified by faith apart from the deeds of the law.
Rom. 3:29	Or is He the God of the Jews only? Is He not also the God of the Gentiles? Yes, of the Gentiles also,
Rom. 3:30	since there is one God who will justify the circumcised by faith and the uncircumcised through faith.
Rom. 3:31	Do we then make void the law

Original Graphic of Paul's Train of Thought

See Page 109

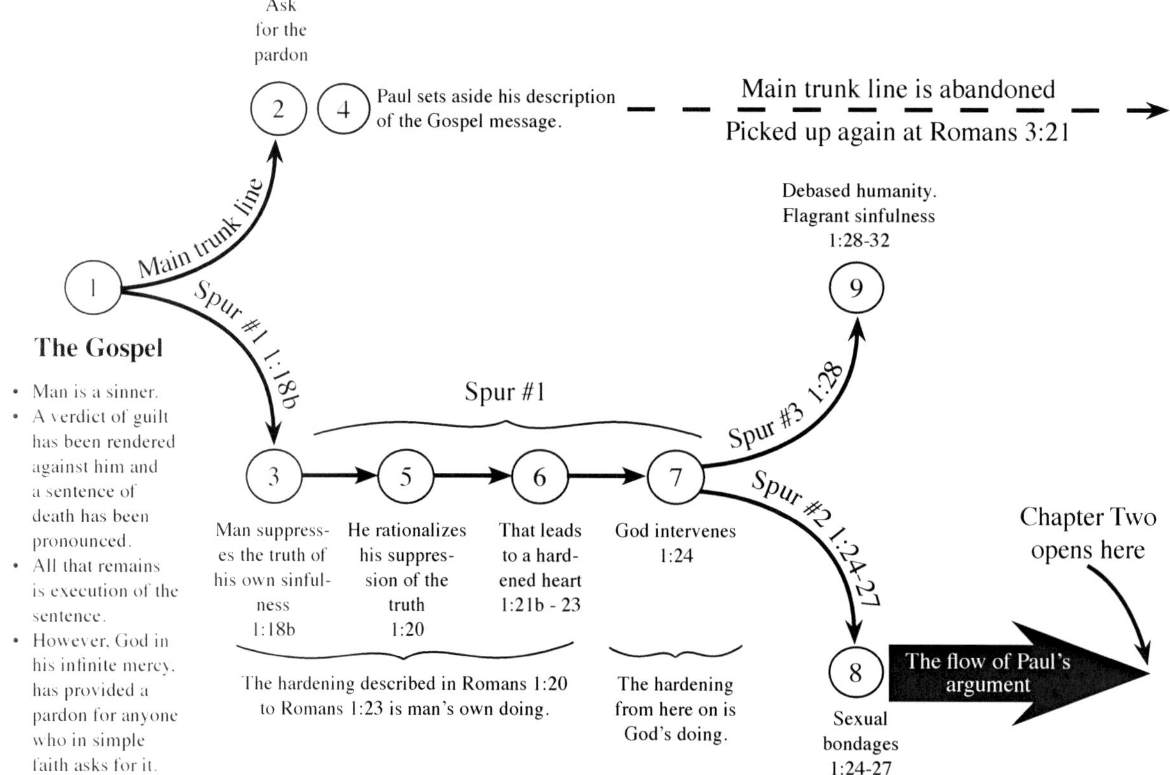

through faith? Certainly not! On the contrary, we establish the law.

Verse:
Rom. 3:21 But now the righteousness of God apart from the law has been manifested, being witnessed by the Law and the Prophets...

Romans 3:20 is the final verse of Paul's long digression – and Paul is now ready to resume his examination of redemption itself – beginning with Romans 3:21. It has been a long and sometimes labyrinthine digression – packed with often unexpected twists and turns designed to preempt challenges Paul knows will be mounted by his protagonists. The twists and turns are, therefore, unavoidable; nevertheless, we're frequently left gasping for breath and a bit disoriented. Consequently, I want to begin verse 21 using the graphic I sketched out on page 109 at the start of Chapter Five. It will help keep us "on track." That graphic is reproduced on page 162.

We will now complete the graphic – tracing the flow of Paul's argument from Romans 2:1 through Romans 3:20 – adding on "spurs #4 and #5 which describe (1) the hypocrisy which arises from mankind's insistent suppression of the truth, (2) God's sovereign jurisprudence; and (3) the intractable condemnation arising from that jurisprudence – a condemnation that touches both Jew and Gentile.

The Completed Graphic

(Explanation on next page)

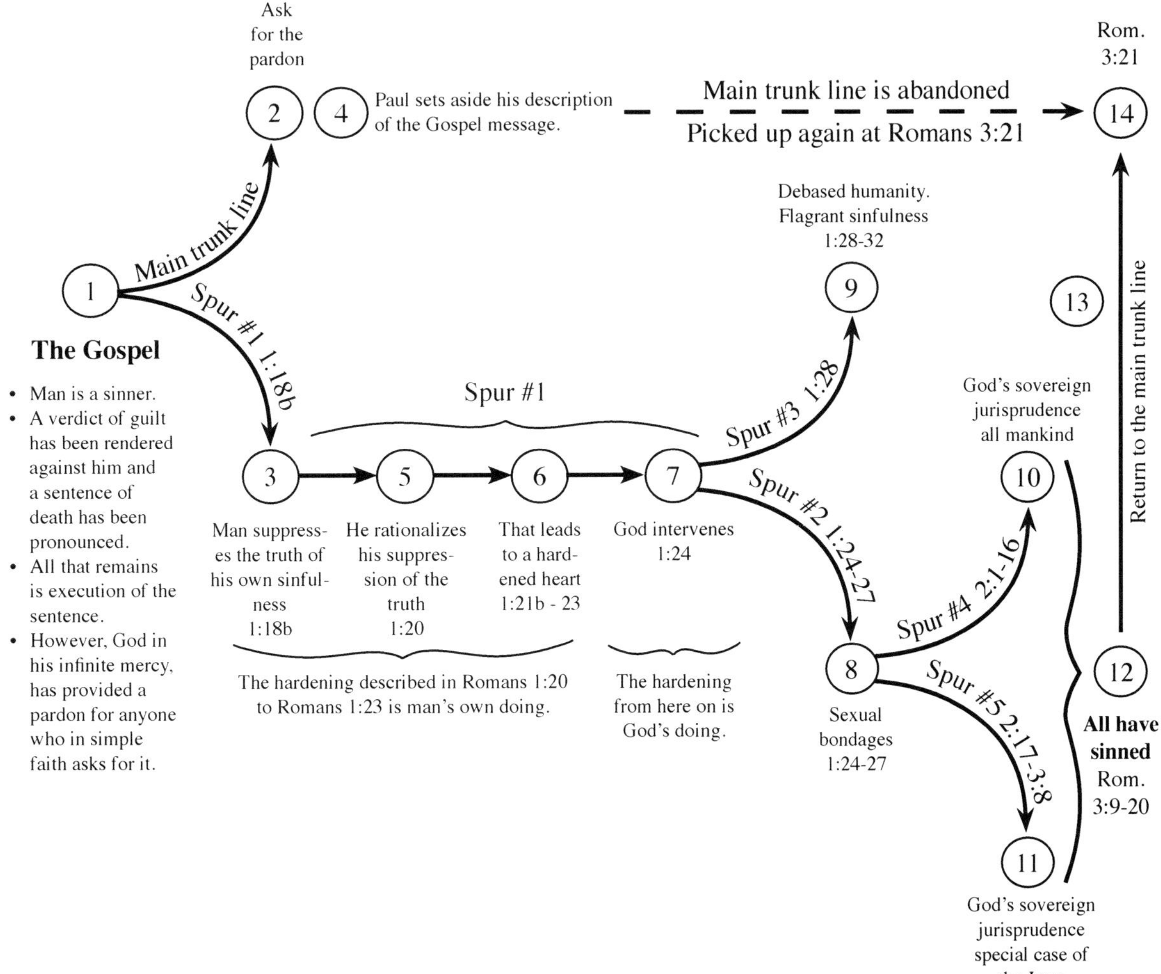

Explanation of the Completed Graphic

1. In Romans 1:16 – 18a, Paul sums up the gospel message (Point #1 on the graphic on page 163) - and, in doing so, reveals the theme of the epistle:
   - Man is a sinner.
   - A verdict of guilt has already been rendered against him and a sentence of death has already been pronounced.
   - All that remains is execution of the sentence.
   - However, God, in his infinite mercy, has provided a pardon for anyone who in simple faith asks for it.
2. The next step should be obvious: ask for the pardon (Point #2 on the graphic on page 163).
3. However, it's not quite that simple: man suppresses the truth of his own sinfulness (Point #3) and is, therefore, blind to his need for a pardon.
4. Paul, therefore, sets aside his description of the Gospel message (Point #4) and doesn't pick it up again until Romans 3:21 (Point #14),
5. and takes up instead the issue of man's sinfulness - what it means to suppress the truth - its nature and consequences. We've now left the "main trunk line" and are on "spur #1."
6. Suppressing the truth leads us to rationalize our sinfulness (point #5) – which, in turn, hardens our heart (Point #6) – meaning our conscience can no longer generate sufficient conviction to hold lust at bay. The hardening here is man's doing, not God's.
7. That prompts God to personally intervene with three judgments (Point #7) – each of which is designed not merely to inflict punishment, but to bring the person undergoing judgment back to his senses. God is "shoving man's face into the sin" he has been toying with – to make him feel the full weight of its horror. If he's brought back, it's because of the anguish and suffering he undergoes, not because of conviction. Each judgment is listed in order of its severity – with the first the least severe and the last the most severe (Points #8 and 9). The hardening (what Paul calls "turning over)" here is God's doing, not man's.
8. The first judgment leads to the loss of freedom (Point 8); the second judgment leads to the loss of dignity (also Point #8). That puts us on spur #2. The persons suffering these two judgments are not flagrant sinners – meaning they're ashamed of their sinfulness and try to hide it – which makes them faultfinding hypocrites – an insight Paul elaborates on beginning with Romans 2:1.
9. Paul now turns his attention to the third judgment (Point #9). That puts us on spur #3. Persons who undergo this judgment reject all moral constraints; they acknowledge no norms of human decency; and since man is by nature a moral being, they thereby suffer the loss of their humanity. They sin openly and flagrantly – with no attempt to hide their sinfulness; furthermore, they endorse the sinfulness of others and encourage them to sin still further.
10. At this juncture, Paul turns his attention back to persons who don't sin flagrantly – who, instead, try to hide their sins (back to Point #8). Obviously, they're hypocrites.[175] That backs us out of spur #3 and puts us again on spur #2.
11. At this juncture, Paul takes up the issue of God's jurisprudence – how God adjudicates man's just deserts (Point #10). That puts us on spur 4. God's jurisprudence is universal – and admits of no exceptions; there are no special exemptions that anyone can claim. Paul examines the criterion of God's judgment, the object of God's judgment, and the resulting recompense. The conclusion is inescapable: no one can sustain his own righteousness before the bar of God's holy justice or avoid the recompense his guilt warrants: indignation, wrath, tribulation, and anguish.
12. But what about the Jew? That question arises in 2:17 and is examined in detail through 3:8 – and the conclusion is emphatic: the Jew, like the Gentile, stands helplessly condemned before the bar of God's holy justice. His "chosenness" does not permit him to escape condemnation (Point #11). That puts us on spur #5.
13. Verses 3:9 to 3:20 underscore Paul's finding with a ringing declaration of mankind's guilt and condemnation – bracketed between: "There is none righteous, no, not one..." (Romans 3:10) and "Therefore by the deeds of the law no flesh will be justified..." (Romans 3:20). That's point #12 on the graph.
14. Paul is now ready to resume his examination of

redemption – what it is and how it's secured – the very topic he set aside in Romans 1:18b (Points #13 and #14 on the graph).

Specific words or phrases found in Romans 3:21
"But now..."
The two words "But now..." follow the conclusion of Paul's long digression – and are clearly meant to underscore a dramatic turn in Paul's argument. However, it quickly becomes obvious that Paul is not taking up a new topic; he's merely returning to the topic he broke away from in Romans 1:18b – the meaning and nature of redemption – which, of course, is what "The Good News" is all about – that God has graciously provided a "right standing" before him for anyone who in simple faith asks for it.

The word "but" prepares us for a contrast that Paul is introducing – a contrast that revolves around the distinction between...

- "righteousness secured through the law" (εξ εργον νομου), and
- "righteousness secured through grace by faith"[176] (τη γαρ χαριτι εστε σεσοωμενοι δια πιστεος)

...a conceptual contrast.

However, the word "now," along with the word "manifested," tells us that what Paul has in mind is more than just a conceptual contrast; he has in mind a temporal contrast as well – a contrast grounded in a concrete historical event; specifically, the Cross.[177] In short, the Cross divides time. Since the Cross, a way has been opened for mankind to be reconciled to God apart from law-keeping – a way that displays the utterly incomprehensible mercy of God – a mercy God is willing – even eager – to lavish on mankind – all of us "vessels of wrath fitted for destruction" (Romans 9:22).

Matt. 27:50	Jesus, when he had cried again with a loud voice, yielded up the ghost.
Matt. 27:51	And, behold, the veil of the temple was rent in twain from the top to the bottom; and the earth did quake, and the rocks rent...

In short, the moment Jesus died on the Cross the veil blocking man's entrance into the "Holy of Holies" of the Temple was torn in two – signifying the establishment of a "new and living way" into God's presence: the throne of judgment has now become a throne of grace for anyone who reposes faith in Christ.

Heb. 10:19	Having therefore, brethren, boldness to enter into the holiest by the blood of Jesus,
Heb. 10:20	By a new and living way, which he hath consecrated for us, through the veil, that is to say, his flesh;
Heb. 10:21	And having an high priest over the house of God;
Heb. 10:22	Let us draw near with a true heart in full assurance of faith, having our hearts sprinkled from an evil conscience, and our bodies washed with pure water.

Specific words or phrases found in Romans 3:21
"...apart from law..."
In the original Greek, there is no definite article before the word law – which suggests that quite possibly Paul means not just the Mosaic Law, but, instead, the law in general – including the law of the Gentiles – the law of our conscience – in short, any standard of righteousness against which man's moral fitness can be measured. But, whichever it is, Paul is telling us that God has established a means of justification not founded on "law keeping." That's the whole point underlying Paul's use of the word "apart."

Specific words or phrases found in Romans 3:21
"...the righteousness of God..."
The phrase "...the righteousness of God" is, grammatically, a genitive of origin, not a subjective genitive - meaning what Paul has in mind here is not an attribute of God (i.e., "God is righteous"), but a status God confers. It's the same phrase we found in Romans 1:17.

Romans 1:17	For in it the righteousness of God is revealed from faith to faith; as it is written, "The just shall live by faith."

Paul has effectively proven the impossibility of using the law to justify oneself – whether Gentile or Jew; that all mankind stands condemned – that we've all sinned and have fallen short of God's glory (Romans 3:23). Now begins Paul's explanation of how man can be put in right standing with God apart from "law-keeping" – of how, in short, man is justified by faith.

Specific words or phrases found in Romans 3:21
"...being witnessed by the Law and the Prophets..."
Paul is emphatic: justification by faith is not a new revelation. The Law itself attests to it – a point Paul

elaborates on in Romans Four. It's a serious mistake to assume, therefore, that the New and Old Testaments are at odds or that the Law has been superceded; that faith somehow renders it null and void. No, the continuity between the two testaments is seamless. Indeed, Paul pointedly insists that faith actually upholds the law.

Romans 3:31	Do we then make void the law through faith? Certainly not! On the contrary, we establish the law.

In short, the whole purpose of the law is consummated in faith. Let's be clear: nowhere does Paul pit faith against the law. How can he when the whole purpose of the law is to point us to faith?

Gal. 3:24	Wherefore the law was our schoolmaster to bring us unto Christ, that we might be justified by faith.

What's at odds with faith is not the law itself, but justification grounded in law-keeping.

Verse:

Rom. 3:22	...even the righteousness of God through faith in Jesus Christ for all those who believe; for there is no distinction;

Specific words or phrases found in Romans 3:22
"even the righteousness of God through faith in Jesus Christ..."
Here, for the first time in his epistle, Paul *explicitly* reveals the object of "saving faith": it's Jesus Christ. We're accorded a "right standing before God" and so saved from his wrath (Romans 1:18a) through faith in Jesus Christ.

Specific words or phrases found in Romans 3:22
"for all those who believe..."
What we have here is basically a restatement of the truth first revealed in Romans 1:16...

Romans 1:16	For I am not ashamed of the gospel of Christ, for it is the power of God to salvation for everyone who believes...

The word "believe" in the phrase "for all those who believe," is linked to the word "faith" in the preceding clause, "through faith in Jesus Christ"...

Rom. 3:22	...even the righteousness of God through faith in Jesus Christ for all those who believe...

...just as it is in Romans 1:16-17.

Romans 1:16	For I am not ashamed of the gospel of Christ, for it is the power of God to salvation for everyone who believes, for the Jew first and also for the Greek.
Romans 1:17	For in it the righteousness of God is revealed from faith to faith; as it is written, "The just shall live by faith."

To believe in Christ, therefore, is to have faith in Christ – to repose trust in Christ. Once again, The words "faith," "believe," and "trust" are, quite often, all translations of the same Greek word "πιστις" or one of its cognates. For example...

• faith	a noun	pistis	Matt. 8:10
• I believe	a verb	pisteuo	Mark 9:24
• I trust	a verb	pisteuo	2 Cor. 13:6

That, therefore, gives us the sense of what it means to believe – of what it means to have faith. It means...

- to trust;
- to count on;
- to rely upon;
- to depend upon.

It's clear, then, that when Paul speaks of "believing in Christ" he has more in mind than a mere intellectual assent. Once again, that's not to suggest that an intellectual assent isn't a vital part of what it means to believe – indeed, a sine qua non of belief; nevertheless, it's certainly not the whole of it. James makes that perfectly clear in his epistle.

James 2:19	You believe that there is one God. You do well. Even the demons believe and tremble!

James is saying here that belief in God ("there is one God"[178]) – just that – is not sufficient. Moreover, throughout the Gospels – and most specifically in the Gospel of John – the meaning most often given to the word "believe" is to "rely upon," "to count on," and "to trust." In short, it's possible to believe in God, meaning believe he exists, without at the same time reposing trust in God – and those who suggest otherwise are clearly wrong.[179]

Specific words or phrases found in Romans 3:22
"for there is no distinction..."
It's important to carefully note that verses 23 and 24 restrict the scope of the phrase "for there is no distinction"...

Rom. 3:23	For all have sinned, and come short of the glory of God;
Rom. 3:24	Being justified freely by his grace through the redemption that is in Christ Jesus...

...limiting it to the matter of sin and redemption only. In short, what we have here is merely a restatement of the truth Paul was at pains to highlight beginning with Romans 2:17 and extending through at least Romans 3:19 – that the Jew can claim no privileged status before the bar of God's holy justice; that the same holy jurisprudence that passes judgment on the gentile's standing before God passes judgment on the Jew's standing as well – with the same result: that both stand condemned. And if the Law – whether the Mosaic Law or the Law of Conscience – condemns both, so faith absolves both. In short, neither the law nor faith makes any distinction between Jew and gentile. Both are condemned alike and both are saved alike.

But that certainly doesn't mean that there is no ongoing distinction whatsoever between Jew and gentile. Romans 3:1-2 tells us otherwise...

Romans 3:1	What advantage then has the Jew, or what is the profit of circumcision?
Romans 3:2	Much in every way! Chiefly because to them were committed the oracles of God.

...and still later, Romans 9:4-5...

Romans 9:4	...who are Israelites, to whom pertain the adoption, the glory, the covenants, the giving of the law, the service of God, and the promises;
Romans 9:5	of whom are the fathers and from whom, according to the flesh, Christ came, who is over all, the eternally blessed God. Amen.

Furthermore, Paul's use of the term "to the Jew first and also to the gentile" is ample proof that the Jew's privileged status still stands.

Romans 1:16	For I am not ashamed of the gospel of Christ, for it is the power of God to salvation for everyone who believes, for the Jew first and also for the Greek.
Romans 2:10	...but glory, honor, and peace to everyone who works what is good, to the Jew first and also to the Greek.

Verse:

Rom. 3:23	...for all have sinned and fall short of the glory of God.

Specific words or phrases found in Romans 3:23
"for all have sinned..."
Once again, the word "for" tells us that what we have here is an adverbial clause meant to explain the preceding verse, verse 22. Verse 22 tells us that God has opened a new and living way to achieve reconciliation with God – a new and living way into his presence. And verse 23 tells us why God has provided it: it's because we're sinners – utterly condemned before the bar of God's holy justice – with no possible way of escape other than God's mercy – which is what the new and living way reflects – the foundation upon which it has been established – the righteousness of God, a status, which God freely grants to anyone who in simple faith asks for it.

Specific words or phrases found in Romans 3:23
"and fall short of the glory of God."
In our sinfulness we fall short of the glory of God. That's the basic meaning here. The phrase "the glory of God" (η δοξα του Θεου) is elsewhere translated "the approbation of God"...

John 12:43	...for they loved the approbation of men rather than the approbation of God.

...and it's a translation that accords well with the insights Paul was at pains to underscore in Romans 2 where he so very carefully delineated the dynamics of God's jurisprudence; more specifically, anyone wanting to stand on his own merit must submit his deeds to God's judgment – which, when rendered, leads to a recompense (Romans 2:6-10) - either:

- approbation leading to reward or
- condemnation leading to punishment.

However, it's possible that Paul also has in mind the glory that was mankind's before the Fall – a glory we no longer possess, but which God longs to clothe us

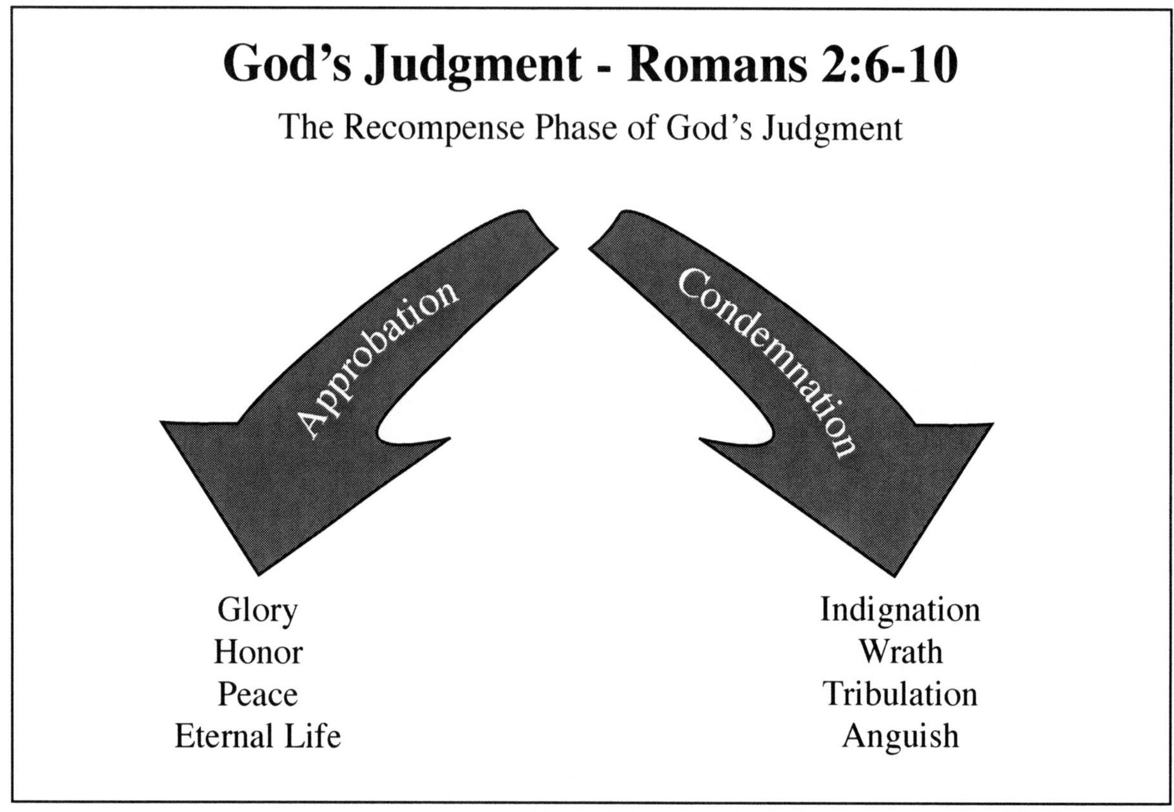

with once again. Indeed, in 2 Corinthians 3:18, Paul likens the progress of sanctification to an ascent from one stage of glory to another – with each stage more glorious than the one before.

2 Cor. 3:18	But we all, with unveiled face, beholding as in a mirror the glory of the Lord, are being transformed into the same image from glory to glory, just as by the Spirit of the Lord.

Verse:

Rom. 3:24	...being justified freely by his grace through the redemption that is in Christ Jesus.

Specific words or phrases found in Romans 3:24
"...being justified freely by his grace..."
In Greek, the word "justify" is derived from the word "righteous;" for example, in verse 26, the word "righteousness" is "διχαιουσυνης;" and here in verse 24, the word "being justified" is "διχαιουμενοι." "Justify," then, means "to make righteous." Here, it's an imputed righteousness; it isn't earned; it's freely bestowed by God whose very nature reflects mercy. "Grace" translates a Greek word (χαρις) meaning "gift" – and so what we have here, "freely by his grace," is an obvious redundancy – a gift, by its very definition is free. The redundancy is clearly intentional and meant to underscore the truth that the justification God bestows is grounded in his mercy and owes nothing to any claim of merit we can assert.

Specific words or phrases found in Romans 3:24
"...through the redemption..."
In Greek, the word "through" (δια) frequently conveys the sense of "agency" – and that's the case here. In short, the righteous status God mercifully confers would not be possible without "the redemption that is in Christ Jesus." That's what lays its foundation and undergirds it.

Let's now take a good look at the word "redemption" and try to grasp its meaning here in verse 24 – and let's take it from the top. Let's begin with mankind's condemnation. It's the Law that condemns man. Once again, that's exactly what Paul made so very clear in Romans 2:6-10.

In short, it's God's own righteousness that cries out

for man to be turned over to indignation, wrath, tribulation, and anguish.

Romans 2:6	who (God) "will render to each one according to his deeds":
Romans 2:7	eternal life to those who by patient continuance in doing good seek for glory, honor, and immortality;
Romans 2:8	but to those who are self-seeking and do not obey the truth, but obey unrighteousness--indignation and wrath,
Romans 2:9	tribulation and anguish, on every soul of man who does evil, of the Jew first and also of the Greek;
Romans 2:10	but glory, honor, and peace to everyone who works what is good, to the Jew first and also to the Greek.

Once again, God's jurisprudence is simple: "You get what you deserve." Here, then, is a real conundrum: if God's very own Law testifies against man – condemning him to indignation, wrath, tribulation, and anguish – declaring that's what he deserves, how can God grant him instead glory, honor, peace, and eternal life and yet hold true to his own righteousness? If God fails to uphold the very Law that reflects his righteousness – that reflects the glory of that righteousness – won't that call into question his Godhood and undermine the moral order of the universe? Of course it will!

The solution is "redemption." The word "redemption" translates the Greek word απολυτροσεους - which is itself derived from the Greek word "λυτρον" meaning "ransom" – used for example in both Matthew 20:28 and Mark 10:45...

Matt. 20:28	...just as the Son of Man did not come to be served, but to serve, and to give His life a ransom for many."
Mark 10:45	For even the Son of Man did not come to be served, but to serve, and to give His life a ransom for many."

Moreover, where "λυτρον" is elsewhere translated "redeem," it can just as correctly be translated "ransom." For example, both Luke 24:21 and Titus 2:14...

Luke 24:21	But we were hoping that it was He who was going to redeem (ransom) Israel...
Titus 2:14	Who gave himself for us, that he might redeem (ransom) us from all iniquity, and purify unto himself a peculiar people, zealous of good works.

Likewise, the Greek word "exagorazo" ("εξαγοραζο"), usually translated "redeem," conveys much the same sense we find in the word "λυτρον." It means to "buy back" – and in some instances can be just as correctly translated "ransom." A good example is Galatians 4:5...

Gal. 4:5	...to redeem (ransom) those who were under the law, that we might receive the adoption as sons.

Finally, the thought of "ransom" is clearly reflected in and both 1 Corinthians 6:20 and 7:23...

1 Cor. 6:20	For you were bought with a price; therefore glorify God in your body and in your spirit, which are God's.
1 Cor. 7:23	You were bought with a price; do not become slaves of men.

And what's true of Greek is true also of Hebrew. The Old Testament frequently equates the two words "ransom" and "redeem." Hosea 13:14 is a good example...

Hosea 13:14	I will ransom them from the power of the grave; I will redeem them from death. O Death, I will be your plagues! O Grave, I will be your destruction!

Hosea 13:14 is cast in the form of classic Hebrew poetry – the characteristic feature of which is synonymous parallelism. Synonymous parallelism is a well developed poetic technique: one line of verse is followed by another that declares the same truth, but using different words the meaning of which is essentially similar. Here in Hosea 13:14 the first line is "I will ransom them from the power of the grave;" the second line is "I will redeem them from death." Synonymous parallelism is found in the words "ransom" and "redeem"[180] – and so we conclude

that the two words, "ransom" and "redeem," convey essentially the same meaning.

But not only does the Old Testament equate the word "ransom" with the word "redeem," it also equates "ransom" with the word "atonement." For example, in Exodus 30:11-12 "ransom money" is used to redeem the children of Israel; and what's called "ransom money" in verse 12 is called "atonement money" in verse 16. Likewise, throughout the Pentateuch the sacrifices used in the ceremonial rituals effect "atonement." (Taken from the Septuagent)

Premodern cultures are shame-based - meaning behavior is governed less by the threat of concrete punishment than by the threat of shame, i.e., the loss of honor and dignity crime entails in a culture built around the priority of the community rather than the priority of the individual. Moreover, it's not just the perpetrator who suffers the loss of honor; the victim does as well. The victim is demeaned. He's shamed. His worth – meaning his honor – is undercut and his standing within the community is called into question. That's why the Old Testament principle of restitution addresses not simply the restoration of any material loss suffered, but, more importantly, at least in a shame based culture, the restoration of honor as well. When tendered, the victim's wrath, arising primarily from the shame he has suffered, is appeased – which is the meaning of the word "propitiation." Old Testament restitution, then, is a form of ransom meant to appease (propitiate) the wrath of a person whose honor has been demeaned by the sin perpetrated against him.

The Old Testament deems some sin, e.g., murder, so heinous that restitution is not permitted. Why? Because a ransom of sufficient value can't be found to atone for the loss suffered.

If the perpetrator is unable to restore what has been lost – either because he can't afford it or no restitution is permitted – he is required to suffer an equal loss – which is the rationale underlying "lex talionis"[181] – "Eye for eye, tooth for tooth, hand for hand, foot for foot, burning for burning, wound for wound, stripe for stripe" – and, of course, life for life. (Exodus 21:23). Once again, if the loss suffered by the perpetrator is not made equal to the loss suffered by the victim, the victim's worth – meaning his honor – is not restored and his wrath is left unappeased. The equal loss suffered by the perpetrator serves to end the victim's shame and restore his honor – and so quench his wrath – or, in the case of murder, the wrath of his kin.

Restitution accompanied by a fine and lex talionis serve essentially the same purpose: what's stolen is restored, the victim's honor is recovered, and his standing within the community is re-established.

The ultimate form redemption assumes in the Old Testament is not, however, either restitution or lex talionis. It's the Levitical sacrifices. No other form is so compelling or quite so dramatic. Several of the sacrifices are said to "soothe" God – meaning appease his wrath – most especially the Whole Burnt Offering,

The Ineffectiveness of Church Discipline in American Culture

A Sobering Insight

Biblically based sanctions, especially excommunication, are not apt to provide an effective means of enforcing congregational discipline for churches here in America. The reason is simple: Biblically based sanctions are built largely around the threat of shame and dishonor - a threat that derives its efficacy from the ties that bind together a church congregation. In short, it's the *priority of the community* that lends credibility to sanctions built around shame and dishonor. But it's precisely that priority which is absent in all modern societies and, therefore, largely absent in Amercian churches as well. Individualism, the ideological linchpin of all modern societies, like an acid, eats away at the ties binding together church congregations and therefore vitiates the impact of sanctions built around shame and dishonor.

Moreover, any church here in America that actually employs excommunication as a means of enforcing church discipline is apt to be cast in the guise of a cult. Americans, wedded to individualism, refuse to ascribe any legitimacy to it.

The Grain Offering, and the Peace Offering. For example...

Lev. 1:9 ...but he shall wash its entrails and its legs with water. And the priest shall burn all on the altar as a burnt sacrifice, an offering made by fire, a sweet aroma to the Lord.

Lev. 2:9 Then the priest shall take from the grain offering a memorial portion, and burn it on the altar. It is an offering made by fire, a sweet aroma to the Lord.

Gordon Wenham, whose study of Leviticus is, in my opinion, without parallel, points out that the word "sweet" conveys the sense of "soothing." In short, the sacrifices delineated in the Old Testament served to appease God – meaning propitiate his wrath.

Leviticus 4:31, which describes the peace offering, is especially instructive. In a single verse, we find the words "sacrifice," "sweet aroma" meaning "soothing," "atonement," and "forgiven."

Lev. 4:31 He shall remove all its fat, as fat is removed from the *sacrifice* of the peace offering; and the priest shall burn it on the altar for a *sweet aroma* to the Lord. So the priest shall make *atonement* for him, and it shall be *forgiven* him.

Paul himself was well aware that the Old Testament sacrifices served to propitiate God's wrath – because in his Ephesian epistle he uses that very paradigm in describing the sacrifice of Christ on the Cross...

Eph. 5:2 And walk in love, as Christ also has loved us and given Himself for us, an offering and a sacrifice to God for a sweet-smelling aroma.

Clearly, then, the word "redemption" found in Romans 3:24 carries forward from the Old Testament a whole array of complexities and nuances that link it to "ransom," "atonement," "restoration," "honor," "wrath," "propitiation," and "sacrifice."

Specific words or phrases found in Romans 3:24
"...that is in Christ Jesus..."

The redemption noted in verse 24 is "in Christ Jesus" – meaning Christ himself is the ransom – a truth highlighted in both the Gospels and the epistles.

Matt. 20:28 Even as the Son of man came not to be ministered unto, but to minister, and to give his life a ransom for many.

Mark 10:45 For even the Son of man came not to be ministered unto, but to minister, and to give his life a ransom for many.

1 Tim. 2:6 Who (i.e., Christ) gave himself a ransom for all, to be testified in due time.

In short, Christ is the centerpiece of mankind's redemption – meaning redemption is found in Christ alone; that without Christ redemption is not possible.

Finally, given the context, the thought here in verse 24 is not a spiritual union with Christ, as some commentators would have it, but the life and ministry of Jesus Christ – most especially culminating in his Death, Resurrection, and Ascension – concrete historical events. Redemption, then, is not a mystical, esoteric event; it's an event grounded in time and space.

Verse:
Rom. 3:25 ...whom God set forth as a propitiation by His blood, through faith, to demonstrate His righteousness, because in His forbearance God had passed over the sins that were previously committed...

Specific words or phrases found in Romans 3:25
"...whom God set forth..."
Here we have a relative clause linked to "Christ" in the preceding verse, verse 24. The word translated "set forth" is the Greek word "proetheto" (προεθετο). However, "set forth" is not the only translation that's possible. "Proetheto" can also be translated "purpose;" for example, Ephesians 1:9...

Eph 1:9 Having made known unto us the mystery of his will, according to his good pleasure which he *has purposed* in himself...

And there's good reason for deciding in favor of "purpose" rather than "set forth." It's certainly true that "set forth," meaning "display," picks up on the public nature of the Cross – that the Crucifixion was a plainly visible event. But that translation obscures the more important truth that the Cross was predestined[182] by God; that God planned it from everlasting. In short, the Cross is not some afterthought on God's part – concocted at the last moment to overcome the unforeseen consequences of sin.[183] It's God's provision for mankind's redemption formulated long ago in eternity past[184] – for all who believe – who repose their trust in God's mercy and look to him for their salvation. ***God, in other words, is eternally merciful and gracious.***

Rev. 13:8	... the Lamb slain from the foundation of the world.
1 Pet. 1:18	...knowing that you were not redeemed with corruptible things, like silver or gold, from your aimless conduct received by tradition from your fathers,
1 Pet. 1:19	but with the precious blood of Christ, as of a lamb without blemish and without spot.
1 Pet. 1:20	He indeed was foreordained before the foundation of the world, but was manifest in these last times for you.

Finally, Paul also makes it plain here that it's God the Father who formulated the redemption of mankind. It's at his behest and initiative that Christ was sent to rescue man from the condemnation he so justly deserved. In short, redemption is no less the work of the Father than the Son.

Specific words or phrases found in Romans 3:25
"...as a propitiation..."
Once again, the word "redemption," when set against the backdrop of the Old Testament, incorporates the meaning of "propitiation" – just as it does the meaning of "ransom," of "atonement," of "restoration," of "honor," of "wrath," and of "sacrifice." Consequently, it should be no surprise that Paul, after using the word "redemption" in verse 24, uses the word "propitiate" in verse 25. The one, "propitiate," flows from the other, "redemption."

The clear meaning here is...

- that mankind's redemption is secured through appeasing the wrath of God; and
- that Christ on the Cross achieves exactly that.

Many Christians find it inconceivable that God can be wrathful – notwithstanding Paul's blatant use of the word "wrath" in Romans 1:18 – a verse inextricably linked to Romans 1:16-17, the theme statement of the entire epistle.

Rom. 1:18	For the wrath of God is revealed from heaven against all ungodliness and unrighteousness of men, who suppress the truth in unrighteousness...

It's used again in Romans 2:5 – where he not only warns the unrepentant that they're "treasuring up wrath" for themselves, but speaks of a "day of wrath" that lies in the future...

Rom. 2:5	But after your hardness and impenitent heart treasure up unto yourself wrath against the day of wrath and revelation of the righteous judgment of God...

...and again in Romans 5:9 where he assures us that, having been justified, we will never face the wrath of God[185]...

Rom. 5:9	Much more then, being now justified by his blood, we shall be saved from wrath through him.

They[186] prefer substituting for the word "propitiate," meaning appease, the word "expiate," meaning "cover" or "absolve" – believing that wrath is beneath God. But that's obviously a foisted interpretation – a clear example of eisegesis – and reflects a failure on their part to distinguish divine wrath from either (1) human wrath or (2) the capricious, irrational wrath of the Homeric gods: the same evil that invariably permeates both human wrath and the wrath of the Homeric gods does not permeate God's wrath. God's wrath is untainted by any evil. The word "wrath" serves to *personalize* God's hatred of sin. Once again, God is not a Platonic archetype. The execution of God's justice will not be administered by "The Principle of Truth," but by God himself – whose whole being is repulsed by sin – and is so because holiness and righteousness comprise his very nature.

That wrath does not occasionally characterize the attitude and behavior of God is clearly at odds with the witness of the Old Testament as well. In Exodus 32:12, Moses pleads with God to turn away from not just his wrath, but his "fierce wrath"...

Ex. 32:12	Wherefore should the Egyptians speak, and say, for mischief did he bring them out, to slay them in the mountains, and to consume them from the face of the earth? Turn from thy fierce wrath...

Likewise, in 1 Samuel 28:17-18, Saul is rebuked for not having "executed God's fierce wrath upon Amalek."

1 Sam. 28:17	And the Lord has done for Himself as He spoke by me. For the Lord has torn the kingdom out of your hand and given it to your neighbor, David.
1 Sam. 28:18	Because you did not obey the voice of the Lord nor execute His fierce wrath upon Amalek, therefore the Lord has done this thing to you this day.

Specific words or phrases found in Romans 3:25
"...by his blood..."
The phrase "by his blood" is a euphemism for "by his death." The same thought is found in Romans 5:9-10 where Paul equates "blood" in verse 9 with "death" in verse 10...

Rom. 5:9	Much more then, being now justified by his blood, we shall be saved from wrath through him.
Rom. 5:10	For if, when we were enemies, we were reconciled to God by the death of his Son, much more, being reconciled, we shall be saved by his life.

Here, quite clearly, Paul is drawing the Old Testament meaning of "sacrifice" into the New Testament meaning of "redemption" – just as in previous clauses and in other verses, he has drawn in the meaning of "ransom," "atonement," and "propitiation." In short, the ransom Christ's life reflects assumes the form of an Old Testament sacrifice – replete with all the rich significance the Old Testament gives it.

Specific words or phrases found in Romans 3:25
"...through faith..."
The meaning here is that redemption is secured only by faith – which shouldn't surprise us because Paul is merely restating a truth he has already highlighted in verse 22...

Rom. 3:22	...even the righteousness of God, through faith in Jesus Christ, to all and on all who believe...

...which is itself a restatement of Romans 1:17 – which, once more, together with Romans 1:16, summarizes the theme of the entire epistle.

Rom. 1:16	For I am not ashamed of the gospel of Christ, for it is the power of God to salvation for everyone who believes, for the Jew first and also for the Greek.
Rom. 1:17	For in it the righteousness of God is revealed from faith to faith; as it is written, "The just shall live by faith."

Specific words or phrases found in Romans 3:25
"...to display his righteousness..."
Here the word "righteousness," unlike the word "righteousness" in verse 22, is clearly a subjective genitive – meaning not a status God confers, but an attribute of God – "God is righteous."

The antecedent of the pronoun "his" is "God" at the beginning of the verse.

Rom. 3:25	...whom God set forth as a propitiation by His blood, through faith, to demonstrate His righteousness...

In short, it's God the Father's righteousness, not Christ's righteousness, that's at issue here in verse 25 – and again in verse 26.

The Greek word "endexis" (ενδειξις) is frequently translated "to demonstrate" – meaning "display;" but it can also be translated "to prove." And the context here suggests that "to prove" is the better translation. Why? Because it's not just a matter of God displaying his righteousness, but proving that he is righteous notwithstanding the underserved mercy he's lavishing on mankind. Once again, if God's very own Law testifies against man – condemning him to indignation, wrath, tribulation, and anguish – declaring that's what he deserves, how can God grant him instead glory, honor, peace, and eternal life and yet hold true to his own righteousness? That's the conundrum redemption is meant to resolve.

Once more, the basic meaning of the word "redemption" is "ransom" – and in the Old Testament the most common form it assumes is sacrifice – though it can also assume other forms as well, including restitution, the ransom money paid to redeem the first born, etc. The cost of the sacrifice – meaning the ransom – is obviously the key: the more costly the ransom the greater its efficacy – meaning the greater its atoning value.[187]

The life of Christ is a ransom of such infinite value that it wholly suffices to restore God's honor and vindicate – meaning prove – his righteousness – even as God passes over mankind's sin. And a little thought reveals why Christ's life – *and only Christ's life* – poured out on the Cross is a ransom sufficiently adequate to purchase our redemption. Why no other ransom suffices. It's because, in the end, only God himself is able to uphold his own honor and vindicate his own righteousness. What other sacrifice could possibly suffice? Offer all creation on an altar of sacrifice – it's wholly insufficient. Can creation amass a ransom of such value that it can restore the Creator's honor and vindicate his righteousness? No! Creation does not undergird and uphold the Creator. It's the Creator who undergirds and upholds creation. The lesser cannot vindicate the greater. If a sacrifice is to be offered that upholds God's honor and vindicates his righteousness, it must be the sacrifice of God himself. Christ, the Second Person of the Triune God, himself fully God and co-equal with the Father – is just such a sacrifice.

Does God hate sin? That's the question God's mercy raises – the very mercy God affords sinners. And it's a question that strikes at the very heart of God's being: because calling into question God's hatred of sin is tantamount to calling into question God's righteousness – which is itself tantamount to calling into question his Godhood. Christ on the Cross proves God hates sin – notwithstanding the mercy he lavishes on sinful mankind. How much does God hate sin? Christ on the Cross proves it's an infinite hatred. Clearly, then, anyone (e.g., Mormons, Jehovah's Witnesses, etc.) who denies that Christ is co-equal with the Father cannot sustain an atonement that secures genuine redemption.

But not only does the Cross vindicate God's righteousness, it also declares his love of mankind. Who can imagine the love that prompted God the Father to deliver up God the Son to the Cross - and there, on the Cross, as mankind's sins were laid upon the Son, turn his back on him?

Matt. 27:46	And about the ninth hour Jesus cried with a loud voice, saying, Eli, Eli, lama sabachthani? that is, My God, my God, why have you forsaken me?

Imagine, for one moment in all eternity the everlasting, immutable fellowship between Father and Son was broken - that the Godhead was, in a sense, however incomprehensible, torn asunder. Who can fathom the horror of the Cross and the love it reflects!

Revelation 5:6 is one of the most profoundly disturbing passages in the Bible – a passage that should fill us with both wonder and horror - and seize our imagination.

> And I beheld, and, lo, in the midst of the throne and of the four beasts, and in the midst of the elders, stood a Lamb as it had been slaughtered, having seven horns and seven eyes, which are the seven Spirits of God sent forth into all the earth.
>
> *Rev. 5:6*

The verb "having been slain" is the Greek word "esfagmenon" ("εσφαγμενον"). It's the perfect passive predicate participle of "sfazo" ("σφαζω"), a word used to indicate the slaughter of sacrificial victims. The term "seven horns" is an Old Testament symbol for kingly authority.[188] Clearly, what we have here, then, is the Resurrected and Ascended Christ – clothed in full power, but still bearing the marks of the Cross. Imagine, for all eternity the Enthroned Christ bearing the marks the Father's wrath inflicted on him as the Lamb of God! Who can fathom it...

- the Father sending his beloved Son to die in our place?
- the love of the Son whose will was in perfect harmony with his Father's and who graciously condescended to lay aside his dignity, majesty, and power to ransom us from the claims of the law and vindicate his Father's rightousness?

Yes, for mankind redemption is a gift – made freely available to anyone who in simple faith asks for it; but for God, the cost is beyond comprehension. Who can plumb its depths? The cost God paid to ransom

Is Belief Itself Praiseworthy?

Calvinists contend that belief - meaning faith - is a gift God imparts to the elect; otherwise, so they insist, salvation is not wrought by God alone, but is instead a shared venture – implying that the praise and glory of salvation is likewise shared - which, so they claim, is impossible because the human heart is wholly incapable of producing anything that's genuinely praiseworthy. J. I. Packer, for example, comments, "The two theologies (Arminianism and Calvinism) ... conceive ... of salvation in quite different terms. ...One gives all the glory of saving believers to God, *the other divides the praise between God and man* ..." (Italics mine) Packer, however, is wrong on both logical and exegetical grounds.

Let's take a good look.

- ***Faulty logic***
  To suggest that the mere choice on the part of a sinner to avail himself of God's mercy - *that* mere choice alone - is itself meritorious and deserving of praise is logically absurd - and is so on its very face. Anyone who opts for God's mercy does so because merit, which affords praise its only genuine rationale, is beyond his reach. Is Richard Nixon praiseworthy merely because he seized the pardon President Gerald Ford granted him – and so escaped the consequences of his guilt? Of course not! Quite the contrary: the pardon afforded Nixon actually confirmed his guilt and underscored his complete lack of merit; after all, only the guilty avail themselves of a pardon; the innocent insist on a new trial to vindicate themselves.

- ***Faulty Exegesis***
  In Romans 3:27, Paul concludes that salvation, because it originates in God's mercy, slams the door shut on pride and the boasting it invariably provokes. Paul, however, suspects that the Jews will trot out Abraham to prove that his conclusion is wrong. And his concern is well founded: the rabbis acknowledged it was faith that secured for Abraham God's favor, *but only because belief, so the Jews insisted, is itself meritorious – exactly what the Calvinists contend.*

  Paul's whole point in Romans 4:1-5, therefore, is to make it plain that belief, in and of itself, is not a "good work" - meaning it is not meritorious; that therefore belief does not warrant a "wage." In short, whatever God's response to our faith might be, it does not arise from a debt he has incurred. It secures God's favor; but it doesn't earn God's favor. The implication here is obvious: the fact that belief arises from within the human heart does not mean that man can claim a share in the glory and praise which is salvation's due. God alone is the author of salvation and to him only all praise, honor, and glory belong.

us from his wrath and vindicate his righteousness will stagger our imaginations throughout eternity.

Specific words or phrases found in Romans 3:25
"...because in his forbearance God had passed over the sins that were previously committed..."
The Greek word "dia" (δια), here translated "because," is perhaps better translated "on account of" – and is meant to explain why redemption is so necessary: it's because God, in his forbearance, has passed over the sins of mankind up to the time of the Cross – meaning he, by and large, permitted those sins to go unpunished – and, in so doing, seemed to condone evil – which, once more, is exactly the point Paul was highlighting back in Romans 2:3-5: that God's forbearance – meaning his reluctance to pour out on sinners the full measure of his wrath – quite frequently leads those very sinners to conclude that God is indifferent to sin. Redemption, though, secured through the propitiatory sacrifice of Christ on the Cross, proves that he isn't indifferent to sin – that he doesn't condone evil – that his hatred of sin is unabated.

Romans 3:25 makes it plain that God restrained his wrath and, by and large, let sin go unpunished because all along he planned to resolve the matter of sin once and for all through the Cross – and it's a plan he

Election and Reprobation vs. the Cross

W.G.T. Shedd, a renowned Presbyterian theologian who preached, taught, and wrote at the end of the 19th Century, alleges quite unabashedly: "(God) ... permitted, but did not *cause* or *compel* (italics his) the fall of angels and men, *with the intention* (italics mine) of guiding the issue of it all to an ultimate and worthy end of himself - namely, the *manifestation of his two great attributes of mercy and justice (italics mine):* of mercy, in the salvation from sin of a 'great multitude whom no man can number;' of justice, in leaving a multitude that can be numbered to the sin which they love and prefer, and its righteous punishment."

Let's take a good look.

That, then, according to Calvinists, is the whole purpose of election and reprobation - to highlight and proclaim God's mercy and justice. *But that's exactly the purpose of the Cross - to cast a brilliant, altogether illuminating light upon God's mercy and justice.* Is that light somehow inadequate? Does it require the additional light election and reprobation supposedly provide? To pose the question is to answer it! No additional light is required! The Cross is wholly sufficient!

Scripture is quite clear. It's the Cross - a single event occuring at a single moment in time - that most vividly displays God's wrath and God's mercy...

- God's wrath poured out on Christ; and
- God's mercy poured out on mankind.

In short, the revelation of God's wrath and God's mercy finds its ultimate consummation in Christ on the Cross, not as Shedd and other Calvinists would have it, in reprobation and election.

Two Different Interpretations

Christ Crucified

The revelation of God's wrath and God's mercy

Christ on the Cross

God's wrath poured out on Christ
God's mercy poured out on mankind

Double Predestination

The revelation of God's wrath and God's mercy

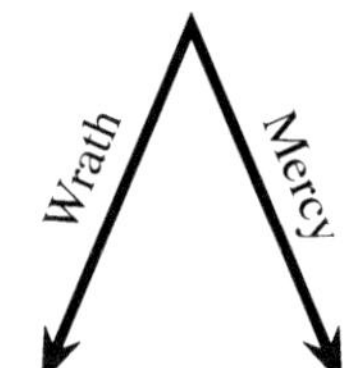

Some men predestined to hell

Some men predestined to heaven

formulated in eternity past – a truth to which, once again, Revelation 13:8 and 1 Peter 1:18-20 provide ample testimony...

Rev. 13:8	... the Lamb *slain from the foundation of the world.*
1 Pet. 1:18	...knowing that you were not redeemed with corruptible things, like silver or gold, from your aimless conduct received by tradition from your fathers,
1 Pet. 1:19	but with the precious blood of Christ, as of a lamb without blemish and without spot.
1 Pet. 1:20	He indeed was *foreordained before the foundation of the world,* but was manifest in these last times for you.

The phrase "God had passed over sins that were previously committed" has led some Christians to mistakenly limit the efficacy of Christ's atonement to sins committed before their conversion, not sins following their conversion. That's far from the meaning Paul has in mind here. Paul means only that up to the time of the Cross *"sins were neither punished as they should be nor atoned for as they were going to be."*[189]

Specific words or phrases found in Romans 3:25
"...in his forbearance..."

Romans 3:25...

... because in His forbearance God had passed

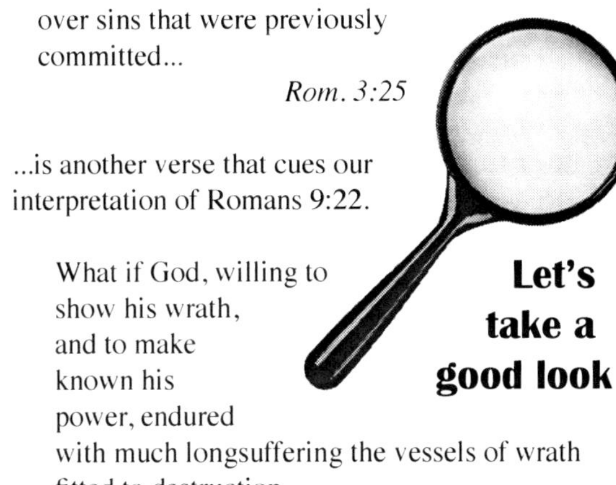

> over sins that were previously committed...
>
> *Rom. 3:25*

...is another verse that cues our interpretation of Romans 9:22.

> What if God, willing to show his wrath, and to make known his power, endured with much longsuffering the vessels of wrath fitted to destruction...
>
> *Rom. 9:22*

The key phrase in both verses is essentially similar:
- Romans 3:25 - "in his forbearance"
- Romans 9:22 - "endured with much longsuffering."

Connection to Romans 9-11

Romans 9-11

Here

Both phrases reveal God suppressing his wrath.

We know that for Romans 3:25...
- the cause of God's wrath is sin; and, because every man is a sinner,
- the object of his wrath is all mankind – no exceptions.

After all, that has been the gist of Paul's entire argument since Romans 1:18 – culminating with Romans 3:19 and Romans 3:23.

Rom. 3:19	...that every mouth may be stopped, and all the world may become guilty before God.
Rom. 3:23	...for all have sinned and have fallen short of the glory of God...

We quite naturally assume, of course, that what's true of Romans 3:25 is true also of Romans 9:22 – that the cause and object of God's wrath are the same in both verses. It's hard to imagine otherwise – that the cause and object of God's wrath in Romans 9:22 could possibly be any different from the cause and object of God's wrath in Romans 3:25. The inconsistency would be glaring.

But for Calvinists that's exactly the case. Calvinists insist that the term "vessels of wrath" in Romans 9:22 pertains only to men God has predestined *from eternity* to damnation (reprobation). Those chosen *from eternity* for salvation (election) are "vessels of mercy" and, as such, are not and never have been the objects of God's wrath.

Rom. 9:23	...that he might make known the riches of his glory on the vessels of mercy, which he had afore prepared unto glory,

In short, God has sovereignly chosen to love the one and hate the other – which is exactly the conclusion Calvinists draw from Romans 9:13...

Rom. 9:13	As it is written, "Jacob I have loved, but Esau I have hated."

There we have it: while the object of God's wrath in Romans 3:25 is clearly all men – again that has been the gist of Paul's entire argument since Romans 1:18 – the object of God's wrath in Romans 9:22 is not all men, but only those men God has predestined for damnation. It's a conundrum Calvinists are either at a loss to explain or, what's more likely, they simply ignore.

And that's not the end of it: there's more to it than just that.
- If all men are not initially the objects of God's wrath – though, incontrovertibly, all men are sinners – then clearly it's not really sin that occasions the wrath of God.
- Or, put a little differently, if it's sin that provokes the wrath of God, wouldn't God hate both Jacob and Esau alike? After all, both are sinners.

The inconsistency that plagues Calvinist thinking is striking indeed. And, once again, it's an inconsistency they ignore; they ignore it because, given the constraints of their underlying bias, they can't resolve it. It can be resolved only if it's faith, not God's sovereignty, that distinguishes Jacob's fate from Esau's. And, clearly, that's the case. Once again, it's elegantly simple: what was true of Abraham...

Rom. 4:3	... Abraham believed God, and it was accounted to him for righteousness.

...became true for Jacob as well.
- Jacob's faith, like Abraham's faith before him, transformed him from a "vessel of wrath" into a

"vessel of mercy;"
- Esau, on the other hand, spurned faith – leaving his standing unchanged, a "vessel of wrath."

That's what underlies Romans 9:13...

Rom. 9:13 As it is written, "Jacob I have loved, but Esau I have hated."

- not God's sovereign will,
- but Jacob's faith and Esau's lack of faith...

...meaning the cause and object of God's wrath in Romans 9:22 is, after all, no different from the cause and object of God's wrath in Romans 3:25; that, more specifically, Romans 9:22 should be interpreted in light of Romans 3:25.

Verse:
Rom. 3:26 ...to demonstrate at the present time His righteousness, that He might be just and the justifier of the one who has faith in Jesus....

Specific words or phrases found in Romans 3:26
"...to demonstrate at the present time his righteousness..."
The word "demonstrate" here in verse 26 is the very same Greek word translated "display" in verse 25: "ενδειξιν." And just as in verse 25, so here in verse 26, the more accurate rendering is "to prove" – meaning what God is most concerned about is not displaying his righteousness, but proving he is righteous.

What's new about verse 26 is the prepositional phrase "at this present time." It's meant to draw attention to the truth that our redemption is grounded in a concrete historical event that had just occurred at the time Paul was writing, the death and resurrection of Jesus Christ – the very event that not only justifies those who repose their faith in Christ, but, in addition, proves that God is just in justifying them! In short, the Cross leaves no room to doubt that in passing over our sins God has not compromised his righteousness; that his justice is unblemished and wholly intact. In other words, the Cross proves that God has *justified justly*.

Verse:
Rom. 3:27 Where then is boasting? It is excluded. By what kind of law? Of works? No, but by the law of faith.

Specific words or phrases found in Romans 3:27
"...Where then is boasting? It is excluded."
The whole thrust of Paul's argument, extending all the way back to Romans 1:18, leads to this conclusion – put in the form of a rhetorical question calling for the obvious answer that Paul supplies: "Where then is boasting? It is excluded."

Boasting implies merit – suggesting...
- that our redemption is founded upon "just desserts;"
- that we've earned it;
- that it's grounded in a right that compels God's favor.

But that's clearly not true. Our redemption is founded on God's mercy, not God's justice; and no one ever deserves mercy. Once again, that's a non-sequitur. There are no "rights" grounded in mercy, only in justice. Therefore, boasting is not just uncalled for, it's both ludicrous and morally repulsive. It reflects a mind-set that fails altogether to grasp either the desperate plight of the human condition or the significance of what God has done in our behalf.

Self-adulation – which is what lies at the heart of boasting – reflects a stubborn refusal to acknowledge our need for mercy; but more than just that, it reflects a desire to stand before God on our own. There's a line in an old New Orleans funeral dirge, *The Saint James Infirmary Blues*, that perfectly sums up this sentiment: "Put a twenty dollar gold piece in my pocket and tell the Lord that I'm standing pat." Boasting marks out a man crossing the threshold to hell.

Specific words or phrases found in Romans 3:27
By what kind of law? Of works? No, but by the law of faith."

Some commentators suggest that the phrase "the law of faith" should be rendered "the principle of faith" – making it stand in contrast to the "principle of the law" which, they claim, underlies "justification grounded in works." In short, what we have here, they insist, is "the law" pitted against "faith." But that's a contrast Paul never draws. Paul has already made that perfectly clear back in Romans 3:21 – where he maintained that justification by faith is not some new revelation; that, quite the contrary, the Law itself – meaning the entire corpus of the Old Testament – attests to it. No, the continuity between the two testaments is seamless. The whole purpose of the Law, Paul insists, is actually consummated in faith – a point that Paul is about to make in verse 31.

Rom. 3:31 Do we then nullify the Law through faith? May it never be! On the contrary, we establish the Law.

In short, the Law is meant to lead mankind to faith – to a justification that's founded on faith – which, once again, is exactly what Paul is at pains to spell out in Galatians 3:24.

Gal. 3:24 Wherefore the law was our schoolmaster to bring us unto Christ, that we might be justified by faith.

Once again, what's at odds with faith is not the law itself, but justification grounded in law-keeping – and that's actually a perversion of the Law.[190]

Paul is saying here, then, that the Law itself makes boasting wholly untenable – that, in other words, the "law of faith" is the Law itself – that the two are one and the same – in the sense that...

- the one, the Law, is meant to lead to the other, faith;
- that the one, the Law, is consummated in the other, faith.

Verse:

Rom. 3:28 For we maintain that a man is justified by faith apart from works of the Law.

Specific words or phrases found in Romans 3:28

"...For we maintain that a man is justified by faith apart from the works of the Law."

Verse 28, as a whole, supports verse 27 – and underscores the point I've already noted: that the contrast Paul draws is not between faith and the law, but between faith and the "works of the Law"– meaning justification grounded in law-keeping.

Verse:

Or is God the God of Jews only? Is He not the God of Gentiles also? Yes, of Gentiles also...

Rom. 3:29

Connection to Romans 9-11

Here → Romans 9-11

Specific words or phrases found in Romans 3:29

"Or is God the God of the Jews only?"

The Jews never doubted that God is the God of the gentiles – in the sense that he's their Creator and Judge. But, by and large, they limited his mercy to themselves; that though he is indeed the God of the gentiles, his mercy is restricted to the Jews only.[191] Paul, however, reveals here in verse 29 just how absurd that notion is. The Cross discloses that God is as merciful as he is righteous and holy – that mercy is as much a part of God's nature as is righteousness and holiness. Therefore, if the consequences arising from God's righteousness, i.e., moral accountability and justice, extend to all mankind – because righteousness is God's nature – so also does his mercy – because mercy is likewise his nature. Or, put a little differently: because mercy defines who God is, he can't be a merciful God to the Jews without at the same time being a merciful God to the gentiles as well.

Let's take a good look

A better rendering of Romans 3:29 is provided with a few changes made in its wording...

Rom. 3:29 Or is God the merciful God of the Jews only? Is he not also the same merciful God of the Gentiles? Yes, of the Gentiles as well.

Here we have another truth that Calvinism is unable to accommodate: if mercy defines who God is – that is, if mercy is at the very core of God's being – how can God tender an offer of mercy to Jacob without correspondingly tendering that very same offer to Esau? Or, put a little differently: if God refuses to tender Esau the exact offer of mercy he tenders Jacob, how is he the same God? He can't be one way with Esau and another way with Jacob. "God is one" – the very truth Paul highlights in the next verse. The inconsistencies that plague Calvinism are indeed glaring.

Once again, Romans 9:13...

Rom. 9:13 As it is written, "Jacob I have loved, but Esau I have hated."

...is not about God's sovereignty, as Calvinists

would have it; it's about faith. It's not that Jacob was sovereignly predestined to God's love and Esau sovereignly predestined to God's hatred – meaning his wrath. It's that Jacob, unlike Esau, believed God; and, like Abraham before him, that belief altered wholly and completely his standing before God; that is, it transformed him...

- from a "vessel of wrath" (Romans 9:22)
- into a "vessel of mercy" (Romans 9:23).

Once again, how elegantly simple: what was true of Abraham...

Romans 4:3	... Abraham believed God, and it was accounted to him for righteousness.

...became true for Jacob as well

Esau, on the other hand, refused to embrace faith – leaving his standing unchanged, a vessel of wrath.

Verse:

Rom. 3:30	...since indeed God who will justify the circumcised by faith and the uncircumcised through faith is one.

Specific words or phrases found in Romans 3:30

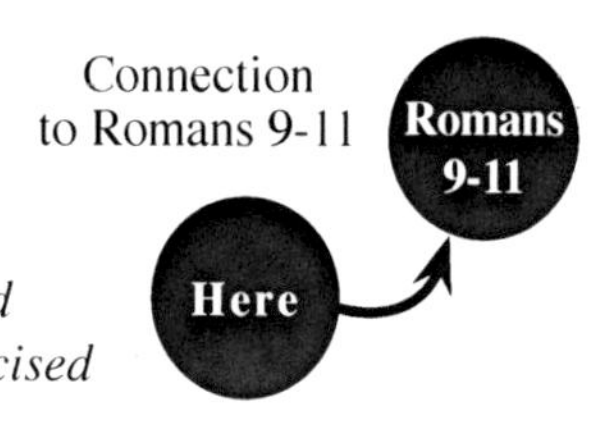

"...since indeed God who will justify the circumcised by faith and the uncircumcised through faith is one."

- The word "circumcised" is a metonymy clearly meaning "the Jews;"
- likewise, the word "uncircumcised" is a metonymy clearly meaning "the gentiles;" and
- the phrase "God is one" recalls the truth Paul highlighted in verse 29 – that because God is by nature merciful, he is necessarily merciful to the gentiles as well as the Jews. ***It's an imperative grounded in the "oneness" of his being.***

Verse:

Rom. 3:31	Do we then nullify the Law through faith? May it never be! On the contrary, we establish the Law.

Specific words or phrases found in Romans 3:31
"Do we then nullify the Law through faith? May it never be! On the contrary, we establish the Law."
Paul has already pointed out that the Law was never designed to provide mankind a means of justifying himself; quite the contrary: it was meant to reveal our innate corruption and to convince us that justification grounded in lawkeeping is a hopeless undertaking...

Rom. 3:20	because by the works of the Law no flesh will be justified in His sight; for through the Law comes the knowledge of sin.

...and, in so doing, point us to justification grounded in faith – a truth perhaps best summed up in another of Paul's epistles, the Book of Galatians.

Gal. 3:24	Wherefore the law was our schoolmaster to bring us unto Christ, that we might be justified by faith.

The Law, then, is consummated in faith. And it's in that sense that faith establishes the Law. In short, faith in Christ is the Law's telos – which is exactly the point Paul makes in Romans 10:4...

Rom. 10:4	For Christ (meaning "faith in Christ") is the end (telos) of the law for righteousness to everyone who believes.

The meaning here is that "faith in Christ" is the ultimate form the Law is meant to assume. The "law of faith," then, is the Law itself – the two are one and the same" (Romans 3:27).

Let me put it a little differently: Romans 10:4, like so many other verses in Romans, can't be interpreted correctly without imbedding it within a teleological framework – and when that's done, it's not that Christ – meaning "faith in Christ" – terminates the law – which is the meaning some commentators give Romans 10:4; it's that "faith in Christ" is the very purpose the Law is meant to serve.

The Wounds of Love and the Scars They Leave Behind

The scars of the Crucifixion left behind on the Lamb prove God's love of mankind. That's what Revelation 5:6 is all about. And just as Christ bears scars from the terrible wounds he suffered in our behalf at the Crucifixion, so we are given the inestimable privilege of bearing scars from the wounds we suffer in his behalf.

> For unto you it is given in the behalf of Christ, not only to believe on him, but also to suffer for his sake...
>
> *Philippians 1:29*

Those scars will, for all eternity, mark out Christ's special few - a "band of brothers" whose love of Christ is beyond question - drawn into an inexpressible intimacy with him and seated at the head of his table.

It's a paradigm that's often drawn upon in the canon of Western literature: *The love we profess is measured by the scars we bear in its behalf.* Shakespeare's Henry V is an unforgettable example. It's based upon the Battle of Agincourt fought in 1415. Henry V, along with his entire army, had been trapped by the French near the small town of Agincourt in Flanders, not far from the English Channel. The English army was worn down from a long seige it had mounted against the port of Harfleur. It had suffered terrible attrition and was, consequently, outnumbered by the French army arrayed against it. Hundreds of Henry's troops had deserted him - escaping through the French lines and crossing the channel to the comfort and safety of their own homes and beds in England. In Act 4, Scene 3 of Shakespeare's play, Henry's war council, in his absence, is recommending surrender with honor. At this crucial juncture, Henry arrives; and the lines Shakespeare gives him to speak are among the most memorable ever penned.

What's he that wishes so?
My cousin Westmoreland? No, my fair cousin;
If we are mark'd to die, we are even now
To do our country loss; and if to live,
The fewer men, the greater share of honour.
God's will! I pray thee, wish not one man more.
By Jove, I am not covetous for gold,
Nor care I who doth feed upon my cost;
It yearns me not if men my garments wear;
Such outward things dwell not in my desires.
But if it be a sin to covet honour,
I am the most offending soul alive.
No, faith, my coz, wish not a man from England.
God's peace! I would not lose so great an honour
As one man more methinks would share from me
For the best hope I have. O, do not wish one more!
Rather proclaim it, Westmoreland, through my host,
That he which hath no stomach to this fight,
Let him depart; his passport shall be made,
And crowns for convoy put into his purse;
We would not die in that man's company
That fears his fellowship to die with us.
This day is call'd the feast of Crispian.
He that outlives this day, and comes safe home,
Will stand a tip-toe when this day is nam'd,

And rouse him at the name of Crispian.
He that shall live this day, and see old age,
Will yearly on the vigil feast his neighbours,
And say 'To-morrow is Saint Crispian.'
Then will he strip his sleeve and show his scars,
And say 'These wounds I had on Crispian's day.'
Old men forget; yet all shall be forgot,
But he'll remember, with advantages,
What feats he did that day. Then shall our names,
Familiar in his mouth as household words -
Harry the King, Bedford and Exeter,
Warwick and Talbot, Salisbury and Gloucester-
Be in their flowing cups freshly rememb'red.
This story shall the good man teach his son;
And Crispin Crispian shall ne'er go by,
From this day to the ending of the world,
But we in it shall be remembered -
We few, we happy few, we band of brothers;
For he to-day that sheds his blood with me
Shall be my brother; be he ne'er so vile,
This day shall gentle his condition;
And gentlemen in England now-a-bed
Shall think themselves accurs'd they were not here,
And hold their manhoods cheap whiles any speaks
That fought with us upon Saint Crispin's day.

"Then will he strip his sleeve and show his scars..." Imagine, no scars to show at the Wedding Supper of the Lamb! No admittance to that special "band of brothers" - those "happy few" who shed their blood in the cause of Christ - that small company of warriors seated closest to King Jesus. How much do we love Christ? The scars we bear on that day will tell the truth!

Just as in Shakespeare's play, the many who keep themselves safe and risk little or nothing - their possessions, their lives, their loved ones, their careers - will *"hold their manhood cheap"* in the august company of those whose bodies are marked and pitted from the wounds of battle - whose lives were cut short in the cause of Christ - whose possessions were drained away - whose families were put in jeopardy - whose careers were compromised. If given another chance, how gladly on that day would they trade away the many years they added to their lives - the wealth they preserved - the families they kept safe - the careers that brought them honor and recognition. But too late! Tears in their eyes and shame in their hearts, they will keep their sleeves rolled down - no scars to show.

... that, when he shall appear, we may have confidence, and not be ashamed before him at his coming.

1 John 2:28

Chapter Nine

Verses for Chapter Nine

Rom. 4:1	What then shall we say that Abraham our father has found according to the flesh?
Rom. 4:2	For if Abraham was justified by works, he has something to boast about, but not before God.
Rom. 4:3	For what does the Scripture say? Abraham believed God, and it was accounted to him for righteousness.
Rom. 4:4	Now to him who works, the wages are not counted as grace but as debt.
Rom. 4:5	But to him who does not work but believes on Him who justifies the ungodly, his faith is accounted for righteousness,

Verse:

Rom. 4:1	What then shall we say that Abraham our father has found according to the flesh?

Specific words or phrases found in Romans 4:1
"What then shall we say that Abraham our father has found"
Paul has concluded in Romans 3:27 that no man can boast before God...

Romans 3:27	Where is boasting then? It is excluded.

Why? Because mankind's salvation is not based upon merit, but upon the undeserved favor of God, appropriated through faith in Jesus Christ.

Paul suspects, however, that the Jews will "trot out" Abraham to prove that his conclusion in Romans 3:27 is untenable – claiming that Abraham's obedience justified him; that, in other words, it was merit that secured Abraham's standing before God.

And Paul's suspicions are well founded. The Jews' assessment of Abraham is spelled out quite clearly in their commentaries on the Old Testament. Jubilees 23:10 provides a striking example: *"Abraham was perfect in all his deeds with the Lord, and well-pleasing in righteousness all the days of his life."* The rabbis go on to assert that not once did Abraham ever need to confess a sin or ask to be forgiven.

Paul knows that the Jews' opposition to the gospel won't be overcome until their assessment of Abraham's standing before God is proven wrong; that, in point of fact, Abraham was not justified on the basis of merit, but solely on the basis of faith. That's the matter Paul's taking up here.

Specific words or phrases found in Romans 4:1
"... according to the flesh"
The meaning of this phrase has been hotly debated. The question is: does it modify "found" or "father"? It seems clear to me that it modifies "father" - that, Paul is laying the groundwork for the truth he underscores a bit further on. But doesn't that make the phrase redundant? The word "father" has already established Paul's kinship with Abraham. Why tack on the phrase *"according to the flesh"?*

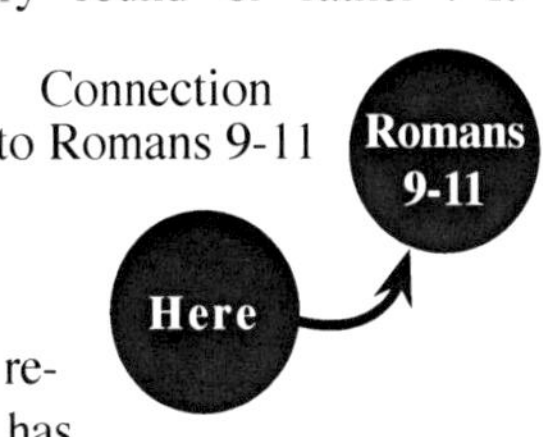

The answer is found several verses further on, specifically, verses 9 – 12. There Paul points out that Abraham is not just the forefather of the Jews, but the forefather of anyone – Jew or gentile – who makes faith the ground of his relationship with God. Paul, therefore, uses the phrase "according to the flesh" here in verse 1 to distinguish between those two "paternities:"

- he's the forefather of the Jews *"according to the flesh,"* and
- he's the forefather of anyone – Jew or gentile – who *"walks in faith"* (Rom. 4:12).

It's a distinction that underlies the meaning of the "root and branches" metaphor in Romans Eleven. (See the next page.)

The truth Paul's highlighting in verses 9 – 12 is the very same truth he points out in Galatians 3:7...

Gal. 3:7	Know therefore that they who are of faith, the same are the children of Abraham.

...and, therefore, it shouldn't catch any of us by

(Continued on page 185)

Abraham's Two Paternities

Romans 9-11

Here

Connection to Romans 9-11

Abraham is the father of both...
(1) ethnic Israel and all the individual Jews who comprise her, and
(2) all who believe whether Jew or Gentile.

Romans Eleven

The key to understanding the "root and branches" metaphor of Romans Eleven lies in making Abraham, not Israel per se, the root - and not just Abraham as the father of Israel, but Abraham as the father of all who believe - in other words, *the father of faith*. In the metaphor, Jewish believers are called "the natural branches" because they boast a lineage derived from *both* paternities: they are the "children of Abraham" by birth *and* the "children of Abraham" by faith. The Gentiles, on the other hand, are the "children of Abraham" *only* by faith, not by birth; hence they are called "the wild branches." It's faith that determines inclusion, not ethnicity; therefore, unbelieving Jews are "broken off" and only believing Jews retained - the *"Israel of God"* - Galatians 6:16. However, it's ethnicity that determines priority - which, at bottom, is what underlies the distinction between "the natural branches" and "the wild branches." The metaphor is entirely consistent with Paul's teaching throughout all of Romans.

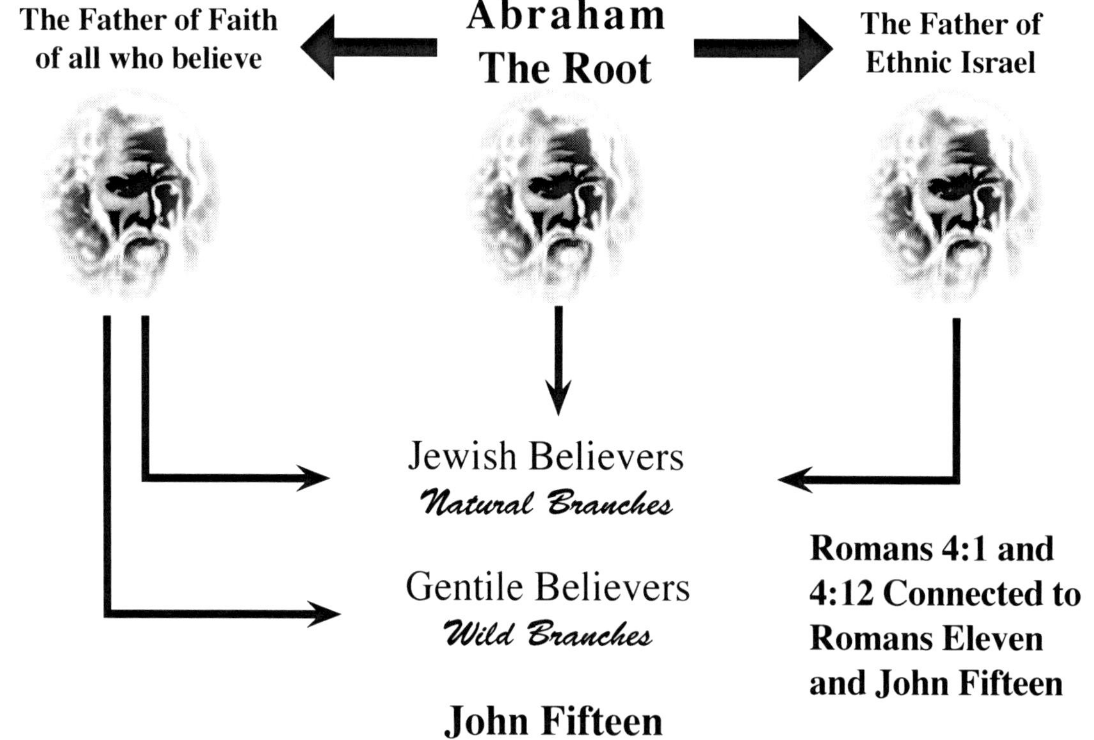

John Fifteen

Throughout the Old Testament, Israel is likened to a vine with many branches (e.g, Psalm 80:8 and 14, Isaiah 5:2, Jeremiah 2:21, Ezekiel 17:8, Hosea 10:1). And that's the metaphor Jesus is using in John Fifteen. It's basically the same metaphor used by Paul in Romans Eleven. Therefore, when Jesus says he's the vine, he's declaring that he is Israel's telos (see page 24) - *the consummation of Abraham's faith*. It necessarily follows, then, that a Jew who repudiates Christ does not walk "according to Abraham's faith" and is, therefore, "cast forth" from Israel (the Israel of God) and burned - exactly the point Paul makes in Romans Eleven when he tells us that unbelieving Jews are "broken off." It's the very truth Paul highlights in Romans 9:6 when he tells us, *"...for they are not all Israel, who are of Israel."* In John Fifteen, Jesus is speaking only to Jews; hence, there's no need there to distinguish between "natural branches" and "wild branches" - whereas in Romans Eleven that distinction is clearly called for.

surprise. A little thought about it adds to the significance we normally ascribe to Genesis 12:1-3...

Gen. 12:1	Now the Lord had said unto Abram, depart from your country, and from your kindred, and from your father's house, unto a land that I will show you:
Gen. 12:2	And I will make of you a great nation, and I will bless you, and make your name great; and you shall be a blessing:
Gen. 12:3	And I will bless those who bless you, and curse him who curses you: and in you shall all families of the earth be blessed.

We're accustomed to think that the blessing mentioned in Genesis 12:1-3 is found in Christ – that and that alone. But there's more to the blessing than that. Abraham is a blessing both...

- because Christ is Abraham's seed (Hebrews 2:16), and
- because "walking in the steps of Abraham's faith" (Romans 4:12) appropriates for us the unsearchable riches God has deposited in Christ (Ephesians 3:8).

Verse:

Rom. 4:2	For if Abraham was justified by works, he has something to boast about, but not before God?

Specific words or phrases found in Romans 4:2
"For if Abraham was justified by works, he has something to boast about..."
Here Paul is facing head on the challenge posed by the Jews' assessment of Abraham's standing before God – specifically, that his obedience justified him. The first phrase, "For if Abraham was justified by works," is clearly a protasis leading to an apodosis found in the very next phrase, "he has something to boast about..." In short, Paul is acknowledging that if Abraham's standing before God is founded on obedience, then the Jews are right: Abraham has good cause to boast.

Specific words or phrases found in Romans 4:2
"but not before God..."
What we have here is an idiomatic expression meaning "but that's not how God sees it." In other words, the protasis is untrue: Abraham was not justified on the grounds of his obedience; consequently, even for Abraham, boasting is out of the question – there's no basis for it.

Verse:

Rom. 4:3	For what does the Scripture say? Abraham believed God, and it was accounted to him for righteousness.

Specific words or phrases found in Romans 4:3
"For what does the Scripture say?"
Having made it clear in Romans 3:21...

Rom. 3:21	But now the righteousness of God apart from the law has been manifested, being witnessed by the Law and the Prophets...

...that the continuity between the new and old testaments is seamless – that the one, the Law and the Prophets, clearly attests to the other, the Gospels and the Epistles – it stands to reason that Paul, to make his point, would resort to the Law and the Prophets – which is exactly what he does here.

Specific words or phrases found in Romans 4:3
"Abraham believed God, and it was accounted to him for righteousness."
Paul is quoting Genesis 15:6.

Genesis 15:6	And he (Abraham) believed in the Lord; and he counted it to him for righteousness.

Genesis 15:6 would seem to settle the matter: Abraham's rightousness is an imputed righteousness grounded in faith, not an earned righteousness. But that's not how the Jews interpreted Genesis 15:6. *For them, Abraham's belief was itself meritorious; it earned him God's favor.* In short, rabbinic Judaism merely lumped faith alongside a whole welter of other meritorious deeds that warranted God's approbation. There's nothing special or unique about it. Rabbi Shemaiah's commentary on Exodus 14:16 is typical...

> The faith of your father Abraham merits that I (the Lord) should divide the sea for them...

Verse:

Rom. 4:4	Now to him who works, the wages are not counted as grace but as debt.

Calvin on the Ropes

Specific words or phrases found in Romans 4:4
"Now to him who works, the wages are not counted as grace but as debt."
Here begins Paul's argument against Rabbinic Judaism's interpretation of Genesis 15:6. Paul acknowledges...

- that "work" and "grace" are mutually exclusive;
- that "work" warrants a "wage" – a wage arising from a debt that's justly incurred;
- that grace, on the other hand, is not deserved;

...and that sets up verse 5.

Verse:

Rom. 4:5	But to him who does not work but believes on Him who justifies the ungodly, his faith is accounted for righteousness,

Specific words or phrases found in Romans 4:5
"...does not work but believes..."
Clearly, Paul is distinguishing between "work" and "belief." He's saying that the two are not the same; that the one, "belief," cannot be subsumed under the other, "work;" that faith is in a class all its own; that it's sui generis. In short, Paul is...

- breaking the unity the Jews have forged between "work" and "belief;"
- he's telling us that "belief" is not a "work;"
- that, therefore, "belief" does not warrant a "wage" – ***meaning whatever God's response to our faith might be it does not arise from a debt he has incurred.***

Specific words or phrases found in Romans 4:5
"...on him who justifies the ungodly..."
Clearly, the word "believes" in the previous clause, "does not work but believes," finds its object here in the word "him." There's no obvious antecedent that supplies the identity of "him;" but that's no problem because the relative clause which follows, "who justifies the ungodly," does precisely that: clearly, it's God.

Specific words or phrases found in Romans 4:5
"...his faith is accounted for righteousness."
Here Paul links faith in God to righteousness; but because in the previous two clauses he has broken the link the Jews have forged between "work" and "faith," insisting that faith is not itself meritorious, what's obviously meant here is an imputed righteousness, not an earned righteousness. In short, the righteousness God confers on anyone who believes is not deserved; it arises from God's mercy – his grace (Romans 4:4).

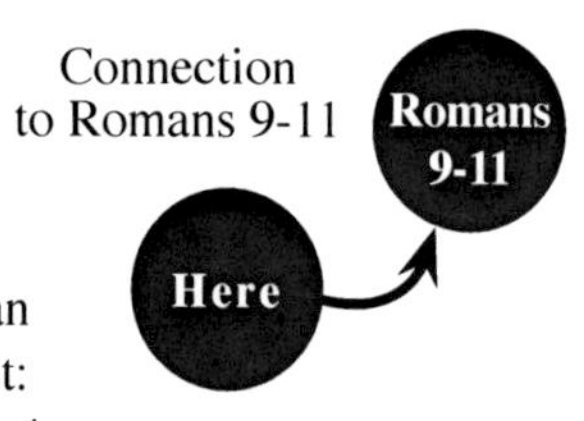

Here again we encounter a flaw in Five Point Calvinism – a flaw that's not immediately obvious, but, with a little thought, can be ferreted out from the text: Paul's argument in Romans 4 hangs on the distinction he draws between "work" and "faith;" that "faith" is not, in and of itself, meritorious – meaning it doesn't warrant God's favor.

- *It secures God's favor;*
- ***but it doesn't warrant God's favor.***

God's favor arises from his mercy – and mercy, by definition, is never warranted. That's a non-sequitur. But...

- if belief doesn't warrant God's favor,
- neither does unbelief warrant God's condemnation.

In short, unbelief – in the limited sense that it amounts to a rejection of the imputed righteousness of Jesus Christ – isn't a sin per se. It's not a person's unbelief – again, in the limited sense of a person disavowing his need for the mercy of God – that sends him to hell; it's his sins that send him there – or, more specifically, the just condemnation arising from those sins. ***His unbelief amounts only to turning down God's offer to pardon him.***

Let me put it differently. All mankind is shuffling down a road leading to hell – that's because we have all inherited both Adam's corruption and his condemnation. Jesus stands alongside that road with a fistful of pardons in his hand – eagerly pressing them into the hands of every man, woman, and child who asks for one. For those who reject it, it's not their rejection that sends them to hell; ***they're already on their way.***

Calvinists, however, disagree. John Piper is a good example. In his defense of limited atonement, he lists three statements and then asks which one is true...

1. Christ died for some of the sins of all men.
2. Christ died for all the sins of some men.
3. Christ died for all the sins of all men.

The first, he acknowledges, no one would suggest is true. The third is affirmed by Arminians – Christ died for the sins of all men.

"Why, then," asks Piper, "aren't they all saved?"

"Because," answer the Arminians, "not all men believe."

"But," asks Piper, convinced he has backed the Arminians into a corner, "isn't unbelief one of the sins for which Christ died?" Certain he has asked nothing more than a rhetorical question the answer to which is obviously "yes," Piper delivers his carefully crafted coup de grâce: "Therefore, if he died for the sins of all men – including the sin of unbelief – why aren't all men saved?"

In short, because all men aren't saved, Christ must not have died for the sins of all mankind, but only for those God has sovereignly elected to salvation.

Piper, though, is wrong. Unbelief is not itself a sin. Let's go over it again - with a slightly different twist: imagine for a moment the impossible – that there's one righteous man milling about in a mass of condemned humanity. Jesus is walking among the men and women huddled there – distributing pardons to every person who asks for one. Some gratefully seize the pardon; others don't. Among those who don't is the one righteous man. Will his refusal send him to hell? Of course it won't. Why? Because God's justice won't permit it – proving that rejecting God's pardon isn't, *in and of itself*, a sin; *it merely forecloses to an already condemned sinner the possibility of availing himself of God's mercy*. Once again, faith is not subsumed under work. It's in a class of its own. It's sui generis.

What Piper doesn't realize is that he has stumbled over the same intellectual snag that tripped up the Jews in their interpretation of Genesis 15:6 – the very mistake Paul exposes in Romans 4:4-5. Just as the Jews forged a link between belief and merit, so has Piper with unbelief and condemnation.

Piper points to Romans 14:23 and insists that it supports his argument that unbelief is itself a sin.

Rom. 14:23	But he who doubts is condemned if he eats, because he does not eat from faith; for whatever is not from faith is sin.

That kind of exegesis, however, only puts him further behind the eight-ball.

- To begin with, the scope of Romans 14:23 is very limited – restricted to portions of the ceremonial law and its continued relevance for Christians. That's its context. There's little justification for expanding the point Paul's making into a principle that's more general in nature.
- Secondly, there's good reason to believe that here in Romans 14:23 the word "pistis" (πιστις), which is usually translated "faith," is better translated "conscience." Why? Because the whole Fourteenth Chapter revolves around how far a Christian should push his freedom from the ceremonial law. There's no doubt that for Paul Christians are free from the strictures of the ceremonial law. However, some Christians – though they may intellectually acknowledge that they're free – haven't yet reached the point of actually being able to walk out that freedom. In other words, their minds may tell them that they're free, but inwardly there's no *sense* of that freedom; the fact that they're free hasn't sufficiently taken root in them – meaning their consciences are still bound. And for them to violate their consciences puts in jeopardy their walk with the Lord – because, as Paul points out in 1 Timothy 1:19, a troubled conscience "shipwrecks" faith - and leaves believers vulnerable to sin – precisely the issue Paul takes up in Romans Seven.
- Finally, here in Romans 14:23 the context in which the word "sin" is imbedded alters its usual meaning. Ordinarily, Paul uses the word "sin" in a wholly objective sense – meaning sin is sin regardless of whatever our minds or consciences may tell us. But Paul is clearly not saying that it's objectively sinful to disregard the ceremonial law. He's simply saying that for "weaker" Christians to disregard the ceremonial law may so damage their consciences that they're put in danger of succumbing to self-condemnation and the ravages that produces – once again, a topic he takes up in Romans Chapter Seven.

The meaning of Romans 14:23 is far better rendered with a few changes in the wording...

Rom. 14:23	But he who doubts is condemned by his own conscience if he eats, because his conscience is troubled thereby; for whatever doesn't arise from an untroubled conscience leads to sin.

Clearly, Romans 14:23 does not support Piper's argument that unbelief is sin. Respectfully, that's bad exegesis. And John Piper's better than that.

That brings us to the one answer Piper and his fellow Calvinists insist is correct: Answer #2, Christ died for all the sins of some men. But that's wrong too. Paul put that argument to rest back in Chapter 3, verses 29-30...

Rom. 3:29	Or is God the God of Jews only? Is He not the God of Gentiles also? Yes, of Gentiles also
Rom. 3:30	since indeed God who will justify the circumcised by faith and the uncircumcised through faith is one.

There Paul pointed out that the Cross proves God is as merciful as he is righteous and holy – that he's *ontologically merciful* just as he's *ontologically righteous* – meaning mercy arises from his very nature. Therefore, if the consequences arising from God's righteousness – moral accountability and judgment – extend to all mankind, so too does God's mercy – because *God is one*. In short...

- God can't be merciful to the Jews without being merciful to the gentiles. *God is one*.
- He can't tender an offer of mercy to Jacob without at the same time tendering that same offer to Esau. *God is one*.
- He can't tender an offer of mercy to some men without tendering that same offer to all men. *God is one*.

No, John Piper and his fellow Calvinists are wrong on both accounts...

- Statement #3, "Christ died for all the sins of all men" is correct (with the added caveat that the forgiveness his death affords must be appropriated by faith); and
- Statement #2, "Christ died for all the sins of some men," is incorrect.

Appendix I
The Relationship between Idolatry and Fornication

Romans Chapter One clearly links fornication and idolatry; but it's a link that American Christians very seldom think about let alone take to heart. The result has been catastrophic. This sermon, preached in the early 1990s, was meant to highlight that link and spell out its dynamic. It was designed to help both Christian lay persons and leaders get beyond simply shouting out warnings against the danger of fornication, and, instead, equip them to explain *why* it's so terribly dangerous. I have left it in a sermon format - just as I preached it close to twenty years ago.

Figures are sometimes hard to come by - and often they're not entirely consistent; nevertheless, let me cite some for you - saving the most recent figures for last.

- 40% of all adolescents will undergo the trauma of witnessing their parents divorce. And the majority of those divorces involve sexual infidelity; consequently, more and more children are being "cued" to sexual promiscuity by their own parents.
- One out every seven teenage girls becomes pregnant - that's pregnant. We're not speaking here about how many engage in sexual intercourse without becoming pregnant, we're talking about how many actually become pregnant - and that's one out of seven.
- In late 1993, a survey of 2000 high school students revealed that 19% of the boys and 27% of the girls (more girls than boys) were engaged in regular, on-going sexual intercourse. Here, we're not including high school students who only occasionally engage in sexual intercourse. The figure for the girls is up from 5% reported in 1970.

Let me provide you with a concrete example to flesh out these figures: recently in Hempstead, Texas, four girls on Hempstead High's cheerleading squad were found to be pregnant. They were all suspended, not dismissed, from the squad pending the birth of their babies. However, one of the four girls decided to abort her baby and she was reinstated within a week of the abortion. There was little moral outrage; just a sort of "let's get this behind us" attitude.

Now, for the most disturbing of all the surveys - conducted just this last month - and reported on all three of the national networks. It found that three out of ten 6th, 7th, and 8th graders, fully 30%, have engaged in sexual intercourse. Not high schoolers, that's 9th through 12th graders, but junior high schoolers, 7th and 8th graders, and even grade schoolers, 6th graders! And what's particularly surprising about this finding is that there were no distinctions pertaining to scholastic achievement, family, financial status, or race. It didn't matter whether the child was getting good grades or bad grades; was from an intact family or a ruptured family; was financially well off or poverty stricken; or was Black, White, Latino, or Asian - the likelihood of his or her having engaged in sexual intercourse was the same - 30%. And, again, we're talking about 6th, 7th, and 8th graders.

In other words, what we're talking about here is not rooted in deprivation; it's not the result of an on-going pattern of discrimination, it's not due to an emotional trauma. It can't be traced back to any kind of hardship. What does it reflect then? It's the result of changing ethics.

Frankly put, sexual promiscuity is no longer frowned upon. It's no longer enveloped in shame. Its commission no longer prompts conviction and guilt. Thirty years ago, or, more likely, forty and fifty years ago, sexual intimacy on the part of anyone who wasn't a married adult - let alone 6th, 7th, and 8th graders - generated moral outrage. Anyone caught engaging in promiscuous sexual intercourse was ostracized - and if that person was a child, the parents were left bewildered, shocked, and stupefied - and their standing in the community was seriously undermined. But today, there's almost no sense of moral outrage - that is, there's very little sense of shame - either on the part of the child or on the part of the parents. There's a single prevailing attitude:

- It's not that the child has behaved shamefully; it's that the child has behaved stupidly.
- It's not that the child is immoral; it's that the child is not behaving in his own best interests.

Let me ask you, "what's likely to occur to a child

caught today engaging in sexual promiscuity?" He'll be told that...

- he's unaware of the implications of his conduct;
- that he's not ready to shoulder the responsibilities that an active sexual relationship necessarily entails;
- that an unwanted pregnancy might result;
- that, at the very least, a condom should be used - both to prevent a pregnancy and to ward off AIDs or venereal disease.

Then father and son or mother and daughter might have a good cry together. And the whole matter is set aside. What's avoided at all costs is the inculcation of guilt. And without the inculcation of a searing sense of guilt, there can be precious little in the way of actual repentance. The two go hand in hand. No guilt, no repentance - and without repentance, prompted by guilt, there's little likelihood of any lasting change in behavior. Oh, there may be tears, but those tears are not the tears of repentance - however much sorrow might be gripping both parent and child. Compassion is almost always extended before repentance is proven.

There's a never ending scenario that's played out in my office - again and again. I wish sometimes you could sit in with me. This scenario is played out not just in my office, but in the office of every pastor I know. A man or a woman is caught engaging in sexual promiscuity - sometimes even resulting in a pregnancy. And the very first issue that's raised by that person's friends in the church or by his relatives is not guilt, or shame, or repentance; it's the need to extend compassion. And, yes, compassion is a uniquely Christian virtue; but the Bible never encourages compassion in the absence of shame, conviction, and repentance.

In fact, the Bible demands not just a verbal repentance; its demands are much more severe than mere words can evidence; it demands that we prove our repentance with deeds. And then compassion can be legitimately conveyed - and restoration and healing can be brought to bear.

Let me remind you of the rebuke Jesus hurled at the Pharisees in Matthew 3:8.

Matt. 3:8	...bring forth fruit in keeping with repentance...

And the same point is made by Paul in his conversation with King Agrippa...

Acts 26:20	...but (I) kept declaring both to those of Damascus first, and also at Jerusalem and then throughout all the region of Judea, and even to the Gentiles, that they should repent and turn to God, performing deeds appropriate to repentance.

No, what we're witnessing today - rampant sexual promiscuity on the part of not only adults but children - is not the result of material hardship or emotional trauma, it's the result of changed ethical standards. Sexual promiscuity is no longer considered shameful. There's no appeal made to moral outrage. There's no real sense of guilt. It's still considered to be unwise - even stupid - and most certainly dangerous; but that's all. And what that means is that the conscience has been deactivated. The moral energy of the conscience is left untapped.

Our children - and I do mean "children" - are being assaulted by a media that hypes up erotic behavior - that appeals brazenly to their developing sexual drives - sexual drives that they only barely understand but feel keenly; and, inadvertently, we've stripped them of their best defense - the moral energy of an acutely sensitive conscience. The conscience can no longer be enlisted in their struggle against sexual promiscuity - because sexual promiscuity is no longer cast in the guise of sin - and all in the name of compassion.

Sexual temptations have assaulted every generation; but our children, unlike past generations of children, have been left defenseless - because we've deactivated their consciences. And that's why there's such an increase today in sexual promiscuity.

But let's not blame only our schools - or the federal government - or Hillary Clinton - or Molly Yard - or the National Organization of Women - or the American Civil Liberties Union. That's too easy. And, furthermore, it's not right. The church has played a major role. Let me give you a concrete example - drawn from a church right here in Sacramento. A good church. A Bible believing church. And it's an example that's repeated scores of times each month throughout the Sacramento area. Several years ago a person was caught engaging in on-going sexual promiscuity. Not once did that person truly repent - bringing forth evidence of changed behavior. The immorality continued. Oh, there were tears; but there was no change. Eventually the person simply ceased attending church - and withdrew from all fellowship. And what happened? Again and again, the pastors of the church were condemned by an influential segment of the congregation for lack of compassion. And several families left the church as a result.

What do we have here? It's the same dynamic that's at work among the unsaved:

- the press to extend compassion without requiring repentance;
- the same refusal to allow searing conviction to finish its course.

Whenever the church seeks to protect a sinner from the pain of conviction in the name of compassion, she strips believers of perhaps their single most powerful defensive mechanism - an acutely sensitive conscience.

My first point this morning, then, is that we must recover our sense of moral outrage. I'm not countenancing cruelty or malice. I'm not encouraging you to form sin patrols to ferret out sexual promiscuity in the church. All I'm asking you to do is...

- call sexual promiscuity "sin," not just an addiction or a disease, but sin. It offends God - and it puts the sinner in jeopardy of judgment.
- Resist the temptation to dampen too quickly the pain of conviction afflicting the conscience of a person caught in sexual immorality; let the Holy Spirit finish His work. Even if that person is your best friend or your own child! Don't seek to dampen the pain of conviction too quickly.
- Do not extend the right hand of fellowship to anyone who claims to be a brother or sister, but who excuses sexual immorality in his or her own life - and refuses to acknowledge that it's a moral outrage. I'm not asking you to shun such a person; but you are not to treat that person as a fellow Christian. That's the real meaning of 1 Corinthians 5:11.

Clearly, once conviction has run its course and genuine repentance is evidenced, then compassion, healing, and full restoration should be extended quickly. Furthermore, the person must be accepted back into fellowship not as a second-class citizen, but as a first class citizen.

Now, building upon this insight, let's move on to my second point this morning: that what sexual intercourse is meant to be is far different from what you've probably been taught. It's not only an act, it's a special language. Let me begin with a passage of scripture you may be familiar with, but perhaps you've never really fully understood. It's Revelation 2, verse 14...

Now we're going to have to get a bit technical here; it's unavoidable. What I'm trying to do this morning is not simply shout at you that sexual promiscuity is sinful, but to explain to you why. OK, let's turn now to Revelation 2:14

> Rev. 2:14 But I have a few things against thee, because thou hast there them that hold the doctrine of Balaam, who taught Balac to cast a stumblingblock before the children of Israel, to eat things sacrificed unto idols, and to commit fornication.

There are several terms and phrases I want you to take note of here in this verse:

- The first is the phrase "hold the doctrine of Balaam" - or, a better translation would be "cling to the teaching of Balaam." What's that?
- The second is the word "stumblingblock."
- The third is "things sacrificed to idols."
- And the fourth and last term is "fornication."

It's apparent from the verse that all four terms and phrases are linked. But how? You can pick up the story of Balak and Balaam in the Old Testament; more specifically, in the Book of Numbers - beginning with chapter 20 and extending through chapter 25. But let me sum it up for you here briefly: Balak was the King of Moab, a country which butted up against the boundaries of Canaan, just east of the Dead Sea. He was King at the time Israel, under Moses, was passing through the Wilderness into the Promised Land. Balak was fearful of Israel; so, he hired the prophet Balaam, from Midian, to curse her - hoping that in so doing he would destroy her. But God prevented Balaam from cursing Israel; and each time Balaam sought to pronounce a curse, God forced him to utter a blessing.

Nevertheless, Balaam wasn't finished. His first strategy - to curse Israel - had failed; but he hit upon a second strategy that ultimately proved to be successful. He advised Balak, King of Moab, to send out the women of Moab into the camp of Israel - enticing the men of Israel to commit fornication. And we read about that in Numbers 25.

Num. 25:1	And Israel abode in Shittim, (which is part of Moab just opposite of Jericho on the Jordan planes) and the people (i.e., the men of Israel) began to commit whoredom (i.e., fornication) with the daughters of Moab.
Num. 25:2	And they (i.e., the women of Moab) called the people (i.e., the men of Israel) unto the sacrifices of their gods: and the people did eat, and bowed down to their gods.
Num. 25:3	And Israel joined himself unto Baalpeor (i.e., the god of the Moabites): and the anger of the Lord was kindled against Israel.

So, Numbers 25:1-3 give us much of the meaning pertaining to the terms and phrases we noted in Revelation 2:14

- The phrase "the teaching of Balaam," found in Revelation 2:14, is Balaam's advice to Balak, King of Moab.
- The stumblingblock - is, of course, fornication. The word "stumblingblock" translates the Greek word "skandalon" - from which we derive our word "scandal." And it means a "trap," or more accurately, "the bait used in a trap." Fornication is bait for a trap. That's its meaning here in Revelation 2:14.
- But the trap itself is idolatry, not fornication. Fornication is the bait; idolatry is the trap.

At this point, we've unraveled much of the meaning of Revelation 2:14; but we still aren't quite there yet; and that's because most of us don't really understand the meaning of "idolatry." That term has lost its meaning to our 20th century minds. When we think of an idol, we imagine a statue of some kind - a stone statue or a carved image. For me, almost inevitably, what pops into my mind is a Buddha - with his legs crossed - in a Japanese garden. But that image does nothing to convey the real meaning of idolatry. Let's turn to the Bible again - and read several verses in Isaiah and the Psalms. And it may be that from these verses we can begin to catch the meaning of "idolatry" or the "principle of idolatry" - because that's what we're talking about here - a principle - a spiritual principle.

Ps. 95:3	For the Lord is a great God, And a great King above all gods...
Ps. 97:9	For Thou art the Lord Most High over all the earth; Thou art exalted far above all gods.
Is. 40:25	To whom then will ye liken me, or shall I be equal? says the Holy One.
Is. 44:6	Thus says the Lord, the King of Israel And his Redeemer, the Lord of hosts: I am the first and I am the last, And there is no God besides Me.
Is. 46:5	To whom will ye liken me, and make me equal, and compare me, that we may be like?

Do you catch now the principle of idolatry? Each of the verses we've just read stresses the utter transcendence of God. He is unique - so utterly unique that He's incomparable. That's His nature. There is none like Him. Indeed, it's sinful to even attempt comparisons with God. The very act of comparison profanes God. Do you know what it means to "profane" God? Do you understand the technical meaning of the word "profane"? Let me read two more passages of scripture with you...

Is. 48:11	...for My own sake, I will (vindicate myself); For how can My name be profaned? And My glory be given to another?
Ezek. 20:39	As for you, O house of Israel, thus says the Lord God, Go, serve everyone his idols; but later, you will surely listen to Me, and My holy name you will profane no longer with your gifts and with your idols.

Do you see how the word "profane" is used in conjunction with idolatry? That's because idolatry is an act of profanity. And profanity simply means to "make common." That's its technical meaning. The very act of comparing God profanes Him - because it reduces God to the level of the item to which He's being compared. God is incomparable - beyond comparison. And any attempt to compare Him reduces His awesome majesty.

All of us know the Ten Commandments, right? How many of you know that four of the ten commandments warn mankind against profaning God - reducing His majesty? And those four commandments are the first four. Turn with me to Deuteronomy, Chapter five.

Deut. 5:7	Thou shalt have none other gods

before me.

Deut. 5:8 Thou shalt not make thee any graven image, or any likeness of any thing that is in heaven above, or that is in the earth beneath, or that is in the waters beneath the earth...

So the first two commandments essentially forbid comparison. God will not tolerate being brought alongside other gods. Nor will He tolerate anyone making a statue of Him or an image of Him - because that presumes comparison. The third commandment is like the first two - in that it prohibits another form of profanity - blasphemy - taking the Lord's name in vain - which drags down the name of God to a common level - and serves, therefore, to undermine its utter transcendence.

Deut. 5:11 Thou shalt not take the name of the Lord thy God in vain: for the Lord will not hold him guiltless that takes his name in vain.

Idolatry profanes God Himself; and blasphemy profanes the name of God. Both are acts of profanity. And even the fourth is akin to the first three - in that it's designed to set aside one day of the week to worship God - and call to mind His utter uniqueness - His transcendent nature.

Deut. 5:12 Keep the Sabbath day to sanctify it, as the Lord thy God hath commanded thee.

Let's go over this very carefully - because it's an important key to solving our riddle. Idolatry puts God on a par with other gods. The principle of idolatry does not aim at replacing the worship of Jehovah with the worship of another god. All it aims at is to include the worship of other gods alongside the worship of Jehovah - Jehovah worshipped alongside Baal, alongside Bel, alongside Ashtaroth, alongside Istar, alongside a whole pantheon of other gods - the gods of the heathen. And in putting Jehovah alongside the gods of the heathen, it drags Him down to their level. It profanes Him. True worship - the kind of worship God sanctions and accepts - is, therefore, exclusive. Worship not only expresses adoration and praise, but, in addition, it promises God exclusive adoration and praise. The act of worship is an act of "exclusivity;" it's an act which declares total commitment. Worship is not just an act of passion - an act of adoration and praise; it is, in addition, a declaration - a declaration of total commitment. It's both an act and a declaration. And for the act to be meaningful and acceptable, the declaration must be authentic and truthful.

How important is idolatry in the Old Testament? In many respects, it's the story of the Old Testament. The children of Israel never quite seemed to "catch on." God would not allow Himself to be worshipped alongside the gods of the heathen. It's the story of the Book of Judges. It's the story of Elijah at Mount Carmel. Not even Solomon, with all his wisdom, caught on - and at the close of his reign, idolatry was rampant. The specific sin that called forth God's judgment upon the Northern Kingdom was idolatry. And, likewise, the specific sin that led to Judah's demise a century later was idolatry. It was the sin the prophets most singled out and condemned.

But how does all this fit into sexual promiscuity? Well, let's go back to Revelation 2:14. We've already established that fornication is the bait the devil uses to draw believers into idolatry - the act of profaning God. But how are fornication and idolatry related? What's the link? How does fornication bait the trap? Ask yourself, "What do fornication and idolatry have in common?" We've already made the point that worship is not just an act of adoration and ecstatic praise - drawing God and His people into oneness, but, in addition, it's a declaration of total commitment. Worship is not just an act; it's a declaration. And for the act to be meaningful, the declaration must be authentic and truthful.

And that's true of sexual intercourse as well. Sexual intercourse, like worship, is not just an act; it's a declaration. And for the act to be meaningful, the declaration must be authentic and truthful. If the declaration of total commitment and exclusivity can't be made in truth, the act loses its meaning. Let me put it another way. We've been taught that sexual intercourse - and all that leads up to sexual intercourse - is merely pleasurable. That it's an act that gives pleasure. But sexual intercourse is not first an act which gives pleasure; it's first and foremost a language that speaks of total and exclusive commitment. And then it's an act that gives pleasure. Just as worship is not first and foremost an act of adoration and praise, it's first and foremost a declaration of total and exclusive commitment. Therefore, if you're a fornicator, you can't speak the language of love. Sexual intercourse loses its meaning. Why? Because you've profaned it. The words it speaks come out garbled. If you've engaged in repeated acts of fornication, you've profaned sexual intercourse - and, therefore, can no longer use it to declare love to your spouse. It has become a garbled language.

And that's the tragedy of fornication. We have a whole generation of men and woman for whom sexual intercourse is not the pure language of love it was meant to be. Spouses can no longer use it to declare love to one another. It has been profaned. It has been made common. That's what fornication does: it makes common what was meant to be sanctified and pure - set aside for one person only. When you make love to your spouse, you can no longer authentically declare to your spouse, "I belong to you alone. I share this joy with you alone. I belong to no one else. I have reserved myself for you only." And if that declaration can't be made, the act loses its meaning - and the pleasure becomes very elusive. Let me repeat myself: we've been taught that sexual intercourse is merely an act which arouses pleasure. But that's wrong. Of course, it should produce an ecstatic joy - that's God's intention; but it's meant first and foremost to be a declaration of total and exclusive commitment. And if it can no longer speak that message, the passion and joy it's meant to convey are likely to vanish as well.

Again, I wish that some of you could sit in my office and hear what I hear - so many husbands and wives who find no real joy in sexual intimacy. I remember when I was young - around 18 or 19 - I couldn't figure out why husbands and wives didn't spend all 24 hours a day making love to one another. To me - at 18 - sexual intimacy was merely an act that promised unending ecstasy and passion. But later I discovered that it's meant to be a language. And the pleasure of the act depends upon the purity of the language. I have counseled with some married couples who engage in sexual intercourse no more than once or twice a year. That's not common; but it's not as uncommon as you might imagine. More frequently, I've counseled with married couples who engage in sexual intercourse no more than once a month. And though certainly better than once a year, it's still far from God's intention. Why the infrequency? Because it has lost its pleasure! And why's that? Because they've profaned it. Keep the language pure, and you'll keep the act pleasurable.

Anything that profanes sexual intimacy jeopardizes its long-term pleasure - anything at all - not just fornication and adultery, but pornography, illicit thoughts - yes, even trashy soap operas. Moreover, it's not just the sins a person commits himself or herself, it's sins committed against him or her as well; e.g., incest and rape.

It's not that sexual intimacy once defiled can't be recovered and sanctified. God is more than able to cleanse whatever stains have tarnished it; however, it can't be "swept under the rug" and ignored. Once again, sexual intercourse and worship are inextricably linked. And that's why fornication baits the trap that leads to idolatry. Both idolatry and fornication are acts of profanity. And once you've engaged in profanity at any level, it spills over onto all other levels. Fornication always leads to idolatry. Balaam knew that principle - and that's why he advised Balak to entice the men of Israel to commit fornication with the woman of Moab - because he knew that profanity at one level always leads to profanity at all levels. He knew that fornication would lead to idolatry. And it did. And this is one of Satan's master plans for the Last Days. Fornication not only ruins marriage; but, in addition, it turns hearts away from God. What a master strategy! One thing the devil isn't. And that's dumb.

Now, I'm not through yet. I want to conclude my warning today with a few principles concerning dating. Let's turn to 1 Corinthians 7:5. Here Paul is speaking to married couples - and, specifically, he's speaking about sexual intercourse.

1 Cor. 7:5 — Defraud ye not one the other, except it be with consent for a time, that ye may give yourselves to fasting and prayer; and come together again, that Satan tempt you not for your incontinency.

This is another passage of scripture which, like Revelation 2:14, is so much more than it appears. Now, the verse here is specifically addressed to married couples, not singles; but there's a principle here that we can apply to singles - and which will shed light on what kind of behavior should be avoided in dating. I want you to take special note of the word "defraud." It translates the Greek word "apostereo." Some translations substitute the word "deprive" for the word "defraud." And that's accurate up to a certain point. We've lost the meaning of the word "defraud" - and "deprive" seems to come closer to what Paul is conveying here. But the word "defraud" implies deceit as well as deprivation - which the word "deprive" doesn't. And that's the problem with the word "deprive" - it misses the element of deceit. Here's my point in a nutshell - it's very simple and straightforward: marriage incorporates by its very nature the expectation of sexual intercourse.

Everyone who gets married looks forward to sexual intercourse. Marriage establishes that expectation. It certainly did for me. It certainly did for Sita. Didn't it for you? Of course it did. In light of that expectation, then, don't deprive one another. Indeed, such a deprivation is more than merely an act of holding back, it's fraud. Why is it fraud? Because the expectation is so clearly established. And that's the principle I want to draw out here. Any setting which establishes the expectation of sexual intimacy - and then fails to provide it is fraud. And fraud is a sin.

Marriage is not the only setting that can establish the expectation of sexual intimacy. It's the only legitimate setting; but it's certainly not the only one. And singles dating one another over an extended period of time - spending a great deal of time alone with one another - encounter those settings again and again. They reach a point of profound emotional intimacy - and that emotional intimacy presses them almost inexorably toward sexual intimacy. Just about every moment alone becomes a setting which establishes the expectation of sexual intimacy. And they find themselves defrauding one another again and again and again. Now, are we going to kid ourselves at this point?

Singles who have been dating one another for a long time and who have established a profound emotional intimacy with one another become trapped between two sins: fornication on the one hand and fraud on the other. If fornication is avoided, fraud is committed. And if fraud is avoided, fornication is committed. They find themselves bouncing back and forth between these two sins. Soon, their whole relationship turns sour. What should be done? Get married, doggone it. Or break off the relationship. But don't continue simply dating one another.

A boyfriend/girlfriend relationship cannot endure indefinitely. It's merely transitional in nature. I'm amazed at how often singles attempt to prolong a boyfriend/girlfriend relationship. Too many men these days are outright wimps. They want an emotional relationship with a woman, but they don't want to pay the price for it - marriage. And too many woman these days are outright suckers: they'll continue indefinitely with a boyfriend/girlfriend relationship with hardly a murmur of protest. Listen, ladies, throw the bum out. Drop him. He doesn't deserve you. Don't play the fool for him. If he's not willing to marry you, send him packing. Is he a real man? Then he'll marry you. The point is stop playing the fool. So many times I hear the excuse: "We just don't have the money to get married." Sita and I got married with hardly a dime to our names. Yes, it was tough. But we managed it. The lack of money is just an excuse. And what does it excuse? Does it excuse fornication, ladies? Does it excuse fraud? A boyfriend/girlfriend relationship is going in one of three different directions: (1) courtship and marriage; (2) fraud; or (3) fornication.

Men, come to grips with what you want. If you want the emotional intimacy a woman can provide, then marry her. And if you're unwilling to marry her, stop dating her. All this business of prolonging boyfriend/girlfriend relationships is morally wrong. And nowhere in the Bible is it countenanced. In fact there are many passages which warn against it. Let me give you a couple:

2 Tim. 2:22	Flee also youthful lusts: but follow righteousness, faith, charity, peace, with them that call on the Lord out of a pure heart.
Rom. 13:14	But put ye on the Lord Jesus Christ, and make not provision for the flesh, to fulfill the lusts thereof.

And you married men - never look to establish emotional intimacy with a woman other than your own wife. Emotional intimacy always develops into a press toward sexual intimacy - always. Stop lying to yourself. And you married woman, I have the same advice for you. I have only one woman with whom I share any kind of real emotional intimacy - and that's my wife Sita. And that's because with her, that emotional intimacy can and, indeed, should lead to sexual intimacy.

Now what about those of you in junior high school and high school? Am I suggesting that you don't date? Not necessarily. It depends on what you mean by "dating." If by dating you mean a bunch of guys going out with a bunch of girls, then the answer is "no." I don't want to discourage that. Not at all. But if you mean going steady - spending a lot of time alone together - to the point that girls are drawn away from their girl friends and guys are drawn away from their guy friends, then the answer is "yes." Don't date. Serious dating is meant to lead to courtship. If you're in junior high school or high school, you have no business thinking about marriage.

I know of too many young men and woman who feel almost destitute unless they're "going steady." And that sense reaches down to the grade schools. Don't cheat yourself like that! It's a delusion. Girls, spend your time learning how to make good girl friends. If you can't establish intimate friendships with other girls, you won't be able to establish an intimate relationship in marriage. The one lays the foundation for the other. And the same holds true for you guys. Loners and introverts don't make good marriage partners. What you learn in making friends throughout your childhood and teen years carries over into marriage. Marriage is not a cure-all for loneliness. Indeed, it only exacerbates loneliness for the lonely.

You say I'm being a prude. Oh no I'm not! If you sat where I sit, you'd think that maybe I'm not being sufficiently prudish. The devastation the devil has perpetrated on your generation is too awful for words. He's spoiling your generation for marriage. He's undermining your relationship with God. He's getting you to profane life itself. And that's his master plan. Keep yourself pure. You'll never regret it.

Now, let's review the main eight points:

1. We have got to recover our sense of moral outrage. Sexual promiscuity is evil. We must reactivate our consciences.
2. We must not seek to dampen the pain of conviction in the lives of those who have engaged in sexual promiscuity. We must allow the Holy Spirit to complete His work.
3. We must not allow ourselves to extend compassion before shame, conviction, and repentance are manifested.
4. Do not extend the right hand of fellowship to anyone who claims to be a brother or sister, but who excuses sexual immorality in his or her own life.
5. Worship and sexual intercourse are not just acts which lead to ecstasy and passion, they're declarations of total commitment. And if the declaration loses its authenticity, then the act loses its meaning - and the pleasure of both soon diminishes. Keep the declarations pure, and the acts will always retain both their meaning and their pleasure. Both for worship and for sexual intercourse!
6. Fornication always leads to idolatry. Profanity can't be contained. If it's committed on one level, it always spills over to other levels.
7. Any setting which establishes the expectation of sexual intimacy - and then fails to provide it is fraud. The only legitimate setting is marriage.
8. Any two persons who have dated one another for a long period of time inevitably find themselves bouncing back and forth between two sins: either fornication on the one hand, or fraud on the other. If fornication is avoided, fraud is committed; and if fraud is avoided, then fornication is committed. There are only two ways out of this dilemma: either break off the relationship or get married.

Take these eight principles and begin to apply them in your lives - and we will enjoy a degree of spiritual health we've never before known - as individuals, as married couples, and as a church family.

End Notes

1. It's certainly not that I've changed from expositing scripture – and switched over to topical studies; it's that I've changed the way I exposit scripture. This will become clearer.
2. Persons born between 1982 and 1995.
3. Once again, (1) reading a passage of scripture and drawing out the general principles embedded there, (2) spotting those very principles at work within our own cultural milieu, and then (3) applying those principles to our own personal lives.
4. Not, of course, their academic value; only their potential to change lives.
5. So also the gen-Yers – that cohort is obviously assumed.
6. Some expository studies do that already, but not to the extent I think is called for; and often it's more incidental than a consciously contrived strategy.
7. I'm fully aware that some teachers ask such a question only to stimulate dialogue – and that's fine. Still, for those of us who can remember back three or four decades, the question most often posed by teachers seeking to stimulate dialogue wasn't, "What does Romans 2:2-16 mean to you?" It was, "What do you think Paul means here in Romans 2:2-16?" Both stimulate dialogue, but one keeps the focus on Paul's meaning while the other shifts the focus to the listener's.
8. Once again, I'm not suggesting that the reasons I've delineated here are the "be all and end all" – only what has caught my attention over the last twenty years or so.
9. A long-running ad featuring André Aggasi sums up perfectly their mind-set: "Style – that's all that counts – style!"
10. Sentence diagramming, of course, presumes a translation of the Greek that retains, as much as possible, the original grammatical structure. I've relied on several commentaries to assure exactly that; the one I've found to be the most helpful is Cranfield's.
11. A good example of the error that's frequently made is found in the confusion that so often swirls about Romans 2 – where a straightforward reading of Romans 2:6-10, 12-16, and 25-29 seems to make salvation a matter of merit, not faith. The actual theme of those verses, however, is not salvation; it's the dynamics underlying God's jurisprudence.
12. Kafka's play The Trial is reviewed for its Biblical relevance at the end of Chapter Two.
13. The same point David makes in Psalm 51:5.
14. James Montgomery Boice's answer is an emphatic "No." God's mercy is not the ground of mankind's hope; it's God's sovereign choice – that alone. He writes, "...because God chooses me, I can know that I am secure..." And why? Boice goes on to say, "...because (his choice is grounded in) his eternal and sovereign determination." Boice, James Montgomery, Romans: Volume 3, God and History, Romans 9-11 (Grand Rapids: Baker Books, 1993), p. 1058.
15. Also what's called "final cause" – distinguishing it from Aristotle's other three causes: material, formal and efficient.
16. The term he preferred was "archetype" or "ideal;" and his best description of it is given in his well-known "Allegory of the Cave."
17. Though, once again, for Plato, the term he uses is not "telos," it's "archetype;" furthermore it's static, not dynamic. Nevertheless, it still conveys the sense of a "fixed destiny."
18. Once again, I'm not at all suggesting that Paul was either a Platonist or an Aristotelian, only that teleological presuppositions were imbedded in 1st Century thought.
19. Cf "American Culture and the Evangelical Church"
20. Individualism is a product of the 17th Century "Age of Reason" – an era that set the stage for the "Enlightenment" one hundred years later. Historically, it has not been the predominant mind-set throughout the world – certainly not in the Middle East, and most certainly not in 1st Century Palestine. It has only been within the last three and a half centuries that individualism has been pushed and shoved into ascendancy – and then only within Europe and North America. It was first clearly articulated by Thomas Hobbes in his book, The Leviathan, published in 1651, and three decades later by John Locke in his book Two Treatises on Government, pub-

lished in 1688.

21. The Greek city-state.
22. So too, in Plato's Republic, the "philosopher king."
23. Socrates willingness to commit suicide at the behest of the Athenian magistrates, notwithstanding his innocence, reflects the profound identity between Socrates and Athens.
24. James Montgomery Boice writes concerning portions of Chapters 9-10, "...I have called Romans 9-11 the most difficult portion of the Bible." Ibid. p. 1057
25. I'm sticking to Western culture only because I'm familiar with both its literature and art; but I'm not at all familiar with other cultures; e.g., Indian, Chinese, pre-Columbian, etc. I leave that to others.
26. Once again, teleology is the study of design or purpose in creation. It presupposes an intelligent First Cause – that creation is not random – that it reflects an underlying purpose – an underlying plan. All pre-modern cultures employ linguistic forms that reflect teleological presuppositions. However, Western culture has jettisoned teleological presuppositions – especially since David Hume and Immanuel Kant. Why? Because Western culture is founded on the empirical sciences the epistemology of which is wholly indifferent to First Causes. It's not that the principle of a First Cause is rejected outright, it's simply ignored.
27. "Subjugate" – the exact word used in Genesis 1:28 "Then God blessed them, and God said to them, "Be fruitful and multiply; fill the earth and subjugate it; have dominion over the fish of the sea, over the birds of the air, and over every living thing that moves on the earth."
28. The issue of God's wrath isn't, however, raised until verse 18.
29. Cf. Cranfield, C.E.B., The International Critical Commentary, Romans Volume I (Edinburgh, Scotland: T&T Clark, 1975), inter alia, pp. 487 and 497.
30. Boice, op. cit. On page 1066 Boice explicitly declares that reprobation (i.e., damnation) preconditions election (i.e., God's mercy). He goes on to quote Calvin: "Election (cannot) stand except as set over against reprobation." Cited from Boice, ibid., p. 1060.
31. ...which occurred on the Cross. The Cross is where God displayed at one and the same moment both his wrath and his mercy (His power to save.) Cf. the graphic on pages 28 and 138.
32. Romans 1:16 – Cranfield's conclusion
33. Cranfield, op. cit., p. 98. What's particularly interesting is that John Walvoord in his widely read commentary on the New Testament insists that the term "righteousness of God" is a subjective genitive, not a genitive of origin; but his conclusion is no different from Cranfield's; specifically, what Paul means is a righteous status that justifies a believer. Walvoord and Zuck, The Bible Knowledge Commentary (Wheaton, Illinois: Victor Books, 1986), p. 441.
34. Cranfield, reflecting the opinion of a majority of Protestant scholars, writes, "there seems to us to be no doubt that, as used by Paul ("righteousness of God"), means simply 'acquit,' 'confer a righteous status on'... This conclusion is surely forced upon us by the linguistic evidence." Ibid., p. 95.
35. The term "righteousness of God" is used frequently in Romans - sometimes to indicate an attribute of God, God's righteousness, a subjective genitive, a trait, e.g., Romans 3:5; and sometimes to indicate a status God confers in justification, a genitive of origin, e.g., Romans 3:21, 22, and Romans 10:3.
36. Cf. Excursus on Faith beginning on page 42.
37. Some scholars shy away from making "faith" mean more than merely an intellectual assent; they want to preserve the sense that "faith alone in Christ alone" is the means of salvation. And, yes, that's true – as long as we don't forget that the very definition of faith (i.e., "trust") incorporates not only an intellectual component, but a volitional, existential component as well. C.f. Dillow, Joseph, Reign of the Servant Kings (Hayesville, Schoettle Pub.,1993), p. 489.
38. Meaning deliver us from the penalty of our sins.
39. Meaning deliver us from the power of our sins.
40. The kind of faith that makes us pleasing to God in our daily lives – that not only delivers us from the penalty of sin, but delivers from the power of sin as well.
41. The Greeks never conceived of their gods in any other terms: they were peevish – and subject to fickle, erratic temper tantrums – tantrums which subjected humans to an uncontrolled fate not bound by moral constraints of any kind. Both Plato and Aristotle complained bitterly against conceptualizing God in such terms.
42. Cf., Ephesians 2:3 – which tells us that man is by nature a "child of wrath" – implying clearly

that he has already been found guilty and sentenced to death; cf., also Isaiah 53:6; Isaiah 64:6; Romans 3:10; Galatians 3:22; etc.

43. Romans 2:2 begins an examination of God's judgment - the dynamics that underlie it.
44. ...which is precisely the meaning of Romans 3:19 – where man is left dumbfounded – unable to respond to God's judgment – aware at last of his helplessness before God.
45. Boice, James Montgomery, Romans: Volume 3, God and History, Romans 9-11 (Grand Rapids: Baker Books, 1993), p. 1058.
46. ...which, of course, is the definition of mercy. Mercy is love that's not earned.
47. Erickson, Millard J., Introducing Christian Doctrine (Grand Rapids: Baker Book House, 1995), p. 288. Erickson writes, "Calvinism's second major concept is the sovereignty of God. He is the Creator and Lord of all things; and consequently he is free to do whatever he wills. He is not subject to or answerable to anyone. Humans are in no position to judge God for what he does. One of the passages frequently cited in this connection is the parable of the laborers in the vineyard" (italics mine).
48. Not that God had ceased to exist - which unfortunately is what the phrase is commonly taken to mean. The only point that Nieztche wanted to make in coining the phrase "God is dead" is that God's existence was no longer of any concern to him or his colleagues. And Nieztche was right. Not only was God "dead" among European intellectuals, he was also "dead" among rank-and-file Europeans as well. Church attendance was minimal at the close of the 19th Century and passion completely absent. Europe had become a religious wasteland. All Nietzsche did was acknowledge that fact.
49. I was a speaker myself – though not a featured speaker.
50. Bernard, J. H., International Critical Commentary, page 9.
51. Other examples abound...

John 14:1	Let not your heart be troubled; you believe in God, believe also in Me.
John 16:8	And when He has come, He will convict the world of sin, and of righteousness, and of judgment:
John 16:9	of sin, because they do not believe in Me...
John 17:20	I do not pray for these alone, but also for those who will believe in Me through their word...
Acts 24:24	And after some days, when Felix came with his wife Drusilla, who was Jewish, he sent for Paul and heard him concerning the faith in Christ.
Gal. 2:16	...knowing that a man is not justified by the works of the law but by faith in Jesus Christ, even we have believed in Christ Jesus, that we might be justified by faith in Christ and not by the works of the law; for by the works of the law no flesh shall be justified.
Gal. 3:26	For you are all sons of God through faith in Christ Jesus.
Philip. 3:9	...and be found in Him, not having my own righteousness, which is from the law, but that which is through faith in Christ, the righteousness which is from God by faith;
Col. 1:4	since we heard of your faith in Christ Jesus and of your love for all the saints...
Col. 2:5	For though I am absent in the flesh, yet I am with you in spirit, rejoicing to see your good order and the steadfastness of your faith in Christ.

52. Cf. the May, 2006, edition of Christianity Today.
53. As Weiser ("πιστευω" TDNT 6:186-90) has shown, faith involves more than mere acceptance of fact and includes overtones of confidence built on a personal relationship.
54. Once again, there's no doubt that the distinction between knowing God and knowing about God can be pressed too far. But the plain and simple fact is that there is a distinction. It's a distinction that's actually incorporated into the linguistic structure of most languages – for example, in French the distinction between "Je connais" and "Je sais" and in Spanish, "Yo conozco" and "Yo se´."
55. Romans 1:18a.
56. The Book of Leviticus uses two terms almost interchangeably: qorban (offering) and olah (sacrifice).
57. Some of the concepts delineated here are drawn from insights developed by Gordan J. Wenham's exegesis of Leviticus. Wenham draws upon recent archeological studies concerning the use of ritual in primitive cultures. Mary Douglas' studies are especially informative.
58.. Except for the hide, which is given to the officiating priest.
59. Gordon Wenham is very emphatic here: all five sacrifices, to some extent, point to atonement; however, the Whole Burnt Offering is the primary atoning sacrifice.
60. It's from this perspective – the Grain Offering – that Christian giving can, at least in part, be understood. Giving expresses homage, submission, loyalty. It reflects gratitude for God's

protection. A Christian who gives generously is declaring to God: "I am your vassal and you are my Lord. I am your faithful servant." It's a declaration that helps establish an intimate relationship between God and the believer (John 14:21).

61. God's share is the portion consumed on the altar in smoke and flame. The rest is removed from off the altar and becomes a meal.

62. When the Germans defeated the French army in the spring and early summer of 1940, they divided France into two regions, occupied and unoccupied. Occupied France was ruled directly by the Germans from their headquarters in Paris. Unoccupied France was ruled from the little resort city of Vichy in the south. Marshal Petain, the hero of Verdun during the First World War, was designated the head of "Vichy" France. He had replaced the last Prime Minister of France, Monsieur Reynaud, in a coup d'état on June 16th and had immediately sued for peace at any price with the Germans. Vichy symbolized for the French humiliation, shame, and disgrace - made all the more painful because Petain, the greatest of France's World War I heroes, was the head of it - and was, in effect, a collaborator.

63. Though Sartre affirmed the existence of evil, he denied the existence of God. The proof, Sartre insisted, is the Holocaust. The Holocaust proves that evil exists and that God doesn't. "I do not believe in God...but in the internment camp (meaning evil)." Sartre's argument – that the presence of evil proves that God doesn't exist – is based upon a common misconception of the "human condition." See box entitled "A Common Fallacy"at the end of Chapter Two.

64. Anyone familiar with sentence diagramming will note that I've taken a few short-cuts here; nevertheless, the point is clear.

65. The diagram I've sketched out here is abridged – because I've simplified some of the classic rules governing "sentence diagramming" – which, quite unfortunately, has become a lost art. Nevertheless, it serves its purpose. An "unabridged" diagram of verses 18b through 23 would run on for many pages.

66. We've already noted that Romans 1:18b is a relative clause modifying the word "men" in Romans 1:18a.

67. It might at first seem a bit incongruous for a "judgmental" Jew to be guilty of idolatry – which is what prompts the second of God's "giving overs" described in Romans 1:26. It seems self-evident that a judgmental Jew would assiduously avoid idolatry. But that's exactly the accusation Paul hurls in the faces of the judgmental Jews in Romans 2:22.

Rom. 2:22 You who abhor idols, do you rob temples?

The clause, "...do you rob temples?" is a figure of speech meaning "commit sacrilege" – which is the principle underlying idolatry.

68. • Man is a sinner – he's guilty of unrighteousness.
• Man's only hope is to throw himself on God's mercy.

69. The Bible never describes God in impersonal terms. He is never reduced to a mere principle; e.g., a First Cause. He is given a distinct personality – without ever compromising his infinite holiness. Even John's two well known aphorisms "God is love" (1 John 4:8 and 1 John 4:16) and "God is light" (1 John 1:5) don't reduce God to a mere principle. To suggest otherwise would ignore John's whole point in his opening sentence:

1 John 1:1 That which was from the beginning, which we have heard, which we have seen with our eyes, which we have looked upon, and our hands have handled, concerning the Word of life...

70. Much of nature's exquisite beauty remains – notwithstanding the curse God pronounced against it in Genesis.

71. The story of Ruth provides several illustrations; so also the Book of Daniel.

72. So John Murray in his study of the Book of Romans; so also Cranfield.

73. Ontology is the study of being – its nature and structure.

74. "sui generis" is a Latin phrase meaning "of the same nature" or "belonging to the same class or genus."

75. At least not manifestly. It may be justifiably argued that some residual of that original image remains.

76. Though not sui generis – meaning that though we bear his likeness and reflect his glory, we do not become, in and of ourselves, God.

77. All it requires is "turning away" from God – which, in and of itself, falls short of actual worship and, hence, short of actual idolatry. The issue of idolatrous worship isn't raised until verse 25.

78. Remember that the Greek word "εις" often conveys the sense of purpose - which is the

sense it conveys here. The "giving over" is unto impurity - that's it's purpose - that's what it's meant to do.

79. See Appendix I on Idolatry and Fornication.
80. The whole issue of mankind's basic morality is taken up again by Paul in Romans Chapter Two, verses 12-16. There he points out that God has imparted to all mankind a moral sensitivity - a conscience - that reflects many of the very truths found in the Mosaiac Law.

    Romans 2:14 For when the Gentiles who do not have the Law do instinctively the things of the Law, these, not having the Law, are a law unto themselves.

    Romans 2:15 in that they show the work of the Law written in their hearts, their conscience bearing witness...

81. Bear in mind that the second punishment does not leave persons without a capacity to empathize with others or feel shame; but the third judgment entails precisely that loss: they can no longer empathize with others nor do they feel shame.
82. In Genesis 15:16 we encounter the puzzling expression "...for the iniquity of the Amorities was not yet complete." Its meaning is found in the principle we're elucidating here – that sin, when left unchecked and unchallenged, eventually dehumanizes not just single, individual persons, but whole societies, cultures, and nations. It's then that God's judgment can no longer be withheld or postponed – and whole nations are overthrown and sometimes thoroughly "extinguished."
83. It has been reported that David Berkowitz, the infamous "Son of Sam" killer, has committed his life to Christ. It's also reported that Ted Bundy asked God to forgive his sins in Christ just before he was executed.
84. At least up to verse 28 – where God turns us over to a "debased mind."
85. Cf., "Summing up Verses 13-15 at the end of my exegesis of Romans 2:15.
86. Scripture occasionally portrays the gentiles exhibiting a moral sensitivity that exceeds the Jew's – even the Jewish Patriarch's; e.g, Abraham and Pharaoh (Gen. 12:10-20); Abraham and Abimelech (Gen. 20:1-18); and Isaac and Abimelech (Gen. 26:6-11).
87. Cf. exegesis of Romans 2:6-12.
88. Though I'm not at all an Arminian and find fault with a good many of their conclusions, both Romans 1:24-32 and Romans 2:14-15, inter alia, provide a basis for ascribing genuine credibility to the Wesleyan doctrine of "prevenient grace."
89. ...in Torah Law.
90. The problem with most Calvinists is that they rely exclusively on systematic theology to make their case – meaning they're likely to begin with a series of "first principles" – and then stretch the Bible out on the procrustean bed those principles comprise. The result is quite predictable – and is the same result any "dogmatism" is likely to produce: "the facts be damned." Hegelians and Marxists have made the same mistake: the facts of human history are stretched out on the procrustean bed of dialectical materialism – and damn whatever facts don't fit. It's a common mistake that all scholars – Christian or otherwise – are prone to make.
91. The doctrine that some men are predestined to salvation while others are predestined to damnation – and that individual choice plays no role.
92. Erickson, Millard J., Introducing Christian Doctrine (Grand Rapids: Baker Book House, 1995), p. 288.
93. The other supporting pillars are, of course, unconditional election, limited atonement, irresitible grace, and perseverance of the saints.
94. Ibid. p. 1057.
95. Ibid. p. 1057.
96. Ibid. p. 1057.
97. Ibid. p. 1057.
98. Boice and the Calvinists make much of what Theodore Beza, Calvin's successor at Geneva, calls the "Golden Chain" of Romans 8:29-30 – a chain consisting of five links: foreknowledge, predestination, calling, justification, and glorification. For Beza, the argument does not revolve around the doctrine of total depravity; it's more a matter of God's sovereign determination – with each link in the chain leading inexorably to the next. But Beza's argument, like total depravity, is fraught with weaknesses – most especially a misunderstanding of "telos."
99. Once again, they are wholly and completely under bondage to sin – and cannot live righteously or hope to justify themselves before God. Cf. graphic to the right.
100. Boice himself acknowledges his own difficulty with it: "It is easy to distort this doctrine (the doctrine of double predestination)... We must proceed slowly and humbly, recognizing our own limited understanding. Still we must try to see what the Bible does teach about reprobation, since the subject cannot be avoided (italics

mine)." Boice, ibid., p. 1060. Also, "When I began ... I pointed out that, in my judgment, we are examining the most difficult portion of the entire Bible (Romans 9-11). Not only because it deals with election, which troubles many, but even more because it deals with reprobation (italics mine), the doctrine that God rejects or repudiates some persons to eternal condemnation in a way parallel but opposite to the way he ordains others to salvation." Ibid., p. 1059.

101. Cf. the graphic entitled "Two Different Interpretations" in my exegesis of Romans 1:16 and in the graphic entitled "Election and reprobation vs. the Cross" in my exegesis of Romans 3:25.
102. There's simply no way the Calvinists can soften the portrait "double predestination" paints of God – though many of them struggle strenuously to do so. Boice himself acknowledges that it seems "a 'monstrous' doctrine that turns God into an indifferent deity who sits in heaven arbitrarily assigning human destinies, saying, as it were, 'This one to heaven, and I don't care. This one to hell, and I don't care.'" He calls it a caricature, but confesses that there's a lot truth underlying it; that there's simply no way to entirely expunge that kind of portrayal. As wrong as I think Boice is, I can't help but admire his profound intellectual honesty. Ibid., p. 1060.
103. And, of course, their collective expression, Israel.
104. Murray, John, The New International Commentary on the New Testament, The Epistle to the Romans, (Grand Rapids, Michigan: Eerdmans Publishing Co., 1965) Chapter 9, p. 18.
105. Some Calvinists deny that they're "double predestinarians;" that though God elects some to salvation, he doesn't actually send the rest to hell; he simply passes over them. But that's merely a bit of artful sophistry. In passing over them, he is, in point of fact, consigning them to hell. There's simply no way to skirt that conclusion – and only the disingenuous will try. Boice, much to his credit, acknowledges that double predestination is the mark of a genuine Calvinist. Again, though I most certainly disagree with many of his conclusions, I can't help but admire Boice's intellectual honesty.
106. Romans 9:6 – 13.
107. "Jacob have I loved."
108. "Esau have I hated."
109. Again, it's wrong to suggest that Romans 9:10 – 13 can be used as a paradigm for salvation. The point Paul is making does not turn upon salvation, but the priority he assigns Israel and the Jewish people.
110. Op cit. Boice, p. 1062
111. Op cit. Murray, Chapter 9, p. 22.
112. Haldane, Robert, An Exposition of the Epistle to the Romans (MacDill AFB: MacDonald Publishing, 1958), p. 467.
113. Haldane is clearly an exception. He's at pains to point out Jacob, no less than Esau, begins as a child of wrath.
114. Nor, for that matter, does predestination. I've already pointed out in Chapter One in my discussion of "predestination" - that it's not the fate of specific individuals that biblical predestination turns upon; it's God's eternal plan and the purpose that plan reflects.
115. ...that man should stand before God in love, holy and blameless (Ephesians 1:4) – the telos God has assigned mankind.
116. Specifically, "love that's got to be earned isn't love at all" – a truth Jesus himself spells out most comprehensively in the Beatitudes; e.g., Luke 6:31-36. I've touched on this matter at the end of Chapter One.
117. Once again, it's my opinion that all intellectually honest Calvinists are double predestinarians; that it's little more than a bit of artful sophistry to suggest that "passing over" some men isn't tantamount to consigning them to hell.
118. Which, of course, is the meaning of Romans 3:19 – where Paul graphically depicts man standing helplessly mute before the bar of God's holy justice – knowing that his condemnation has been proven beyond doubt...

    Rom. 3:19 ... that every mouth may be stopped, and all the world may become guilty before God.

119. The other truly grievous consequence it leads to is the denigration of the Cross – a consequence I've taken pains to describe elsewhere.
120. Boice, op. cit., p. 1060
121. Once again, as we pointed out, Paul is making a clear distinction between the sinners described in Romans 1:24-27 and those described in Romans 1:28 - 32. In short, Paul is developing a typology of sin.
122. Synonymous parallelism is a well developed poetic technique used in the Psalms: one line of a verse is followed by another that declares the same truth, but using different words the meaning of which is essentially similar.

123. Clearly, the phrase "such things" here in verse 2 and the word "same" in verse 3 refer to specific, concrete deeds.
124. Clearly, not his real name.
125. Romans 5:9 tells us that believers are safe from God's wrath: "Much more then, having now been justified by his blood, we shall be saved from wrath through him." However, Hebrews 12:5-11 tells us that salvation doesn't keep God from correcting saved sinners - sometimes to the point of "scourging" them. (verse 6).
126. Erickson, Millard J., Introducing Christian Doctrine (Grand Rapids: Baker Book House, 1995), p. 288.
127. I'm not elaborating on this point here largely because I've already discussed it sufficiently elsewhere.
128. Romans 1:18a
129. We dare not push the distinction too far, however. Why? Because the distinction is not that sharply drawn; it's more that the one, lust, shades into the other, sin. As a mentor of mine was fond of saying, "Evil, lustful thoughts are like birds that circle around our heads and occasionally land there. The fact that they land is not a sin; it's only when we fail to chase them off, when, instead, we allow them to make a nest there that we lapse into sin."
130. Normally translated "Not at all."
131. Cranfield insists that "δε" (here translated "but") puts "verses 17ff in an adversative relationship to verses 12-16." But that's clearly not the case. Verses 12-16 amount to nothing more than a continuation of Paul's line of thought extending back to verse 2 – specifically his elucidation of God's sovereign jurisprudence. And verses 17ff merely apply those principles to the specific case of the Jew. Moreover, his insistence that "δε" always denotes a disjunction – what he calls "an adversative relationship" – is simply not true. Occasionally it indicates a follow-up.
132. Once again, this phrase "to the Jew first and also to the Greek" is not found in Romans 2:17-3:20. Why? Because, unlike Romans 2:1-16, the focus of Romans 2:17-3:20 is exclusively upon the Jew. That phrase clearly distinguishes the two passages – the first, Romans 2:1-16 touches upon both Jew and Gentile and outlines the nature and consequences of God's jurisprudence, while the second, 2:17-3:20, touches only upon the Jew – making the Jew a special case of the general principles spelled out in Romans 2:1-16. (Romans 3:9 which does indeed mention the Gentile is part of an address directed to the Jew alone – and does not, therefore, invalidate what I'm saying here.)
133. And is so in both the KJ and the NKJV.
134. Romans 2:13.
135. I'm reminded here of Paul's exclamation in 2 Corinthians 12:7... "And lest I should be exalted above measure by the abundance of the revelations, a thorn in the flesh was given to me, a messenger of Satan to buffet me, lest I be exalted above measure." Privilege can prove to very dangerous.
136. I can claim no credit for this insight. Walter Kaiser first brought it to light in his remarkable study of the Old Testament entitled simply *The Old Testament*.
137. The phrase "I will be your God" is first found in Genesis 17:7.
138. The phrase "You shall be my people" is first found in Exodus 6:7.
139. The phrase "I will dwell in the midst of you" is first found in Exodus 29:44-46.
140. The phrase "Therefore, be holy; for I am holy" is first found in Leviticus 11:45.
141. The entire formula is found in many Old Testament passages; but it's also found in the New Testament as well:
2 Corinthians 6:16-18 is one of several examples...

    2 Cor. 6:16-18 And what agreement has the temple of God with idols? For you are the temple of the living God. As God has said: "I will dwell in them and walk among them. I will be their God, and they shall be My people. Come out from among them and be separate, says the Lord. Do not touch what is unclean, and I will receive you. I will be a Father to you, and you shall be My sons and daughters, says the Lord Almighty.

142. ...though, of course, his conscience provided some guidance.
143. The study of how knowledge is acquired.
144. The study of the nature and structure of being.
145. In the Platonic sense – in the sense of Plato's *Allegory of the Cave*.
146. Though the Alexandrian Jews did indeed eventually succumb to neo-Platonism – championed especially by Philo.
147. 425 AD marks the date Rome was sacked by the Visigoths and the last Roman Emperor in the West was dethroned.
148. Having forsaken its Christian heritage and eschewed its Christian principles. There's no

doubt that we're living in a post-Christian era.
149. Weariness and emptiness.
150. It's clear that Moses has more in mind here than just "numbers." Numbers here reflect power, glory, and rank. And judged in those terms, the Jews were the "least" of all nations.
151. Ephesians 6:12 – "For our struggle is not against flesh and blood, but against the rulers, against the powers, against the world forces of this darkness, against the spiritual forces of wickedness in the heavenly places."
152. After all, Philip of Macedonia brought none other than Aristotle himself to tutor his son Alexander, who, following his ascension to the throne, became conqueror of the whole known world.
153. Though Aristotle transformed the word "telos" into a formal philosophical category, the concept itself is certainly not unique to Greek culture. Almost all pre-modern cultures employ linguistic forms which reflect teleological presuppositions – including Hebrew culture. Christian doctrine reflects it as well. Paul's frequent use of the term "new man" is proof positive. So also Peter's use of the term "seed" in 1 Peter 1:23. Both terms are charged with the sense of "telos" – meaning a fixed, preordained destiny.
154. The difference between Plato and Aristotle is found here. Plato, Aristotle's teacher, insisted that all concrete, empirical phenomena are mere shadows of eternal, transcendent archetypes – which exist on an entirely different plane of reality. One reality, the empirical, is a shadow world of the other, the transcendent - and the two can never co-exist. Aristotle, however, repudiated that claim – and, instead, insisted that the two realities do indeed co-exist. How? Each concrete, existential phenomenon is impregnated with the transcendent – in the form of what Aristotle called "telos." (1 Peter 1:23 conveys this very sense.) But telos is not simply an embodiment of the transcendent realm, it's also a kind of engine that propels a single, existential phenomenon toward its telos. What Aristotle did was quite simple. He seized Plato's archetypes and inserted them into concrete, empirical phenomena – and, in so doing, rescued the empirical realm from the insignificance into which Plato's philosophy had cast it.
155. ...which is only possible given the Law.
156. The term "rob temples" is an idiom meaning "commit sacrilege."
157. Romans 2:1. All of Chapter Five is devoted to this one issue: hypocrisy.
158. Romans 11:25 "For I do not desire, brethren, that you should be ignorant of this mystery, lest you should be wise in your own opinion, that blindness in part has happened to Israel until the fullness of the Gentiles has come in."
159. Obviously, the syllogism here is partly masked by Paul's rhetorical question.
160. That's the "value" (verse 25, i.e., the "meaning") the Jews ascribe to circumcision. And it's a gross misconception.
161. There are four deductive systems in use; the one we're using here is the most common – called the "Categorical Language" – and is derived from principles first brought to light by Aristotle.
162. In formal logic, this is what's called a "stipulative definition" – meaning a hitherto somewhat vague definition that has been rendered more precise.
163. Meaningless only in terms of justification – which is the sense the Jews have cast for it – clearly a misconception. Obviously, however, circumcision is not meaningless in terms of what God intended – specifically, that the Jews – Abraham's descendants – are God's Covenant People (Genesis 17:7).
164. ...which, of course, he isn't – proving that Paul is being rhetorical here in verse 27.
165. ..."null and void" only in the limited and obviously misconstrued sense that the Jew has cast for it – specifically, as a mark of justification! Paul is not calling into question here the continued viability of God's covenantal relationship with Israel – which is founded on God's faithfulness alone (Romans 3:3-4), not the Jew's!
166. A feat only the Spirit of God can effect.
167. It's a tendency that, of course, plagues all mankind, not just the Jews.
168. The Greek word, "απιστια," here translated "unbelief" can also be translated "unfaithful" or "untrustworthy" – and probably should be in light of the word "entrusted" ("επιστευθησαν") in verse 2.
169. Obviously, in condemning it.
170. Obviously an imaginary protagonist – a rhetorical device only.
171. Normally translated "Not at all," rather than "Not altogether."
172. The Septuagint is the Greek translation of the Hebrew scriptures completed during the 2nd Century B.C. The word "Septuagint" means

"seventy" – and the word was thought an appropriate name of the translation because seventy rabbis took a hand in its completion.

173. Otherwise known as "The Sin Offering."
174. See exegesis of Romans 2:12-16
175. Once again, as we pointed out, Paul is making a clear distinction between the sinners described in Romans 1:24 - 27 and those described in Romans 1:28 - 32. In short, Paul is developing a typology of sin.
176. I've intentionally avoided using "law" and "grace" simply because that's not the distinction Paul wants to make here. Indeed, Paul insists that the law points to grace; that the two are not incompatible. The contrast is between two means of justification: one by "grace through faith" and the other through "law keeping" (εξ εργον νομου).
177. The term "the Cross" includes, of course, not just the death of Christ, but his resurrection and ascension as well.
178. A Jewish euphemism for "belief in God" – taken from Deuteronomy 6:4. Adamson in his commentary on this verse suggests that the verbal construction of "believe" here in 2:19 makes it clear that it's only God's existence that the demons acknowledge. They certainly don't trust him or repose faith in him. Adamson, James B., The New International Commentary on the New Testament, The Epistle of James (Grand Rapids: Eerdmans Publishing Co., 1976) p. 125.
179. e.g., Zane Hodges
180. As well, of course, in the words "death" and "grave."
181. The law of retribution.
182. Bearing in mind the teleological definition of "predestination" – that the focus of predestination is not specific individuals, but God's eternal plan and purpose; cf., Chapter One, my discussion of predestination.
183. Exactly what's suggested by the proponents of "Open Theism."
184. I'm well aware the term "eternity past" is a contradiction in terms; but given the limits of the human mind – that time and space comprise its very medium – it will have to do.
185. And at least three more times in the Book of Romans
186. C.H. Dodd is perhaps the best known proponent.
187. It's certainly true that the cost of some of the sacrifices stipulated in the Levitical ceremonies varied greatly (e.g., the cost of a turtledove was far less than the cost of a bullock) – though all served to propitiate God's wrath and secure forgiveness of sin. However, the symbolic import of each of those sacrifices pointed to Christ – a truth clearly attested to in the Book of Hebrews – meaning that from God's viewpoint all cost the same – the life of Christ. The difference in cost served to afford individuals from every economic and social strata of Jewish society an opportunity to avail themselves of the benefits arising from the sacrifices.
188. e.g., 1 Samuel 2:10; 1 Kings 22:11; Psalms 112:9; Daniel 7:7, 20
189. Elegantly put by Cranfield, C.E.B., The International Critical Commentary, Romans Volume I (Edinburgh, Scotland: T&T Clark, 1975).
190. Cf. "Excursus on the Real Purpose of the Law."
191. That the Jews believed God's blessing – most especially his mercy – is restricted to the Jews only is precisely the point Paul takes up in Romans Chapter 4 - in his discussion of Genesis 15:6 and Psalm 32:1ff.

Index

D

E

F

G

H

Calvin on the Ropes

CPSIA information can be obtained at www.ICGtesting.com
Printed in the USA
BVOW060613191011

274027BV00001B/205/P

9 781606 479797